The Ecology of Gender

Fourth Edition

Barbara Collamer
Western Washington University

Harcourt Brace *Custom Publishers*
Harcourt Brace College Publishers
Fort Worth Philadelphia San Diego New York Orlando
Austin San Antonio Toronto Montreal Sydney Tokyo

Custom Publisher   Kathleen Abraham
Senior Production Manager   Sue Dunaway

The Ecology of Gender, Fourth Edition
Copyright © 1999 by Barbara Collamer

Permissions Department
Harcourt Brace & Company
6277 Sea Harbor Drive
Orlando, FL 32887-6777

Portions of this Work were published in previous editions.

Acknowledgements begin on page 263 and constitute an extension of this copyright page.

Printed in the United States of America

0-15-567334-3

Table of Contents

THE ECOLOGY OF GENDER

Chapter 1

Chapter 1 *Barbara E. Collamer*, **Introduction**

Where we begin in terms of gender ideology is an interesting reflection of our cultural development. Where we end up is determined by an introspective journey into our own personal lives. As a guide to this journey, this book starts with an historical glimpse into cultural shifts considered responsible for important changes in roles for women and men, and ends with solutions to several of the persistent gender-based problems we still face today. The authors and scholars that contribute to this text trace the cultural and political route Americans have traveled to establish the state of the gender field as it stands today. This is an interdisciplinary collaboration from sociologists, ethnographers, biologists, historians, psychologists, educators and political activists. It was obvious from the start that one discipline (and especially one author) cannot explain, interpret, or resolve the issues of our gendered world.

Section I of this book invites us into the study of gender through a review of economic and social shifts during America's industrial revolution. The responsibilities that men and women would take on within this new democratic system were born out of necessity from the changing social, political, and economic conditions. What evolved from the redefinition of roles for men and women at that time ultimately expanded into the first rise of feminism. In 1848 the first women's rights convention was held in Seneca Falls, NY. From that time the campaign for social change in women's and men's roles was an organized venture with a life and definition of its own. Seventy two years later, in 1920, the 19th amendment was ratified giving women the right to vote, thus granting official United States citizenship for women. After that event, for the most part, there was a 35-year lull in organized gender-based activity while Americans struggled with the disruption and instability of wars and major economic crisis.

In section II of this book, interpretive perspectives on gender are introduced that arose during the flurry of scholarship amid the 1970s and 1980s. This activity spawned various models, or ideologies, in a state of the field that was politically alive with stable democratic process and jurisprudence. Amid provocative movements, controversy, conflict, and reactionism, Americans chiseled out the rules of the gender game using human rights, civil rights, and legal rights as platforms. As a general ideology emerged, the parties of the movement revisited the assumptions about differences between the sexes. What, if any, are the biological differences between women and men? What universal psychological differences are there and how stable is gender identity? How prevalent and powerful is the sex-typing of children in our modern culture? The selections for this segment of text are a journey through responses to these questions and investigations, mostly academic, into the era of women's liberation; the second rise of feminism.

During this activity, there was new research into what particular areas of behavior are seen as "feminine" and which areas of behavior are seen as "masculine". Attempts were made to equalize the sexes by identifying what stressors men and women experience from sex-typed socialization. The thinking was that because of socialization, both women and men are faced with unrealistic and sexist expectations about their role in our culture. Sex role socialization was viewed as so much cultural baggage. Sex role theory, as it is called, had its advocates but also attracted some critics and it is this struggle between two models of definition that lend much of the intellectual content to our current study. However, knowing the historical details of the second rise of gender is vital to participating in any debate or discussion on today's gender world. For example, in the early 70s, it was apparent that there needed to be a distinction between the concept *sex* and the concept *gender*. The term *sex* refers to physical and biological characteristics of an individual. Biology includes the typical physical traits of being male or female such as body build and genitalia, prominent hormones, secondary sexual characteristics such as facial hair and breasts, and chromosomal make-up. *Gender*, on the other hand, refers to the social and cultural dimensions of being male or female, that is, (in our culture) characteristics such as aggressiveness, competitiveness, nurturance, and expressiveness. Making this separation, conceptually, say advocates of sex-role theory, helps us in our gendered discourse. Case in point, a new chapter in an adolescent textbook stated: "Possibly one of today's adolescent females will become the head of a large corporation several decades from now and the appointment will not make headlines by virtue of her gender."[1] By the above definition, we don't know her gender, we only know her sex, so more accurately the statement should read "by virtue of her sex."

Section III, titled "social symptoms", addresses the persistent social dilemmas we have come to know as "gender issues". Scholars and activists alike say that these problems persist, in good part, due to a hierarchical social order and our attachment to prescribed roles for each sex. It is proposed that this social order is responsible for the conflict we see acted out in the routine interpersonal relations of women and men. There are other interpretations, of course, and it is important to be reminded of the assumptions and biases, and to use powers of critical thinking. It is also important to manage the emotional reaction to these volatile issues and try to maintain concern with the ultimate task of testing problem-solving strategies and finding solutions. But the evidence is clear; there are unresolved issues to be dealt with before there can be a genuine bilateral alliance of the sexes. The point of this segment is to reiterate the issues that constitute serious unresolved gender-based problems in our society today.

After setting the stage for problem resolution in section III, that is, defining the problem, we launch into the task of constructing a model of intervention in Section IV. This segment involves contrasting common approaches to such interventions and ultimately setting out a plan for testing problem solutions. In a combination of anthropology, sociology and psychology, a solution pathway is proposed as a vehicle for further thinking, discussion, and problem-solving. Here we can put our scholarship to use. We can explore strategies to problem solving as an academic exercise within the personally relevant and lively content area of gender.

In this segment of the book, we revisit sex role theory and construct an alternative ideology. The alternative to sex role theory (often referred to as the *ecological model)* is more accurately viewed as an extension of sex role tenets and derives most of its substantive matter from sociology. Sex role theory resides at the macrostructural level of analysis. Components of the macro-level of a society are the institutional and governmental systems and structures that rule such as, the Constitution of the United States and various laws. Ecological theory adds to that the micro-level, with concerns that are personal and intimately connected to our daily lives such as family, jobs, and social network of friends. Without a doubt, sex-role socialization has, as its directive, the macrostructual elements likely to show up in mass media, economic conditions and courts of law. But how the socialization, per person, *ends up* and where it is acted out to our benefit or dismay, is in our microstructure. Thus, the modification of sex role socialization, if it is necessary or desirable, takes place more efficiently and effectively in our personal lives: our choices, situations, and relationships, *not* in changing our social directives (e.g., not changing sexist TV programming, advertising, schoolbooks, etc.). In the controversy that follows, our reading takes us through the arguments about where the changes should take place. Within the ecological perspective, the micro-level becomes a proposed site of resolution for the social symptoms identified in Part III. This contrasts with the long-standing sex role theory that the changes need to take place at the macro-level. There are no right or wrong conclusions, just plenty of things to consider, and the challenging task of clarifying the two contrasting models for further gender discourse and practice.

I believe we have reached a point in our social transformation of gender prescriptions where we have, in place, all the cultural artifacts and political pieces necessary for a bilateral alliance of women and men. It appears to me that we have already traversed several levels of prior conditions. These levels can be defined in five stages:

Stage I: Gender stratification—distinct and enforced roles for men and women. Men are expected to be the dominant provider, women are expected to be the subordinate nurturer. The prevalent assumption is that men and women are unequal in basic ability with women being less capable than men

Stage II: Gender uniformity—the idea that men and women are exactly the same; no different. The guiding thought is that anything men can do women can do as well. Generally used to break down barriers to education, training, and employment opportunity for women.

Stage III: Gender differentiation—the understanding that there are distinct behavioral differences between men and women. Recognizing that gender socialization and cultural expectations create capabilities and talents unique to each sex.

Stage IV: Gender equality—fair and equal value is assigned to the characteristics of both femininity and masculinity; placing balanced importance on the traits that men and the traits that women bring to gender-role enactment.

Stage V: Gender dualism—the capacity to effectively use the distinct contributions that both genders bring to a situation. The ability to integrate the talent of each gender role or any combination of roles expressed through the phenomenon of role flexibility by any given individual.

To the student:

Keep in mind as we explore the gender domain that if authors of these articles make sweeping statements about men and women they are usually referring to the statistical 68% of individuals under the bell-shaped curve that fall between one standard deviation below and one standard deviation above the mean on any particular issue. For example, if research indicates that "Women have better proximal senses than men", this means that women, as a group, scored higher on this dimension than men, as a group. That, of course, leaves us the latitude to cite the "exception".

Your task as student is to conceptualize, sort and consolidate the information, including a variety of terminology, into the two-part standard categories labeled "individualist" and "ecological". In the most basic sense, the two distinctions are illustrated through the nature/nurture debate. For example, how does the nature vs. nurture paradigm contend with our culture's definition of today's gender-based division of labor (men as providers, women as homemakers)? The nature perspective of the division of labor is viewed through the biological lens and, additionally, by way of psychological characteristics (gender identity) of women and men. Are most women biologically motivated by a strong maternal urge to be homemakers and mothers? Are most men "hard-wired" with the drive to be breadwinner and head of household? If not specifically biologically predisposed, then are men and women socially predisposed to adhere to a sex-typed gender identity? In other words, is our gender behavior individualist? From the nurture perspective, has our culture established the gender division of labor through the social, economic and political needs of our environment? Whether resources are plentiful or scarce, whether one sex outnumbers the other, whether political climate is liberal or conservative--do these conditions, in consort or separately, influence how resources and responsibilities are distributed? Simply put, is gender behavior ecological? These questions require your critical thinking.

My belief is that we are just now entering the forth phase (gender equality) of our attitudes toward women's and men's roles. That is, culturally (socially and politically) we have traversed a path consisting of several previous eras in gender-role ideology. It is now incumbent on each of us, *personally*, to establish the rules of our relationships, build necessary support systems, accept role flexibility, and so on.

This suggestion of the two-part standard, though greatly simplified here to the nature/nurture issue, is woven throughout all of the selected articles. It is only one of the colorful threads on this theme. Each chapter preface is designed to help weave the content into a fabric of multiple colors, the result of which is this unique tapestry: *The Ecology of Gender.* I hope you enjoy reading, thinking, talking, and writing about men and women, our conflicts and our resolutions.

---

[1] Santrock, J. W., *Adolescence*, 1998, McGraw Hill.

Chapter 2

The feminization of love. We begin our historical overview of the study of gender in the United States with an article by prominent author and researcher, Francesca Cancian. Dr. Cancian is a professor of sociology at the University of California at Irvine. This chapter is a revised selection from her book, Love in America, Gender and Self-development. *Roles and responsibilities shifted for women and men when our country rapidly transformed its economic basis during the middle to late 19th century. Men's lives focused on paid work in growing industry and women's lives shifted to solely caring for home and family. The definition of love changed to a feminine style of caring and expression.*

Chapter 2 *Francesca M. Cancian, Love and the Rise of Capitalism*

Love is a personal experience, but it is socially constructed, shaped by economic institutions that structure our daily activities and by cultural understandings about the meaning of love, gender, and self. A historical analysis of conceptions of love in nineteenth century America clarifies how our love relationships are socially structured. With the transformation from an agrarian to a capitalist economy, love also was transformed.

Two aspects of capitalist society have been most important in shaping marital love (which is the type of love relationship on which I am focusing). The first aspect, associated with early capitalism, is the separation of the home and the workplace. This structural change intensified the split between the feminine sphere of love and the family versus the masculine sphere of achievement and work. Men's and women's activities became separated, leading to a division of personality characteristics by gender, so that women were expected to be compliant, tender, and dependent, while men were expected to be assertive, rational, and independent. Love became feminized, controlled by women and identified with feminine qualities like tenderness and weakness. Although this split has softened in recent decades, it continues to structure marital love.[1]

The second aspect that has transformed personal relationships, associated with late capitalism, is the cultural emphasis on individualism and emotional self-expression for both women and men. With wives increasingly joining the labor force, the growth of leisure and consumerism, the improving standard of living, and the rise of wives' employment, men and women came to value self-development and internal experience. Ideals of marital love became more intimate and androgynous. But these trends did not emerge strongly until the third or fourth decade of the twentieth century. In this paper I will focus on the first transformation -- the feminization of love that accompanied the separation of the home and the workplace during the nineteenth century.[2]

Love in Agrarian New England

Before the nineteenth century, the dominant image of family life was that women and men were both responsible for love, and family members were dependent on each other both materially and emotionally. The ideal of the independent individual was still weak; gender roles were not polarized, and the private sphere of family life was closely integrated with the public community.[3]

In the colonial communities of New England, the household was the arena for affection, economic production, education, and social welfare. The typical family was, in the words of the historian John Demos, "a little commonwealth," a miniature community governed by the same rules as the wider community.[4]

The integration of activities in the family produced a certain integration of instrumental and expressive traits in the personalities of men and women.[5] Husbands and wives were involved in similar economic activities, and shared the task of caring for household members. The patriarch was expected to guide and nurture all the dependents in his household, which often included apprentices and servants, and both sexes were instructed by their ministers to be loving and affectionate within the family. Benjamin Wadsworth's book, *The Well-Ordered Family*, published in 1712, advised that "the duty of love is mutual, it should be performed by each to each of them." Husbands were instructed to temper their authority with love: "Though he governs her, he must not treat her as a servant but as his own flesh, he must love her as himself." And love included sexuality. Men were told, in the words of the Bible, to "rejoice with the wife of thy youth. Let her breasts satisfy thee at all times. And be always ravished with her love."[6]

Men did monopolize almost all the property and positions of power in the community, while women were responsible for the care of infants and of the sick and disabled, but the activities and personality traits associated with love were not highly differentiated by gender. As the historian Mary Ryan summarizes the evidence:

> When early Americans spoke of love they were not withdrawing into a female byway of human experience. Domestic affection, like sex and economics, was not segregated into male and female spheres... The reciprocal ideal of conjugal love... grew out of the day-to-day cooperation, sharing, and closeness of the diversified home economy.[7]

The Separation of Men's and Women's Activities in a Cash Economy

By the end of the eighteenth century, a great transformation was occurring. The family and personal relationships were being separated from economic production, and there was a parallel separation of human personality traits by gender. Love and family attachments were being defined as women's sphere while economic production and individual achievement were in men's sphere. The feminization of love and the masculinization of work intensified the divergence between men's and women's activities and personalities, and produced ways of loving that were more congenial to women than to men. Mary Ryan describes how this transformation took place in upstate New York. A similar transformation has occurred in much of the world during the past two centuries.[8]

At the beginning of the nineteenth century, Oneida County was a sparsely populated frontier, where most families lived on subsistence farms. Households were headed by the patriarch and produced their own food and clothing, bartering some of their produce for spices, liquor, and other luxury goods in one of the few local stores. The household also conducted family worship, educated its children, and took care of the sick and the indigent. The church and town watched over the household and tried to ensure that it carried out these duties.[9]

Personal relationships within the household were relatively formal and hierarchical. Obedience of the wife and apprentices to the household head and of children to their parents was a primary virtue, and all adults were expected to be hardworking and religious. Children were viewed as miniature adults, and stern discipline was used to break a child's will and turn the child from individual desire to obedience to parents and church. The emotional bonds between husband and wife were not emphasized, and there was little physical privacy in the house for the couple. Marital intimacy, in the modern sense of emotional expression and verbal disclosure of personal experience, was probably rare. Instead, husband and wife were likely to share a more formal and wordless kind of love, based on duty, working together, mutual help, and sex.

The activities of both men and women focused on productive work near the home and on caring for household members. Women had a major role in economic production, usually taking charge of planting the family vegetable garden, caring for poultry and cattle, and making thread, cloth and clothing, and other products. Men as well as women were responsible for the well-being of household members, and for their religious education, although men were doubtless expected to be more severe and demanding. Men worked near their homes, often assisted by family members, and were home during the day for meals and other family activities. Moreover, there was no sharp distinction between "private" and "public." The household was a hierarchical work group supervised by church and town, and intimate attachments or individual self-expression were not cultivated; thus people behaved much the same at home and in the community.

The patriarchal household began to disintegrate between 1815 and 1840. As land became scarce, shops and crafts began to replace agriculture as the major economic activity. Cash replaced barter as a mode of exchange, and merchants in the 1830s lured farmers with advertisements such as "cash for wool."[10] The new economic opportunities to work as artisans, shopkeepers, or commercial farmers were mostly open to men, but the cotton mills offered employment to young unmarried women. At first, the factories were small; families worked together under the father's leadership and were often paid in kind rather than cash. Thus an advertisement in the Utica *Patriot* in 1813 announced, "A few sober and industrious families of at least five children each, over the age of eight years, are wanted at the Cotton Factory."[11] But by 1840, the factories were larger; workers were all recruited individually, not as families, and they were paid in cash. Husbands in the towns typically worked as craftsmen or shopkeepers in establishments that were attached to the homes, but the most prosperous merchants worked away from home. Wives stayed at home and did not work for money.

As the workplace became more separate from home and family, relationships at work became impersonal. The distinction between the warm, personal private sphere and the cold, public sphere was emerging. Paul Johnson describes the changes in the shoe factories and building crews of Rochester, New York, a community that became the fastest growing city in the nation in the 1820s as agriculture became commercialized and the Erie Canal was completed. In 1820, merchants and master craftsmen "lived above, behind, or very near their places of business, and employees boarded in their homes." The master was responsible for the moral behavior of his workmen; they were defined as dependents in his household. "Work, leisure and domestic life were acted out in the same place and by the same people..."[12]

In the following decade, the size of workshops grew larger, and workmen increasingly lived apart from their employer. For example, while in 1827 one in four shoemakers lived with his employer, only one in twenty was doing so by 1834.[13] Masters were becoming businessmen, spending most of their time away from the workshops buying labor and raw materials and selling finished goods. At the same time, they were demanding new standards of discipline at work. "Masters increased pace, scale, and regularity of production, and they hired young strangers with whom they shared no more than contractual obligations."[14]

By the 1840s, the split between men's sphere at work and women's sphere at home was well under way. The male world of business and public life had become an unpredictable arena of competition among individuals. People moved from farm to town and from one town to another in search of work, competing with the growing number of foreign workers and fearful of recurrent business slumps. Men's daily work increasingly became divorced from personal relationships and cooperation, and men also became separated from religion, as they stopped attending church and leading family prayers. Historians detect a mood of expansiveness and unlimited opportunity in American public life in the early nineteenth century. At the same time, there was an undercurrent of fear, a sense of slipping away into a chaos of "individual men devouring each other in the struggle for success."[15]

As public life became more impersonal, immoral, and uncertain, the female world of the family was becoming more intensely personal, pure, and circumscribed. Households became smaller as the birth rate declined and fewer households had apprentices and boarders. The ties between household, church, and town diminished, as husbands withdrew from the family and from the church, and town governments became more impersonal. The family less often acted as an efficient work team, and economic production, education, and health care moved out of the home into factories, offices, schools, and hospitals. Women continued to work hard at home, producing clothing, preparing food, and caring for the family members, but the focus of their lives was to care for their children and their husbands.

8

Women's task of child rearing expanded as children were defined as vulnerable innocents in great need of care. Moreover, the proper raising of children became increasingly important to the middle class as the class position of sons and daughters came to depend more on character and education than on inheritance of land. Child rearing, according to Paul Johnson, "fell more and more to mothers. They were warned not to beat their children..., but to mix discipline with love, and to develop moral sensibilities that would make them useful citizens of a Christian republic."[16] The relationship between mother and child became emotionally intense and oriented to the individual development of the child (but not the mother). In Ryan's words, the center of the household shifted "from patriarchal authority to maternal affection."[17]

Between the worlds of work and home, a new arena of lodges, clubs, and missionary societies was developing. Young men joined lodges to have a place to stay when they left home and went to clubs for fellowship. Women joined religious and moral reform societies as a way to have an impact on the wider society and find a context for carrying on close friendships with women. These sex-segregated voluntary organizations bridged the growing gap between the public and private spheres.

The Ideology of Separate Spheres

As the daily activities of men and women grew farther apart, a new world view emerged. It exaggerated the differences between "the home" and "the world" and polarized the ideal personalities of women and men. It was an ideology that was adopted by affluent Americans as well as the working class and is still influential today.[18]

The ideology of separate spheres is clearly evident in the magazines, church newsletters, and sermons of the nineteenth century, and has been well described by several historians.[19] In brief, this ideology portrayed the home as an "oasis in the desert," a spiritual "sanctuary." A New England minister proclaimed in 1827 that

> it is at home, where man... seeks a refuge from the vexations and embarrassments of business, an enchanting repose from exertion, a relaxation from care by the interchange of affection: where some of his finest sympathies, tastes, and moral and religious feelings are formed and nourished;-- where is the treasury of pure disinterested love, such as is seldom found in the busy walks of a selfish and calculating world.[20]

Home is good and pure in this image and also somewhat immaterial and unreal -- home centers on feelings and ideals, not productive physical activities like preparing meals or caring for infants.

In contrast, in the tough, material outside world "we see the general good, sacrificed to the advancement of personal interest," according to the *Ladies' Magazine* in 1820. "We behold every principle of justice and honor, and even the dictates of common honesty disregarded, and the delicacy of our moral sense is wounded."[21]

These two different worlds were dominated by two different personalities -- the feminine and the masculine. The ideal woman was pious, pure, domestic, and submissive, in the words of historian Barbara Welter; a pious, emotional giver of care who depended on her husband to provide money and to deal with the threatening outside world. The ideal was described in a sermon on women:

> How interesting and important are the duties devolved on females as WIVES... the counselor and friend of the husband; who makes it her daily

study to lighten his cares, to soothe his sorrows, and to augment his joys; who like a guardian angel, watches over his interests [and]... constantly endeavors to render him more virtuous...[22]

A letter from General William Pender to his wife during the Civil War illustrates how husbands expected their wives to be moral arbiters:

Honey, whenever I try to reflect upon the future and to resolve to do better, I think of you first and your image rises up... so that I have almost come to feel that you are a part of my religion. Whenever I find my mind wandering upon bad and sinful thoughts I try to think of my good and pure wife and they leave me at once. My dear wife you have no idea of the excellent opinion I have of your goodness and sweetness. You are truly my good Angel.[23]

Motherhood was the key to being a real woman. The virtues of motherhood were extolled in *The Ladies' Companion* in 1838. Fathers could not inculcate morality in children because the father

weary with the heat and burden of life's summer day or trampling with unwilling foot the decaying leaves of life's autumn, has forgotten the sympathies of life's joyous springtime... The acquisition of wealth, the advancement of his children in worldly honor -- these are his self-imposed tasks.

It was his wife's duty to develop the child's character, to form "the infant mind as yet untainted by contact with evil... like wax beneath the plastic hand of the mother."[24] An ideal woman centered her life on love of husband and children, a love expressed mostly through emotions and piety, not practical action.

The ideal woman could also be powerful, both as the ruler of her domestic domain and as a moral reformer working with other women to help the weak and punish the wicked. Thus popular magazines between the mid-eighteenth and mid-nineteenth century portrayed women as increasingly powerful, especially in child rearing, morality, and courtship.[25] But if she were to avoid censure, her power had to be based on her special feminine qualities -- her superior ability to love, to be good, and to serve others -- and not on masculine qualities such as self-interest, anger, or a desire for control.[26] According to an 1839 article on matrimony, "The man bears rule over his wife's person and conduct. She bears rule over his inclinations: he governs by law; she by persuasion... The empire of the woman is an empire of softness... her commands are caresses, her menaces are tears."[27]

The masculine ideal, tailored to fit the emerging capitalist economy, was to be an independent, self-made man. Key male virtues included self-control, economic success, courage, and upright character. *A Voice to the Married*, published in 1841, advised young men that "a good character must be formed, it must be made -- it must be built by our individual exertions." Nineteenth century writers called on men to be disciplined and courageous and to concentrate their energies, in order to prosper in the world outside the home, which was "a vast wilderness" where they were "naked and alone surrounded by savages" in "a rage of competitive battle."[28] Thus Demos identifies the central masculine virtues as strength, cunning, and endurance.

Men's strength depended on controlling and restraining their emotions and their sexuality. A medical text counseled men that "reserve is the grand secret of power everywhere. Be noble, generous, just, self-sacrificing, continent, manly in all things -- and no woman worthy of you can help loving you in the best sense of the word."[29] An abundant medical literature described the dire consequences of masturbation and excessive sexual intercourse. One text warns that with masturbation "all the intellectual faculties are weakened. The man becomes a coward; sighs and weeps like a hysterical woman. He loses all decision and dignity of character."[30] With the polarization of gender roles, male vices are female virtues, as Charles Rosenberg has commented.

The masculine conception of self-development that is still influential today is rooted in this nineteenth century male ideal. Independence, self-control, and achievement are the major values of this ideal self; while intimacy, emotional expression, and other feminine qualities are devalued.

An ideal man was not perfectly suited for family life. Trained for competitive battles and self-reliance, he might well suffocate in a cozy Victorian home. This conflict was reflected in the existence of two contradictory male ideals: the family man and the independent adventurer. From the point of view of most mothers, ministers, and prospective brides, the ideal man was probably a dependable family man who was a good provider and a devout Christian. Nineteenth century marriage manuals defined the ideal husband as a home-loving Christian and a man of good character who avoided "idleness, intemperate use of intoxicating drinks... licentiousness in every form, gambling, swearing, and the keeping [of] late hours at night."[31]

But many of the nineteenth century heroes -- the mountain men, ships' captains, and cowboys -- were undomesticated adventurers. They had abandoned the civilized world of women and the family for a life of danger and comradeship among men. According to Leslie Fielder's analysis of novels, the central myth of American culture is the tale of a boy or man who escapes from society to an island or wilderness where mother can't come and where he can enjoy innocent, violent adventures with a special male companion.[32] In this myth, marriage represents captivity and emasculation by sexless, virtuous women. The ideal is heroic action with men, not passionate love with women, as it usually is in European novels. Heroes from Tom Sawyer and Captain Ahab to the contemporary private eye all fit this pattern, which is an extreme version of the myth of male independence from women and families.

In sum, the ideology of separate spheres reinforced the new division of labor, and portrayed a world of independent, self-made men and dependent, loving women. The ideal family was portrayed as a harmonious, stable, nuclear household with an economically successful father and an angelic mother.

The reality of family life in the nineteenth century was of course much more diverse and turbulent than this ideal, even among the white middle class. Death disrupted many families. Marriages were just as likely to be broken in 1850 as 1950, if we combine the effects of death and divorce, because in 1850 so many people died young. Not until the 1960s was there a substantial rise in broken marriages, because of a sharp increase in divorce. Many households included other people besides the nuclear family. Affluent families usually had servants, while poorer families took in boarders.[33] Husbands some-times rebelled against the provider role and deserted their wives, and wives were often less docile and more interested in sex than the Victorian image of "the angel in the house." Many women retreated into illness or rebelled against their confinement at home by joining religious or reform organizations or by remaining single.[34]

For the working class, immigrant groups, and black slaves, reality was probably farther from the ideal, although the evidence for these groups is scanty. Working-class men and their families often moved from city to city in search of work. For example, only 40 percent of the unskilled laborers who had lived in Newburyport, Massachusetts, in 1850 were still there in 1860.[35] When work was available, the husband's wages often could not support his family, and his children and wife had to work. Less than 36 percent of the men working in Massachusetts factories in 1897 earned enough to support their families.[36] Immigrant groups often maintained the family patterns of their homelands, and slave families also had special traditions as well as a unique burden of oppression. Despite this diversity, however, these families too were strongly influenced by Victorian ideals. According to historian Carl Degler:

> The majority of Afro-American children in the 19th and 20th centuries lived in a nuclear family with both parents present, in which the father was not only the recognized head of the household but the primary breadwinner as well... Among the immigrants, as among the Black and native families, the wife and mother was the heart of the home; it was she who managed the home and reared the children. Upon her fell the responsibility for seeing that the home was a proper place for the children and an attractive place for the husband.[37]

The Feminization of Love

With the split between home and work and the polarization of gender roles, love became a feminine quality. A Unitarian minister described the female as "accustomed to feel, oftener than to reason." An Episcopalian praised women for possessing "all the milder virtues of humanity," and "a more exquisite sensibility than men... The God of heaven has more exquisitivly [sic] attuned their souls to love, to sympathy, and compassion."[38] Women's superior ability to love was seen as enabling them to comfort and care for their children and husbands.

As women gained control of love, the cultural images of love shifted toward emphasizing tenderness, expression of emotion, and weakness. When mothers replaced fathers as the parent with day-to-day authority, the methods of child rearing shifted from the stern will-breaking methods of agrarian times to socialization through giving and withholding love. Conceptions of God's love also shifted toward sweetness and tenderness. God was seen as an "indulgent parent," a "submissive, meek, and forgiving" Christ.[39] In religious revivals, and in women's friendships, there was a new emphasis on recognizing private feelings and communicating them in an intimate relationship in which one could unfold one's whole heart.[40] Conceptions of marital love also shifted toward greater emphasis on affectionate feelings.

In *The Feminization of American Culture*, Ann Douglas argues that religion and popular literature were dominated by middle-class women and Protestant ministers in the nineteenth century. Women's status was declining as the household lost many of its functions, and ministers were becoming less powerful as the church lost its control over daily life and society became secularized. Excluded from effective public action, they took over activities devalued in industrializing America, and created an ineffectual, sentimental mass culture reflecting their own powerlessness. The literature and the religion they produced emphasized subjective feelings and suffering, and opposed virile action, rebellion, and objective analysis. As this simplified outline of her argument may show, Douglas is more admiring than I am of "masculine" assertion and independence, more critical of "feminine" emotion, and less interested in integrating the two spheres. But her analysis suggests how love was changed and distorted by being identified with women.

Feminized love was defined as what women did in the home; it had nothing to do with how men related to each other at work. Love became a private feeling, disassociated from public life, economic production, and practical action to help others. Many middle-class women challenged this private conception of love in the latter part of the nineteenth century. They expanded domestic love to include being "social housekeepers" and "mothers of the world." In the name of feminine love, hundreds of thousands of women organized to stamp out the vice of liquor, and smaller numbers worked to help the poor or abolish child labor.[41] But by the 1920s women's love was private once again.

Equating woman's activities with love and men's activities with work produced a distorted perception of the activities of both sexes. Men's attachments and dependency were obscured, and women's productive labor was labeled love. A great deal of work remained to be done at home, especially for the majority of women who lacked servants. But women's domestic labor was less visible and less respected than it had been in the agrarian economy.[42] Women were not paid for housework, while outside the home people usually worked for wages. The labor involved in women's expanding new task of shopping -- spending money for goods -- was especially obscured by identifying work with getting money. There was also an increasing divergence in the quality of work experience. Women's work at home "retained the irregularity, the responsiveness to immediate and natural demands, and the intermixture with social occasion common to pre-industrial occupations."[43] Outside the home, work was regulated by clock time and the demands of machines. Gradually the concept of work excluded women's labor in the home and emphasized the masculine ideals of individualism, achievement, discipline, and competition.

Another effect of the feminization of love was the encouragement of a florescence of intimate friendships between women in the late eighteenth century and the nineteenth century. The historian Nancy Cott points out that "the identification of women with the heart... implied that they would find truly reciprocal interpersonal relationships only with other women."[44] Moreover, the equality between women compared favorably to women's subordination to men. Friendship among women was also encouraged by the sociability among women in all-female schools and charitable and religious societies.

Frontier women bitterly complained about the absence of female friends, and the correspondence of educated women often reveals a passionate, enduring commitment to a life-long woman friend. Luella Case, a married woman from Massachusetts, wrote to her old friend Sarah in the 1830s after discovering a poem that Sarah had written to her: "Words seem inadequate to express the sense I feel of your -- what shall I say *friendship*? No, I will rather call it affection, for you know I confessed as one of my weaknesses an inordinate desire *to be loved*." And as a visit from Sarah ended, she felt "most lonely" having "no gentle voice to talk with, or read to me, no sweet beaming countenance to echo the feelings expressed, none of that gentlest of all sympathies, that of a pure, and true hearted female..."[45] Intense love between women friends, more accepted in the nineteenth century than now, was expressed in fondling, endearments, and love letters, concludes historian Lillian Faderman, but rarely included genital sex.[46] Victorian women thus turned to other women and to their children for love, more than to men.

Love, Dependency, and Power

Power relations in the family and the economy were also affected by the new beliefs in feminine love and masculine independence. These beliefs strengthened men's power advantage at home. They also covered up the material dependency and exploitation that were the major causes of power differences in the family and the workplace.

Women in the nineteenth century became extremely economically dependent on their husbands, probably more so than before or after the Victorian era. In the colonial period, women were actively involved in the domestic economy; after the Victorian era, increasing numbers of women entered the workforce. But in the nineteenth century it was shameful for a wife to work, even if she was a widow. An advice book for married women pointed out that "the average woman recognizes the value of money," but her desire to make money "battles perpetually with her desire to do nothing which is strong-minded and unladylike."[47] Married women who had worked as teachers usually would not be rehired after they married, and offices and stores often would not employ older married women.[48][49] Three-quarters of the female industrial workers in large cities in the 1880s were younger than twenty-five and 96 percent of them were single.[50]

Other family relationships became less dependent with the transition to capitalism. Economic survival was no longer based on working in the family farm or shop; individual wage labor was an alternative. Sons and daughters no longer depended on inheriting land from their father, and family members increasingly turned to outside government and private organizations rather than each other for education and health care. But wives became more dependent on husbands.

For example, Emma Goldman reports matter-of-factly that despite the poverty of her family, she quit her factory job in 1887 when she married the young man who worked next to her in the shop. After describing her reactions to her husband's impotence, she continues:

> My own passion subsided. The material anxiety of making ends meet excluded everything else. I had stopped work: it was considered disgraceful for a married woman to go to the shop. Jacob was earning fifteen dollars a week... Life became insupportable.[51]

Increasing economic dependency was the basis for what many social historians see as a decline in the power of wives during the Victorian era,[52] but the connection was obscured by the ideology of innate differences between the sexes. In this world view, women were powerless because they were naturally affectionate and docile, as an article by the antislavery writer Lydia Maria Child illustrates:

> The comparison between women and the colored race is striking. Both are characterized by affection more than by intellect; both have a strong development of the religious sentiment; both are exceedingly adhesive in their attachments; both, comparatively speaking, have a tendency to

14

submission, and hence, both have been kept in subjection by physical force, and considered rather in the light of property, than as individuals.[53]

This perspective denies the material basis of women's dependency, and emphasizes women's need for affection and their natural morality and submissiveness. Part of the feminization of love was the belief that women had an enormous need for love and tenderness while men were naturally independent and had much less need for enduring, nonsexual love. This imbalance in emotional dependency bolstered the power of men over women.

In the workplace, too, relations of material dependency were obscured by polarized gender roles. Men were defined as naturally independent, amoral, and isolated, the other side of defining women as naturally dependent, moral and affectionate. This ideology of the isolated (male) individual accompanied and justified the rise of capitalism, as Marxist scholars have pointed out.[54] Workers were encouraged to see themselves as independent, competitive, and self-made. If they were rich or poor, it was the result of their own individual merit, not relations of dependency with other people. And if they were real men, they would thrive on the impersonal, competitive relationships that prevailed at work. Personal, caring relationships were restricted to women and the home; they should not be expected in the public sphere.

The ideology of independent individuals and "free" workers replaced the old patriarchal model of dependent workers who were subordinate members of their master's household. Johnson describes how new ideals of independence and self-control emerged in Rochester in the 1820s and 1830s, fueled by a religious revival that emphasized the "moral free agency" of each individual to reject evil and choose Christ.[55] This ideology implied that employers had no responsibility to their workers beyond paying them a minimal wage:

> the belief that every man was spiritually free and self-governing enabled masters to present a relationship that denied human interdependence as the realization of Christian ideals... workmen who continued to drink and carouse and stay away from church were no longer considered errant children; they were free moral agents who had chosen to oppose the Coming Kingdom. They could be hired when they were needed, fired without a qualm when they were not.[56]

Thus the new division of labor in the family and the workplace intensified the material dependency of wives and of workmen, but these relations of unequal resources and power were covered over by an ideology that focused on the characteristics of individuals. The economic dependency of women was masked by the belief that women were inherently loving. The economic dependency of workers was masked by the belief that men were independent and self-made and free to determine their own social position.

The ideals of love and self-development that emerged in the nineteenth century justified inequality, especially at the workplace, by denying the material dependency among people. Twentieth century ideals of love and self continue to ignore material interdependence, perhaps because recognizing this interdependence would threaten the legitimacy of our economic system.

Androgyny and Intimacy

As we have seen, the transition from an agrarian to a capitalist society polarized gender roles, feminized love, and led to a masculinized ideal self. But in the long term, the transition led to more androgynous conceptions of gender love, and self, and more intimacy between husband and wife. The new androgynous ideal combined masculine autonomy and feminine affection. Emotional expression became more valued for both sexes and intimate relationships in the private sphere became the main arena for developing one's unique self. In contrast, the masculine ideal self that accompanied the rise of capitalism emphasized independence, emotional control, and success in the public sphere. Conceptions of love also became more androgynous, as feminized love was superseded by new ideals of husband-wife companionship and open-communication. Ideals of intimacy and androgyny did not become powerful in American culture until the twentieth century, in my view, although these ideals were visible much earlier, during the transition to capitalism.

Lawrence Stone, a historian of the English family, argues that the rise of capitalism was accompanied by new values of "affective individualism" that emphasized self-development and intimate bonds with others. Stone describes how "human relationships were increasingly seen in economic terms, governed by the rules of the free market" because of the growth of a market economy and wage labor, together with other trends such as urbanization and geographical mobility. In the old-world view, "the purpose in life was to assure the continuity of the family, the clan, the village or the state, not to maximize the well-being of the individual."[57] The new-world view emphasized

> firstly, a growing introspection and interest in the individual personality;
> and secondly, a demand for personal autonomy and a corresponding
> respect for the individual's right to privacy, to self-expression, and to the
> free exercise of his will within limits set by the need for social cohesion...

Combining individualism with a focus on personal experience and feelings, the new-world view was manifest in warmer, more affectionate family relationships and in "a wholly new scale and intensity of interest in the self."[58]

However, affective individualism probably did not predominate until much later than Stone asserts. The evidence that he cites primarily shows that love became feminized, not androgynous, with the rise of capitalism. For example, he notes the enormous popularity of romantic novels (read mostly by women) and the greater intimacy of the mother-child relationship.

Other scholars have noted signs of affective individualism during the rise of capitalism in nineteenth century America. William Goode argues that with industrialization the American family became more affectionate and egalitarian, increasingly emphasizing the need for all its members to develop their unique selves. Eli Zaretsky discusses the emergence of a new sphere of personal life in nineteenth century America as work became less satisfying and people turned to personal relationships and internal experiences for gratification.[59] And Robert Bellah and his colleagues describe the "expressive individualism" that began to develop in the mind-nineteenth century. In this new perspective, "the expansive and deeply feeling self" was the mark of a successful life, along with rich experience and the freedom to express oneself. In contrast, the older "utilitarian individualism" advocated "a life devoted to the calculating pursuit of one's own material interest."[60]

16

Some historians argue that this trend to affection produced more intimate and equal marriages in the nineteenth century, and they cite letters and diaries exhibiting a high degree of mutual love and dependency in marriages.[61] However, my reading of the evidence is that intimacy between wife and husband remained rare as long as their activities were so different and their power was so unequal. Thus Nancy Cott points out that "exaggerated sex-role distinctions may have succeeded in making women uncomfortable with men (and visa versa) as often as rendering the two sexes complementary."[62] She also argues that marital love was weakened by the subservience of women to men in a period in which traditional dependency relations were dissolving and peer relationships were increasingly valued.

Evidence of the lack of intimacy between husband and wife comes from nineteenth century marriage manuals, which rarely mention affection or companionship. According to these manuals, a sound marriage is based on being religious, industrious, and healthy, and sex is for the purpose of procreation only. Women are advised to seek a husband who values home life and has good morals and then to obey him and be hardworking and good tempered. The quality of the relationship between husband and wife is relatively unimportant.[63] Other signs of marital estrangement include the complaints of married people in their letters and diaries, the disapproval of sexuality, the enormous rise in prostitution, and the decrease in the marriage rate toward the end of the nineteenth century.[64] In sum, the primary effect of the rise of capitalism in the nineteenth century was to create inequality and estrangement between the sexes, and a split between feminine love and masculine self-development.

In the twentieth century, these marital patterns reversed. As wives joined the labor force and women's education increased, husband and wife became more equal; they also probably developed more similar personalities and became more capable of intimacy, as their daily activities converged. Emotional experience and self-development in the private sphere became more important, fueled by the growth of advertising and consumerism, which encouraged people to develop new personal needs and try to fulfill them.

By the 1920s, the new ideal of "companionship" marriage emerged, emphasizing marital intimacy and the personal development of both partners. By the 1970s, intimate, open communication of feelings had become the most important part of marital love. Self-development was a major goal in life, and love had become the joint responsibility of both partners, who were now expected to diligently "work on" their relationship.

We are now (1980s) in the midst of this change toward intimacy and androgyny, caught between new cultural ideas of androgyny and intimacy, and the reality of persisting differences in men's and women's job opportunities and family responsibilities. These cultural understandings and structural arrangement will continue to shape our experience, as they have in the past.

References

Bane, Mary Jo (1976). *Here to Stay: American Families in the Twentieth Century*. New York: Basic Books.

Barker-Benfield, G. J. (1976). *The Horrors of the Half-known Life: Male Attitudes Toward Women and Sexuality in 19th Century America.* New York: Harper and Row.

Bellah, Robert, Richard Madsen, William Sullivan, Ann Swidler, and Steven Tipton (1985). *Habits of the Heart.* Berkeley: University of California Press.

Braverman, Harry (1975). *Labor and Monopoly Capital: The Degradation of Work in the 20th Century.* New York: Monthly Review Press.

Calhoun, Arthur W. (1917). *A Social History of the American Family.* Cleveland: Arthur Clark.

Cancian, Francesca (1985). *Marital Conflict over Intimacy.* Pp. 277-292 in G. Handel (ed.), *The Psychosocial Interior of the Family*, Third Edition. New York: Aldine.

Cancian, Francesca (1987). *Love in America: Gender and Self-Development.* New York: Cambridge University Press.

Cott, Nancy F. (1977). *The Bonds of Womanhood.* New Haven: Yale University Press.

Degler, Carl N. (1980). *At Odds: Women and the Family in America from the Revolution to the Present.* New York: Oxford University Press.

Demos, John (1974). "The American Family in Past Time." *American Scholar.* 43: 422-446.

Demos, John (1979). "Images of the American Family: Then and Now." Pp. 43-60 in V. Tufte and B. Myerhoff (eds.). *Changing Images of the Family.* New Haven: Yale University Press.

Douglas, Ann (1977). *The Feminization of American Culture.* New York: Knopf.

Faderman, Lillian (1981). *Surpassing the Love of Men.* New York: William Morrow.

Fiedler, Leslie A. (1966). *Love and Death in the American Novel,* Revised Edition. New York: Stein and Day.

Flexner, Eleanor (1974). *Century of Struggle.* New York: Atheneum.

Goldman, Emma (1931). *Living My Life.* New York: Knopf.

Goode, William (1963). *World Revolution and Family Patterns.* New York: Free Press.

Gordon, Michael (1978). "From Unfortunate Necessity to a Cult of Mutual Orgasm: Sex in American Marital Education Literature, 1830-1940." Pp. 59-84 in J. Henslin and E. Sagarin (eds.), *The Sociology of Sex.* Revised Edition. New York: Schocken.

Gordon, Michael and M. Charles Bernstein (1970). "Mate Choice and Domestic Life in the Nineteenth Century Marriage Manual." *Journal of Marriage and the Family* 32: 665-674.

Jacoby, Russell (1975). *Social Amnesia.* Boston: Beacon Press.

Johnson, Paul E. (1978). *A Shopkeeper's Millennium.* New York: Hill and Wang.

Kett, Joseph (1977). *Rites of Passage.* New York: Basic Books.

Lantz, Herman R.; Jane Keyes; and, Martin Schultz (1975). "The American Family in the Preindustrial Period: From Base Lines in History to Change." *American Sociological Review* 40:21-36.

Lyons, John O. (1978). *The Invention of the Self.* Carbondale, IL: Southern Illinois University Press.

Marcuse, Herbert (1964). *One-Dimensional Man.* Boston: Beacon Press.

Parsons, Talcott (1954). "The Kinship System of the Contemporary United States." Pp. 177-197 in *Essays in Sociological Theory*. Revised Edition. Glencoe, IL: Free Press.

Poster, Mark (1978). *Critical Theory of the Family*. New York: Seabury Press.

Rose, Willie Lee (1982). "Reforming Women," *New York Review of Books*. October 7.

Rosenberg, Charles E. (ed.) (1975). *The Family in History*. Philadelphia: University of Pennsylvania Press.

Rosenberg, Charles E. (1980). "Sexuality, Class and Role in 19th Century America." In Elizabeth Pleck and Joseph Pleck (eds.), *The American Man*. Englewood Cliffs, NJ: Prentice-Hall.

Rothman, Sheila M. (1978). *Woman's Proper Place: A History of Changing Ideals and Practices 1870 to the Present*. New York: Basic Books.

Ryan, Mary P. (1979). *Womanhood in America: From Colonial Times to the Present*, Second Edition. New York: New Viewpoints.

Ryan, Mary P. (1981). *The Cradle of the Middle Class: The Family in Oneida County, N.Y., 1790-1865*. New York: Cambridge University Press.

Shorter, Edward (1975). *The Making of the Modern Family*. New York: Basic Books.

Smith-Rosenberg, Carroll (1975). "The Female World of Love and Ritual." *Signs* 1:1-29.

Stone, Lawrence (1979). *The Family, Sex, and Marriage in England, 1500-1800*. New York: Harper Colophon.

Swidler, Ann (1980). "Love and Adulthood in American Culture." Pp. 120-147 in N. Smelser and E. Erikson (eds.), *Themes of Work and Love in Adulthood*. Cambridge, Mass.: Harvard University Press.

Thernstrom, Stephan (1964). *Poverty and Progress: Social Mobility in a Nineteenth Century City*. Cambridge, Mass: Harvard University Press.

Wahlstrom, Billie Joyce (1979). "Images of the Family in the Mass Media." Pp. 193-229 in Virginia Tufte and Barbara Myerhoff (eds.), *Changing Images of the Family*. New Haven: Yale University Press.

Welter, Barbara (1966). "The Cult of True Womanhood: 1820-1860. *American Quarterly,* Summer: 151-174.

Zaretsky, Eli (1976). *Capitalism: The Family and Personal Life*. New York: Harper Colophon.

Zweig, Paul (1968). *The Heresy of Self-Love*. Princeton, NJ: Princeton University Press.

Notes

[1] This is a revised version of Chapter 2 in Francesca Cancian's *Love in America: Gender and Self-Development*. (Boston: Cambridge University Press, 1987). For an analysis of feminized love in contemporary marriage, see Cancian, 1985.

[2] The change to androgyny and intimacy in the twentieth century is examined in my book *Love in America*.

[3] The historical description, which focuses on the white middle class in New England and in other Eastern states, is based primarily on the work of Ryan, 1979; Cott, 1977; Welter, 1966; and Degler, 1980.

[4] Demos, 1979.

[5] This description of family and gender roles in the Colonies draws heavily on Ryan, 1979.

[6] *Ibid.*, pp. 23-24.

[7] *Ibid.*, pp. 24.25.

[8] Ryan, 1981. See Stone, 1979, on the transportation in England; and also Goode, 1963, and Shorter, 1975.

[9] Thus the Oneida Baptists pledged to "extend a faithful watch over all its members, also in every private relation," and to "promote true piety and family religion." In a typical court case, the Oneida County Court ordered a man to support his aging father in order to avoid expense for the town. Ryan, 1981, pp. 39 and 24.

[10] *Ibid.*, p. 9.

[11] *Ibid.*, p. 44.

[12] Johnson, 1978, p. 43.

[13] *Ibid.*, p. 46.

[14] *Ibid.*, p. 57.

[15] Demos, 1974, p. 433. Also see Johnson, 1978.

[16] Johnson, 1978, p. 7; Degler, 1980; and Ryan, 1981, describe childbearing in the nineteenth century. For an incisive analysis of mother-child intimacy and its relation to Freudian theory, see Poster, 1978.

[17] Ryan, 1981, p. 102.

[18] Both Degler, 1980 and Cott, 1977, conclude that this ideology was widely accepted in different social classes.

[19] See especially Welter, 1966; Cott, 1977; Degler, 1980; and Ryan, 1979. See also Rosenberg, 1975, and Demos, 1979. An interesting analysis of how the ideology was created in female religious groups in the early nineteenth century is presented by Ryan, 1981.

[20] Quoted in Cott, 1977, p. 64.

[21] *Ibid.*, pp. 64-65.

[22] Welter, 1966, p. 325.

[23] Degler, 1980, p. 31.

[24] Quoted in Welter, 1966, p. 326.

[25] Lantz *et al.*, 1975.

[26] Some historians argue that the separation of spheres increased women's status; see, for example, Cott, 1977, and Degler, 1980.

[27] Welter, 1966, p. 325.

[28] The quotes are from Ryan, 1981, p. 147; and G. J. Barker-Benfield, in Gordon, 1978, p. 374.

[29] Demos, 1974. The quote is from Rosenberg, 1980, p. 229. Historians tell us about the masculine ideals in the nineteenth century because there is as yet no male equivalent to the feminist-inspired research on women's roles.

[30] Rosenberg, 1980, p. 237.

[31] Gordon and Bernstein, 1970.

[32] Fiedler, 1966. Also see Swidler's 1980 discussion of male aversion to domestic love in our culture. Wahlstrom, 1979, shows how this image persists in contemporary mass media portrayals of men. The psychoanalyst Erik Erikson has also noted that American myths and folk songs glorify the womanless, unattached man without roots.

[33] See Bane, 1976, on marital dissolution, and Degler, 1980, p. 155, on household composition. Around 1870, 1 out of every 6.6 white families had servants. Taking in boarders was a popular way for a woman to bring in income, and about 20 percent or urban households had lodgers.

[34] This discussion relies on Ryan, 1979; Degler, 1980; and Flexner, 1974.

[35] Thernstrom, 1964.

[36] Calhoun, 1917, p. 74.

[37] Degler, 1980, pp. 131 and 136.

[38] Quoted in Cott, 1977, p. 160.

[39] Douglas, 1977, p. 149.

[40] Cott, 1977, p. 186.

[41] Women's reform activities are well described by Ryan, 1979 and Rothman, 1978.

[42] See Ryan, 1981, for a description of the domestic work of women in the nineteenth century and men's devaluation of this work. Douglas, 1977, also describes the increasing invisibility of women's domestic work in the nineteenth century.

[43] Cott, 1977, p. 60. See Braverman, 1975, for a description of increasing discipline and alienation at

work.

[44] Cott, 1977, p. 168. Smith-Rosenberg, 1975, and Faderman, 1981, describe women's friendships.

[45] Cott, 1977, p. 185.

[46] Faderman, 1981.

[47] Quoted in Rothman, 1978, p. 86.

[48]

[49] See Rothman, 1978, p. 85.

[50] From Ryan, 1979, p. 124.

[51] Goldman, 1931, p. 23.

[52] Historians who take this position include Ryan, 1979; Demos, 1974; and Douglas, 1977. A related change in the nineteenth century was that children became more dependent on their parents as schooling increased and apprenticeships declined; see Kett, 1977.

[53] Quoted in Rose, 1982.

[54] For example, see Jacoby, 1975, and Marcuse, 1964.

[55] Johnson, 1978, p. 7.

[56] *Ibid.*, pp. 138 and 141.

[57] Stone, 1979, pp. 172-173.

[58] *Ibid.*, pp. 141 and 155. Stone avoids clear causal arguments and does not assert a necessary connection between individualism and affect (see Chapter 6 of his book). For other evidence on the rise of individualism and a concern with the self and psychological perspective, see Lyons, 1978, and Zweig, 1968.

[59] Goode, 1963. Goode labels this the "conjugal" family system. Another sign of affective individualism is romantic novels, which were extraordinarily popular in America in the mid-nineteenth century, while in England they became very popular at the end of the eighteenth century; see Zaretsky, 1976, and Ryan, 1979. The religious revivals that swept over the northern states in the 1820s and 1830s might also be considered as a sign of affective individualism.

[60] Bellah *et al.*, 1985, pp. 33-34.

[61] It is possible that intimacy increased as patriarchal authority based on the family farm declined, as the family no longer functioned as a productive, formally organized work group, and as the values of freedom and individualism spread. Degler sees the family of this period as characterized by affection and respect between spouses along with an increasing separation of men's and women's spheres, a growing focus of women on child rearing, and a decrease in family size. See, for example, Parsons, 1954; Goode, 1963; Degler, 1980; and Shorter, 1975.

[62] Cott, 1977, p. 190.

[63] Gordon and Bernstein, 1970.

[64] On the decrease in the marriage rate, see Degler, 1980, p. 152; Stone, 1978; and Goode, 1963. On the decline in husband-wife affection, see Ryan, 1979; Barker-Benfield, 1976; and Demos, 1974. The increase in intimate friendships among women also suggests that women may have been missing something in their relations with their husbands; such friendships were rare for wives who had very affectionate marriages, according to Degler, 1980, Chapter 7.

Chapter 3

Advice about marriage. This work from 1904 has been included to illustrate the climate of our culture toward the end of the Victorian Era in the United States. While it is often humorous, it is also poignant in its relevance to some of our enduring problems and issues even now, at the dawn of the 21st century.

Chapter 3 *J. H. Greer*, Talks on Nature: Important information for both sexes (1904)

Courtship

It is a most delightful period, this time when lovers are about deciding life will not be worth much unless the other shares it. It is an important period as well, for all inharmonies in thought and character must be made to blend.

In the choosing of a life companion all feelings aside from the intellectual should be kept dormant for the time being, and the necessary requisites for a perfect union looked for. For instance, a woman who aspires to purity and goodness should not be linked to a man in whom a love for purity and goodness is deficient. A man with social faculties largely developed should marry a woman who also cares for society. A man or woman having a desire for wealth or position should mate with one of similar taste. Otherwise discord would result.

In physical make-up the law of opposites should rule. The tall and the short, the fair and the dark, the plump and the slender should marry. Every young man and woman, or every uninformed person should take a course of reading on Phrenology and the law of

23

choice, before deciding on whom they will marry (provided that person's consent can be obtained)[1].

Man and woman, in the plan of nature are complements.

> " 'As unto the bow the cord is,
> So unto the man is woman.
> Though she bends him, she obeys him,
> Though she draws him, she follows,
> Useless each without the other!'
> Thus the youthful Hiawatha said within himself."

The modern woman has had the word "obey" stricken from the marriage ceremony, having outgrown the idea of submission shared alike by Hiawatha and others equally primitive.

Having, however, consulted the law of mental and physical adaptation and selected a companion of suitable years, our young people begin courtship. What is it? A few evenings out of each week spent together intermingling the magnetic elements which make the very being together a dear delight. Amusements are enjoyed the more because enjoyed together. The hand clasp, the lover kisses, all tend to convince one that

> "There is nothing half so sweet in life
> As love's young dream –"

The precarious economic outlook which at present confronts young people is a serious stumbling block. The young man whose salary is just enough to meet his own expenses will ponder long as to how he can make it answer for two. He may not have been prudent in the use of funds up to this time, but he has had no incentive to do so till now. He cannot save very much in the city out of six, eight or ten dollars a week, but perseverance will enable him to accumulate enough to furnish a home nest in time; a place that will be a haven of refuge and rest from the storms of the active business world.

If the young woman also be earning a livelihood, perhaps she will hesitate before deciding to give up an independent career to begin home-making. Home-making will, in the end, win most women; women are dominated to such a great extent by their affections and emotions. Having decided to unite her life with a worthy young man she can add to the fund for making a common home by little self-denials. A prominent writer says "successful love takes a load off our hearts and puts it upon our shoulders." In the courtship days the load will not rest heavy while the heart is light in expectation of the culmination of their cherished hopes.

Who should be happier than the young pair with a fair life opening before them like

> "A rose with all its sweetest leaves yet folded,'

and all the glorious possibilities of mutual confidence and helpfulness and mutual love.

Too much stress cannot be laid upon the idea that information regarding the marriage relation is a necessity before marriage. To their great discredit be it said that most parents allow their children to grow up untrained in matters relating to sex, or give whatever information in such a way as to make that part of the body seem indecent. A morbid curiosity is aroused, just as would be regarding any other part of the body, if the true knowledge of its functions were smuggled away. Until purity of thought and knowledge on this question is engendered in youth we can not hope for men and women to be much cleaner spiritually.

Nothing can make up for a lack of education in youth, but a help that will greatly assist is books. Young people should glean all possible information between the time they decide to marry and the date of marriage, selecting with care their reading. All books will not do, because all authors do not treat of marriage, except in its physiological sense, and there is so much more in true wedlock than the mere physiologic.

Another point for the consideration of lovers. The tide of passion sometimes will run high in these days of close association. All familiarities which would tend toward over-stepping the bounds of prudence and propriety should be avoided. The consequences of transgression are such that no young person wishes to assume the load.

Be honest and sincere one with another. Truth should be the foundation of all dealings. Especially in money matters. Food and clothes are more intimately connected with happiness than most lovers are inclined to think. A whole after life of uprightness may not be able to expunge the effect of a single misrepresentation before marriage. It would be foolish to jeopardize the happiness of future years for a little effect in the present.

It is safe to say ninety-nine young men out of every hundred will choose for a wife one whose character is without spot or blemish, and not consider the justice or the need of having the same personal test applied to their own, as regards health, chastity and morality.

A young man may have been thrown into the filthy stream of impure social life by circumstantial ignorance; he may have gone on with the current without being befouled thereby, but that is hardly probable. Some men go on for life, destroying the beauty and usefulness of both body and soul.

Assuming, however, that he swims ashore, having seen the folly of his former course, is he a fit associate for any pure young woman until he has lived in a state of mental quarantine for some time, in order to be sure he has escaped finally from the thralldom of sensuality?

Dr. Dio Lewis has a plan for eradicating sensual thoughts which is worth the experiment. He says, "While striving to help young men into the habits of clean thinking, I have tried many expedients. With intelligent persons what I call the 'card plan' has often proved successful. That is, to write on a card a number of words, each suggesting a subject of interest or a familiar train of thought. When an impure notion obtrudes itself, the idea of danger which has been associated with it will arrest attention; the card is taken out, and a glance at it will help to shift the switch at once." A patient who had profited by this prescription of the doctor's said, "I cannot tell you how clean and manly I feel. I would not go back for a mine of gold. I believe that this expedient might help the worst victim of sexual filth into purity and manliness, if he would only try it with a good strong will."

One idea further for this period of courtship. The young man must make up his mind to try to preserve the depth and sweetness and delicacy of the attraction that brought them together, by treating his wife with the same consideration he gives his sweetheart. Many a young husband supposes that the nuptial ceremony gives him the fullest power over the person of his wife. Nothing more disastrous to their future happiness from every possible point of view can be imagined. The most innocent and affectionate young wife will feel that she has been abused through the holiest impulses of her nature if she yields to excessive sexual demands on the part of her spouse. This is not an intentional wrong on the part of husbands – only lack of correct information, and that is the reason for bringing up the subject for consideration during courtship. Knowledge as to the way to live a pure married life is worth more before mistakes are made. "An ounce of prevention is worth a pound of cure."

Persons who would not be persuaded to enter a business career without a preparatory course, enter the matrimonial career blindfolded, having no guide for passion. The shipwrecks of so many barks of health and happiness can testify to the mistaken idea that ignorance is purity.

Marriage

Ralph Waldo Emerson says, "We are not very much to blame for our bad marriages; we live amid hallucinations, and this especial trap is laid to trip up our feet with, and all are tripped first or last. But the mighty Mother Nature who had been so sly with us, as if she felt she owed us some indemnity, insinuates into the Pandora box of marriage some deep and serious benefits and some great joys."

Every one will agree that there is a vast difference between marriage as it is and marriage as it should be. A marriage properly entered into by chaste partners understanding the natural laws which should govern the conjugal relation, is probably the happiest condition upon earth.

But the divorce record, which almost keeps pace with the weddings, is a testimonial that few reach the ideal state. The ideal can never be reached so long as we are dominated by passion, or while the gratification of passion or the results attending gratification is the aim of the institution of marriage. Marriage is of the mental and spiritual as well as the physical, a blending of all three elements for the uplifting of man and woman. It is called a lottery because reason and judgment are so seldom exercised in connection with sex attraction; hence the responsibilities should not be assumed in haste, lest never-ending unhappiness be brought upon two individuals.

Matrimony gives the opportunity and the occasion for the high faculties of the mind to unfold, while a single life offers self as the chief object of consideration. The Buddhist says there can be no such thing as happiness until self is lost sight of.

There are many arguments used to prove marriage is a failure by those who either have made mistakes in choice or who, by a violation of natural laws in the conjugal relation, have not tasted happiness. The fact still remains unshaken that it is the doorway through which the real life with all its blessings is attained. No argument is needed to prove it to be the natural condition of adult life, and that the best successes of life are reached through a harmonious marital union.

Among those living in "single blessedness" the strongest supporters are they who have not loved. They wonder what there is to induce anyone "to commit matrimony"; from their standpoint the pros and cons are considered in a material vein, and the decision rendered accordingly. The bachelor says a wife divides his pleasure and doubles his sorrows. That the world is divided into two classes – those who are unmarried but wish they were and those who are married but wish they were not.

It is true the unmarried have opportunities for learning not possible, unless under the best financial conditions, for the married. They may surround themselves with books and other means of study, and broaden their intellect until the world does them honor. There is the beautiful story of Faust, who had spent a lifetime in delving into the mysteries of nature, and found one lifetime was not enough to fathom them. They he longed for a taste of human joy which his studious life had not allowed him, and sold his soul to the devil for the restoration of his youth, and for love. But Mephisto was finally vanquished after producing untold misery and death for Faust and Marguerite, by the great strength and purity of their love.

Not every one is wedded to learning who lives a celibate life, but those who are surely perpetrate bigamy in marrying a woman. No woman likes second place in her husbands thoughts, and the wife of a man absorbed in public work, or business, or learning, feels she is defrauded of attentions that should be hers; that she has been wooed and won as a matter of convenience, and there surely will come a time of rebellion in any spirited woman. Do not be bigamists.

A woman student can better think her way through without the little cares of wifehood and possible motherhood. St. Stockham has made clear the idea that the maternal desire can be gratified by giving to the world child thoughts – thoughts born of the mind – instead of children born of the body.

Marriage is a school of itself, as life is a school. Even if everything has beforehand been studied as how to attain the best conditions for these relations, it yet remains that few men and women will really and truly know each other until the intimacy of wedded life begins. There are little things to be overlooked in each other, and little discrepancies to be pruned out of one's own character. Pages and pages have been written on "Advice to Wives" and "Advice to Husbands," beginning with "don't do this" or "don't do that." But no one set of rules will apply. Each husband and each wife is an individuality, and if wise they can be a law unto themselves. "Of all actions of a man's life his marriage does least concern other people," says Selden, "yet, of all actions of our life, it is most meddled with by other people." Now, the object of this chapter is not to meddle with any individual marriage, but to point out a few of the pitfalls common through ignorance.

Eternal vigilance is the price of love as well as of liberty. Like all fire it needs constant fuel; so while the ups and downs of life come and go, do not neglect the courtesies and sweet expressed sentiments toward one another. "I love you" is just as sweet to the wife of five, ten or fifty years, accompanied by lovers kisses and embraces, as it was in the earliest days of courtship. It is a mistake to apply the fuel only once in awhile. Sometimes the fire for want of it may smolder away and die, and the rekindling will be no easy task. Guard well this holy flame that makes marriage sacred.

As to the other means of preserving the fineness of true marriage, here are some suggestions of a material order and yet so closely related to the ethical that there should be no separation:

Let no married lovers think of habitually occupying one bed. It can do no good, and it is undoubtedly one source of inharmony and lack of physical hardiness. What one may gain in vitality the other loses. The magnetic attraction is neutralized, if not destroyed. Aside, and above all other reasons, is the one that separate beds will in a great measure help overcome sexual excesses. The close bodily contact under a common bed-clothing is a constant provocation to amorous ideas and sensations. It is the purely sensual that needs to be put one side that the spiritual may have chance for growth. This idea of separate beds cannot be combated on any other than the ground of the sensualist. Children will be less liable to come unless wished for by both its parents. The mere gratification of sex desire is a very poor excuse for calling a soul into being, and a very poor heritage to bestow upon the little lives that should be occasion for purest thought before as well as after they are called into life.

The world looks on in disapproval of any who attempts to handle the social question without gloves. It prides itself in its ignorance, and calls itself pure. Purity is not ignorance and never will be; it is a great insight. If ignorance were purity why are the sins of ignorance against natural laws visited with the same severity as sins of any other king? People are constantly sinning against their bodies when a little light of knowledge would enable them to see wherein lay their offense. But the world has so ordained it that those who seek light must find it in hidden places. Not a single text-book on physiology treats of the sex organs any more than if they did not exist; not a teacher, even if he be awake to the necessity of knowledge regarding that part of the body, dare mention it. And youth is not clean. Schools are even called hotbeds of vice.

When youth shall know himself he will be less liable to consider marriage a cloak for lust. He will then steer right his course in order to preserve happiness.

At present a girl before marriage is kept from nearly all knowledge regarding wifely or maternal duties. If the young man is informed it is usually of not one whit more practical character. He has probably no idea that there should be a limit to sexual gratification before exhaustion.

The young wife who is rudely approached on her wedding night will always carry in her memory a nightmare of repulsion.

All men do not go to the excess of brutality, it is true. Those in whom passion is strongest and who look upon marriage as the door of gratification are the worst sinners, even if they do not so recognize themselves.

A well-known woman writer on this subject who is brilliant in her denunciation of ignorance, asks these pertinent questions: "Is there one man in ten who does not insist on the payment of the conjugal debt on the first night of marriage, be his wife's reluctance and terrors what they may? Is there one man in a hundred who will give his new-made bride a week to become acquainted and reconciled to the idea of the new relation to which she is pledged? Is there one in one thousand who is willing to wait with the same patience and to use the same art that the libertine in his superior wisdom knows so well how to employ – arts perfectly proper and commendable in lawful wedlock – even though it may take months before his purpose is gained, so that his wife shall be a willing partner to the consummation of marriage?"

This, young man, is something for your consideration from a reliable source. Only a woman knows a woman's needs.

And, young woman, consider now some of your rights. There was a fine attraction drew you to the young man about to be your husband, aside from a kinship of ideas and similarity of tastes. An attraction so exquisite as to be a delight to you. Do not feel it to be your duty to give yourself over to your companion on the wedding night unless there is a perfect spontaneity on the part of yourself. Do not pretend to enjoy the sexual embrace because you love and are fearful of being misunderstood if you do not. Prostitutes imitate desire, either out of wedlock or in it. Women have always been weakest on this point when their love has been strongest, and yielded their bodies when their souls rebelled.

To call forth passion in most women it is necessary to bring out the love and tender graces of kindness and consideration, otherwise she is repelled. And it is her right to demand this consideration or withhold herself. She belongs to herself alone, and no man has any moral claim to sexual congress with her when she does not freely and lovingly give him the right. If this were recognized in the marriage relation there would soon be fewer women sick in both soul and body.

Another point that must be looked to by newly married lovers is the frequency with which they come together in the new relation. Avoid temptation now as you did before marriage, remembering "satiety blunts passion and clips the wings of love." Every natural appetite is for a good purpose, but excessive gratification is surely depraving. Hunger for food shows the system needs fuel, but eating because the food tastes well brings on dyspepsia and kindred ailments. The habit of indulging any appetite too frequently rivets upon the sinner chains too strong to be broken, and brings in its train disaster.

Each sex sees in the other that which it demands and craves. If they are mutually agreeable they are drawn toward each other with impulses for which they forsake all other ties. Therein is great danger, for no other appetite binds its victims more strongly than does the sexual passion when given unbridled sway.

Some thinkers are inclined to the belief that procreation is the sole cause for the marital embrace, but that is the other extreme from the present idea of indulgence to the point of exhaustion. Persons of different temperaments and habit or occupation are benefited by this love feast at intervals of varying lengths. For the hardiest and fullest of vitality no less time than a week should elapse. Occupying separate beds will help those who will make their lives chaste. Chastity in the sense used here means, not an entire abstinence from sex relation, but a union in which mere sensuality is lost sight of.

Children will be but the outcropping of the pure love of any well developed married pair, the number to be limited, of course, to the desire for and ability to provide good pre-natal and post-natal conditions.

Reproductions of the species is certainly not the end and aim of marriage. The world needs a better quality of people rather than larger numbers. But more of this in another chapter.

Here is a stanza written in the dear true spirit of welcome parenthood:

"We used to think how she had come
    Even as comes the flower
The last and perfect added gift
    To crown Love's morning hour;
And how in her was imaged forth
    The love we could not say,
As on the little dew-drops round
    Shines back the heart of day."

With children conceived and welcomed in love, a married life is one of happiness, and a life worth living for.

Collamer's Notes

1.   Dr. Greer is referring to a theory originated by Joseph Gall (1758-1828), an Austrian anatomist who thought personality and character traits were reflected in the development of different areas of the brain and could be "read" by noting the shape of the skull.

Chapter 4

Backlash to early feminism. During the first rise of feminism men were concerned about the changes in our culture and the accompanying changes in women's roles and attitudes. This concern led to a defined crisis in masculinity that Dr. Kimmel delineates here in his discussion of the three of the most common ways that men felt during this time of change.

Chapter 4 *Michael S. Kimmel,* From Separate Spheres to Sexual Equality: Men's Responses to Feminism at the Turn of the Century

> Doubt is in the air. There is an upheaval of traditions and conventionalities...
> With no firm ground to stand upon, the self-confidence of the past has vanished.
> Disbelief in everything involves disbelief in one's self. -- A. W. Warner, 1909

The emergence of the modern feminist in the late nineteenth and early twentieth century is a well-documented and much celebrated phenomenon. Less well understood and far less well documented are the variety of reactions to her emergence by American men. Such a lacuna can be explained by the convergence of several problems in the historical study of gender in the United States. For one thing, students of gender have most frequently adopted a "sex-role" model to study masculinity and femininity, a model that is designed to specify the ways in which biological males and biological females become socialized as men and women in any particular culture. This model can be labeled "individualist" (Risman, 1987) because it focuses on learned personal behaviors. This paradigm implies an ahistorical inevitability, which is contradicted by its emphasis on cultural relativity; in each culture, the researcher can identify a kind of static sex-role container into which all biological males and females are forced to fit. As such, the paradigm ignores the extent to which our conceptions of masculinity and femininity -- the content of either the male or female sex role -- is relational, that is, the product of gender relations that are historically and socially conditioned. Masculinity and femininity are relational constructs; the definition of either depends upon the definition of the other. "Male" and "female" may have some universal characteristics (though even

33

here, the research on biological dimorphism suggests a certain fluidity), but one cannot understand the social constructions of either masculinity or femininity without reference to the other. The sex-role socialization paradigm has been critically discussed and evaluated in detail (see, for example, Gerson and Peiss, 1985; Gould and Kern-Daniels, 1977; Lopata and Thorne, 1978; Shapiro, 1982; Stacey and Thorne, 1985; and Tresemer, 1975). These writers, though, tend to stress the problems with the model as it applies to the study of gender in general, or more often to women in particular. Little, if any, attention has been paid specifically to men and masculinity as a social scientific problematic, which is my intention here.

The sex-role socialization model is ahistorical in another sense. Almost all sex-role research focuses on attributes, indicating behavioral or attitudinal traits that are associated with the particular sex role. Thus, changes in sex roles appear as changes in the list of traits or attitudes associated with masculinity or femininity. But masculinity and femininity are more the products of role enactments; instead of specifying traits, research might detail the ways in which people negotiate their "roles," the historically fluid and variable enactments of specific role prescriptions. Such a focus on gender relations allows articulation of traits at separate times, but also the processes by which the changes occur.

The sex-role paradigm also minimizes the extent to which gender relations are based on power. Not only do men as a group exert power over women as a group, but the historically derived definitions of masculinity and femininity reproduce those power relations. Masculinity becomes associated with those traits that imply authority and mastery; femininity with those traits that suggest passivity and subordination. By undervaluing the historical and social bases for gender relations, then, the sex-role paradigm can reproduce the very problems it seeks to understand.

An emphasis on gender relations as historically and socially constructed also sheds different light on another problem. (The gender relations model is similar to the "microstructural" model proposed by the editors.) The sex-role model has assumed fixed, static, and mutually exclusive role containers with no interpenetration. Further, bipolar mutual exclusivity of sex roles reinforces oppositional assumptions about masculinity and femininity; though defined in reference to abstract ideals, sex roles reinforce the popular notions of the "otherness" of the "opposite" sex.

I believe therefore that the sex-role socialization model is theoretically inadequate on conceptual grounds. But its explanatory weakness is best revealed when one looks at those historical movements in the public consciousness, moments in which gender issues assume a prominent position of gender confusion and the vigorous reassertion of traditional gender roles against serious challenges to inherited configurations -- moments, we might say, of "crisis" in gender relations, historical moments not unlike our own.

The late nineteenth and early twentieth centuries were also such an historical moment of crisis in gender relations, when the meanings of both femininity and masculinity were challenged and various groups attempted to reconstitute gender along different relational lines. The rise of feminism and the emergence of the New Woman and the articulation of distinctly different identities for the heterosexual and the homosexual -- prior to the late nineteenth century, identity did not inhere in sexual behaviors, and especially in the gender of one's sexual partner -- explicitly challenged inherited constructions. And responses to these challenges ranged from frightened retreat to traditional configurations to demarcating institutional spheres for the vigorous assertion of renewed masculinity, to the rise of sex-role theory itself, an historical popularization of the Freudian notion that appropriate gender organization and sexual orientation were products of cultural interventions in the child's life, that the development of personality was, as he put it, "a work of culture -- not unlike the draining of the Zuider Zee" (Freud, 1965: 80).

When, in the late nineteenth and early twentieth centuries, gender relations were challenged, men were suddenly confused; no one knew what it meant to be a "real man." (Fortunately for the scholar, such periods of confusion yield a rich set of texts that give popular readers advice on how to recapture or reconstruct their gender identity.) Men's responses can be organized into three separate categories, which suggest three alternate strategies for the reconstitution of gender. Some men, whom I call the "anti-feminists," demanded the return of women to the private sphere of hearth and home, yearning nostalgically for a mythic separation of spheres that helped to keep women from explicit challenges to men in the public realm. Other men, though not entirely indifferent to women's invasion of the public sphere, sought solutions in developing separate public institutions for men. This "pro-male" response could combat the perceived "feminization" of American culture (Douglas, 1977) through institutions to train young men in a virile hardiness appropriate to their gender. Finally, a small but visible group of men believed that the solution to the gender crisis at the turn of the century rested on embracing the feminist model of social reconstruction. These "pro-feminist" men actively supported campaigns for women's public participation, especially suffrage, as well as more personal demands for sexual autonomy.

The explication of these three distinct trajectories of men's responses to feminism at the turn of the century provides an historical counterpoint to sex-role socialization models, revealing that model's conceptual inadequacy to fully encompass shifting gender relations. For example, though historically linked, the anti-feminist and the pro-male responses articulate different strategies for restoring the traditional balance between women and men, which rest on the shifting relations between public and private spheres. The sex-role socialization model, resting on acquisition of individual psychological traits, is particularly ill-suited to account for these two trajectories. Nor is it well equipped to account for the historical emergence of pro-feminist men at specific historical junctures and not at others. One could resort to a sex-role deviant model that questions the appropriateness of fit between these men and the male self-role, which is precisely what many antagonists of pro-feminist men actually did. But the historical question of the emergence of pro-feminist men at some times and not at others would remain.

To the historical sociologist, crises in gender relations occur at specific historical junctures, when structural changes transform the institutions of personal life, such as marriage and the family, and hence the possibility for gender identity. In this paper, after specifying these structural shifts, I shall turn to the rise of the New Woman, who became the target for the three male responses to feminism. Understanding these responses requires discussion of several ideological currents of the period, especially the rise of scientific discourse as a counter to anti-modernist sentiments. In its nineteenth century incarnation, feminism represented a paragon of modernist thought, and male responses to feminism were inextricably bound to responses to modernity.

One sociological implication of a gender relations model is that it allows the observer to specify not only the reconstitution of gender over time, but also the directionality of changes in gender relations. The historical evidence suggests that though both masculinity and femininity are socially constructed within an historical context of gender relations, definitions of masculinity are historically reactive to changing definitions of femininity. Such a claim runs counter to traditional formulations of gender -- such as David Riesman's comment that "characterological change in the West seems to occur first with men" (1950: 18). Instead, my argument suggests that since men benefit from inherited definitions of masculinity and femininity, they would be unlikely to initiate change. In fact, it would appear that men as a group have benefited from the sex-role socialization model that has governed behavioral science's treatment of gender, since it uses masculinity as a normative standard of reference and maximizes the distance between the two genders while it minimizes the extent to which these definitions reproduce existing power relations, are historically variable, and are therefore open to challenge.

The New Woman challenged traditional gender relations, which called into question the definition of masculinity, which, in turn, prompted a set of male responses at the turn of the century. Let us begin the explication of these responses by examining the circumstances under which the New Woman emerged.

35

Structural Changes and the Erosion of Traditional Gender Arrangements in the Late Nineteenth Century

The early nineteenth century provided a fertile environment for an expansive American manhood. Geographic expansion -- the taming of the West and the "pacification" of its native population -- combined with rapid industrial and urban growth to fuel a "virile" optimism about social possibilities. The Jacksonian assault on "effete" European bankers, and the frighteningly "primitive" Native American population, grounded identity in a "securely achieved manhood" (Rogin, 1975: 162).

By mid-century, though, "the walls of the male establishment began to crack," as social and economic changes also transformed the social institutions in which gender relations were negotiated (marriage, family, sexuality). Westward expansion came to an abrupt end as the frontier closed; the unspoiled virgin land that "gave America its identity" (Rogin, 1975: 79) was gone. "For nearly three centuries," wrote Frederick Jackson Turner in 1896, "the dominant fact in American life has been expansion. And now the frontier is gone, and with its going has closed the first period of American history."

Rapid industrialization in the late nineteenth century radically transformed men's relationship to their work. The independent artisan, the autonomous small farmer, the small shopkeeper, were everywhere disappearing. Before the Civil War, almost nine of every ten American men were farmers or self-employed businessmen; by 1870 that figure had dropped to two-thirds, and by 1910, less than one-third of all American men were so employed. Increased mechanization and the routinization of labor accompanied rapid industrialization; individual workers were increasingly divorced from control over the labor process as well as dispossessed of ownership. Thus Henry George wrote in *Social Problems* (1883) that labor-saving devices were "absolutely injurious" and result in "positive evils" for the working man, "degrading men into the position of mere feeders of machines:"

> rendering the working man more dependent; depriving him of skill and the opportunities to acquire it; lessening his control over his own condition and his hope of improving it; cramping his mind, and in many cases distorting and enervating his body (Trachtenberg, 1982: 43).

In such an atmosphere, the dramatic international economic collapse of 1873 was especially powerful. A series of bankruptcies, bank failures, and foreclosures sharpened political conflict. (In 1874 alone, over 6,000 businesses closed, and 900 closed every month during one quarter in 1878.) In the South, Southwest, and Midwest, dispossessed farmers fought back against big capital through the Farmers Alliance and the Populist movement, perhaps the United States' only genuine mass leftist political movement. In the burgeoning cities, a widening class rift and waves of immigrants fueled hostilities, which erupted in a wave of strikes and revolts in 1877 that brought the nation to the brink of armed insurrection. "Sudden as a thunderburst from a clear sky the crisis came upon the country," wrote journalist J,. Dacus in 1877. "It seemed as if the whole social and political structure was on the very brink of ruin" (Trachtenberg, 1982: 70-71).

And indeed it was. During the last decade of the century, American men were increasingly restless, besieged by a seemingly endless string of structural problems: "the failures and corruption of reconstruction, the longest depression in American history, insatiable trusts, swarms of what were held to be sexually potent and racially inferior immigrants, and a government discredited at all levels" (Barker-Benfield, 1976: 84).

One set of responses to this cultural crisis was the anti-modernist critique of American culture. A convulsively anti-modernist sentiment captured the imaginations of many groups, although it was often expressed in contradictory ways. For some, anti-modernism glorified individual achievement; for others, it revealed a desperate longing for community. Resurgent medievalism, a fascination with oriental culture, and religious revivalism all celebrated the annihilation of the ego and its immersion into a transcendent community. The anti-modernist vision thoroughly rejected the city, with its "dark satanic mills," as the breeding ground for both "idleness" and "vicious classes" according to Wendell Phillips (Leah, 1980: 334). Frank Lloyd Wright's tirade against New York captures part of the anti-urban sentiment. He described it in *The Future of Architecture* as

> a place fit for banking and prostitution and not much else... a crime of crimes... a vast prison... triumph of the herd instinct... outgrown and overgrown... the greatest mouth in the world... humanity preying upon humanity... carcass... parasite... fibrous tumor... pig-pile... incongruous mantrap of monstrous dimensions... enormity devouring manhood, confusing personality by frustration of individuality. Is this not anti-Christ? The Moloch that knows no God but *more*? (cited in Muschamp, 1983: 15).

To others, the city was less a sinkhole of vice and violence than an enervating seductress, skillfully sapping men of their virility. In contrast to the frontier, "the city represents civilization, confinement, and female efforts to domesticate the world" (Pugh, 1983: 150). Its effect, as Ernest Thompson Seton put it, was to make us "degenerate. We know money grubbing machine politics, degrading sports, cigarettes... false ideals, moral laxity, and lessening church power, in a word 'city rot' has worked evil in the nation" (Macleod, 1983: 32). The city was cast as cultural villain, either because of its effete feminizing refinement, or because of the ominous danger lurking in the rows of working-class tenements that housed the unwashed immigrant hordes. Each strain of thought saw a threat to masculinity.

Responses to Structural Change by Women and Men

Feminism and the New Woman

Against this background of dramatic structural change and ideological developments, the family and the relations between women and men were undergoing upheaval and conflict in the late nineteenth century (Rosenberg, 1980: 235). Rapid capitalist industrialization "increasingly subverted the older sexual division of labor... [and] created conditions favorable to the emergence of women into the public realm with men" (Leach, 1980: 123). Women were involved in arenas that directly touched the lives of men

> in temperance, social science, and moral education; in the reforms... of the marriage laws... that legally permitted women to transact their own business, keep their own separate earnings, and retain ownership of their separate estates; in the reform of many state laws... that sanctioned the rights of women, whether married or single, to employment of large numbers of women in the industrial sector of the economy and... in the professions, especially medicine, journalism, and education (Leach, 1980: 123).

Women's increased public presence was buttressed by changes in the family, such as shrinking family size, increasing nuclearization of family structure, and a clear demarcation between workplace and household as separate units of production and consumption, respectively (Chafetz and Dworkin, 1986: 4). The median age for marriage for men was higher in 1890 than in any subsequent year until 1986, and a statistical imbalance between the sexes, with women out-numbering men, was observed (*New York Times*, 10 December 1986, and Todd, 1867: 20). Motherhood was increasingly professionalized, cast as a "calling," which coincided with a decline in the number of household servants and greater absence of busy fathers from the home, which "made the mother-son relationship appear threatening to proper masculine socialization" (Hantover, 1980: 290). Everywhere, "motherhood was advancing, fatherhood was in retreat" (Rotundo, 1983: 30).

Such changes placed contradictory demands on a woman; she was to be both the True Woman, "emotional, dependent, and gentle -- a born follower," and the Ideal Mother, "strong, self-reliant, protective, an efficient caretaker in relation to children and home" (Smith-Rosenberg, 1985: 199). By "combining piety and domesticity with submissiveness and passivity," the notion of the True Woman "controlled women and narrowed their options" (Degler, 1980:26-27). But both the Ideal Mother and the True Woman were confined to the home and other arenas of social reproduction, so that culture became "increasingly the sphere of women, of ladies of charity as well as schoolteachers and librarians" (Trachtenberg, 1982: 145). That American culture was increasingly "feminized" became a dominant theme in the discourse between women and men. The separation of work and home, the privatization of family life, and other changes meant that childhood socialization -- by parents, teachers, and religious leaders -- was increasingly the work of women, as mothers, schoolteachers, and Sunday school teachers (Douglas, 1977). By the late nineteenth century, "women were teaching boys to be men" (Rotundo, 1983: 32).

Several social changes -- the rise of women's colleges, increased literacy, delayed age of marriage, an ideology of upward mobility, and capitalist development -- gave rise to the New Woman, a single, highly educated, economically autonomous woman who "challenged existing gender relations and the distribution of power" (Smith-Rosenberg, 1985: 245). Since, as Sarah Norton observed in 1870, the "inequality of women finds its origins in marriage," and to make political equality possible, "social equality of the sexes must precede it" (Leach, 1980: 190), the New Woman eschewed marriage and "fought for professional visibility, espoused innovative, often radical economic and social reforms, and wielded real political power" (Smith-Rosenberg, 1985: 245). The New Woman was an avowed feminist, who campaigned for suffrage and asserted her autonomy in the world of men. "My aim," said one, "is to make myself a true woman, one worthy of the name, and not to be one of the delicate little dolls or the silly fools who make up the bulk of American women, slaves to society and fashion" (Lasch, 956: 67). Such expressions of autonomy carried serious costs for women; many believing that the price of independence was femininity, took on men's names, dressed as men and behaved as men. "The determination to be a 'true woman' forced one in effect to lead a man's life" (Lasch, 1965: 68). The rise of the women's movement is a direct outcome of those structural change, arising "during times of, and in response to, general socioeconomic and cultural change, changes that include, but are not restricted to alterations in the family and the roles of women" (Chafetz and Dworkin, 1986: 38).

The Crisis of Masculinity

Thus the stage was set for a new "crisis of masculinity," in the late nineteenth and early twentieth century United States. Structural changes had transformed the structure of gender relations; both men and women struggled to redefine the meanings of masculinity and femininity.

> What did it mean to be masculine or feminine? What did the adjectives signify? The intensity of the speculation about these questions discloses anxieties which lie much deeper than anything associated with the greater leisure of the modern woman or the flight of household from the home (Lasch, 1965: 57).

One historian argues that, in fact, the "real gender drama in this period involve[d] the changes in men's lives and their reactions to them" (Hartman, 1984: 13). Writers acknowledged that "their readership was hungry to be told of what true manhood and true womanhood consisted," and though they often "flew to the simplest, most extreme kind of definitions" (Barker-Benfield, 1976: 210) a serious reexamination was also under way. Men felt themselves besieged by social breakdown and crisis, as "the familiar routes to manhood [became] either washed out or roadblocked" (Hartman, 1984: 13), and as male anxieties intensified by democracy and industrialization.

Men... were jolted by changes in the economic and social order which made them perceive that their superior position in the gender order and their supposedly "natural" male roles and prerogatives weren't somehow rooted in the human condition, that they were instead the result of a complex set of relationships subject to change and decay (Hartman, 1984: 13).

At both the textual and the institutional levels -- in works of fiction, sermons, and scientific tracts as well as in public policy and voluntary associations -- the late nineteenth century crisis of masculinity revealed three important reactions to perceived feminization of American popular culture. First, there was a considerable anti-feminist backlash, which, casting women as the source of men's troubles, sought to reestablish the male dominance that was perceived to have eroded. Second, we can observe a pro-male backlash, which sought to vigorously reassert traditional masculinity, especially as a cultural and political ethos, against social and political trends of which feminism was but a symptom, not a cause. Finally, a small but important group of men openly embraced feminist ideas and ideals as the signposts pointing toward a radically different future.

The Anti-Feminist Backlash

For some men, the need to redefine masculinity was caused by women's ill-advised challenge to their traditional role; if masculinity was in crisis, it was women's fault, and the solution to the crisis was the revival of a hypermasculine subordination of women. A strongly misogynist current runs through a number of religious tracts, medical treatises, and political pamphlets of this period, as the assault against women's gains came largely from the religious and medical spheres and from the opposition to women's suffrage. All three discourses resorted to a revivified emphasis on the "natural" differences between men and women as the basis for social differentiation; opponents of increasing economic, political, and social equality between men and women almost always resort to arguments about the "natural order of things" as counters to progressive social trends.

For example, pamphlets about women and sexuality written by women and clergy "played with stereotypic sex distinctions," providing "a testament of sexual tension, of covertly stated hatred of women by men and the reverse" (Douglas 1977: 228). A new "muscular Christianity" hailed a remasculinized Jesus: He was "no dough-faced, lick-spittle proposition," proclaimed Billy Sunday, but "the greatest scrapper who ever lived" (Douglas, 1977: 327). Texts such as Thomas Hughes's *The Manliness of Christ* (1880) and Carl Case's *The Masculine in Religion* (1906) echoed this remasculination of Jesus. And the Right Reverend John L. Spalding, Catholic bishop of Peoria, fused political repression and sexual repression of women when he wrote:

> Sensuality and love, though mysteriously related, are contrary as religion and superstition. The baser passion grows upon the grave of the finer virtue. Woman, like religion, appeals to what is highest in man. Her power over him is that of sentiment, and to seek to place her in rivalry with him in the rude business of life is an aim worthy of an atheistic and material age (Gardella, 1984: 116).

Men's anti-suffrage organizations sprang up around the nation to rally men behind the masculine cause. Suffrage was seen as the "ultimate invasion of the male domain by women in their drive to save the Republic" (Dubbert, 1979: 86). Some organizations, like the Man Suffrage Association, were composed of men representing the industries that had been active in the anti-suffrage cause (Flexner, 1975: 311; see also Chafetz and Dinorkin, 1986: 31). Horace Bushnell, a mid-nineteenth century reformer, went so far (1867) as to claim that women would be physiologically damaged if they got the vote, growing larger, developing heavier brains, and losing their unique feminine mannerisms, and features. It wasn't so much, he argued, that they should be deprived of the vote as *exempted* from it, because of their lofty position and female role (see Frothingham, 1890: 177).

Opposition to women's suffrage reasserted a natural division between women and men and often rested on a distinction between natural right and civil right. "It would seem best," wrote John Todd (1867: 25), "for those who, at any hazard or labor, earn the property, to select the rulers, and have this responsibility." Opposition to suffrage was hailed as a patriotic act. "The American Republic stands before the world as the supreme expression of masculine forces" claimed the Illinois Association Opposed to Women's Suffrage in 1910. Those who supported women's advance, or progressive reformism generally, were considered less than American and hence less than real men.

> Reformers and genteel intellectuals who stood above party battles invited the scorn of the regulars, a scorn couched frequently in images fusing anger at feminizing culture with sexual innuendo, and manly braggadocio of the stalwarts: "political hermaphrodite," "miss-Nancys," "man-milliners." Nonpartisans were a "third sex," "the neuter gender not popular in nature or society" (Trachtenberg, 1982: 163).

Men used the "natural" division between the sexes as the justification for opposition to women's education. "I think the great danger of our day is forcing the intellect of woman beyond what her physical organization will possibly bear," wrote John Todd (1867: 23). He counseled (1867: 25) giving women "all the advantages and all the education which her organization so tender and delicate, will bear; but don't try to make the anemone into an oak, nor to turn the dove out to wrestle with storms and winds, under the idea that she may just as well be an eagle as a dove."

Medical texts revealed the twin terrors of sexuality and women's advances, and many manuals conflated their effects, casting women as both lustful temptresses and pious guardians of home and hearth. The male response to the New Woman underscores how scientific discourse came to dominate the arguments over women's equality. Men first attacked the New Woman for her rejection of motherhood. Edward Bok, editor of *Ladies Home Journal*, linked this to structural changes when he wrote that "[t]wenty years ago, a change in economic conditions, caused chiefly by the invention of labor saving devices, found thousands of women suddenly thrown with leisure on their hands." As a result, women were drawn away from the "great and fundamental problems directly touching the marriage relation and the home" (Bok, 1910: 5-6). Soon, armed with new medical evidence, the New Woman was attacked for her rejection of femininity in general. Thus Dr. Alfred Stille observed in his presidential address to the American Medical Association in 1871:

> Certain women seek to rival men in manly sports... and the strong minded ape them in all things, even in dress. In doing so, they may command a sort of admiration such as all monstrous productions inspire, especially when they tend towards a higher type than their own (Ehrenreich and English, 1979: 65).

Rejecting motherhood and femininity, the New Woman was also cast as rejecting men. She was a third sex, an intermediate sex, a "mannish lesbian." By linking social protest to biological differences, male anti-feminists could claim that this war against the socially constructed gender was really a war against nature.

> Men's growing sense of vulnerability after the Civil War -- their notion of social crisis and the concomitant gynecological crescendo -- cannot be disassociated from the increasing vociferousness of women at the same time, most noticeably on the suffrage front. Doctors like other men also displayed persistent anxiety over the growing numbers of the new, conspicuously consuming, fashionable life style of city women, their style dangerously attractive to all women (Baker-Benfield, 1976: 123).

From this growing fear came an episode of reactionary myth-making; commentators "clothed gender distinctions specific to late nineteenth century industrial countries in the unchangeablity of human biology," making the social appear natural and immutable (Smith-Rosenberg, 1985: 289).

On the other side, physicians warned against feminized boys, and spent tremendous energy in advising parents on proper socialization to manhood. In the same presidential address cited above, Dr. Stille, warned that "a man with feminine traits of character or with the frame and carriage of a female is despised by both the sex he ostensibly belongs to and that of which he is at once a caricature and a libel" (Barker-Benfield, 1976: 86). One physician wrote that "a woman admires in a man true manliness, and is repelled by weakness and effeminacy. A womanish man awakens either the pity or the contempt of the fair sex" (Rosenberg, 1980: 231). And Dr. Augustus Kinsley Gardner stressed the imperative of different childrearing techniques for boys and girls. His extensive consideration of male masturbation in *Our Children* (1872) led him to argue against feather beds for boys, because "the very softness is not desirable, while the very excess of heat conduces to a frame of mind not desirable, engenders and ferments lascivious thoughts in the adolescent, and is otherwise very objectionable" (Barker-Benfield, 1976: 232). Parents had an enormous responsibility, and manuals proliferated to help them guide their children through the perilous journey to maturity. Several cautioned against dancing, book-learning, and even fraternities, since they would corrupt the young, (see McKeever, 1913: passim). Barely concealed were views of children, especially young boys, as increasingly impressionable and vulnerable to feminine wiles, and of women as dangerous and tempting threats to masculinity. Male anti-feminists were wary of the feminizing clutches of mothers and teachers, whose refined civility would be the undoing of American masculinity, and they sought to push women out of the public domain and return them to the home passive, idealized figurines, so that their influence could no longer sap the vitality of the nation.

Nowhere is the male anti-feminist backlash better expressed than in Henry James' novel *The Bostonians* (1886), whose hero, the dashing Basil Ransom, is afraid that the natural masculinity of political leaders would be rendered impotent by meddling, aggressive women; he "projects his anxiety onto women and provides... an explicit literary example of the castration complex" (Pugh, 1983: 109).

> The whole generation is womanized; the masculine tone is passing out of the world; it's a feminine, nervous, hysterical, chattering canting age, an age of hollow phrases and false delicacy and exaggerated solicitudes and coddled sensibilities, which, if we don't soon look out, will usher in the reign of mediocrity, of the feeblest and flattest and most pretentious that has ever been. The masculine character, the ability to dare and endure, to know and yet not fear reality, to look the world in the face and take it for what it is... that is what I want to preserve, or rather... recover; and I must tell you that I don't in the least care what becomes of you ladies while I make the attempt! (James, 1965: 343).

The assertion of masculinity required the resubordination of women.

The Pro-Male Response

Other men were equally anxious and distressed about masculinity, but saw solutions to gender crisis in a vigorous reassertion of traditional masculinity in other, more public domains. Women, themselves, were not the enemy; women's increased power was but symptomatic of cultural changes that had reduced the importance and visibility of masculinity. Masculinist sentiments countered feminization as a cultural process, rather than women, either as a group or as individuals. Several well-known authors jumped on the masculinist bandwagon. Melville argued that masculinity was a "resistance to sentimentalism," and "effort at a genuinely political and philosophical life" (Douglas 1977: 294), and Harvard senior John Dos Passos complained to a friend in 1917:

> I think we are all of us a pretty milky lot, don't you? With our tea table convictions and our radicalism that keeps up so consistently within the bounds of decorum.... And what are we to fit when they turn us out of Harvard? We're too intelligent to be successful businessmen and we haven't the sand or the energy to be anything else (Filene, 1984: 10).

41

William James wrote that there was "no more contemptible type of human character than that of the nervous sentimentalist and dreamer, who spends his life in a weltering sea of sensibility and emotion, but who never does a concrete manly deed" (Bellah *et al.*, 1985: 120).

Several antidotes to this perceived feminization were offered, antidotes that would increase male fellowship and instill those masculine virtues that could rescue an enfeebled nation. Whereas anti-feminist men wanted to press women back into the private sphere, pro-male men were concerned about women's dominance of the private sphere, and sought to dislodge her in the home by creating distinctly male agencies of socialization. There was something "mentally enervating in feminine companionship" (Dubbert, 1979: 97). The separation of boys and girls became a "kind of mania"; Hartman (1984: 11) notes that in some libraries it was normative to segregate the volumes authored by men from those authored by women. William James prescribed a stiffening of American ideals with the tonic of the common laborer's "sterner stuff of manly virtue." Such an infusion of masculinity into the predominantly feminine precincts of refinement would allow the entire society to "pass toward some newer and better equilibrium" (Trachtenberg, 1982: 141-142). Senator Albert Beveridge of Indiana counseled, in his *Young Man and the World* (1906), one of the many manuals that advised parents and children on the proper behavior of boys and girls, that boys should "avoid books, in fact avoid all artificial learning for the forefathers put America on the right path by learning from completely natural experience" (Dubbert, 1980: 310).

Curiously, pro-male men believed that separation of the sexes would also serve as an antidote to increasing homosexuality. If the sexes mingled, these authors claimed, then men would become feminized, and hence homosexual. Separation of the sexes -- or homosociality -- was the necessary precondition of heterosexuality. As G. Stanley Hall, the eminent psychologist, argued in his textbook *Adolescence*, familiarity and camaraderie produced a disenchantment and diluted the "mystic attraction of the other sex" (1904: 641).

This compulsive reassertion of traditional masculinity resonated with the anti-urbanism and the reactivated martial ideal that characterized a strain of anti-modernist sensibility at the turn of the century. "Get your children into the country," one real estate advertisement for Willmington, Delaware, urged potential buyers in 1905. "The cities murder children. The hot pavements, the dust, the noise, are fatal in many cases, and harmful always. The history of successful men is nearly always the history of country boys" (Jackson, 1985: 138).

Revived martial idealism also pushed the nation even closer to war. If, as Maurice Thompson wrote in 1898, "the greatest danger that a long period of profound peace offers to a nation is that of [creating] effeminate tendencies in young men" (610), then war could be a sensible policy for the nation and a remedy for feminized men. The building of empire through military domination was fueled by an emotional fervor to prove masculinity. The *Washington Post* editorialized in 1898:

> A new consciousness seems to have come upon us -- the consciousness of strength, and with it a new appetite, a yearning to show our strength... Ambition, interest, land-hunger, pride, the mere joy of fighting, whatever it may be, we are animated by a new sensation... The taste of empire is in the mouth of the people, even as the taste of blood in the jungle (Booth, 1982: 27).

General Homer Lea linked the two explicitly, when he noted that "[as] manhood marks the height of physical vigor among mankind, so the militant successes of a nation mark the zenith of *its physical greatness*" (Roszak and Roszak, 1975: 92). At least some writers believed that it worked. "The slouching, dissipated, impudent lout who seemed to typify young America has disappeared," editorialized the *Washington Post* in 1918 at the end of the First World War (Filene, 1980: 325).

Perhaps no one better captures this militarist strategy and the view of the soldier as moral exemplar than Theodore Roosevelt, who elevated compulsive masculinity and military adventurism to the level of national myth. Roosevelt's triumph over his own youthful frailty and his transformation into a robust vigorous man served as a template for a revitalized American social character; he "symbolized a restoration of masculine identity at a time... when it appeared to be jeopardized," and "typified the male oriented conquest of the wilderness that seemed to be the new 'safety valve' or 'frontier'," (Dubbert, 1980: 313); Green 1986: 237). William Allen White, a Kansas newspaper editor, praised Roosevelt's "hard muscled frame" and his "crackling voice"; here was a "masculine sort of person with extremely masculine virtues and palpably masculine faults" (Dubbert, 1980: 131). Roosevelt's foreign policy was military expansion; his style was hypermasculine, proven in imperial adventures in the Caribbean and the Philippines. "The nation that has trained itself to a cancer of unwarlike and isolated ease is bound, in the end, to go down before other nations which have not lost *the manly and adventurous virtues,"* he thundered. "There is no place in the world for nations who have become enervated by the soft and easy life, or who have lost their fibre of vigorous hardiness and masculinity" (Roszak and Roszak, 1975: 92).

The masculinist response to the crisis of masculinity also manifested less bellicose institutional responses, such as the founding of the Boy Scouts of America in 1910. The Boy Scouts celebrated a masculinity tested and proven against nature and other men, removed from the cultural restraints of home, hearth, school, and church. Scouting could "counter the forces of feminization and maintain traditional manhood," Hantover (1980: 293) writes. Here was "a boy's liberation movement, to free young males from women, especially from mothers" (Dubbert, 1979: 152). "Manliness can only be taught by men," observed Lord Baden-Powell, the founder of the organization in England, "and not by those who are half men, half old women" (Rosenthal, 1986: 226). If "spectatoritis" had "turned robust, manly, self-reliant boyhood into a lot of flat-chested cigarette smokers with shaky nerves and doubtful vitality," according to Chief Scout Ernest Thompson Seton in his *The Boy Scouts of America* (1910), then the BSA could counter the forces of feminization and maintain traditional manhood (Macleod, 1983: 49). Americans found in the BSA "an institutional sphere for the validation of masculinity previously generated by the flow of daily social life and affirmed in one's work" (Hantover, 1980: 299). Here was the place to re-create an ideal boyhood an its natural small-town setting, masculine preserves against the urban world of enfeeblement, refinement, civility, and women. To the BSA fell the "noble ideal of restoring the primitive past" (Dubbert, 1979: 156), resolving a cultural Oedipal angst by removing boys from mothers and reinserting them back into nature with the band of the brothers, the primal horde, re-created in the American small town. As Walter Lippman put it, the Boy Scouts made boys' gangs "valuable to civilization" as a "really constructive reform" (1962: 41-43).

Such organized "primitiveness" requires quotation, because the goal of the BAS was hardly to encourage political rebellion against an enervated culture, but it was a "quest for disciplined vitality," to redirect male anxieties, to channel and sublimate adolescent sexual yearning -- "the curse and bane of boyhood" as health reformer Horace Fletcher put it (Green, 1986: 261) -- and to reassert a traditional masculinity, but all within the bounds of an extended complacency and obedience to the emerging industrial order (Green, 1986: 262). Lord Baden-Powell understood this campaign for moral redemption well. England was "shamed by the Boer War, concerned about the vulnerability of its vast empire and the specter of social unrest among its own laboring classes," when Baden-Powell wrote that the brotherhood of scouts consisted of

> real *men* in every sense of the word... the understand living out in the jungles, and they
> can find their way anywhere... they know how to look after their health when far away
> from any doctors, are strong and plucky, and ready to face any danger, and always keen
> to help each other (Rosenthal, 1984: 46).

Neither anarchistic nor individualistic, Scouting's cult of masculinity requires that they "give up everything, their personal comforts and desires, in order to get their work done. They do not do all this for their own amusement, but because it is their duty to their king, fellow country-men, or employers" (Rosenthal, 1984: 45-46). In the United States as well, the goal of all this "stodgy fun" was therapeutic, to turn boys into docile middle-class workers, tuned to middle-level occupations, with some responsibility, but subordinate and able to take commands from superiors (Macleod, 1983; see also Rosenthal, 1984: 30). If boys were provided a place away from the city, from women, and from culture -- where they "could be boys" -- then they would surely become the "real men" required by early twentieth century industrial capitalism.

The Pro-Feminist Response

Although fewer in number and less influential institutionally, a significant group of American men openly embraced feminist principles as a potential solution to the crisis of masculinity. Inspired by women's increasingly visible public presence (in reformist movements such as abolition, populism, and labor, and socially redemptive groups such as the WCTU and the Social Purity movement), many men believed that women's political participation, symbolized by the extension of suffrage to women, would be a significant gain for all Americans, male and female. Other men supported feminist women's goals to revolutionize the relations between men and women in the family and in sexuality. Still others maintained a firm belief in the division of the sexes, but argued that increased feminization might prove a palliative to the dangers of compulsive masculinity.

Male support for women's public participation came first from the founders and early leaders of the newly opened women's colleges. Matthew Vassar, William Allan Neilson, and Joseph Taylor (both of Smith), and Henry Durant (Wellesley) were articulate champions of women's citizenship. Durant wrote that "the real meaning of the Higher Education for Women" was "revolt."

> We revolt against the slavery in which women are held by the customs of society --the broken health, the aimless lives, the subordinate position, the helpless dependence, the dishonesties and shams of so-called education. The Higher Education of Women... is the cry of the oppressed slave. It is the assertion of absolute equality it is the war of Christ.. against spiritual wickedness in high places (Horowitz, 1984: 44).

Vassar President Henry Noble MacCracken chartered trains at his own expense to transport Vassar students to suffrage demonstrations in New York, where he proudly led the college's contingent, holding one end of the Vassar College Suffrage Association banner before a jeering crowd.

The movement for coeducation was also supported by pro-feminist men, whose political views were often based upon scientific advances. John Vleck, for example, who presided over Wesleyan's experiment with coeducation, believed that "egalitarian coeducation represented the true index of the scientific advancement of the race" (Leach, 1980: 73). Floyd Dell argued that the patriarchal system had "labored under a.. disadvantage of having to assert that it artifices were laws of nature" (Dell, 1930: 131) while pro-feminist men had science on their side. And Burt Green Wilder, a scientist at Cornell, condemned the "barbaric cruelty" and "repression" that had "crushed" women's spirit and transmuted sexual "equivalence" into sexual disequilibrium. "The real creed of the future," he wrote in *Atlantic Monthly*, "is equal but not identical; diverse yet complementary; the man for the woman, and the woman for the man" (Leach, 1980: 49).

Men also directly supported women's suffrage, believing with Dr. Charles Taylor that the repression of women was "the greatest evil of modern society" (Degler, 1980: 256), and that political equality might relieve the world of oppressively masculine politics. The Men's League for Women's Suffrage had both English and American branches; in the United States, Greenwich Village radical Max Eastman was its guiding light. His pamphlet *Is Woman Suffrage Important,* linked a socialist economic critique of the leisured class with an analysis of the social construction of gender differences; these combine to turn women's "enforced feebleness into a holy thing," he wrote (Strauss, 1983: 229).

Men participated regularly in suffrage demonstrations as well. An editorial from *LaFollette's* (May 1911) praises the 85 "courageous and convinced men" who marched in a demonstration, among them John Dewey, Hamilton Holt, Oswald Garrison Villard (editor of the *New York Evening Post*), and Edward Markham. Although "hooted and jeered," and "guyed in the streets," one counted being "booed and hissed down the Avenue... a very thrilling and inspiring experience. I am determined," he continued, "that if I can help to that end, there shall be a thousand men in line next year." He wasn't very far off target. An editorial in the *New York Times* the next year predicted 800 men would march in a suffrage demonstration the next day, and suggested, somewhat smugly, that these "courageous" men would face an "unsympathetic multitude" as they stood publicly for what they believed.

But suffrage was but a public expression of a deeply social challenge that feminists had issued to the social order that bound them to unattainable ideals and repressive social conditions. "Woman's suffrage is not primarily a political but a social question," wrote Jesse Jones, a Boston Unitarian minister, in the *Woman's Journal*, "and means a profounder revolution in the whole structure of society that many advocates seem ever to have dreamed of" (Leach, 1980: 15). Within the personal sphere, men sought to resolve the crisis of masculinity by supporting women's claims for autonomy, both within the family and the marriage relationship, and in their demands for sexual freedom.

Many men supported feminists' repudiation of the traditional hierarchical principles of patriarchal authoritarianism. "For them personal love was the determinant factor in marrying. The problem for them was how to transform sexual love into an egalitarian relation while at the same time preserving social order and community" (Leach, 1980: 126). In fact, Floyd Dell argued that since modernity eliminates necessity, it could reestablish "family life on the basis of romantic love" (Dell, 1930: 7). Reverend Jesse Jones championed the notion of divorce "so far as women take the initiative in it [as] one phase of the revolt of women against the harem idea." Although it seemed "corrupting," he wrote in the *Woman's Journal*, it was a "movement for good, for it is a movement to escape out of tyranny into freedom" (Leach, 1980: 145). Many men followed Henry Blackwell's earlier admonitions that women's maintaining careers after marriage was essential to the survival of their equal union (Leach, 1980: 196). In the language of the late nineteenth century magazines, the pro-feminist man married neither "drudge nor ornament." He would not try to transform his wife into a woman chained to "sexual servitude or bodily toil" or to conditions in which "her mind rises no further than the roof that shelters it" (Leach, 1980: 30). Dell linked work and marriage explicitly:

> The recognition of women's work outside of home, and of educational preparation for
> such was *being a part of the marriage system, and not something alien and hostile to it*,
> would modernize our social and economic system at this point (1930: 357; italics in
> original)

Birth control reformer Margaret Sanger's husband William actively supported her participation in the public sphere. "You go ahead and finish your writing," she quotes him as saying, "and I'll get the dinner and wash the dishes" (Foster, 1985: 252).

The sex radicals who clustered around Greenwich Village in the first two decades of the twentieth century supported women's sexual equality while they challenged traditional notions of masculinity and wrestled with these issues of equality and autonomy in their own lives. They believed that sexual repression was an essential underpinning of capitalism, and based their critiques on socialist politics and scientific advances, both of which posited an equality of sexual desire between women and men. Sex radicals tried to transform the entire sexual relation between men and women. Denlow Lewis wrote in 1900 that "the sexual act must be performed with satisfaction to both participants in the conjugal embrace" (Degler, 1980: 274). Ben Reitman, a Greenwich Village Bohemian and longtime lover of Emma Goldman, supported her work in birth control reform, and was well identified with the feminist cause himself. When Reitman was on trial, one prosecutor denounced him as "an Anarchist, who comes to our fair city to defy our laws... If you let him break the law on birth control, our property and our wives and daughters will not be safe... [from their] dirty, filthy, stinking, birth control literature" (Falk, 1985: 254).

Floyd Dell, who believed that feminism was the only antidote to ruling-class pretense and materialistic value culture, also claimed that men were "tired of the subservient woman -- the pretty slave with all the slave's subtlety and cleverness" (Strauss, 1983: 249). The liberation of women from the oppressive bonds of traditional femininity -- women were "world builders" to Dell -- implied the liberation of men from the restrictive moorings of traditional masculinity. Such a pro-feminist sensibility required women's access to birth control. "Modern contraceptive methods are not yet all that might ideally be desired," he wrote, "but *they do enable people to live sexual lives which they need not be ashamed to think about*" (Dell, 1930: 196; italics in original). And in a 1914 essay entitled "Feminism for Men," Dell made this connection explicit.

> The home is a little dull. When you have got a woman in a box, and you pay rent on the box, her relationship to you insensibly changes character... It is in the great world that a man finds his sweetheart, and in that narrow little box outside of the world that he loses her. When she has left that box and gone back into the great world, a citizen and a worker, then with surprise and delight he will discover her again and never let her go (Trimberger, 1984: 136).

Conclusion

These three responses to late nineteenth and early twentieth century feminist claims for reconstruction of gender relations -- anti-feminist, pro-male, and pro-feminist -- presented different strategies for the reconstruction of masculinity, but all agreed that masculinity was in crisis because of profound structural transformations. Does it surprise us today, in the wake of transformations of work, the closing of the imperial frontier, and new gains for women, that masculinity is seen as an "endless trial" (Emerson, 1985: 188) and although books, films, and even presidential addresses counsel us on appropriate behavior for "real men," we again find these three responses to the crisis of masculinity. Some men suggest a return to traditional gender differences (through a distortion of "scientific" evidence of "natural" differences); others proclaim a reinvigorated masculinity and support for wounded men (as well as anti-feminist challenges to divorce, alimony, child-custody, and abortion rights); and an increasing number often who, recognizing the ways in which their ability to transform masculinity is inspired by and made possible by the women's movement, have joined their sisters in the difficult and painful process of dismantling masculinity in order to create a vision of sexual equality and gender justice.

References

Barker-Benfield, G. J. (1976). *The Horrors of the Half Known Life: Male Attitudes Toward Women and Sexuality in 19th Century America*. New York: Harper and Row.

Bellah, Robert, Richard Madsen, William Sullivan, Ann Swidler; and Steven Tipton. *Habits of the Heart*. Berkeley: University of California Press.

Bok, Edward (1910). "My Quarrel with Women's Clubs," *Ladies Home Journal*, 27.

Booth, John (1982). *The End of the Beginning: The Nicaraguan Revolution*. Boulder, CO: Westview Press.

Bushnell, Horace (1867). *Woman's Suffrage: A Reform Against Nature*. Boston: Picknor.

Chafetz, Janet Saltzman, and Anthony Gary Dworkin (1986). "In the Face of Threat: Organized Antifeminism in Comparative Perspective." Paper presented at the annual meetings of the Southern Sociological Society, April.

Degler, Carl (1980). *At Odds: Women and the Family in America from the Revolution to the Present.* New York: Oxford University Press.

Dell, Floyd (1930). *Love in the Machine Age: A Psychological Study of the Transition from Patriarchal Society.* New York: Farrar and Rinehart.

Douglas, Ann (1977). *The Feminization of American Culture.* New York: Knopf.

Dubbert, Joe (1979). *A Man's Place: Masculinity in Transition.* Englewood Cliffs, NJ: Prentice-Hall,

_____ (1980). "Progressivism and the Masculinity Crisis," in Elizabeth Pleck and Joseph Pleck, eds., *The American Man.* Englewood Cliffs, NJ: Prentice-Hall.

Ehrenreich, B., and D. English (1979). *For Her Own Good.* New York: Doubleday.

Emerson, G. (1985). *Some American Men.* New York: Simon and Schuster.

Falk, Candace (1985). *Love, Anarchy and Emma Goldman.* New York: Holt, Rinehart and Winston.

Filene, Peter (1980). "In Time of War," in Elizabeth Pleck and Joseph Pleck, eds., *The American Man.* Englewood Cliffs, NJ: Prentice-Hall.

_____ (1984). "Between a Rock and a Soft Place: A Century of American Manhood." Chapel Hill, NC: unpublished manuscript.

Flexner, E. (1975). *Century of Struggle.* Cambridge: Harvard University Press.

Forster, Margaret (1985). *Significant Sisters: The Grassroots of Active Feminism.* New York: Knopf.

Freud, Sigmund (1965). *New Introductory Lectures in Psychoanalysis.* New York: W. W. Norton.

Frothingham, O. B. (1890). "The Real Case of the Remonstrance Against Woman Suffrage," *The Arena II,* July.

Gardella, Peter (1985). *Innocent Ecstasy.* New York: Oxford University Press.

Gerson, Judith and Kathy Peiss (1985). "Boundaries, Negotiation, Consciousness: Reconceptualizing Gender Relations," *Social Problems* 32(4).

Gould, Meredith, and Rochelle Kern-Daniels (1977). "Toward a Sociological Theory of Gender and Sex," *The American Sociologist* 12.

Green, Harvey (1986). *Fit for America.* New York: Pantheon.

Hall, G. Stanley (1904). *Adolescence,* Vol. II. New York: Appleton.

Hantover, Jeffrey P. (1980). "The Boy Scouts and the Validation of Masculinity," in Elizabeth Pleck and Joseph Pleck, eds., *The American Man,* Englewood Cliffs, NJ: Prentice-Hall.

Hartman, Mary (1984). "Sexual Crack-Up: The Role of Gender in Western History." New Brunswick, NJ: unpublished paper, Rutgers University.

Horowitz, Helen Lefkowitz (1984). *Alma Mater: Design and Experience in the Women's Colleges from Their 19th Century Beginnings to the 1930s.* New York: Knopf.

Jackson, K. (1985). *Crabgrass Frontier.* New York: Oxford.

James, Henry (1965). *The Bostonians.* New York: Modern Library.

Lasch, Christopher (1965). *The New Radicalism in America, 1889-1963.* New York: Knopf.

Leach, William (1980). *True Love and Perfect Union: The Feminist Reform of Sex and Society.* New York: Basic Books.

Lippman, Walter (1962). *A Preface to Morals.* New York: Harper and Row.

Lopata, Helena Z., and Barrie Thorne (1978). "On the Term 'Sex Roles'," *Signs 3.*

"Marrying Later in Life" (1986). *New York Times,* 10 December 1986 (chart).

Macleod, David (1983). *Building Character in the American Boy: The Boy Scouts, YMCA, and Their Forerunners, 1870-1920.* Madison: University of Wisconsin Press.

McKeever, William (1913). *Training the Boy.* New York: Macmillan.

Muschamp, Herbert (1983). *Frank Lloyd Wright and the City.* Cambridge: Massachusetts Institute of Technology Press.

Pugh, David (1983). *Sons of Liberty: The Masculine Mind in Nineteenth Century America.* Westport, CT: Greenwood Press.

Riesman, David (1950). *The Lonely Crowd.* New Haven, CT: Yale University Press.

Risman, Barbara J. (1987). "Intimate Relationships from Microstructural Perspective," *Gender and Society* 1(1).

Rogin, Michael (1975). *Fathers and Children.* New York: Pantheon.

Rosenberg, Charles (1980). "Sexuality, Class and Role in 19th Century America," in Elizabeth Pleck and Joseph Pleck, eds., *The American Man.* Englewood Cliffs, NJ: Prentice-Hall.

Rosenthal, Michael (1984). "Recruiting for Empire: Baden-Powell's Boy Scout Law," *Raritan* 4(1), Summer.

_____. (1986). *The Character Factory: Baden-Powell's Boy Scouts and the Imperatives of Empire.* New York: Pantheon.

Roszak, Theodore, and Betty Roszak (1975). *Masculine/Feminine.* New York: Harper and Row.

Rotundo, E. Anthony (1983). "Body and Soul: Changing Ideals of American Middle Class Manhood, 1770-1920," *Journal of Social History* 16(4).

Shapiro, Judith (1982). "'Women's Studies: A Note on the Perils of Markedness," *Signs* 7.

Smith-Rosenberg, Carroll (1985). *Disorderly Conduct: Visions of Gender in Victorian America.* New York: Knopf.

Stacey, Judith, and Barrie Thorne (1985). "The Missing Feminist Revolution in Sociology," *Social Problems* 32(4).

Strauss, Sylvia (1983). *Traitors to the Masculine Cause: The Men's Campaign for Women's Rights.* Westport, CT: Greenwood Press.

Thompson, Maurice (1898). "Vigorous Men, A Vigorous Nation," *Independent*, September 1.

Todd, John (1867). *Woman's Rights.* Boston: Lee and Shepard.

Trachtenberg, Alan (1982). *The Incorporation of America: Culture and Society in the Guilded Age.* New York: Hill and Wang.

Tresemer, David (1975). "Assumptions Made About Gender Roles," In Marcia Milman and Rosebeth M. Kanter, eds., *Another Voice: Feminist Perspectives on Social Life and Social Science.* Garden City, NY: Anchor.

Trimberger, Ellen Kay (1984). "Feminism, Men and Modern Love: Greenwich Village, 1900-1925," in Ann Snitow, Christine Stansell, and Sharon Thompson, eds., *Powers of Desire: The Politics of Sexuality.* New York: Monthly Review Press.

Wright, Frank Lloyd (1970). *The Future of Architecture.* New York: Dover.

Chapter 5

The social movements. The women's movements of the turn of the century and the more recent resurgence of women's liberation that arose during the 60s and 70s are briefly summarized. After that, this chapter focuses on the men's movements of the 1990s. The review of material and inquiry into men's response to today's social and political changes in roles and expectations has resulted in this outline of three segments to the current men's movement that appear to roughly parallel the earlier reaction to the first rise of feminism described by Michael Kimmel in Chapter 4.

Chapter 5 *Barbara E. Collamer*, The Social Movements

The First Rise of the Women's Movement

Launching the first rise of feminism in the mid 1800s, Elizabeth Cady Stanton used the Declaration of Independence as the framework for writing what she titled a "Declaration of Sentiments." Stanton connected the nascent campaign for women's rights directly to that powerful American symbol of liberty. In the Declaration of Sentiments, Stanton enumerated areas of life where women were treated unjustly.[1]

> "The history of mankind is a history of repeated injuries and usurpations on the part of man toward woman, having in direct object the establishment of an absolute tyranny over her. To prove this, let facts be submitted to a candid world."[2]

Stanton's declaration then went into specifics:

- Married women were legally dead in the eyes of the law

- Women were not allowed to vote
- Women had to submit to laws when they had no voice in their formations
- Married women had no property rights
- Husbands had legal power over and responsibility for their wives to the extend that they could imprison or beat them with impunity
- Divorce and child custody laws favored men, giving no rights to women
- Women had to pay property taxes although they had no representation in the levying of these taxes
- Most occupations were closed to women and when women did work they were paid only a fraction of what men earned
- Women were not allowed to enter professions such as medicine or law
- Women had no means to gain an education since no college or university would accept women
- With only a few exceptions, women were not allowed to participate in the affairs of the church
- Women were robbed of their self-confidence and self-respect, and were made totally dependent on men

The draft continued: "Now, in view of this entire disenfranchisement of one-half the people of this country, their social and religious degradation,--in view of the unjust laws above mentioned, and because women do feel themselves aggrieved, oppressed, and fraudulently deprived of their most sacred rights, we insist that they have immediate admission to all the rights and privileges which belong to them as citizens of these United States."[3]

Following the drafting of this declaration in the summer of 1848, Elizabeth Cady Stanton and four of her friends organized the first women's rights convention to be held July 19th and 20th in Senaca, New York.

In the months that followed the women endured a backlash of ridicule. The entire text of the Declaration of Sentiments was often published and publicly satirized with cartoons; made fun of in attempts to embarrass the women involved. Through all the negativity the new Women's Movement survived and the second Women's Rights Conference was held in Salem, Ohio in 1850. It was there that the men who were in attendance were ruled out of order if they rose to speak and the women experienced solidarity for the first time. However, the campaign for suffrage was one of the most resisted issues for women and met with such stanch opposition that it took 72 years for the women and their male supporters to be successful in winning women the right to vote.

After the ratification of the 19th amendment in 1920, many women who had lobbied and marched for women's vote felt satisfied and activism diminished considerably. A few notable events occurred at that time, however, that are linked to the second rise of women's issues. In 1920, the Women's Bureau of the Department of labor was created to investigate the situation of women in the workplace. Another piece of the puzzle was developed around the issue of birth control. A public health nurse, Margaret Sanger, launched a movement around birth control, endorsing the education of women about birth control methods. As an eventual result of this effort, in 1936, a Supreme Court decision declassified birth control information as obscene. Still, it was not until 1965 that married couples in all states could obtain contraceptive products legally.[4]

The Second Rise of the Women's Movement

A second wave of activism was ushered into our cultural consciousness during the 1960s. President Kennedy convened a Commission on the Status of Women, naming Eleanor Roosevelt as its chair.   The report that the commission issued in 1963 documented discrimination against women in virtually every area of American life. Also, in 1963, Betty Friedan published her book, *The Feminine Mystique*, that compelled thousands of American women to look for fulfillment beyond the role of homemaker. In 1964, Title VII of the Civil Rights Act was passed prohibiting employment discrimination of the basis of "race, religion, national origin and *sex*"(my italics). But this alone was not enough to bring about change. The implementation and enforcement of Title VII was disappointing. When women found themselves stifled and unheard as they brought their issues to the government agencies assigned to their concerns, numerous organizations formed, including the National Organization for Women in 1966.[5]

In 1972 came the most monumental legislation of the movement. With the inclusion of Title IX in the Education Codes, equal access to higher education and to professional schools became the law.   The numbers of women doctors, lawyers, engineers, architects and other professionals doubled and doubled again as quotas limiting women's enrollment in graduate schools were outlawed.

Much of the work of the second rise was carried out in political and legal channels. Publicly the backlash was again a strong one. As some women marched and protested against discrimination in the workplace, some men heeled in to underground directives to keep the feminists at bay. There ensued both a covert and overt power struggle in the public sphere. But many of the advances women achieved in the 1960s and 1970s were personal and home-based. Marriages were redesigned to account for more equality with husbands doing more housework and wives getting a long-deserved promotion at work, gaining financial strength, and spending more time away from domestic tasks.

There was one more piece, a direct link between the first and second women's movements, to be dealt with. An activist of the First Rise, Alice Paul, leader of the National Woman's Party, had proposed an equal rights amendment to the Constitution of the United States and it had lain dormant in Congress since 1922. In 1972, Congress finally passed the amendment and it was moved for a vote in the House of Representatives. The wording of the ERA was simple, "Equality of rights under the law shall not be denied or abridged by the United States or by any state on account of sex." Considering the social climate of the time, it was considered a shoo-in. However, opponents organized and they charged that the passage of ERA would lead to men abandoning their families, unisex toilets, gay marriages, and women being drafted. When the deadline for ratification came in 1982, the ERA was three states short of the 38 needed to write it into the U. S. Constitution. It was considered too controversial. There it died and has not been resurrected since.

Today, the women's rights movement of the 1990s recognizes the hard work and sacrifices of the women and men who went before, breaking ground and risking ridicule.

The issues of today are the most resistant and complex of the original articles of sentiment drafted 150 years ago. We are now in territory that is steadfastly controversial. Some of these issues are:

- Women in the military, including military schools and academies
- Pornography and whether it is linked to violence against women
- Domestic violence
- Sexual harassment
- Women's reproductive rights
- Affirmative action
- Images of women in the media

Many women are hesitant to call themselves "feminist" because of the ever-present backlash, and most men would not want to be known as "profeminist". However, most women and men know and respect the legacy of personal freedoms and expanded opportunities we all enjoy because of the women's movements.

Men and Masculinity

Men's roles also have shifted throughout history. Elizabeth and Joseph Pleck divide the male gender role into four parts: The **agrarian patriarchy** (1630-1820) refers to the early colonial years in which America's economy was based in agriculture. As Cancian described in Chapter 2, men were engaged in crop and livestock production. Work was heavy and hours were long but the center of work was at home on the farm. The **commercial age** (1820-1860) was marked by increased industrialization which shifted the economic emphasis to the cities. Men's roles were affected by the harsh and competitive business world.[6] Many men of this era were forced to undergo a transformation in the workplace from the cooperative interdependent family experience of farm life to a fiercely competitive public work world that lacked rules and ethical standards. Rather than being physical, a man's endurance now took the form of the unemotional, calculating, psychologically hardy type.

A dramatic turnabout occurred in the commercial period with respect to the sexual element of the male role. Since the early Christian period, women, not men, were thought to be oversexed. For centuries women were portrayed as the source of passion and sensuality. Of course, men were sexual creatures also, but it was women's nature that was given to carnal desires and, as the church taught, was the cause of the males' downfall. This view shifted during the nineteenth century when men were portrayed as having a stronger sexual tendency than women, who were now viewed as being above sex or at least put off by it. For this reason, men were encouraged to exert themselves in their work, to become successful in their business ventures because though work a man could expend a large portion of his sexual energies on tasks more worthwhile than mere sexual release. After a hard day's work, the passionate husband has little energy or spirit left for baser things, which was perfectly all right with his "cool" wife.[7]

Beginning approximately 1861 over the turn of the century to around 1919, there occurred what the Plecks describe as the **strenuous life**. Led by Teddy Roosevelt, men pursued a hardy and rough role that would help them bolster their masculinity. In response to a concern over a "softened" male, organizations like the Boy Scouts of American were founded on principles believed to foster manhood. In addition to this and other efforts to socialize American boys, men were encouraged to frequent men's clubs, sports, saloons, and various activities to help turn wimps into real men.

A forth shift, the **companionate era**, took place from around 1920 to 1965. After World War I the separate spheres of men and women began to merge. Men turned to women for companionship. They learned to talk to each other. They began to share feelings, thoughts, and responsibilities. Some of this change in men's roles was prompted by the dramatic role shift for women during the war years in which they were expected to take factory jobs and build bombs, aircraft, and other war machinery while the men were away. When men returned from the war they found women had redefined femininity, a new identity which would never be the same again. As men adjusted to this new relationship with women, they had to rethink how they would now direct their own identity. As a consequence they felt they also needed to explicitly define masculinity. Men knew they faced new challenges to their dominant position in society. They began to ask themselves questions about what it means to be a man.[8]

In 1981, Joseph Pleck wrote a book called The Myth of Masculinity. In this sympathetic look at the male role he describes two beliefs concerning masculinity: the **identity paradigm** and the **strain paradigm**. The myth that Pleck refers to is the belief that men are psychologically predisposed to develop the male identity; the identity paradigm. From life's most explicit messages such as "boy's don't cry" to the subtle but potent influence of the dominant/subordinate ideology, the identity paradigm promotes the myth that a real man must internalize such messages to form a healthy sense of himself as a man. That is, a real man's identity is a state of psychological well-being achieved by believing that he fits the male ideal: "I am a real man because I am tough, competent, and in charge of things." Joseph Pleck believes that the identity paradigm is inaccurate. In reality, the male role according to Pleck, is more a product of role strain. The strain is a hazard brought on by our society's unrealistic and often unattainable expectations for men. Men who are attached to the identity perspective are at risk of an identity crisis or psychological maladjustment if they fail to meet the criteria of the "real man"; because the criteria is nearly impossible to achieve. A better outlook for a man would be to view the criteria for manhood as a cultural construction that changes with time and is a product of the conditions of the society: "I am a real man because I am upholding my responsibilities in today's society". That outlook on what it means to be a man is less personal and focuses on issues outside of the individual. The strain can thus be relieved when it is *externalized*.

What becomes apparent when we look at the difference between men's issues and women's issues is that, for women, the task is to exert more control over the external factors that direct their ambitions and for men the task is to control their ambitions by recognizing the external factors that prompt them. Many men today grow up believing that they must meet the often unrealistic expectations of the male role that has grown continually over history. To the modern male it seems that the definition of masculinity has expanded to include multiple role expectations without the benefit of any decrease in responsibility or accountability.

Men of Today

Things are not going well for some men of today. They will tell you that they struggle to maintain their position of sole provider on two microstructural levels. At home, there is added domestic responsibility that they feel unprepared for and a sincere need to connect with their children. At work, some men blame recent political shifts for the competition they experience for promotions and the crowding in of women, ethnic minorities, the physically challenged, and everyone else who previously had been marginalized in the workplace. Today, role clarity and access to resources is clearly not assigned to the average family man as it was in the past. As a result we often hear the refrain, "what does it mean to be a man today?"

The dominant/subordinate paradigm

Joseph Pleck is joined by many other influential scholars in the belief that gender identities are formed by the economic, social, and political needs of a society. Social structures and institutions are the *macro*-level elements guiding the socialization process (the patriarchy, the Constitution of the United States, mass media, and the current political climate as labeled on our ecological diagram in Chapter Eleven). The structure of our society is hierarchical. Individuals fit into designated levels of status and power with some afforded *more* status and some afforded *less* status. For the majority of citizens it is desirable to strive for and achieve a high level of social status. Status achievement is translated into dominance and can be reached, typically, through exercising individual rights and opportunities provided equally to all people through the laws of our land. However, the assumption of equality for all is not always forthright or apparent because each individual will interpret their placement in the hierarchy in a personal, microstructual way. In assessing their everyday lives, men see problems in realizing the goals they strive for that represent, to them, self-esteem and a manly identity. Things are further complicated by the difficulty in determining whether the source of the problem is personal (microstructural) or political (macrostructural). Sometimes, micro-level problems become macro-level influences on our lives as in the case of divorce. Research into divorce can shed light on the culture's influence on gender identity. Arendell reminds us of the importance of intimacy and family on shaping the meaning of masculinity. She reports that some men experience paradoxical goals in marriage: They seek relationships in which they can be the dominant spouse; the position that affords them status with other men. Many young men learned this role from their fathers who never considered it to be ambiguous. At the same time they seek relationships with women in which they are equal partners. They value the modern emphasis on closeness with their children and reciprocity of assistance with their wives. The improbability of achieving both of these goals is obscured by the strength of the dominant/subordinate paradigm in our culture. In fact, the contradictions in these two sets of goals ultimately led to the divorces of many of the men in Arendell's study.[9]

The pressure of unattainable goals may, in part, be responsible for so many failed marriages, but another voice points out the stigma men experience against homemaking and babycare, for those men who volunteer for this role. Warren Farrell says there is a 24-hour psychological responsibility for the family's financial well-being that men can't break out of.[10] Farrell says:

A woman today has three options:
Option 1:   Full-time career

Option 2:   Full-time family
Option 3:   Some combination of career and family
A man today has a slightly different set of options:
Option 1:   Full-time work
Option 2:   Full-time work
Option 3:   Full-time work[11]

Since many women today now earn substantial incomes doesn't that relieve the pressure on men to be "a wallet?" No, says Farrell, because successful women do exactly what less-successful women do—marry up. That is, they marry a man who is more successful than they are.[12] Often if a high-wage earning woman can't marry a man who has even higher wage-earning potential than she does, she does not marry at all. A survey of top female executives, 85% don't get married. The remaining 15% who do almost always marry up. This does not relax the pressure on men to succeed.[13]

The concern that men only have the work option because of society's rules for men is joined by the equally important concern that society has placed constraints on men's expression of emotions. In a 1994 publication, *The Courage to Raise Good Men*, co-authors Olga Silverstein and Beth Rashbaum, are in sympathy with the challenges that men face.[14] Silverstein, a well-known family therapist, describes the expectations for men as cultural chains that train men to be soldiers of war, winners on the athletic field, and then also to be loving husbands and fathers. The conflict of demands is causing men problems.

"Our culture stresses from the beginning that winning is the highest honor. A gentle boy is sent out to play ball so he doesn't turn into a momma's boy. As a culture we overvalue the qualities we call masculine and undervalue the qualities we call feminine--including empathy, caring, and feelings."[15]

Silverstein believes men are allowed only one emotion" "Anger." Never fear or hurt. "A man grows up hating the feminine qualities in himself. He then projects them onto some woman and beats the hell out of her."[16] She blames a competitive society that clamps off the artery that connects a man with his feelings.

The ideologue underlying all of the above issues is the strain paradigm; the ecological role that men and women play in our culture's dominant/subordinate, hierarchical social system.

The Men's Movement

Today's men's movement is all about defining the "new male". This attempt was an inevitable outcome of a women's movement that could not be ignored by anyone. Feminism has been fueled by a media blitz of unprecedented proportions. Most feminist scholars have been articulate and undeniable sensible. The male response is forthright, but it takes several forms.

What's true of men's issues follows a different vein than women's issues. For one thing, the men's movement as such, is relatively new compared to the women's movement. Although the concerns that men have about their role became apparent early in the 20th Century, men did not organize as a "movement" until the 1980s. With the publication of Robert Bly's, *Iron John,* one of the more unwavering issues for men was made explicit: male identity.[17] As far back as the 1920s, men were experiences a crisis of the definition of masculinity in a modern context. Work was no longer rugged or individualistic. Women were abdicating their domestic role and moving into the world of work that had always been clearly male territory. The same is true today. Many men still find the competition oppressive to their role as breadwinner and the shared decision-making leaves them further confused about their role. Throughout all of time, men have had but one objective, to be the provider and protector of territory, abode, and women and children. The direction that the men's movement has taken is as split now as it was during the first rise of feminism. In two main factions, we have the followers of Bly, the *mythopoetic* men's movement, and on the other hand, we have the *pro-feminist* men's movement motivated by a dozen or so scholars. We will discuss the mythopoetic movement, including the Promise Keepers, which uses as its ideology the reestablishment of the hardy, dominant male.

The Mythopoetic Men's Movement

> Many men, in sympathy with the women's movement of the 60s, began to notice what was called their feminine side. This is good and important but I sense there is something wrong. The modern male has become a man concerned with pleasing—not only his mother, but also the woman he is living with. In the 70s, I began to see what we might call "the soft male". This man is not happy. No energy. Many times you see these men with strong women who radiate energy. This strong women, soft man pair has turned the male role from life-giving to life-preserving.
> ---Robert Bly (1990) *Iron John*[18]

The alpha literature for this movement is Bly's, *Iron John.* Around this central publication, there grew a subculture of men who organized focus groups, retreats, sensitivity gatherings, and rituals to help them reconstruct their masculinity. The constituents of these gatherings are mostly white, middle-class, middle-aged men. Mythopoetic leaders attempt to guide men through a spiritual journey to reclaim their deep masculine nature, their "Zeus energy". It is a type of masculinity that is neither the self-destructive hypermasculinity that shortens their lives, nor the feminized softness that saps them of their virility. The movement accentuates men's ties to other men, confronts the "costs of masculinity" (in mythopoetic terms, "men's wounds"), and explores and reconstructs men's inner selves

The book gets its inspiration from a rendition of a fairy tale by the Brothers Grimm. A hairy wild man named Iron John is brought up from the bottom of a pond and imprisoned by a king. The king's son loses a golden ball to the wild man, who will only give it back if the boy releases him from the cage. According to Bly, the boy separates from his mother by stealing the cage key from under her pillow, and begins the work of becoming a man by courageously going off with Iron John into the forest. Bly uses the story to explain why it is important to break the emotional and psychological bond with women, particularly mothers, and for men to find manhood with the help of other men.

Bly explains:

"The boys in our culture need an initiation into the male spirit—
but older men can't offer it and they grow up not getting it. Manhood
doesn't happen all by itself. It needs active intervention by older men
welcoming younger men into the ancient mythological male world. Older
men have a responsibility to interrupt the mother-son unity. A clear break
from the mother is essential and it simply is not happening."[19]

As men explored their place in the modern world they gathered in groups to
discuss and share their stories. The concern with softness is apparent in Bly's words: "I
suggested an acting out of a certain fierceness in these groups. I asked them to lift and
show off a sword. Some of these young men could not bring themselves to extend their
arms with a sword in their hands."[20]

In a slightly different vein but still in the mythopoetic category, author, Sam
Keen, writes to men about how to break out of the constraints of traditional manhood. In
his book, *Fire in the Belly: On being a man*, he implores men to gather in groups to share
their stories; to create a conscious autobiography. In doing this, a man will exchange the
unconscious myth of what it means to be a man with a conscious reality that is more
personal and honest. Keen writes: "Rather than trying to fit into the stories that others
have created for us, begin the process of writing your own story."[21] In other words,
Keen suggests that each man needs to accept who he is right now and make *that* the
definition of what a man is. Sam Keen's work probably more clearly follows from
Joseph Pleck's strain paradigm than does Robert Bly's. Keen joins Pleck in the belief
that society's pressure on men can be ameliorated by recognizing its source. Because of
the emphasis on organizing into sensitivity groups, Keen is considered one of the leading
personalities in the mythopoetic men's movement.

Promise Keepers

In 1997, nearly 500,000 men led by former University of Colorado football coach
Bill McCartney, met in Washington, D. C. to listen to their leaders inspirational talks, to
sing, and to pray about their roles as men. This gathering is one of several that has
become a nationwide network of Christian men who strive, among other things, to
reassert the male head of household and role of leadership as naturally male.

Time Magazine reports that this ten-year old organization, the Promise Keepers,
boasts annual revenues of $87 million, a two-story brick headquarters in Denver and 360
paid staff members. Their plan is to reclaim male responsibility and re-establish male
leadership in a country that they see as badly detoured from a godly and natural course,
falling into the snares of poverty, illegitimacy, drug abuse, juvenile delinquency and
disease because American men have forsaken Christian values. Commitments are called
for in an official guidebook, *Seven Promises of a Promise Keeper*. The organization
declares it has no political agenda but founder McCartney is a stanch conservative who
attacks issues such as abortion, gay rights, and women's liberation. The group's mission
is vague and unsettled regarding its relationships with women. "It calls for men to take
"spiritual leadership" over their wives, for example, and suggests that women follow."[8]

Promise Keepers believe that men and women differ in spiritual constitution. McCartney says that men need a "masculine context that allows them to come clean"; and the group describes itself as a "Christ-centered ministry dedicated to uniting men through vital relationships to become godly influences in their world."[9] Men are expected to view themselves more honestly, take responsibility for any wrong doing they have committed, and begin a cleansing and renewal that includes everything from sexual sin to getting themselves out of debt. In a section of *Seven Promises*, titled "Reclaiming Your Manhood," Tony Evans, a senior pastor of Oak Cliff bible Fellowship in Dallas, puts it this way: "Sit down with your wife and say something like this: 'Honey, I've made a terrible mistake. I've given you my role. I gave up leading this family, and I forced you to take my place. Now, I must reclaim that role'…I'm not suggesting you ask for your role back, I'm urging you (to) take it back…there can be no compromise here. If you're going to lead, you must lead."[22]

This is seen as a threat to many feminists and prompts watch-dog organizations concerned with what they believe may be a patriarchal fervor that sets off their political alarms. Is this a movement toward Christain-male domination? In *Promise Keepers: The third wave of the American Religious Right*, co-authors Alfred Ross and Lee Cokorinos of the Center for Democracy Studies write: "In its conception and execution, Promise Keepers is one of the most sophisticated political movements the right wing has yet conjured up."[23] The suspicion in understandable in the wake of the enormous response and success of Promise Keepers as a part of the men's movement.

There was a similar movement shortly after the first rise of feminism (1911,1912). "Muscular Christianity" swept across the nation in response to the sense that men were being threatened by feminism and the United States was at risk of becoming "soft". Is this the same reactionary movement now witnessed today? Promise keepers deny the reactionary agenda and say that they are merely responding to the moral and spiritual crisis that American men face today. The group has a simple solution to this crisis: shape up in eyes of the Lord, or you're going straight to hell. And if you don't shape up, you'll be responsible for dragging this great land of ours right down with you. "A house divided cannot stand," says Bill McCartney.[24] The men involved in this grass roots campaign see only their souls at stake.

The Profeminist Man

Michael Messner, a professor of Sociology at the University of Southern California, is one of the leaders of the profeminist campaign. Messner views the mythopoetic men's movement as a support system to help men feel good about their "Zeus power" (Messner, 1997). Profeminist men like Messner believe that the distribution of power, itself, is at the heart of the problems that women and men experience in both their macrostructural and microstructural dealings with each other. Messner suggests that rather than reasserting the dominant role, men should bring the definition of masculinity more in line with the goals of the original profeminist men in the early years of the 20th Century; that is, that men and women can be cooperative world-builders utilizing a balance of power.

It's actually getting harder and harder for a young male to figure out how to **be** a man. But this is not necessarily a bad thing. Young men's current fears of other men and the continued erosion of the male breadwinner role might offer a historic opportunity for men—individually and collectively—to reject narrow, limiting, and destructive definitions of masculinity and, instead, to create a more humane, peaceful, and egalitarian definition of manhood.

---Michael Messner (1997, p xiv)[25]

For the pro-feminist men's movement, the task is to redefine the patriarchal system which is traditionally based on the dominant/subordinate ideology. The influence of the dominant/subordinate paradigm should not be underestimated. It has never been eliminated in any society during any time in history, only reduced to varying degrees at rare times. The dominant/subordinate dichotomy has only been reduced with exceptional effort and extraordinary ecological circumstances. In pastoral cultures, for instance, because of the nomadic nature of the people, the fact that women and children accompanied the entire community as it migrated and tended its herds of animals, and the fact that women were taking part in the productive work along side men, these people had low levels of gender stratification.[26]

The profeminist stance seems to evolve much more slowly and consume more intellectual energy for a man than the mythopoetic movement possibly due to the cognitive shift profeminism requires. Messner tells a story about his early years as a student. He remembers a course on social inequality that he took as an undergraduate. He learned that women in the workforce were paid $.59 to the male's dollar for working the same jobs.

For an assignment in this course, he wrote a paper sympathetic to the inequality in the work world for women and in his conclusion he stated that it was only fair that women should enjoy the same status and compensation that men do. He was proud of his "profeminist" position. That summer he was back to his usual job as a parks employee along with about 14 other college students. He noted that the 12 or so women employees were always assigned a shorter work week (20-30 hours per week) at smaller parks, while he and the other two men were getting not only a full 40 hour workweek, but were the only ones asked to work overtime, thus increasing their average workweek to 42 to 46 hours.

> "One week, at a staff meeting, a supervisor routinely invited me and another man to come to the recreation center to do some overtime work. Before we had a chance to say yes, we were interrupted by one of the women workers, who firmly stated, "I don't know why the guys always get the extra hours; we women can do that work as well as them. It doesn't really seem fair." I immediately felt threatened and defensive and broke the uncomfortable moment of silence in the room by whispering—far too loudly, as it turned out—to my male coworker, 'Who the hell does she think she is, Gloria Steinem?' In response, the woman worker glared and pointed her finger at me: 'Don't talk about something you don't know anything about, Mike!'

Immediately, it ran though my mind that I *did*, in fact, know a lot about this topic. Why, I had just written this wonderful paper about how women workers are paid less than men and had taken the position that this should change. Why, then, when faced with a concrete situation where I could put that knowledge and those principles to work had I taken a defensive, reactionary position? In retrospect, I can see that I had not yet learned the difference between taking an intellectual position on an issue and actually integrating principles into my life...I had not yet come to grips with the reality that men—especially white, heterosexual, middle-class men like myself—tend to take for granted certain *institutional privileges".* (his italics).[27]

Messner acknowledges that, to receive equal treatment, the women had to stand up for themselves and make public claims based on values of justice and equal opportunity. He just had to show up. He said what struck him about this in retrospect was how easy it is for members of a privileged group to remain ignorant of the ways that the social structures of which they are a part grant them privileges, often at the expense of others.

What is unique about the new profeminist perspective is that the men involved recognize what Michael Messner did, that our hierarchical patriarchy consists of social structures that grant men special privileges. Within that premise, profeminist men also talk about a hegemonic masculinity that serves mainly middle-class, heterosexual, white males. Profeminists point out that most of the solutions to men's issues are practical only for an employed, often professional, non-marginalized class of men. Profeminist men outline institutional power for men and not women as the issue feminists are most painfully aware of and our hierarchical social system as the culprit for gender and class dilemmas.

When we consider each of the major perspectives of our present-day men's movement it is the profeminist ideology that takes the most time and effort to accommodate. This is a tough transition in thinking for a dominant group. "Our dominance is oppressive and harmful to others" is a very difficult statement to make; a quantum leap in assumptions from the mythopoetic message that men need to learn how to become stronger leaders.

The Men's Rights Campaign

There is another distinct category of men's positions in the state of the field of gender. The contention of this group is that men's rights have been violated and men are discriminated against in many areas of their lives. The men's rights movement organizes its constituency around the belief that men are the real victims of a sexist society. Men suffer oppression from feminist led legal and political reform. Feminism was seen as the proof that women actually have power over men. Men's rights advocates claim that men are victimized by pornography, sexual harassment, false rape accusations, and domestic violence. David Thomas states that there is a cover-up of the massive amount of violence against men by women.[28] Thomas uses stories and anecdotal evidence to assert that in cases of domestic violence it is just as common (if not more common) for wives to injure and kill their husbands than for husbands to batter their wives. This fact is obscured by the shame of the men involved, says Thomas. Other issues include reverse discrimination on the job and also the discrimination that men feel in a court of law in child custody disputes. As a campaign, the organization is openly antifeminist and they don't hide their anger over their sense of oppression. They put their agenda forth forcefully as political and legal in its source and solution. A men's rights activist might rightfully argue that judges often automatically give custody of the children in a divorce settlement to the mother without considering the parental capabilities of the father. But, they view the financial burden of child support as unfair and mandated by an unjust court of law.

Warren Ferrall, who was mentioned previously in our discussion about role strain and the cost of masculinity, speaks out for men's rights. Earlier in his activity of gender discourse he had written articles and a book on the consequences of a sexist society on the lives of both men and women. By the 1990s Ferrall had shifted his attention to an unabashed sympathy for men only. He most recently focused his criticisms on government programs for the protection of women and children and what he sees as institutionalized privilege for women at the expense of men. To illustrate this point in his book, *The Myth of Male Power*, Farrell states that men succeed by finding the right job and moving from job to job until the right opportunity presents itself.[29] But, he says, women succeed by calling in the government or a lawyer and suing the employer to force the opportunity to present itself. Farrell views women as a manipulative, conniving, force supported by our government to reduce men to second class citizens.

When asked to consider that men have disproportionate positions of power in government and corporate America, men's rights leaders such as Richard Haddad state that men don't really have a "monopoly on power" in public life—they are simply "over-represented in decision-making positions in…government and industy"[30]

Men's Declaration of Sentiments

Its apparent that the men's movement, like the women's movement, has its issues and that it also has its factions: conservatives and liberals, moderates and radicals, scholars and activists. If we were to construct a Declaration of Sentiments for the men of today, what would it say? Concerns from all areas of the men's movement need to be addressed. Here is what we've heard men say:

- Men have suffered for lack of an emotional bond to their families.
- It is hard to fulfil the definition of manhood in today's world: "role strain".
- Being too sensitive can undermine their position in society.
- Relinquishing power and privilege is difficult both intellectually and actively.
- The feminist collaboration with law and government has taken away men's rights.

Without a doubt there is a covert and overt power struggle alive and active in today's gender discourse. Let's revisit the two models of interest that help us build an ideology of conflict resolution and problem-solving. In the following chapters we will explore the basic nature/nurture controversy as it applies to our gendered world.

Notes

[1] From *Legacy '98: A Short History of the Movement,* on a wed site about women's history, e-mail: nwhp@aol.com

[2] Ibid., p. 5.

[3] Ibid., p. 6.

[4] Ibid., p.10

[5] Doyle, J. A., 1989, *The male experience* (2nd. Ed.). Dubuque, IA: William C. Brown

[6] Pleck, J & Pleck, E., 1980, *The American Male.* Englewood Cliffs, NJ: Prentice Hall

[7] Pleck, J., 1981, *The Myth of Masculinity.* Cambridge, MA: The MIT Press

[8] Ibid.

[9] Arendell, T., 1995, *Fathers and divorce.* Thousand Oaks, CA: Sage

[10] Time Magazine, *The Pointcast Network,* time-webmaster@pathfinder.com

[11] Quoted in time-webmaster@pathfinder.com, October 6, 1997 VOL. 150 NO. 14, p 3.

[12] Ibid., p.4.

[13] Ibid., p.2

[14] Silverstein, O., & Rashbaum, B., 1994, *The Courage to Raise Good Men.*

[15] Interview with Olga Silverstein by Deirdre Donahue, pulished in USA Today, June 24, 1994

[16] Silverstein, O., & Rashbaum, B., 1994, *The Courage to Raise Good Men.*

[17] Bly, J., 1990, *Iron John: A book about men*

[18] Ibid., p. 12

[19] Ibid.

[20] Ibid.

[21] Keen, S., 1991, *Fire in the Belly: On being a man,* New York, NY: Bantam Books, p. 144.

[22] Time Magazine

[23] Ibid.

[24] Ibid.,

[25] M. Messner, 1997, *Politics of Masculinities: Men in Movements,* Thousand Oaks, CA: Sage

[26] O"kelly & Carney, 1986, *Women & Men in Society: Cross-cultural perspectives on gender stratification,* Belmont CA: Wadsworth

[27] Quoted in Messner, 1997, *Politics of Masculinities: Men in Movements,* pp. 3-4.

[28] Thomas, D., 1994, *Not Guilty: In defense of men,* Freedom Press.

[29] Farrell, W., 1993, *The Myth of Male Power.*

[30] Quoted in Messner, M. & Haddad, R., 1985, Concepts and overview of the men's liberation movement, In R. Baumle (Ed.), *Men freeing men: Exploding the myth of the traditional male,* p. 282.

Chapter 6

The biological perspective. This chapter illuminates the controversy over the use of biological differences to discuss gender during the 1970s and 80s. Feminists of the time thought the focus on biology had historically led to depicting women as inferior to men. Thus, the authors make a strong case using medical evidence from studies showing that women are not physically inferior to men. In fact, they point out, it may be the other way around. This essay and others like it are part of the backlash to earlier attitudes that women were weak and frail.

Chapter 6 *James A. Doyle and Michele A. Paludi,* **The Biological Perspective**

The French say *vive la différence*, facetiously applauding the differences between the sexes. Unfortunately, *la différence* has lost something in translation, and has been interpreted as implying an unfavorable comparison with men in the intrinsic value of the female and in her value to society. In order to use biology to support the premise of the inferiority of women to men, the physiological attributes common to the human species have been ignored or minimized and the differences between the sexes have been exaggerated and misrepresented. -- Anne M. Briscoe

Even the most casual observer can see that women and men differ. They look, move, and sometimes even act differently. Many people believe the differences make for a more interesting world, proclaiming *vive la différence!* It's not enough, however, to note that women and men differ. Rather by how much, in what areas, and more important, why do they differ? Looking at women and men from a biological perspective can afford us with much valuable information.

63

In this chapter we will begin our discussion of biology by briefly noting why the biological perspective remains controversial. We then will focus on the prenatal period. Chromosomes and hormones play a large part in shaping our physical makeup, and we need to be aware of their contributions. Next, we describe sex similarities and differences across the life span. We will also examine hormones and behavior. And, we will discuss one of the more controversial topics in this area, namely, sociobiology.

The Politics of Biology

Why should there be such a struggle between those dedicated to explaining sex and gender differences? The debate over biology (nature) and culture forces (nurture) seems to intensify when, according to Ann Oakley (1972), "the existing roles and statuses of male and female are changing." And certainly, women's and men's statuses and roles have been changing in the last several years. Thus, we shouldn't be too surprised that the nature-nurture debate seems to be at fever pitch nowadays.

Another reason for the continuing controversy is that, historically, biology has been used to defend the so-called natural order of certain social systems. For instance, during the Middle Ages, gross injustices and oppression were justified by what was called the divine right of kings. Many proclaimed the naturalness of these systems with their inequities, stating that nature deemed that some had the right to oppress others. Today, we are becoming aware that many in the past used biological differences to keep women in a subordinate and powerless position.

As a matter of record, during the last century and into the early part of this century, biological differences were used to rationalize women's unequal status in society. About one hundred years ago for instance, it was commonly believed that a woman's "fragile" nature required her to be protected, that a woman's menses destined her to periodic bouts of uncontrolled emotions, and that her small brain limited her intellectual horizons. Consequently, women were prevented from pursuing certain professions such as medicine or law, were not allowed to vote, and were subjected to numerous other restrictions all by virtue of their "fragile" biology. Furthermore, because women gave birth, most believed they were forever destined for child raising as well as household duties. Even when early researchers found women superior to men in certain abilities (e.g., verbal abilities), little was made of such talents. An even more blatant use of a biological principle employed against women was the *variability hypothesis* (Shields, 1975, 1982).

Stemming from Darwin's theory of evolution, the variability hypothesis stated that the more varied and widespread a species' behaviors, skills, and talents were, the more likely that species was to survive and develop. In other words, a species that possessed wide-ranging and adaptive abilities was more likely to survive and pass on its genes than a species whose abilities were more restricted or more rigidly expressed. Those who applied the variability hypothesis to humans thought that men, as a rule, showed more variability in their abilities than women showed. For example, one reason given for the greater number of men geniuses throughout history was the men's greater intellectual variability. Men, according to this line of reasoning, were thought to be naturally predisposed to greater heights of intellectual achievements (and greater deficits also -- but that was never discussed) than women, whose achievements were limited -- neither gifted nor retarded -- to a more narrowly defined range of intellectual endeavors. If women were constrained by their lack of great intellectual achievements, there was little need or reason for more than a cursory or basic education for them. This is only one example of a supposed biological difference used to prevent women from gaining educational opportunities equal to those of men. It is not surprising, then, that biology and biological principles have taken on a controversial air in the discussion of sex and gender differences.

We should also note that there has been criticism of the methodology and reporting of research on the biology of sex and gender differences. Many studies dealing with brain development or hormone function have been done on animal populations and the results generalized to humans (Goy, 1978; Phoenix, 1978). In some research studies, average differences are likely to be statistically significant even when the differences themselves are quite small. Furthermore, researchers have tended to overemphasize biological causation and neglected the importance of cultural values on physical functioning such as the impact of religious views. The search for biological underpinnings of girls' and women's behavior are frequently interpreted as an attempt to set unchangeable limits on their opportunities. On the other hand, attempts to explain all of girls' and women's traits in terms of environmental factors may be seen as a denial of the genetic realities of human behavior. Obviously, an understanding of both the biological concomitants of female and male behavior and the external influences on that behavior are necessary for a psychology of sex and gender (Rathus, 1988).

Prenatal Events and Sex Differences

The *prenatal period* of development is the time elapsing between conception and birth. It averages about 266 days, or 280 days from the first menstrual period (see discussion below). The prenatal period is divided into three stages: the germinal period, embryonic period, and the fetal period.

The *germinal period* is characterized by the growth of the zygote and the establishment of a linkage between the zygote and the woman's support system. The *embryonic period* lasts from the end of the second week to the eighth week. This period is characterized by rapid growth, the establishment of a placental relationship with the woman, and the early structural appearance of all the major organs. Development begins with the brain and head areas and then works its way down the body. This growth trend is referred to as *cephalocaudal development*. The cells in the central portion of the embryo thicken and form a ridge that is referred to as the *primitive streak*. This streak divides the embryo into right and left halves and becomes the spinal cord. The tissues grow in opposite directions away from the axis of the primitive streak. This growth trend is referred to as *proximodistal development*.

The *fetal period* begins with the ninth week and ends with birth. This period is characterized by the continuous development of major organ systems. The organs also assume their special functions.

Determination of sexual characteristics begins at conception. When a woman's ovum (the female reproductive cell with 23 single chromosomes) is fertilized by a sperm cell (the male reproductive cell with 23 single chromosomes) the result is expected to produce the characteristic human cell with a total of 46 chromosomes (23 pairs). Of these pairs only one pair, "the sex chromosomes," controls the genetic sex of the child (Rathus, 1988). The woman's ovum possesses an X chromosome for sex, while the man's sperm cell may contain an X or Y. When an X-bearing sperm cell fertilizes the X-bearing ovum, the genetic pattern is established for a female (XX). When a Y-bearing sperm cell fertilizes the X-bearing ovum, the genetic pattern is established for a male (XY). This explanation of the development of sexual characteristics allows one to conclude that the male sperm cell controls the sex of the offspring, and that chromosomes are the determinants of sexual characteristics. While these are basically correct, other factors may mediate the outcome: female viability and hormonal factors in sex development.

Female Viability

The environment through which the sperm cell must pass to reach the ovum must be considered a factor in sex determination (Rathus, 1988). Genetic researchers have found that the X-bearing sperm appear more viable than the Y-bearing sperm. Women who conceive during times when their vaginal environment is likely to be strongly acidic are more likely to produce girls. This suggests that a strongly acidic environment is detrimental to the Y-bearing sperm.

Hormonal Factors

While the chromosomal pairing of XX or XY occurs in most cases, there are anomalies in which too many or too few chromosomes connect, resulting in physical differences. The female pattern of development is the standard. While male development needs the secretion of male hormones from the testes to stimulate the growth and development of the male reproductive system (approximately the sixth week), female development occurs spontaneously, even in the absence of ovaries and their hormonal secretions (Money, 1987).

Adrenogenital syndrome is a hormonal abnormality. This condition seriously affects genetically normal female fetuses. The adrenogenital syndrome can have several causes. First, some women develop tumors on their ovaries or on their adrenal glands that in turn produce a surplus of androgens. If such a condition develops during pregnancy, some excessive androgen may reach a female fetus via the bloodstream. A second cause may be the fetus's own adrenal cortices. Normally, a fetus's adrenal glands produce a hormone called cortisol, which is similar to an androgen. Some female fetuses have a defective adrenal cortex that produces an abundance of cortisol, which can affect its body much like an androgen. And last, during the 1940s and 1950s, many women with histories of miscarriages were prescribed a synthetic drug (progestin) that affected female fetuses much like androgen. Thus, some female fetuses have suffered the masculinizing consequences of being exposed either naturally or medically to an overdose of androgen or androgenlike chemicals during fetal development. The outcome and extent of adrenogenital syndrome depends on the amount of the androgen substance in the fetus's bloodstream and the time at which it occurs, leading to various degrees of masculinization of the external sex structures.

The external genitalia of the female appear masculine despite the XX chromosomal pair. These girls may be labeled and raised as boys. Although surgical procedures may be necessary at puberty to facilitate development as a boy, these individuals will adjust to the sex designation they were given at birth (Money & Tucker, 1975).

Psychologists Susan Baker and Anke Ehrhardt have conducted several studies on girls with adrenogenital syndrome (Baker & Ehrhardt, 1978; Ehrhardt & Baker, 1978). The adrenogenital girls observed in these studies were all treated soon after birth with cortisol, which prevented further masculinization of their bodies and allowed them to develop normal female secondary sex characteristics. Boys can also be classified as adrenogenital when they are exposed to extremely high androgen levels before birth (Ehrhardt & Baker, 1978).

Androgen-insensitivity syndrome is an abnormal hormonal condition affecting a genetic male and is caused by an X-linked, recessive condition. Because the fetal gonads develop as testes, the Müllerian-inhibiting substance prevents the development of internal female sex structures. However, the androgens produced by the testes do little if anything to foster the development of a male's internal or external sex structures because these tissues, for some yet unknown reason, do not respond to the masculinizing effects of the androgens. But the small amounts of estrogen produced by the testes are able to stimulate female sex characteristics such as a vaginal opening. Consequently, at birth, most of these individuals have what appears to be external female sex structures.

If this condition is not noticed at birth or shortly thereafter, these infants will be labeled as girls, and, more than likely, accept the prescribed feminine gender role behavior (Money & Ehrhardt, 1972). Because they lack the internal sex structures of the female, however, they will not menstruate. Thus, the person who suffers from the androgen-insensitivity syndrome is a genetic male who usually grows up as a female because the embryonic sex tissues did not respond to the masculinizing effects of the androgens.

These hormonal abnormalities show the dramatic influence that the androgens have on either a male or female fetus. Without androgen and its masculinizing effect, or if the body's sex tissues are immune or insensitive to androgen, the fetus will develop as a female. If, somehow, excessive amounts of androgen or other adrogenlike substances happen to occur during the female fetus's development, she will have varying degrees of masculinization of her sex tissues. The key issue in all of these conditions is that the androgens, especially testosterone, play a key role in the development of the internal and external sex structures.

The results of studies of individuals with abnormal genetic or hormonal conditions clearly indicate that biological factors are necessary but not sufficient in producing the characteristics that we attribute to sex. Even in the prenatal period there appears an interaction between physical and social conditions, which will be repeated again and again.

Sex Chromosomal Abnormalities

In the prenatal stage of development, as throughout life, there is an interaction between social and physical conditions. The sex chromosomes' contribution to fetal development is also important. To learn more about the effects sex chromosomes have on the physical structures, we will now turn our attention to three abnormal chromosome patterns: Turner's syndrome, Klinefelter's syndrome, and the double-Y syndrome.

<u>Turner's Syndrome</u>

In approximately one in every ten thousand infant girls, an abnormal sex chromosome pattern is found in which the second female sex chromosome is either defective or missing (Hamerton *et al.*, 1975). This condition is referred to as *Tuner's syndrome*. Since it is the second sex chromosome that directs the development of the gonadal tissue into either functioning ovaries or testes, girls with Turner's syndrome always develop a female body with either underdeveloped ovaries or no ovaries whatsoever. Consequently, they will not menstruate at adolescence, nor will they develop breasts. Their bodies do not produce the estrogen necessary for the development of their secondary sex characteristics during adolescence.

Administration of estrogen will contribute to breast growth. In addition, an artificial menstrual cycle may be produced by administering estrogen for three weeks followed by one week without this treatment (Golub, 1992). This treatment has been reported to be beneficial for girls' self-esteem and self-concept (Ehrhardt & Meyer-Bahlberg, 1975).

A girl with Turner's syndrome usually has a short stature, a weblike configuration around the neck, eyelid folds, and a rather broad or shieldlike chest (Money & Garnoff, 1965). Also, they show little or no impairment in intellectual ability, with some even showing significantly above-normal IQs (Money, 1964).

Klinefelter's Syndrome

One type of sex chromosomal abnormality occurs when there is a surplus of sex chromosomes. For example, there can be too many X or Y chromosomes. We will first discuss those boys with a surplus of Xs (either 47, XXY, or 48, XXXY) who have what is called *Klinefelter's syndrome*. Approximately one or two out of every one thousand infant boys have Klinefelter's syndrome (Hamerton *et al.*, 1975). A boy with Klinefelter's syndrome is usually taller than the average boy and appears rather gangling because of his long arms and legs. During adolescence, their chests usually take on a female-like appearance by becoming larger than normal. Their testes are infertile and produce abnormally small amounts of testosterone (Money & Ehrhardt, 1972).

A boy with Klinefelter's syndrome usually has some impairment in intellectual functioning, and many are classified as mentally retarded. In prison populations, men with Klinefelter's syndrome have been found in greater numbers than expected by chance alone. However, this finding may be attributed to their committing more minor crimes and getting arrested more often -- rather than to some genetic predilection for criminal activity (Witkin *et al.*, 1976).

The Double-Y Syndrome

Approximately one out of every one thousand infant boys has one or more extra Y chromosomes, which is designated as the *double-Y syndrome* (Hamerton *et al.*, 1975). In adulthood, these men are taller than even men with Klinefelter's syndrome. Other than their above-average height, few other obvious physical features set these men off from chromosomally normal men (Owen, 1972). A major psychological feature of the double-Y man, however, is a marked increase in his impulsivity and lack of tolerance for frustration (Nielson & Christensen, 1974). Intellectually, he shows a slightly below-average overall ability (Witkin *et al.*, 1976).

The issue that first caught the public's attention with respect to the double-Y syndrome was the much publicized research that found these men in greater numbers in prison populations than would be predicted by chance alone (Jacobs *et al.*, 1965). The press highlighted this, and soon the public was convinced that the extra Y chromosome somehow predisposed such men to a life of violence and crime. However, the relationship between the extra Y and criminality has proved tenuous. In fact, male prisoners with an extra Y have less violent criminal histories than genetically normal male prisoners (Witkin *et al.*, 1976). Rather than indicting the extra Y chromosome as the cause of violent and criminal behavior, it makes just as much sense to point to the fact that the XYY male's greater impulsivity and excitability, coupled with frequent emotional outbursts, may contribute to many of these men committing crimes. Their psychological profile, rather than their genetic abnormality, may be the more important factor (Noel *et al.*, 1974).

Infancy and Childhood

Boys are more vulnerable to most every type of physical disease, environmental insult, and developmental difficulty (Jacklin, 1989). Approximately 125 boys are conceived for every 100 girls. By the end of the prenatal period, however, there is a significant loss of male concepti: The ratio of boys to girls is 106 to 100 (Strickland, 1989).

In addition, females experience fewer difficulties during the birth process and consequently, fewer birth defects. Carol Nagy Jacklin and Eleanor Macoby (1982) reported that even in unproblematic deliveries, the births of girls take an average of an hour shorter than the deliveries of boys. This shortened length of labor has been correlated with fewer problems in infancy. Girls are thus more viable than boys.

Research has supported the greater *female viability* even after birth. For example, women have an overall life expectancy that surpasses men at every decade of life, regardless of race (Jacklin, 1989; Strickland, 1988). Girls have fewer congenital disorders, are less likely to succumb to *Sudden Infant Death Syndrome* (the death, while sleeping, of apparently healthy infants who cease breathing for unknown medical reasons) and less prone to hyperactivity (Rathus, 1988). All of these findings suggest genetically determined strength.

Infant girls are more mature at birth than are infant boys. Girls have more advanced skeletal and neurological systems (Hutt, 1978; Rathus, 1983). Girls continue to mature between two and two-and-a-half years faster than boys. Their skeletal development at birth is approximately one month ahead of boys'. Development for boys and girls follows the cephalocaudal principle and proximodistal principles. Growth, thus, progresses from the head region, then the trunk, then the leg region. Motor development also follows the cephalocaudal principal. Infants learn to control the muscles of their head and neck, then their arms and abdomen, and finally their legs. Thus, infants learn to hold their heads up before they can sit, and they learn to sit before they learn to walk. Infants' large muscle control develops before fine muscle control.

Height remains equal for both girls and boys until age seven, when girls are, on the average, taller than boys. This difference reverses at age 10. While as a group, boys are physically stronger and weigh more than girls after puberty, there is considerable overlap -- many girls are physically stronger and weigh more than the average boy.

In early and middle childhood, boys are over-represented among children who have speech, behavior, and learning disorders. Approximately twice as many boys than girls exhibit articulatory errors; three times as many boys as girls stutter (Bentzen, 1963). In addition, the incidence of reading problems is almost five times more prevalent in boys than in girls (Knopf, 1979). Mental retardation is higher among boys than girls. And, more boys than girls are autistic and hyperactive.

No consistent differences have been observed in the average of onset of certain developmental tasks, e.g., eruption of teeth, walking, sitting up, or thumb-and-forefinger grasping. Many studies report sex as a factor in performance of motor tasks, but they frequently give the advantage to boys. This assignment of advantage contradicts the fact that girls have more accelerated physical development. It is illogical that biological acceleration may be given as an explanation of girls' rapid acquisition of language skills (Maccoby & Jacklin, 1974) and their ability to excel in fine motor skills, while there remains an expectation of inferior performance in gross motor activities. Bem (1981) concluded that differences in motor performance appear to be influenced by both biological and environmental factors. The low expectations that parents and teachers have with respect to girls' motor performance, in addition to the lack of rewards given to girls for such activities, apparently combine to produce low motivation and low performance levels for girls in the behaviors that have been societally defined as appropriate for boys.

Adolescence and Early Adulthood

The period of *adolescence* is marked by changes in physical development that are part of the passage from childhood to adulthood. These physical changes occur during the stage of development referred to as *pubescence*, which is the period of rapid growth that culminates in *puberty*, or sexual maturity and reproductive capacity.

Pubescence technically begins when the *hypothalamus* (part of the upper brain stem) signals the pituitary gland to release the hormones known as *gonadotrophins*. This usually occurs during girls' and boys' sleep a year or so before any of the physical changes associated with pubescence appear (Schowalter & Anyan, 1981). The obvious physical differences among adolescents of the identical chronological age underscore an endocrinological issue: the hypothalamus does not signal the pituitary to release the gonadotrophins at the same time in every adolescent. The exact factors that activate the hypothalamus are not determined. However, researchers (e.g., Frisch, 1984; Katchadorian, 1977; Tanner, 1962) have argued that the hypothalamus monitors adolescents' body weight and releases the necessary hormones when the body is of sufficient weight. In the United States, the age when puberty is reached has steadily decreased, with the trend now leveling off. Most adolescent girls in the United States begin pubescence at approximately 11 years of age and reach the end of their growth by 17. Their growth spurt starts between 9.5 and 14.5 years. Girls grow fastest in height and weight at approximately 12 years of age. They reach 98 percent of their adult height at 16.25 years. Girls typically mature on the average of two years earlier than boys. As a group, boys are physically stronger, are taller, and weigh more than girls after puberty.

During adolescence girls and boys undergo common physical changes. For example, their lymphatic tissues decrease in size; they lose vision due to rapid changes in eyes between the ages of eleven and fourteen, and their facial structures change during pubescence. Also, their hairline recedes and the facial bones mature in such a way that the chin and nose become prominent. Adolescents' weight nearly doubles during pubescence; girls weigh 25 pounds less than boys as a result of their lower proportion of muscle to fat tissue. There is considerable overlap in the distributions, however (Petersen & Taylor, 1980). By the time they are fifteen, adolescents have lost 20 deciduous teeth. The number of bone masses during pubescence drops from approximately 350 to less than 220 as a result of epiphysel unions (Petersen & Taylor, 1980).

Middle and Later Adulthood

Men's greater vulnerability holds true from conception to old age, and the death rate for American men is higher than that for women in every decade of life. Women have an overall life span expectancy that surpasses men at every age regardless of race (Strickland, 1988; U.S. National Center for Health Statistics, 1987).

Approximately 33 percent more boys than girls die in their first year of life. An equal sex ratio does not occur until eighteen years of age, when 100 men are alive for every 100 women (Strickland, 1988). However, the ratio steadily decreases throughout adulthood: By age eighty-seven, one man is alive for every two women (Williams, 1983). The life expectancy for women in the United States is 78.2 years; for men 70.9 years. Black women live longer (73.8 years) than both black men (64.8 years) and white men (71.4 years).

In adulthood, the mortality rates for men exceed those of women for most disorders, especially heart disease, malignancy, accidents, and chronic pulmonary disease (Strickland, 1988). Lung cancer surpasses breast cancer as the leading cause of cancer death for women (U.S. Department of Health & Human Services, 1982). Smoking interacts with the use of oral contraceptives; consequently the risk of heart attack for women who use oral contraceptives is increased 10 times if they smoke. Women have a higher death rate than men for strokes since they live longer and are thus more likely to suffer cerebral accidents.

Breast cancer is the second leading cause of cancer deaths among women between thirty-five and fifty-five years old. Cancer of the prostrate accounts for 10 percent of the malignancies that occur for men.

In adulthood, women exceed men with Alzheimer's disease by 2 or 3 to 1. In addition, women are more likely than men to be subject to chronic and disabling diseases, e.g., arthritis, rheumatism, hypertension, and diabetes.

The highest male-to-female death ratios occur for AIDS (approximately eight times more men than women), suicide (approximately four times more men), homicide (three time more men), accidents (twice as many men), and chronic liver diseases (twice as many men).

It was believed that as women participate in more male-populated (considered "high stress") careers, they would increase their changes of heart disease. However, research has indicated that women in executive career positions do not show a higher incidence of heart disease than women not in these positions (Haynes & Feinleib, 1980). Heart disease is more likely to be found among women in clerical or low-status jobs where they have poor or no support systems. Role strain is increased for women in low-income jobs with many child care demands and no assistance with housecare (Anderson-Kulman & Paludi, 1986). And, illness and poor health are more likely to be found among individuals of lower socioeconomic status.

Research does point to the negative effects of socialization practices of boys and men. Anxiety associated with conforming to the masculine gender role, including the emphasis on competitiveness and achievement, may lead to the development of compensatory behaviors that are hazardous to men's health: exhibitions of violence, smoking, excessive consumption of alcohol, drug abuse, risk taking behavior. Black men in particular are vulnerable to physical illnesses and death (Strickland, 1988). They may have inadequate access to affordable health care and suffer the added stress of racism.

Black males have higher rates of infant mortality, low birth weight, sickle cell anemia, nonfatal and fatal accidents, elevated blood pressure, and sexually transmitted diseases. Among black men, homicide is the leading cause of death.

Strickland (1988) pointed out that across many cultures with different stressors men still die earlier and have a greater incidence of chromosomal abnormalities than do women. A biological predisposition seems to interact with cultural factors to make men more physically vulnerable than women. Research does suggest that female hormones may be protective (Rodin & Ickovics, 1990; Travis, 1993). Girls' and women's ability to withstand infection may be transmitted via the X chromosome or their lower metabolic rate may contribute to their viability.

Hormones and Behavior

Let's now proceed with our discussion of some of the effects that hormones have on certain behaviors.

Aggression

One of the frequently mentioned gender differences is that boys and men are more aggressive than girls and women. Eleanor Maccoby and Carol Nagy Jacklin (1974) concluded that, "Aggression is related to levels of sex hormones, and can be changed by experimental administration of these hormones" (p. 243). Let's review some of the research on men and see the relationship between aggression and testosterone.

The first correlational study between aggression and testosterone levels using a sample of men was conducted by Harold Persky and several of his colleagues (Persky, Smith, & Basu, 1971). Two groups of physically healthy men were selected for the study. The first group consisted of 18 college men between the ages of seventeen and twenty-eight, and the second contained 15 men between the ages of thirty-three and sixty-six. Each of the men took a battery of tests, including the *Buss-Durkee Hostility Inventory*, a paper-and-pencil test that asks the respondent to check off statements, such as the frequency of losing one's temper and getting into fights, that apply to himself. A significantly positive correlation was found between levels of testosterone and aggression scores among the younger men but not among the older ones. We could argue that aggression on a paper-and-pencil test is one thing, but what about the testosterone levels for those men who actually lose their tempers and get into fights?

In a study of prison inmates, Leo Kreuz and Robert Rose (1972) studied testosterone levels between those inmates who were classified as fighters and those classified as nonfighters. Interestingly, Kruez and Rose found no difference between these two groups of men with respect to their testosterone levels, nor did they find a relationship between their testosterone levels and their scores on the *Buss-Durkee Hostility Inventory*. Others who have used different groups of men and different measures of aggression have found equivocal results, at best, between testosterone levels and male aggression (Doering *et al.*, 1975; Persky *et al.*, 1977; Tieger, 1980; Udry & Talbert, 1988).

In an extensive review of the literature on aggression and testosterone levels, Joseph Pleck (1981) remarked that:

> Given the social importance of aggressive behavior, it is clear that research on its possible biological sources will continue to receive serious

attention. At the present time, the evidence in animals for hormonal factors in male aggression is strong (albeit complex). But comparable evidence for human male aggression is much weaker and less consistent (p. 170).

The Premenstrual Syndrome

Women's testosterone levels remain relatively stable, but their estrogen and progesterone levels show considerable fluctuation during their menstrual cycle. Menstruation occurs in most women between the ages of twelve and forty-five or fifty. Although menstruation is a normal feature of a woman's life, many ancient peoples believed a menstruating woman was unclean. Others believed the menstruating woman unfit to handle food or even dangerous to others' safety and well-being (Delaney *et al.*, 1988). Today, few people think of menstruation or menstruating women as dangerous, but many view menstruation as hindering women from taking on certain responsibilities and being treated fairly in many situations. Karen Paige (1973) noted as much when she wrote:

> Women, the old argument goes, are eternally subject to the whims and wherefores of their biological clocks. Their raging hormonal cycles make them emotionally unstable and intellectually unreliable. If women have second-class status, we are told, it is because they cannot control the implacable demands of that bouncing estrogen (p. 41).

Menstruation carries with it a burden of cultural beliefs, and stereotypes by many men and some women (Golub, 1992; Koeske, 1976; Sherif, 1980). In the last several decades a new element has been added to the issue of the menstruating woman, namely, the *premenstrual syndrome*, or PMS.

First described by an American physician (Frank, 1931), the premenstrual syndrome, or tension, as it was originally called, is thought to occur during the preceding week or two before the onset of menstruation. PMS's symptoms vary among women, but there seems to be a fairly consistent pattern among most who report suffering from PMS. The prevalent psychological symptoms are tension, depression, anxiety attacks, and irritability. Physical symptoms include headaches, backaches, fatigue, tenderness of the breasts, water retention, and cold sores (Hopson & Rosenfeld, 1984).

A considerable amount of controversy has surrounded the premenstrual syndrome. Researchers have failed to agree upon the characteristics of PMS (Golub, 1992; Parlee, 1993). The lack of a definition for PMS makes it difficult to investigate women's symptoms carefully. Furthermore, PMS is controversial because some experts report that all women experience the syndrome while others state that PMS doesn't even exist -- that it is a myth. Both sides of this issue discriminate against women.

One attempt at defining PMS for research purposes was a conference at the National Institute of Mental Health in April, 1983. The criteria agreed to at this conference were that there must be a change of at least 30 percent in the intensity of symptoms measured in days 5-10 of the cycle as compared with the premenstrual phase, and that these changes must be prospectively documented for at least two consecutive cycles.

Research does indicate that some women have mild to severe mood swings that are related to their menstrual cycles. However, certainly not all women experience PMS. The data simply demonstrate a correlation between cycle phase of hormone levels and mood. Thus, it is questionable to infer that hormones *cause* mood changes. We could just as well argue that the mood change associated with a woman's menstrual cycle "appears to be related... to a woman's current psychosocial experience and more enduring features of her psychological experience and more enduring features of her psychological makeup such as attitudes about menstruation and personality factors" (Friedman, Hurt, Arnoff, & Clarkin, 1980, p. 726).

Carol Nagy Jacklin (1989) summarized the literature on hormones and behavior in the following way:

> A word of warning: Correlations between hormones and behavior are typically interpreted as cases in which the biological causes the psychological. It fits our predispositions to assume that hormones cause behavioral outcomes. The hormone system is an open system. Much more empirical work is needed before the direction of the causal arrows are understood (p. 130).

The causes of PMS are not clear nor agreed upon by most researchers. Some point to fluid retention, brain changes, or a decrease in progesterone levels during the premenstrual period as possible factors in negative moods (Dalton, 1964; Janowsky, Berens, & Davis, 1973). Others, however, point out that stress-producing social factors -- being fired from one's job or getting a divorce -- may play a decisive role in PMS symptoms (Parlee, 1973; Sherif, 1980). Whatever the causes for the premenstrual syndrome, few can deny that the culturally defined negative social attitudes about menstruation can seriously influence a woman's perceptions of her own bodily states.

Attitudes about Menstruating Women

Cultural factors contribute to mood shifts. For example, in many cultures and many religions, menstruating women are seen as unclean. The words of Leviticus 15:19-33 speak most clearly of this belief:

> And if a woman have an issue, and her issue in her flesh be blood, she shall be put apart seven days: and whosoever toucheth her shall be unclean until the even.

In this culture, many women may abstain from sexual intercourse during menstruation. Since all women have the same hormone cycles while the correlated psychological cycles are different, the latter must be influenced by cultural attitudes. Girls' and women's attitudes and feelings about menarche are most important.

Brook Gunn and Anne Petersen (1984) reported that adolescent girls who have such negative attitudes toward menstruation will experience the most depression and discomfort in their own menstrual cycles. Adolescent girls with the most liberal attitudes about gender roles and sexuality experience less menstrual pain than adolescent girls with more conservative attitudes. Research has also suggested that girls who reach menarche prior to age 12 feel the most "abnormal" about menstruation.

Many adults as well as media emphasize only the hygienic aspects of menstruation, thus perpetuating the belief that menstruation is unclean and should be hidden from others in an ashamed manner (Gunn and Petersen, 1984). Negative attitudes about menstruation have been found to be related to health problems. Adolescent girls, while attempting to rid their bodies of what they have been socialized to believe are unclean odors, will use vaginal deodorants, deodorized tampons, and douches. These products irritate their genital tissues and may create vaginal infections.

Sociobiology: A Brewing Storm in the Social Sciences

For some time now, there has been a battle over the issue of the relative importance of one's biology versus the impact of one's environment as determinants of human behavior. In the last several years, since the introduction of a new perspective on human social behavior called *sociobiology,* the debate has become especially strong.

Most will agree that our evolutionary heritage has played a significant role in the development of our human species. Some suggest that our early ancestors have more in common with us than many might think. Beatrix Hamburg (1978) suggested this when she wrote:

> The evolution of human behavior and its relation to social organization are best understood in the context of early man in the period of hunting-and-gathering societies. The best available information indicates that out of the roughly 2 million years that hominids have existed, over 99 percent of this time has been spent in hunting-and-gathering societies. Agriculture as a major way of life was instituted only 5,000 to 6,000 years ago. The Industrial Revolution is a recent development of the last 100 years, and only the most minute fraction of humans have lived in an industrial or technological society. Our biological heritage chiefly derives from the era of man the hunter. The long period of man's existence in the challenge of a hunting-and-gathering way of life has afforded the opportunity for those adaptations to become firmly established in the gene pool. It has been postulated that our intelligence, interests, emotions, and species-specific patterns of social interaction are all the evolutionary residue of the success of Homo sapiens in the hunting-and-gathering adaptation. In effect, modern man carries essentially the same genetic heritage as early man (p. 378).

Sociobiology is quickly becoming an established alternative view for explaining human social behavior. We will examine its tenets and then some of the major criticisms directed against it.

The Case for Sociobiology

Edward Wilson (1978), a major proponent of sociobiology, defines this new science as "the systematic study of the biological basis of all forms of social behavior" (p. 16). In their attempt to understand the biological principles underlying social behaviors, sociobiologists draw data from several different disciplines -- genetics, anthropology, psychology, and sociology. Thus sociobiology can be considered an interdisciplinary science.

Basically, sociobiologists believe that certain behaviors are inherited through one's genes, much like one inherits skin color or hair texture. The reason for certain behaviors having a genetic link is simply that these behaviors proved advantageous to the species' survival throughout the evolutionary period.

Sociobiologists, for example, believe the among early human groups, when men banded together and dominated women, there was a greater likelihood of the group's survival and development to higher levels (Tiger, 1969; Tiger & Fox, 1971). The key to sociobiology's view of social behavior is simply that certain social behaviors have "become genetically encoded in a species if they contribute to the fitness of those individuals that have them" (van den Berghe, 1978, p. 20). As Wilson (1978) commented:

> In hunter-gatherer societies men hunt and women stay home. This strong bias persists in most agricultural and industrial societies, and on that ground alone appears to have a genetic origin... My own guess is that the genetic bias is intense enough to cause a substantial division of labor even in the most free and most egalitarian of future societies... even with identical education and equal access to all professions, men are likely to continue to play a disproportionate role in political life, business, and science.

With an eye to their genetic basis, several specific human social behaviors have been examined, such as altruism, aggression, homosexuality, and even ethics. One area that is especially interesting with respect to our preceding discussion of gender differences is that of maternal or nurturant behaviors. A common belief is that women are somehow predisposed to act more nurturant and have special feelings toward the young. In most societies we find that women also act as the primary, if not the sole, caretaker of the newborn infants. But is there anything preventing a man from taking over after the birth and performing many of the caretaking duties? Or are women directed by their genes or something called maternal instinct after birth to continue their care of the young?

And, anthropologist Lila Liebowitz (1989) argued that the early division of labor was molded by socioeconomic considerations, not biological imperatives.

> The "common sense" explanation of the division of labor by sex that is usually offered is that it is related to differences in size and strength between early, proto-human women and men and to the lengthened "biological" dependency of the young. This implies that the sexual division of labor is protocultural and, therefore, "natural." But this notion does not bear up under close inspection... Early hominids of both sexes, despite their difference in size after researching sexual maturity, engaged in the same kinds of productive activities. Adult females just combined these activities with bearing and nursing the young (p. 3).

Sociologist Alice Rossi (1977) believes that biology plays a significant role in the development of a strong mother-infant bond. Rossi believes that, historically, women who have had a greater involvement with and in their children's growth are predisposed for such behaviors. Accordingly then, because men lack the biological bond with their offspring, they never develop the same attachment to the young. Rossi thinks that new mothers exhibit many responses toward their newborns that are not learned. For example, many mothers will automatically hold their infants in their left arms, which brings their infants close to their hearts where the infants can be comforted by the soothing and rhythmic sounds.

Rossi's views have been challenged (Chodorow, 1977, 1978). Rossi, however, believes that biology is far too important a factor in the human experience to dismiss outright because of past misuses by individuals who used biological constructs to oppress others.

The Case Against Sociobiology

Sociobiology has been criticized as "opening the door to justifying the oppression of one group by another on the basis of biological inferiority" (Rogan, 1978, p. 85). Furthermore, there are several obvious flaws in its propositions (Kitcher, 1987).

First, the basis of sociobiology rests on the existence of some as yet unidentified genes. Wilson and others have outlined a whole realm of social behaviors ranging from altruism to xenophobia (i.e., fear of strangers) without so much as identifying even one possible gene that affects these behaviors. It seems somewhat reasonable, then, to postulate that a set of social behaviors are caused by genetic material and then not be able to point to the material in order to study its effects.

The second and most telling criticism of sociobiology, however, is the extreme difference in terms of time when we compare biological evolution to cultural evolution. Several tens of thousands of years are relatively few in terms of biological evolution. But a decade or two can witness preliterate societies whisked into a technological age and the social behaviors of those involved completely revamped. Social customs and rituals thought appropriate only ten, fifty, or a hundred years ago would today be seen as eccentricities at best, if not evidence of aberrant mental states.

Pointing to the contention that women by virtue of their biological makeup make better parents, researchers studied the fathers of first-borns and found evidence of a strong attachment or a bond between the fathers and their new-borns that the researchers called engrossment (Greenberg & Morris, 1974). Although the existence of a father-infant bond has been seriously challenged (Palkovitz, 1985), others have found that fathers do, in fact, give considerable attention to and show affection for their newborn infants (Parke & O'Leary, 1975). Thus, research doesn't support the popular belief that women have some biological edge over men when it comes to nurturant social behaviors.

A major problem with sociobiology is that it relies too much on an overly simple or reductionistic explanation for some very complex issues. Also, sociobiology tends to dismiss alternative explanations for social behaviors as if it were the final authority on such topics (Gould, 1976). Maya Pines (1978) states the argument against sociobiology as follows:

> Sociobiology may give the illusion of offering new insights into the human condition. Yet its methods are still so gross, its notions of "fitness" so primitive (can fitness really be measured by the frequency of copulation or the number of offspring?), our information about animal behavior still so meager, and human culture so complex that sociobiology can provide very little enlightenment about the behavior of real people at this time (p. 24).

Time will tell if sociobiology becomes an accepted part of mainstream social science. For the moment, there appears to be too many scientists who fear that its tenets could be more of a hindrance than a help in trying to make sense out of the issues that surround gender differences. Ethel Tobach and Betty Rosoff (1978) argued:

The recent publication of... Wilson's sociobiology... strengthened the "scientific" legitimacy of "herediatarianism." By hereditarianism we mean the dogma that genes determine an individual's life history in the most significant ways. In other words, each of us has a "genetic destiny" that programs our behavior according to race and sex. Defenses of sexism and racism in the name of evolutionary theory have been used to support the continuing attacks on the few victories won by women in the United States, such as antiabortion legislation, ERA defeats, and legal actions against affirmative employment programs. These events and the attempts to pit women against Blacks, Hispanics, and other minorities in a period of increasing unemployment have made it clear that it is necessary to expose the myth of genetic destiny. That myth says that women are doomed to exploitation because their genes determine their anatomy, physiology, and behavior. This then limits their societal activity and prevents them from overcoming their oppression (p. 7).

Summary

Human development begins with our sex chromosomes and hormones. Several abnormal conditions exist that show the degree to which our biology influences later development, namely, Turner's, Klinefelter's, the double-Y, androgen-insensitivity, and adrenogenital syndromes.

A continuing controversy has arisen over the effects that hormones have on individuals' behavior, for example, aggression and premenstrual syndrome.

In the last decade, the study of sociobiology has caused a stir in the social sciences. Sociobiology has been hailed by some as a new approach to the study of human social behavior using biological constructs; others see it as little more than a scientific way of justifying inequality and discrimination of women.

There are a number of sex differences across the life span, especially in terms of male vulnerability and mortality rates of various illnesses. We need to remember that when sex differences are found, they are to be interpreted as physical only. Biology predisposes but does not predetermine the functions of individuals.

Suggested Readings

Asso, D. (1984). *The real menstrual cycle.* New York: Wiley.

Blechman, E. A. & Brownell, K. D. (Eds.). (1968). *Handbook of behavioral medicine for women.* Elmsford, NY: Pergamon.

Bleier, R. (1984). *Science and gender: A critique of biology and its theories on women.* Elmsford, NY: Pergamon.

Grady, K. E. & Lemkau, J. P. (Eds.). (1988). Women's health: Our minds, our bodies. *Psychology of Women Quarterly, 4,* 381-511.

Hardy, S. (1983). *The women that never evolved.* Cambridge: Harvard University Press.

Hubbard, R., Henifin, M., & Fried, B. (Eds.). (1979). *Women look at biology looking at women.* Cambridge, MA: Schenkman.

Longino, H., & Doell, R. (1983). Body, bias, and behavior: A comparative analysis of reasoning in two areas of biological science. *Signs, 9,* 206-227.

Tobach, E., & Rosoff, B. (Eds.). (1978). *Genes and gender.* New York: Gordian Press.

Wilson, E. (1978). *On human nature*. Cambridge: Harvard University Press.

References

Anderson-Kulman, R. E., & Paludi, M. A. (1986). Working mothers and the family context: Predicting positive coping. *Journal of Vocational Behavior 28*, 241-253.

Baker, S., & Ehrhardt, A. (1978). Prenatal androgen, intelligence, and cognitive sex differences. In R. Friedman *et al.* (Eds.), *Sex differences in behavior*. Huntington, NY: Krieger Publishing.

Bem, S. L. (1981). Gender schema theory: A cognitive account of sex typing. *Psychological Review, 88*, 354-364.

Bentzen, F. (1963). Sex ratios in learning and behavior disorders. *American Journal of Orthopsychiatry, 33*, 9-98.

Chodorow, N. (1977). Considerations on "A bio-social perspective on parenting." *Berkeley Journal of Sociology, 22,* 179-198.

Chodorow, N. (1978). *The reproduction of mothering.* Berkeley: University of California Press.

Dalton, K. (1964). *The premenstrual syndrome.* Springfield, IL: Thomas.

Dalton, K. (1980). Cyclical criminal acts in premenstrual syndrome. *Lancet, 2,* 1070-1071.

Delaney, J., Lupton, M., & Toth, E. (1988). *The curse: A cultural history of menstruation.* Campaign, IL: University of Illinois Press.

Doering, C. *et al.* (1975). Negative affect and plasma testosterone: A longitudinal human study. *Psychosomatic Medicine, 37*, 484-491.

Ehrhardt, A. E., & Baker, S. (1978). Fetal androgens, human central nervous system differentiation, and behavior and social dominance in man. *Psychosomatic Medicine, 36*, 469-475.

Ehrhardt, A. E., & Meyer-Bahlberg, H. (1975). Psychological correlates of abnormal pubertal development. *Clinics in Endocrinology and Metabolism, 4*, 207-222.

Frank, R. (1931). The hormonal causes of premenstrual tension. *Archives of Neurology and Psychiatry, 26*, 1053-1057.

Friedman, R. C., Hurt, S. W., Arnoff, M. S., & Clarkin, J. (1980). Behavior and the menstrual cycle. *Signs, 5*, 719-738.

Frisch, R. (1984). Fatness, puberty, and fertility. In B. Gunn & A. Petersen (Eds.), *Girls at puberty: Biological, psychological, and social perspectives.* New York: Plenum.

Golub, S. (1976). The effect of premenstrual anxiety and depression on cognitive function. *Journal of Personality and Social Psychology, 34*, 99-104.

Golub. S. (1992). *Periods: From menarche to menopause.* Newbury Park: Sage.

Gould, S. (1976, May). Biological potential vs. biological determinism. *Natural History Magazine*, pp. 12-22.

Goy, R. (1978). Development of play and mounting behavior in female rhesus monkeys virilized prenatally with esters of testosterone of dihydrotestosterone. In D. Chivers & J. Herbert (Eds.), *Recent advances in primatology* (Vol. 1), New York: Academic Press.

Greenberg, M., & Morris, N. (1974). Engrossment: The newborn's impact upon the father. *American Journal of Orthopsychiatry, 44*, 520-531.

Gunn, B., & Petersen, A. (Eds.). (1984). *Girls at puberty: Biological, psychological, and social perspectives.* New York: Plenum.

Hamburg, B. (1978). The psychobiology of sex differences: An evolutionary perspective. In R. Friedman *et al.*, (Ed.). *Sex differences in behavior.* Huntington, NY: Krieger Publishing.

Hamerton, J. *et al.* (1975). A cytogenetic survey of 14,069 newborn infants. *Clinical Genetics, 8,* 223-243.

Haynes, S. G., & Feinleib, M. (1980). Women, work, and coronary heart disease: Prospective findings from the Framingham Heart Study. *American Journal of Public Health, 70,* 133-141.

Hopson, J., & Rosenfeld, A. (1984, August). PMS: Puzzling monthly symptoms. *Psychology Today*, pp. 30-35.

Hutt, C. (1978). Biological bases of psychological sex differences. *American Journal of Diseases of Children, 132,* 170-177.

Jacklin, C. N. (1989). Female and male: Issues of gender. *American Psychologist, 44,* 127-133.

Jacklin, C. N., & Maccoby, E. E. (1982). Length of labor and sex of offspring. *Journal of Pediatric Psychology, 7,* 355-360.

Jacobs, P. *et al.* (1965). Aggressive behavior, mental subnormality and the XYY male. *Nature, 208,* 1351-1352.

Janowsky, D., Berens, S., & Davis, J. (1973). Correlations between mood, weight, and electrolytes during the menstrual cycle: A renin-angiotensin-aldosterone hypothesis of premenstrual tension. *Psychosomatic Medicine, 35,* 143-154.

Katchadorian, H. (1977). *The biology of adolescence.* San Francisco: Freeman.

Kitcher, P. (1987). *Vaulting ambition: Sociobiology and the quest for human nature.* Cambridge: MIT Press.

Knopf, I. J. (1979). *Childhood Psychopathology.* Englewood Cliffs, NJ: Prentice-Hall.

Koeske, R. (1976). Premenstrual emotionality: Is biology destiny? *Women and Health, 1,* 11-14.

Kreuz, L., & Rose, R. (1972). Assessment of aggressive behavior and plasma testosterone in a young criminal population. *Psychosomatic Medicine, 34,* 321-322.

Liebowitz, L. (1989). Origins of the sexual division of labor. In D. Kaufman (Ed.), *Public/private spheres: Women past and present.* Boston: Northeastern Custom Book Program.

Maccoby, E. E., & Jacklin, C. N. (1974). *The psychology of sex differences.* Stanford: Stanford University Press.

Money, J. (1964). Two cytogenetic syndromes: Psychological comparisons. 1. Intelligence and specific-factor quotients. *Journal of Psychiatric Research, 2,* 223-231.

Money, J. (1987). Propaedeutics of diecious G-1/R: Theoretical foundations for understanding dimorphic gender-identity/role. In J. M. Reinisch, L. A. Roseblum, & S. A. Sanders, (Eds.), *Masculinity/femininity: Basic perspectives.* New York: Oxford University Press.

Money, J. & Ehrhardt, A. (1972). *Man and woman, boy and girl.* Baltimore: Johns Hopkins University Press.

Money, J. & Granoff, D. (1965). IQ and the somatic stigmata of Turner's syndrome. *American Journal of Mental Deficiency, 70*, 69-77.

Money, J. & Tucker, P. (1975). *Sexual signatures.* Boston: Little, Brown.

Nielsen, J. & Christensen, A. (1974). Thirty-five males with double-Y chromosome. *Journal of Psychological Medicine, 4*, 37-38.

Noel, B. *et al.* (1974). The XYY syndrome: Reality or myth? *Clinical Genetics, 5*, 387-394.

Oakley, A. (1972). *Sex, gender, and society.* New York: Harper & Row.

Owen, D. (1972). The 47, XYY male: A review. *Psychological Bulletin, 78*, 209-233.

Paige, K. (1973, April). Women learn to sing the menstrual blues. *Psychology Today*, pp. 41-46.

Palkovitz, R. (1985). Fathers' birth attendance, early contrast, and extended contact with their newborns: A critical review. *Child Development, 56*, 392-406.

Parke, R., & O'Leary, S. (1975). Father-mother-infant interaction in the newborn period. In K. Riegel & J. Meacham (Eds.). *The developing individual in a changing world* (Vol. II). The Hague: Mouton.

Parlee, M. B. (1973). The premenstrual syndrome. *Psychological Bulletin, 80*, 454-465.

Parlee, M. B. (1993). Psychology of menstruation and premenstrual syndrome. In F. L. Denmark & M. A. Paludi (Eds.), *Handbook on the psychology of women.* Westport: Greenwood.

Persky, H., Smith, K., & Basu, G. (1971). Relation of psychologic measures of aggression and hostility in chronic alcoholics. *American Journal of Psychiatry, 134*, 621-625.

Persky, H. *et al.* (1977). The effect of alcohol and smoking on testosterone function and aggression in chronic alcoholics. *American Journal of Psychiatry, 134*, 621-625.

Petersen, A., & Taylor, B. (1980). The biological approach to adolescence. In J. Adelson (Ed.), *Handbook of adolescent psychology.* New York: Wiley.

Phoenix, C. (1978). Prenatal testosterone in the nonhuman primate and its consequences for behavior. In R. Friedman *et al.* (Eds.), *Sex differences in behavior.* Huntington, NY: Krieger Publishing.

Pines, M. (1978). Is sociobiology all wet? *Psychology Today*, May, 23-24.

Pleck, J. (1981). *The myth of masculinity.* Cambridge: The MIT Press.

Rathus, S. (1983). *Human sexuality.* New York: Holt, Rinehart & Winston.

Rathus, (1988). *Human sexuality.* New York: Hold, Rinehart, & Winston.

Reid, P. T., & Paludi, M. A. (1993). Psychology of Women: Conception to Adolescence. In F. L. Denmark & M. A. Paludi (Eds.), *Handbook on the psychology of women.* Westport, CT: Greenwood Press.

Rodin, J. & Ickovics, J. R. (1990). Women's health. *American Psychologist, 45*, 1018-1034.

Rogan, A. (1978). The threat of sociobiology. *Quest, 4*, 85-93.

Rossi, A. (1977). A biosocial perspective on parenting. *Daedalus, 106*, 1-31.

Schowalter, J., & Anyan, W. (1981). *Family handbook of adolescence.* New York: Knopf.

Schuckit, M. *et al.*(1975). Premenstrual symptoms and depression in a university population. *Disease of the Nervous System, 36*, 516-517.

Sherif, C. W. (1980). A social psychological perspective on the menstrual cycle. In J. Parson (Ed.), *The psychobiology of sex differences and sex roles.* New York: McGraw-Hill.

Shields, S. (1975). Functionalism, Darwinism, and the psychology of women: A study in social myth. *American Psychologist, 30,* 739-754.

Shields, S. (1982). The variability hypothesis: The history of a biological model of sex differences in intelligence. *Signs, 7,* 769-797.

Strickland, B. (1988). Sex-related differences in health and illness. *Psychology of Women Quarterly, 12,* 382-399.

Tanner, J. (1962). *Growth at adolescence.* Oxford: Blackwell.

Tieger, T. (1980). On the biological basis of sex differences in aggression. *Child Development, 51,* 943-963.

Tiger, L. (1969). *Men in groups.* New York: Random House.

Tiger, L., & Fox. R. (1971). *The imperial animal.* New York: Holt, Rinehart and Winston.

Tobach, E. & Rosoff, B. (Eds.) (1978). *Genes and gender.* New York: Gordian Press.

Travis, C. (1993). Women and health. In F. L. Denmark & M. A. Paludi (Eds.). *Handbook on the psychology of women.* Westport: Greenwood.

Udry, J. R., & Talbert, L. M. (1988). Sex hormone effects of personality at puberty. *Journal of Personality and Social Psychology, 54,* 291-295.

U.S. Department of Health and Human Services (1982).

U.S. National Center for Health Statistics (1987).

van den Berge, P. (1978). *Man in society.* New York: Elsevier.

Williams, J. (1983). *Psychology of women: Behavior in a biosocial context.* New York: Norton.

Wilson, E. (1978). *On human nature.* Cambridge: Harvard University Press.

Witkin, H. *et al.* (1976). Criminality in XYY and XXY men. *Science, 193,* 547-555.

Chapter 7

The psychological perspective. In this chapter the author's main premise is that gender identity is learned rather than biological. Evidence presented supports the supposition that gender identity is established in most children at a very early age. It is discussed as a cognitive-developmental issue. For example, there is a reported tendency for children to ignore or forget information that is inconsistent with gender norms and stereotypes. Also, there is evidence that children distort their memories of men engaged in atypical (feminine) roles and occupations, but that these children can accept women and girls in atypical roles and occupations. This and the many other similar concerns discussed in this chapter are compatible with the learning perspective.

Chapter 7 *Carole R. Beal,* The Psychological Perspective

GENDER IDENTITY

What do we know about early awareness of one's sex, that is, the beginnings of gender identity? In the past, researchers have relied on studies in which children are asked whether they are a boy or girl, to point to pictures of boys and girls, and to indicate which they are most like. These techniques required that the child understand language and, as described below, generally led to the conclusion that children knew their own sex between the second and third birthday. However, more recent studies of preverbal infants suggest that gender identity may be forming at the end of the first year of life. This possibility is explored in the following section.

Infancy

The first step in constructing a gender identity would be to discriminate males and females. One needs to establish that there are two groups before identifying the self as a member of one. To test whether the infant can tell men and women apart, the infant is typically presented with examples from one category (e.g., slides of female faces) until the infant becomes bored and merely glances at each new example as if to say, "Oh, another one of those . . . I've seen enough already." An example from another category (e.g., a male face) is then presented to see whether the infant shows renewed interest, implying that the category shift has been detected. Studies using this method have shown that by about the middle of the first year infants can distinguish between male and female (Fagan, 1979; Leinbach, 1991; Walsh, Katz, & Downey, 1991). Babies seem to rely primarily on hair length to make discrimination, as they cannot tell men and women apart if photographs of women with short haircuts are used.

Infants can also discriminate men and women by other sensory systems. Babies can tell the difference between male and female voices by 6 months, even if voice pitch is artificially equalized, suggesting that they notice sex differences in intonation and speech patterns (C. Miller, 1983). Two-month-olds who heard a single syllable spoken by a man noticed the gender change when the same syllable was spoken by a woman (Leinbach, 1991). Babies also match on the basis of gender across sensory modalities: 9- to 12-month-olds look longer at female face when they hear a female voice and longer at a male face when they hear a male voice (Poulin-Dubois, Serbin, Kenyon, & Derbyshire, 1991). Although newborns are highly sensitive to odors, there is so far no evidence that they can make male-female discriminations on this basis, for example, telling Daddy and Mother apart by sense of smell alone. However, babies can tell their own mother from other women by smell when they are only a few days old, so it is not implausible they could make gender discriminations as well.

Babies' early ability to tell males and females apart might be taken to imply that gender is somehow a fundamental or distinctive characteristic of human beings, one so basic that it is perceived before babies have had much social experience or exposure to the surrounding culture. However, this implication is false; infants also easily make other types of distinctions, such as on the basis of facial expressions (e.g., smiling versus frowning faces) or race. For example, 9- to 12-month-old infants show renewed interest and attention to the face of a black person after seeing a series of white faces or to a white face after seeing a set of black faces. This seems to be based on opportunities to observe and learn about people from diverse backgrounds. Black infants recognize race category shifts more quickly than white infants, who are less likely to have seen other-race faces (Walsh et al., 1991). Thus, there does not appear to be anything particularly special about gender as a social dimension for infants.

Early Gender Identity

The beginnings of gender identity appear in the second year, based on evidence that infants start to show a preference for others of their own gender, as if at some level they are beginning to learn that the other person is "like me." M. Lewis and Brooks-Gunn (1979) found that infants 12 to 18 months old looked longer at photographs of babies of their own sex than those of the other sex. Another study also found that infants looked longer at a photograph of a same-sex child as long as the child was dressed in sex-typical clothing. Babies became confused when the other child was cross-dressed, suggesting that they relied on clothing cues to determine the other child's gender. Infants even preferred to watch the pattern of biological motion produced by a same-sex child. The patterns were produced by attaching lights to the joints of a boy and a girl and filming the children walking in the dark (T. Bower, 1982). Slightly different patterns were produced because girls' wider hips give them a more rolling gait. There are also hints in some studies that 6-month-old boys show increased attention to male faces (Kagan, Henker, Hen-Tov, Levine, & Lewis, 1966; Langlois, Ritter, Roggman, & Vaughn, 1991; M. Lewis, 1969; Moss & Robson, 1968). While more research needs to be done to confirm the findings, these studies suggest that our earliest sense of self may be tinted with pink or blue (M. Lewis & Weinraub, 1979). However, it is not yet clear how this knowledge would be acquired. T. Bower (1982) suggests that girls may detect a correspondence between the girl-produced pattern of lights and proprioceptive feedback from their own bodies. Gender identity might also be related to early language comprehension. It is generally thought that many concepts are understood before the corresponding linguistic terms are attached and that the ability to understand language precedes the ability to speak. It is not implausible that being repeatedly called a boy or girl would become a component of early self-concept and that language is a mediator for gender identity in the second year of life when most children are beginning to speak.

The possibility that gender identity is forming in late infancy may also be relevant to the case discussed in Chapter 6--the boy baby who was reassigned as a girl after his penis was damaged in a circumcision accident and who was raised as girl but then returned to the male role as an adult. Since the sex assignment was done when the baby was 17 months old, it is possible that a male identity had already started to become established, with the switch contributing to lingering ambivalence about gender identity. On the other hand, other sex reassignments have been apparently successful up to the time the child uses verbal labels to refer to the self as a boy or girl. More studies will need to be done to learn whether in fact the preverbal infant has a sense of the self as a boy or girl, an if so, whether early gender identity is still malleable enough for sex reassignments to be successful.

The Toddler Period: Using Gender Labels

Once the child begins to use language to express himself or herself and to communicate with others, it becomes possible to test the child's knowledge about gender stereotypes much more directly than can be done with preverbal babies. Slaby and Frey (1975) showed toddlers a series of dolls and photographs of men and women and of boys and girls. The children were asked if the dolls and photographs were male or female and what sex they were themselves. About 80 percent of the 3- to 31/2-year-olds could accurately identify the sex of other people and knew their own sex. Converging results were obtained by Thompson (1975), who asked toddlers to sort photographs by sex and then to add their own picture to the appropriate pile. Some children as young as 21/2 years could do so accurately, and most children knew their own sex by the time they were about 3 years old.

Like infants, toddlers continue to make their judgments primarily on the basis of how people look and what they do, rather than on an understanding of the biological basis of gender. For example, young children initially believe that someone who has short hair, wears pants, and enjoys rough, outdoor games must be a boy. Relying on appearance and activity cues makes sense; the biological information is often not available, and appearance cues are quite reliable indicators of gender in our culture. For example, men rarely wear skirts or cosmetics or push baby carriages. Yet Thompson and Bentler (1971) found that young children continued to rely on appearance cues even when the biological information was also provided. The researchers used a doll that could be modified through the use of snap-on parts to have male or female genitals, large breasts or a flat chest, and long or short hair. Each child in the experiment was shown the doll with a particular combination of masculine and feminine features. For example, the doll might have a penis, a flat chest, and long hair. The child was asked to pick out clothes for the doll (dress or pants), to give it a name, and to say whether it would grow up to be a mommy or daddy. Adults who were shown the doll relied exclusively on its genitals to determine its sex, but the children relied primarily on hair length. Only 16 percent of the children mentioned the doll's genitals as the reason for their gender assignment. One of my graduate school friends had a very short haircut, and one day when she happened to wear overalls to her job at a local preschool, she looked up to see a little girl staring at her with a puzzled expression. The little girl tentatively whispered, "Are you a man?" When my friend said no, the little girl became quite distressed, convinced that my friend was lying to her because she was unable to believe that a woman could have short hair and wear pants.

In addition to establishing a gender identity, young children also quickly acquire an astonishingly extensive set of stereotypical beliefs about males and females (Cann & Haight, 1983; Fein, Johnson, Kosson, Stork, & Wasserman, 1975; J.E. Williams, Bennett, & Best, 1975). Kuhn, Nash, and Brucken (1978) asked 2- and 3-year-olds which sex was associated with particular activities, future roles, and personality traits. To avoid taxing the children's emerging verbal skills, the researchers trained children to point to one of two paper-doll drawings, " Lisa" and "Michael," to indicate their responses. For example, the adult would ask who would most like to play with dolls, and the child would point to either the Lisa or Michael doll. The researchers found that even 2-year-olds had clear beliefs about boys and girls. For example, children thought that Lisa liked to play with dolls, liked to clean house and cook dinner, talked a lot, and never hit, while Michael liked to play with cars and build things, liked to fight, and was loud, naughty, and made girls cry. They thought that Lisa would grow up to clean the house and be a nurse or teacher, while Michael would grow up to mow the grass and be "the boss." Children also hold stereotyped beliefs about more abstract qualities associated with gender, such as color: When shown a set of stuffed toy animals, children selected the pink and lavender animals as the "girls" and the brown, blue, and maroon ones as the "boys" (Picariello, Greenberg, & Pillemer, 1990). Similarly, children assign a fierce bear, fire, and a piece of rough sandpaper to males, while giving butterflies, flowers, and soft textures to females (Leinbach & Hort, 1989). They also associate natural objects such as trees, flowers, and lakes with females, while artifacts such as buildings, sunglasses, and cameras are associated with males (Mullen, 1990). Thus, many of the stereotypic associations about masculinity and femininity are learned early in the life span.

Gender identity seems to provide the impetus for conforming to gender role expectations and learning such stereotypes. In the studies described above, the most stereotyped 2- and 3-year-olds were those who already knew their own sex (Hort, Leinbach, & Fagot, 1991). In addition, once children use gender labels accurately, their actual behavior changes as they try to fit what they think is expected for their own sex. For example, girls and boys initially start out with similar levels of aggression, but girls' aggression rates then decline once they start to call themselves girls, as if they have figured out that such actions are not expected for females. Similarly, boys who call themselves boys begin to avoid girls' toys and activities that they had previously enjoyed, such as playing in the "housekeeping corner" (Fagot, 1985b; Fagot & Leinbach, 1989). Toddlers who know their sex also spend more of their time playing with other children of the same sex than those who have not yet acquired gender identity.

To summarize, toddlers can tell males and females apart, know which sex they are, have learned many cultural stereotypes about the sexes, and have altered their behavior accordingly---all by the time they are 3 years old. No wonder many parents, including the parents of the little girl who insisted on wearing pink pajamas, start to wonder whether sex stereotypes are programmed by nature! By the time most parents even begin to consider the issue of gender stereotyping, much of the learning has already taken place. The rate at which different children acquire stereotypes and gender labels does suggest that these concepts are learned (Reis & Wright, 1982). Brighter children acquire gender stereotypes more quickly than their less intelligent peers. The speed with which toddlers acquire gender labels and stereotypes is also related to how much gender is emphasized in the surrounding environment; children in more traditional homes master these concepts sooner than their peers whose parents place less emphasis on gender (Fagot & Leinbach, 1989; Weinraub, et al., 1984).

The Preschool Period

By the preschool period, children know they are boys or girls, but they still do not really understand why, that is, because they are biologically male or female, and, in particular, that their identity as male or female is permanent. The realization that they will always be the same sex is an important aspect of development because it appears to trigger a renewed and more serious search for appropriate role models and to increase children's conforming to traditional gender role expectations. This realization is marked by several milestones or components of gender permanence which are acquired gradually in an ordered sequence.

Gender Stability and Consistency

Many young children can accurately label themselves as a boy or girl while believing that they could become the other sex if they wanted to, by dressing and behaving like a child of the other sex. Slaby and Frey (1975) found that children first learned to label themselves reliably and accurately as male or female (identity), then learned that they stayed the same gender over time (stability), and finally learned that they stayed the same gender across situations (consistency), including changes in their appearance and activities. This ordered sequence has been observed across several cultures, including children in Belize, Kenya, Nepal, and Samoa, although children from working-class families and those living in nonindustrialized cultures tend to reach the identity, stability, and consistency milestones a year or so later than children from upper-middle-class U.S.samples (Frey & Ruble, 1992; Munroe, Shimmin, & Munroe, 1984).

Gender Permanence

Children can know that they are male or female and that they will not change sex, but their knowledge is still incomplete. Kohlberg (1966) emphasized the importance of gender permanence: understanding that male or female is biologically determined and that while outward signs such as clothing and hairstyle are correlated with one's sex, these characteristics do not determine one's sex. This knowledge has traditionally been assessed by the *sex constancy* task (Emmerich, 1981; Wehren & De Lisi, 1983). The task begins with a drawing or photograph of a boy or a girl which is gradually altered by overlaying sheets or add-on paper-doll clothes so that the picture begins to resemble the other sex. For example, the experimenter might add a long hairstyle to a drawing of a boy and ask the child if "John" is now a boy or girl. Next, a frilly dress might be substituted for John's pants and t-shirt. Finally, a doll and toy baby carriage might be added to the picture. After each change, the child is asked if John is a boy or girl. In order to answer correctly, the child must discount the altered appearance and realize that the changes in hairstyle, clothing, and behavior cannot affect John's status as a male. Sex constancy is a more advanced concept than the previously acquired notions of gender stability and consistency in the following sense: While young children may realize that people do not typically change sex, they might believe that this is a matter of custom or preference, based on observation of those around them, without necessarily understanding that one *cannot* change sex because of one's biology.

When shown the sex constancy task, many preschool children agree that John has become a girl by adopting long hair, a dress, and girls' toys. One of my nephews had hair that had grown quite long one summer. Before he started kindergarten, he asked his mother to cut his hair short; he thought he was turning into a girl and wanted to be a "real boy" again before going to school. As Kohlberg had hypothesized, most children master sex constancy between 5 and 7 years, first realizing that they themselves cannot change sex by changing how they look. This knowledge is then generalized to others (Gouze & Nadelman, 1980; Marcus & Overton, 1978). Among children who were quite sure that they themselves could not change sex, many were considerably less certain when asked about their classmates, particularly when they saw another child actually dressed up to look like the other sex!

Preschoolers' belief that they could change sex seems a little odd, particularly since they seem so knowledgeable about other aspects of gender roles. However, this reasoning is understandable given that they first learn to tell the sexes apart on the basis of appearance cues. This reasoning also may not be unique to gender; there are some indications that a similar phenomenon occurs with children's concepts of ethnicity. Until they are about 7 to 8 years old, children report that a black child could change into a white child by putting on light makeup and wearing a blond wig or that a white child could become a Native American by donning a leather shirt with beaded fringe and a feather headdress (Aboud, 1988; Wyche, 1991). Similarly, children often do not realize that they were born with their skin tone or that a person's skin color is permanent; many children reason that people become black by going out into the sun or white by staying in the shade all the time. Believing that ethnicity is a matter of wearing and doing certain things is analogous to believing that being a boy or girl is due to wearing and doing particular things.

The Role of Biological Knowledge

Children's reliance on outward appearance is quite reasonable given that most do not have the relevant knowledge about the biological basis of gender and ethnicity. Children who have the relevant knowledge about the biological knowledge are more likely to show sex constancy than their peers who lack this knowledge (Bem,1989; McConaghy, 1979). In one study, children were first shown a photograph of a nude toddler, who was referred to with a sex neutral name (e.g., "This is a picture of Gaw") (Bem,1989). Children were asked, "Is Gaw a boy or a girl? Is there a part of Gaws's body that makes Gaw a boy or girl?" The child was then shown another photograph of Gaw dressed as the other sex and was asked if Gaw was a boy or girl. About 40 percent of Bem's sample of 3- to 5-year-olds could accurately tell Gaw's sex, and most of these children also said that Gaw was still the same sex even when dressed in cross-sex clothes. These children were also more likely than others to say that they could not really change their own sex and to refer to their own anatomy as a reason. For example, children said they could not change sex because "that's how I was made"; "Jesus made me a boy"; and "I was born a girl." Children who could not tell if a naked toddler was a boy or a girl relied on dress and hairstyle to determine sex and also reported that people could change their sex if they wanted to. In some cases, however, children who do know the difference between male and female genitals still believe that gender can change; for example, a girl might develop a penis and turn into a boy as she grew up (Frey & Ruble, 1992).

Once children understand that gender is related to biology and is unchangeable they assume that biology is the *reason* that the sexes behave differently and have different interests. In fact, preschoolers are little nativists, believing that sex differences are due to nature rather than to nurture! When told a story about a little girl who was raised on an island with only boys and men, preschoolers thought that despite growing up in an exclusively masculine environment, the girl would still play with dolls, wear dresses, cry a lot, want to be a nurse when she grew up, and be good at taking care of babies (M. Taylor & Gelman, 1991). When asked why the sexes behaved differently children often referred to physical characteristics , such as, "Boys have different things in their innards to girls. Only girls can get milk out of their bosoms, and they haven't got a penis" (J. Smith & Russell, 1984, p.1114). These biological attributes decline in frequency beginning between 7 and 10 years, with most older children and adults saying that boys and girls act differently because their mothers and fathers treat them differently (J. Smith & Russell, 1984; Ullian, 1976). Girls shift from biological to socialization explanations for sex differences sooner than boys, perhaps realizing more quickly that they are physically capable of doing certain things, such as riding their bike home from the library in the evening, but are limited by social conventions or parental restrictions.

The Role of Cognitive Development

In addition to acquiring the relevant biological knowledge, children's greater understanding of sex constancy is also due to their increasing cognitive capacities. With age and experience, children become better able to consider multiple representations of events and discrepancies between appearance and reality, for example, recognizing that someone who appears to be a boy could really be a girl underneath the masculine clothes. Many preschoolers say that John has become a girl as the result of wearing a dress, having long hair, and playing with dolls because the appearance of the altered picture is more salient and compelling than their memory of the initial reality. Because the task involves a conflict between immediate appearance and remembered reality, children can be easily confused about what is being asked. C. Martin and Halverson (1983b) found that when some children claimed that a person had changed sex, they seemed to mean that the person was "dressing up" or "pretending" to be the other sex. When these children were asked if a person could change sex "for real," most said no. Similarly, if reminders of the staring point are available, children tend to perform better. For example, when the same proper name ("John") was used throughout the task, children were more likely to say John was still a boy than when only a neutral phrase ("this child") was used (Beal & Lockhart, 1989). The sex constancy task may therefore underestimate children's knowledge in the sense that some young children may know perfectly well that biology determines one's sex but become temporarily confused when they see the picture transformed to resemble the other sex. Of course, it could also be argued that the reason children become confused by the task in the first place is that they do not really understand what makes one male or female.

Children's reasoning on the sex constancy task is correlated with their general level of cognitive development, as measured by several Piagetian tasks that involve conflicts between appearance and reality (Marcus & Overton, 1978). For example, the child who understands that pouring liquid from a short, wide container into a tall, thin one does not change the amount, and who realized that a sponge painted to look exactly like a piece of black and white granite is still really a sponge, is also likely to realize that a boy does not become a girl by changing into girls' clothing and wearing a ribbon in his hair (S. Brown & Pipp, 1991). A similar correlation has been found between children's understanding of conservation and ethnic constancy (Aboud, 1988). Knowing that external appearances do not necessarily correspond to an underlying reality seems to be the specific aspect of cognitive flexibility that is most important to understanding gender permanence. Another study found no relation between performance on the sex constancy task and another measure of general cognitive flexibility, a test of "divergent thinking" (Carter & Patterson, 1982). This task involves asking the child to think of possible novel uses for a common object, such as a bowl (e.g., use as a bucket or wear as a hat).

Performance on the divergent thinking task is correlated with general intelligence, but not gender permanence.

Gender Identity: Effects on Behavior

One of my students was writing a paper on sex typing in children's play and posed the following hypothetical question to his 8-year-old brother: "Ben, if I gave you a Barbie doll to play with, would you make her play house or would you make her shoot guns and do karate kicks?" Ben's response was, "I wouldn't do it. I wouldn't do it. I wouldn't touch the Barbie doll." When asked to explain why not, he looked at his big brother and said condescendingly, "Because they're for girls, you dumbhead!"

One tenet of the cognitive-development perspective is that as children learn their own sex, they will be motivated to learn more about gender role expectations, to seek out appropriate role models, and to conform to what they think is expected of them as boys or girls. We have already seen an example of this in the earliest stages of gender identity: Toddlers who know their own sex are more stereotyped in attitudes and behavior than their age-mates who have not yet learned to use gender labels accurately. Similarly, preschoolers who have reached subsequent milestones in gender identity become more strongly stereotyped and more selective in their patterns of attention to role models, their willingness to adopt new behaviors, and avoidance of cross-gender behaviors (Eaton, Von Bargen, & Keats, 1981; G.Levy, 1991; C. Martin & Little, 1990; Stangor & Ruble, 1987, 1989). For example, once children master gender consistency, that is, the notion that one stays the same sex across situations, they are more likely to watch same-sex role models. In one study, children were shown a movie of a male and a female actor (Slaby & Frey, 1975). The screen was divided so that the child could watch either the male or female actor but could not see both simultaneously. Children who had not yet acquired sex consistency spent equal amounts of time looking at the two sides of the screen, while children who had mastered consistency spent more time watching the actor whose sex matched their own. Similar patterns have been found in children's attention to male and female actors when they watch TV at home; gender-constant children are more likely to watch the program when same-sex actors are on the screen (Luecke & Anderson, 1993).

Knowing that they are boys or girls also helps children decide whether to adopt new behaviors, since they can match their own sex to the sex of a potential role model. For example, in a study by Ruble, Balaban, and Cooper (1981), children saw a film that included a short commercial for a plastic movie-viewer toy. The viewer had been previously established to be highly attractive to both sexes. Half the children saw the viewer demonstrated by a boy in the commercial, while the remaining children saw it demonstrated by a girl. Later, children were given the opportunity to play with the movie viewer themselves. Children who still thought that they could change sex played with the viewer regardless of the model's sex; for example, a boy would happily play with the viewer even if he had seen a girl use it in the commercial. In contrast, children who knew they would always be a boy or girl carefully avoided playing with the viewer when it had been demonstrated by a model of the other sex. In another study, gender-constant boys played more with an uninteresting toy that had been demonstrated by a male model than a very attractive toy demonstrated by a female model (Frey & Ruble, 1992). Gender constancy did not strongly affect girls' behavior in this study, possibly because girls are generally less strongly sex-typed even after acquiring gender constancy and probably felt less conflict about approaching a highly attractive boys' toy. In contrast, boys were careful to play it safe and leave the girls' toy alone even if they secretly thought it was pretty neat.

In general, gender identity predicts both children's attention to same-sex role models and their avoidance of new behaviors that are perceived to be for the other sex. However, gender identity does not always mean that a gender-stereotyped behavior will increase in frequency, because many behaviors have already been well established by this point. For example, achieving sex constancy does not increase children's preference for same-sex toys because most have already shown this preference for several years (Blakemore, LaRue, & Olejnik, 1979; Bussey & Bandura, 1992; Emmerich & Shepard, 1984; Marcus & Overton, 1978; Stangor & Ruble, 1987). Similarly, girls who had achieved sex constancy were more likely to seek out other girls as play partners than girls who had not yet acquired sex constancy, but no relation was found for boys, probably because the boys had already learned to avoid playing with girls (Fagot, 1985a; Smetana & Letourneau, 1984). In contrast, in the movie-viewer study described above, children had not seen the toy before and were therefore in the position of deciding whether it was appropriate to play with; in this situation, gender identity was clearly influential.

GENDER AS AN ORGANIZING PRINCIPLE

Besides gender identity, the other side to the cognitive-developmental coin is children's use of gender schemas to make sense of their social world. Children learn to organize information in memory according to whether it is associated with males or females. Because gender is thought to be an either-or category, children resist the notion that males and females might sometimes behave in similar ways, are critical of others who deviate from traditional gender roles, and exaggerate the differences between the sexes. Gender thus becomes a sort of mental filter through which children can interpret and evaluate others' behavior. In addition, children begin to guide their own behavior in terms of its perceived appropriateness for their own sex. Over time, children's need to be like others of the same sex and, by definition, different from the other sex leads them to act differently. Children's interests, skills, and even speech styles become increasingly gender-typed as a ways of enhancing their sense of being male or female. In the following sections we look at children's use of gender as an organizing principle for interpreting others' behavior and guiding their own.

Reasoning about Others

Reasoning about other people is much easier when they can be classified as male or female, because schemas organize information in memory under the category labels "male" and "female." These categories or clusters of information allow us to make inferences about what a particular unknown male or female might be like, by looking up the typical characteristics of males or females and assuming that the new exemplar will be similar to those who have already been encountered. Categorical processing is a powerful cognitive mechanism that can be very useful; after all, if we had to treat each person we met as a completely unique individual without being able to make any assumptions about what they might be like, we would not have time to do very much else in life. The corresponding drawback is that our tendency to rely on stereotyped information in our schemas often leads us to ignore the unique characteristics of the individual.

Although adults are susceptible to stereotyping, children are more likely to rely heavily on gender label to make predictions about others, even when more detailed information is available (Berndt & Heller, 1986; Eisenberg, Murray, & Hite, 1982; C. Martin, 1985). For example, when children were told a story about a little boy who liked to play with dolls, they still predicted that he would also like to play with a truck, despite the information that this particular boy had feminine play interests. In contrast, adults reasoned that if this boy happened to like dolls, he might also like to play with a kitchen set. Conversely, children find it very hard to reason about someone's interests when they do *not* know if the person is male or female (C. Martin & Wood, 1987). Even when children are told that the person likes dolls, they cannot imagine what other toys the person might like unless they know whether the person is a boy or girl.

Additional evidence of the inferential power of gender schemas comes from a study in which children were either told that someone was a boy or girl (gender category) or told about a particular characteristic the person had (gender property) (Gelman, Collman, & Maccoby, 1986). In the study, children were first taught that boys had "andro" in their blood, while girls had "estro." Children were then shown a picture of a child that was sex-ambiguous. Some children were told that the picture had andro and were asked if it was a boy or girl. That is, they were given a specific characteristic and had to figure out if it was typical of boys or girls. Most of the children found this very difficult to do. In contrast, children who were told that the picture was a boy and were asked if it had estro or andro easily inferred that it had andro. Gender schemas make it easy for children to make inferences about others, in this case, that if someone is a boy, he must also have various characteristics that are associated with being male.

Memory Effects

Gender schema theory argues that children will attend to, process, and store more information perceived to be sex-appropriate, while information that is inconsistent with the schema will be ignored or forgotten. Several studies have shown that children remember actions and characteristics that fit their stereotypes better than information that is schema-inconsistent (Meehan & Janik, 1990). In one case children were told stories about male and female characters who engaged in both traditional and atypical actions; for example, in one story about a circus, the girl was described as fixing a broken bicycle seat, while the boy sewed a clown costume (Koblinsky, Cruse, & Sugawara, 1978). Later, the children were asked which character had done the different things in the story; for example, did the girl or boy sew the clown costume? Children remembered the gender role-consistent information in the story much more accurately than the inconsistent actions. The same pattern was found in a study of children's memory for pictures. Liben and Signorella (1980) showed children a set of pictures, including some of boys engaged in feminine activities such as sewing and girls in masculine activities such as directing traffic. After a 5-minute delay the children had to pick out the original picture from a larger set; again, they recognized the pictures showing gender-consistent activities more than those showing gender-inconsistent activities. Picture recognition is generally extremely good, so the children's failure to recognize some images that they had seen only a few minutes before was striking. Children even remembered more information about a song if the lyrics were gender role-consistent (Britain & Coker, 1982). C. Martin and Halverson (1981) suggest that children's tendency to recall only stereotype-consistent examples creates an "illusory data base" which leads to gender distinction being exaggerated in the child's image of the world.

How do we know that children's memory is actually being influenced by schemas, rather than that they simply have trouble remembering some stories and pictures? First, the memory errors are highly selective; children do not appear to have trouble remembering information as long as it fits their expectations. Also, information about male characters who had been shown engaged in feminine activities is particularly likely to be forgotten; if memory errors were random, children should remember these example at least as well as those showing females engaged in masculine activities. Second, there is evidence that children with stronger gender stereotypes are more likely to forget the inconsistent information than their peers who had more egalitarian beliefs (Liben & Signorella, 1980; List, Collins, & Westby, 1983; Signorella & Liben, 1984). That is, the stronger the schemas, the more children overlook schema-inconsistent information. This pattern has not been observed consistently, perhaps because most children are already strongly stereotyped at this age and so the relation is hard to demonstrate (Cann & Newbern, 1984; C. Martin & Halverson, 1983a).

In some cases, schema-inconsistent information may attract special attention and be remembered because of its novelty (C. Martin & Halverson, 1981; Trepanier-Street & Kropp , 1986). For example, when children heard a story about a boy who wanted to be a ballet dancer, they recalled more details from the story than those who heard the same story about a girl (Jennings, 1975). Although they remembered it better, many children did not like the male version of the story, called it "stupid," and asked for a different story!

Whether schema-inconsistent information will be remembered or forgotten depends on how long it is before children are asked to remember and on whether they must recall the information or recognize it. Recognition is generally easier and more accurate, Trepanier-Street and Kropp (1986) showed kindergarten and second-grade children photographs of children playing with various toys, including some toys that were atypical for the models' sex (e.g., a boy playing with a Barbie doll). When the children were asked to pick out the original photographs from a larger set of distractor pictures a week later, even the kindergartners were quite good! When children have to recall the information instead of recognize it, they are more likely to rely on schemas to fill in gaps and missing information, leading to distorted memories. C. Martin and Halverson (1983a) showed children pictures of boys and girls engaged in gender role-consistent and -inconsistent activities. For example, some children saw pictures of a boy fixing a stove and a girl cooking at a stove, while others saw a girl fixing a stove and a boy cooking. Recalling the inconsistent pictures accurately on an immediate memory test, children showed that they had noticed the gender role reversals. However, after a week's delay they often reversed the sex of actors to be consistent with the activity (e.g., the picture of the boy cooking was remembered as a picture of a girl cooking). Often seeming completely unaware that their memories had changed, the children were very confident that they had seen a girl cooking and explicitly denied that they had seen the picture of a

boy at a stove. In general, children who have relatively strong gender stereotypes are more likely to show such memory distortions than are less stereotyped children (Liben & Signorella, 1980; C. Martin & Halverson, 1983a).

Such memory distortions can occur very quickly (Cordua, McGraw, & Drabman, 1979; Drabman et al., 1981). In one study, children saw one of four films depicting a doctor and nurse examining a patient (Cordua et al., 1979). Actually, there were four versions of the film: one showed a male doctor and female nurse, and the second a male doctor and nurse, the third a female doctor and male nurse, and the fourth a female doctor and nurse. The respective roles were clearly emphasized in the script: the nurse took the patient's temperature, and the doctor came in, examined the patient, and wrote a prescription. After watching the film, the children were asked to describe what they had seen a few moments before. All the children who had seen the film of the male doctor and female nurse recalled the film correctly, as did 91 percent of those who saw the film of the female doctor and female nurse. However, when the role of the nurse was played by a man, there were many memory errors. Only 22 percent of those who had seen the male nurse and female doctor identified them correctly, and most reversed the information in memory and said that they had seen a male doctor and a female nurse. Similarly, when children saw a male doctor and male nurse, half said that both men in the film were doctors. Note that the distortions centered around the male character; many children accepted that the woman could be a doctor but not that the man could be a nurse!

Not only can gender schemas induce memory distortions, they can interfere with learning new information. Carter and Levy (1991) taught children to play a game in which they had to pick the "right one" out of a pair of pictures of toys. The picture sets varied along two dimensions: size and gender typicality. For example, on one trial a child would be shown a picture of a small doll and a picture of a large truck and on the next trial a large kitchen set and a small baseball bat and ball. On each trial the child guessed which picture was "right" and received feedback. Although the children were not told explicitly what made one picture right and the other wrong, they quickly figured out that choosing the toy that was typical for their sex was the right strategy. After the game had been played for a while, the adult switched from rewarding one dimension (i.e., gender typicality) to the other (i.e., size). Thus, a child who had figured out to always choose the sex-typical picture suddenly found that this was no longer the "right one." Most children quickly picked up on the shift and began choosing on the basis of the other dimension, that is, size. However, individual children who were highly stereotyped took significantly longer to recognize a shift away form gender to size than other children who were less sex-typed. Strong gender schemas made the gender typing of the pictures highly salient, making it hard for children to ignore the gender information when it was no longer relevant to the game.

Exaggerated Stereotyping

Gender schema theory also helps explain why many children go through a period of rigid stereotyping. Many parents have heard their children say that only women can be teachers or only men can drive cars, remarks that are puzzling when parents know perfectly well that the children have encountered male teachers and female drivers. One mother reported that her little girl said one day, "Women don't fish," although they lived on a canal, had often seen women fishing, and the girl had asked for a fishing rod of her own only a few day before (Statham, 1986). While children's cognitive capacities are still fairly limited, it is easier to ignore the exceptions than to revise their emerging gender schemas to include them. Maccoby (1980) suggested that children may even temporarily exaggerate gender distinctions in an effort to get them clearly in mind. Confronted with an apparent exception to a gender stereotype, they often mark it as special. When children were asked to label pictures of people performing various jobs, such as nurse, carpenter, pilot, secretary, with each occupation being illustrated once with a man and once with a woman, they either mislabeled the picture (e.g., calling a female doctor a nurse) or used a linguistic marker (e.g., saying, "It's a *lady* spaceman"). The errors and linguistic markers occurred as often for males in gender-atypical occupations as for females (D. Rosenthal & Chapman, 1982).

In addition to trying to deny that exceptions exist, children at this stage can also be quite critical of others who deviate from traditional gender roles. Damon (1977) told children a story about a little boy named George who liked to play with dolls and who wanted to wear a dress to school. Children were asked what they thought of George's behavior, if his parents should make him stop playing with dolls, and what they thought he should do instead. Four-year-olds generally thought that George should do whatever he wanted to. As one child eloquently put it, "It's his mind, not mine." Yet by the time children were 5 or 6 they had become quite critical of George. They thought that he was wrong to play with dolls or wear a dress to school and argued that his parents should punish him to make him to stop. Many preschoolers are made uneasy by deviations from expected roles because they do not yet really understand what makes someone male or female--that is, they have not yet mastered sex constancy concepts. Children often become more tolerant when they realize that being a boy or girl depends on biology, not on how one is dressed or what one does (Ullian, 1976; Urberg, 1982). Eight- and nine-year-olds thought that George was not really doing anything wrong and should be allowed to continue, although they pointed out that other children would probably tease him. One child said that George's parents might be disappointed if he kept playing with dolls but that they should be more understanding and try to remember what it was like to have a favorite toy!

Stereotyping eventually declines when children realize that many gender role behaviors are merely social conventions adopted out of convenience, habit, or custom (Carter & Patterson, 1982). At first, children view them as moral imperatives, and so violations are perceived to be very serious. Stoddart and Turiel (1985) told kindergartners and elementary school students several stories that included gender role transgressions (e.g., a boy who wore barrettes and nail polish) as well as other types of social transgressions (e.g., a boy who pushed another child off a swing or a girl who broke school rules by eating a cookie in class). The kindergartners thought the gender role violations were just as bad as hurting other children or breaking school rules, while the older children regarded them as comparatively harmless matters of personal choice.

In-Group, Out-Group

In children's minds, the same-sex and other-sex schemas are not equal; their own is better. One father was horrified to overhear his 5-year-old son tell his little sister, "Too bad you're a girl. Boys are better" (Meltz, 1991). C. Martin and Halverson (1981) term this the "in-group, out-group" phenomenon and suggest that it increases children's motivation to fit in with one group and to avoid the behaviors that characterize the other group. This begins almost as soon as children learn that they are boys or girls; for example, toddler girls think that girls are nice and boys are mean, while boys think that boys are nice and girls are mean (Kuhn et al., 1978). Older children often simply assert that their own sex is better, tossing out negative remarks about the other sex, such as, "boys are the best, girls have no brains"; "girls have brains, boys are just dirt" (J. Smith & Russell, 1984, p. 1114). Children also claim various socially desirable traits (e.g., sticks with a problem, is clever) are more typical of their own sex than the other sex (Albert & Porter, 1983; Koblinsky et al., 1978). Part of the motivation for learning to be a member of one group probably comes from constructing that group as superior.

Of course, the in-group, out-group phenomenon eventually creates a conflict for little girls, who start out believing that being a girl is better but later realize that feminine characteristics are less valued within the surrounding culture (Kohlberg, 1966). Girls do acquire certain stereotypes more slowly than boys, perhaps as a result of this conflict. For example, 3- and 4-year-old girls do not yet believe that certain careers, such as fire fighter, doctor, and pilot, and certain personality attributes, such as independence and bravery, are exclusively masculine, but 3- and 4-year-old boys do (Albert & Porter, 1983; Kuhn et al., 1978). Five- to nine-year-old girls claim that both sexes would like certain toys, while boys are more likely to say that particular toys are only for boys (Frey & Ruble, 1992). Older girls recognize the advantages of being male: Baumgartner (1983) asked elementary school children to describe how their lives would change if they became a member of the other sex and found that girls often thought they would be better off as boys; in particular, many girls mentioned that they thought they would have had closer relationships with their father if they had been a boy. One said, "If I were a boy, my Daddy might have loved me." In contrast, boys thought that girlhood would be a fate worse than death; one wrote, "If I woke up and I was a girl, I would go back to sleep and hope it was a bad dream" (Tavris & Wade, 1984, pp. 209-210). Girls generally are more flexible and more aware of the costs of rigid stereotyping than boys. Since boys' beliefs that they are superior to girls are reinforced by their observations of the surrounding culture, they have little motivation to change. A similar pattern has been observed in studies of children's developing sense of ethnic identity. Identification with one group often seems to involve a corresponding denigration of other groups. In contrast to children of minority groups, white children have been found to identify with their own group and to be biased against other groups relatively early, because these tendencies are reinforced by discriminatory attitudes in the surrounding culture (Aboud, 1988; Kleinke & Nicholson, 1979).

Self-Regulation of Behavior

We saw that children who are advanced in gender identity concepts are more careful to avoid other-sex activities than their peers. Generally, children's behavior depends on their perceptions of whether an action is sex-appropriate and enhances their sense of themselves as belonging to one gender role rather than the other. The either-or nature of gender roles is apparent in that if children think a new toy or activity or behavior is for the other sex, they will avoid it for themselves. Children also tend to exaggerate differences in how the sexes act, for example, in their ways of talking.

New Interests

Children's willingness to adopt a new activity is determined by its perceived gender-appropriateness. If they know that other children of the same sex have played with a toy, they tend to choose it also, and their interest and persistence in an activity is higher if they think it is something that others of the same sex have done (Bradbard & Endsley, 1983; Liebert, McCall, & Hanratty, 1971; Perry & Perry, 1975; A. Stein, Pohly, & Mueller, 1971). In one case children were asked to try out a new game which involved tossing marbles into the body cavity of a plastic clown as it spun around on a rod (Montemayor, 1974). Some of the children were told that the game was "a toy for boys, like basketball," others were told it was "a toy for girls, like jacks," and the remaining children were told only that it was a brand new toy, with no gender-related information provided. When children thought the clown game was appropriate for their sex, they rated it as much more fun than those who perceived it as gender-inappropriate, and they actually played the game better, in the sense that they tossed significantly more marbles into the clown. Perceived appropriateness thus predicts both interest and task performance, a finding that has considerable implications for girls' difficulties with math and boys' problems with reading in school. In other words, if you believe that a task such as husking corn is something that the other sex typically does and does well, then you will not try quite as hard to learn how to do it, and you will accept lower performance as being about the best you can expect--even though you actually had the ability to be a star corn husker if you thought it was something your own sex usually did. One international track coach noticed that female athletes' times were now low enough to suggest that a woman could run a 4-minute mile and suggested that only the psychological barrier of being considered unfeminine was preventing a woman form doing so (Turnbull, 1988).

Speech: Talking like a Lady

Children regulate other aspects of their behavior to conform to their ideas about what is appropriate for their gender role and to distinguish themselves from the other gender. For example, boys and girls learn to speak differently, with girls generally using more correct and polished speech than boys. (Andersen, 1984; J. Coates, 1986; Edelsky, 1977; Graddol & Swann, 1989). The differences reflect the assumption that gender roles should be opposites: Boys should talk "rough" and girls should talk "posh." Most of the research on boys' and girls' speech has been conducted in England where there are strong regional and social class accents, making it easier to see how sex differences in speech styles emerge over childhood and adolescence.

One way boys and girls learn to differentiate their speech is by adjusting the pitch of their voices. Among adults, the average pitch of male voices is lower that that of female, but there is so much overlap in range that the two sexes could speak at the same pitch if they chose to do so. With practice, women can adjust the pitch of their speaking voice to fall within the typical range for males. For example, the actress Lauren Bacall

100

acquired her distinctive husky voice by sitting in her car and reading aloud. Margaret Thatcher had professional speech training to lower her voice into the male range for her political speeches, because lower voices were considered to be more authoritative (Graddol & Swann, 1989). Conversely, there are cases of men whose voices had apparently never dropped at puberty. However, when they spoke through a masking device that prevented them from hearing their own voice, their pitch dropped, suggesting that they had unconsciously trained themselves to speak in the pitch range typical for women (Graddol & Swann, 1989). These findings suggest that the sexes tend to choose pitch ranges that will clearly distinguish women's and men's voices. In some cultures the differences are exaggerated, for example, Japanese women speak at a much higher pitch than men, while in other cultures the differences are not as extreme (Loveday, 1981).

In addition to learning to speak at different pitches, girls generally use more correct, standard speech, while boys adopt more "vernacular" speech, which involves slang, stronger accents, and more use of nonstandard grammatical constructions, such as "ain't": "How come that ain't working?" or "You ain't been around here." Vernacular forms of "what" and "be" are found in working-class British English and U.S. black English: "The new record what they've got out" and "Sometime she be fighting in school" (Romaine, 1984). Differences in boys' and girls' use of vernacular speech are apparent by middle childhood and early adolescence. Cheshire (1982) studied a group of adolescents in Reading, an English town where people spoke with a very strong regional accent and used many nonstandard grammatical constructions. Vernacular speech can be difficult to study because people usually shift into more formal, correct speech when talking to a stranger. To get around this problem, Cheshire hung around the local playground with a tape recorder for several weeks; she explained that she had a job to find out what people thought of the town, shared her candy and cigarettes with the boys and girls who played there, and recorded their speech. She found that while both boys and girls used nonstandard speech with their friends, boy did so more than girls, often to display their masculinity and "toughness." Similar patterns of girls using more polite and "correct" speech than boys of the same age have been observed among schoolchildren in Scotland, Sweden, and Japan and among Italian-American children in Boston. In some languages, such as Japanese, males and females must use different terms and grammatical forms for the same sentence, and parents and teachers correct Japanese schoolgirls who use boys' words by saying, "You're a girl, don't forget" (Rudolph, 1991).

Girls not only speak more grammatically, they tend to lose regional accents as they get older. Margaret Thatcher's accent became noticeably more "refined" over the years of her career in British politics. In contrast, boys tend to retain distinctive regional or working-class accents. In fact, linguists who study vanishing dialects try to find elderly men as informants because they are the only ones who are likely to still have their childhood accents (Romaine, 1984). Why do girls lose their accents while boys retain them? For males, a strong working-class accent and slang speech are associated in listeners' minds with physical labor and, thus, masculinity (Trudgill, 1972). In contrast, a woman's femininity is enhanced by sounding more wealthy and educated--more like a lady of leisure. Listeners do interpret stronger accents as more masculine. In one study, adults listened to tape recordings of young boys' and girls' speech and tried to guess whether the speaker was male or female. Half the children were from working-class families, while the others were from British aristocratic families. Adults could usually tell if the speaker was a boy or girl, but when they made a mistake, working-class girls were usually mistaken for boys, while upper-class boys were thought to be girls (Edwards, 1979). So boys who keep their lower-class accents are in fact emphasizing their masculinity in a way that listeners recognize.

Two lines of evidence suggest that boys and girls actually learn to speak differently to enhance their identity as a boy or girl. First, most children can switch from standard to vernacular speech when the situation calls for it, showing that they choose to speak in a particular style in order to fit in with a particular group. Most of the Reading children recorded by Cheshire (1982) used standard English in school but switched to the vernacular style when with their friends. There are also some situations where boys speak more correctly than girls. One study of Swedish students found that when rehearsing for job interviews, boys were less likely than girls to use the local dialect. The researchers suggested that boys were more concerned with making a good impression on a prospective employer. Second, children themselves are conscious of the sex differences in pitch and grammar. Children raise their voices when pretending to be a female, and even babies babble at a higher pitch when near a woman instead of a man (Anderson, 1984; Graddol & Swann, 1989). Children associate grammatical, nonaccented speech with being ladylike. One child said, "The boys just talk any old way. The girls take more care in talking" (Romaine, 1984, p. 131). Some 12- to 14-year-old British girls denied they had a Birmingham accent (a broad, nonprestigious accent) even when hearing themselves on tape. Children also disapprove of girls using slang (de Klerk, 1990). Cheshire found that "good" girls used more standard speech than "bad" girls, that is, those who skipped classes, smoked, and engaged in petty crimes. Thus, girls who have rejected the traditional feminine role also avoid some of the speech patterns typically associated with girls.

At this point it should be clear that children are not passive recipients of gender role socialization messages from parents and other adults; rather, they actively observe the world around them, notice that males and females tend to do different things, figure out their own gender assignment, and then alter their behavior accordingly. Some of the otherwise-puzzling aspects of children's behavior, such as their attempts to deny that men can be nurses and their assumption that their own gender is superior, can be explained by the notion of gender schemas, cognitive structures that are organized around the assumption that the sexes are different. Schemas influence children's view of the social world, increasing their convictions that males and females do different things and that they had better figure out what is appropriate for their gender and be careful to avoid behaviors associated with the other gender. This process begins early in children's lives, and gender becomes part of their sense of who they are, with being a boy or girl forming one of the building blocks of their developing self-concept.

References

Aboud, F. (1988) *Children and prejudice.* New York: Basil Blackwell.

Albert, A. A., & Porter, J. R. (1983) Age patterns in the development of children's gender role stereotypes. *Sex Roles,* 9, 59-67.

Andersen, E. S. (1984) The acquisition of sociolinguistic knowledge: Some evidence of children's verbal role-play. *Western Journal of Speech Communication*, 48, 125-144.

Baumgartner, A. (1983) *"My daddy might have loved me"*: *Student perceptions of differences between being male and being female.* Unpublished paper, Institute for Equality in Education, Denver, CO.

Beal. C. R., & Lockhart, M. E. (1989). The effect of proper name and appearance changes on children's reasoning about gender constancy. *International Journal of Behavioral Development, 12,* 195-205.

Bem, S. L. (1989). Genital knowledge and gender constancy in preschool children. *Child Development, 60,* 649-662.

Berndt, T. J., & Heller, K. A. (1986). Gender stereotypes and social inferences: A developmental study. *Journal of Personality and Social Psychology, 50,* 889-898.

Blakemore, J. E. O., LaRue, A. A., & Olejnik, A. B. (1979) Sex-approapriate toy preference and the ability to conceptualize toys as sex-role related. *Developmental Psychology, 15,* 339-340.

Bower, T. G. R. (1982). *Development in infancy* (2nd ed.) San Francisco: Freeman

Bradbard, M. R., & Endsley, R. C. (1983). The effects of sex-typed labeling on children's information-seeking and retention. *Sex Roles, 9,* 247-260.

Britain, S. D., & Coker, M. (1982). Recall of sex-role appropriate and inappropriate models in children's songs. *Sex roles, 8,* 931-934.

Brown, S. R., & Pipp, S. (1991, April). *The role of the appearance-reality distinction and the genital basis of gender constancy.* Paper presented at the biennial meeting of the Society for Research in Child Development, Seattle, WA.

Bussey, K., & Bandura, A. (1992). Self-regulatory mechanisms governing gender development. *Child Development, 63,* 1236-1250.

Cann, A., & Haight, J. M. (1983). Children's perceptions of relative competence in sex-typed occupations. *Sex Roles, 9,* 767-773.

Cann, A., & Newbern, S. R. (1984). Sex stereotype effects in children's picture recognition. *Child Development, 55,* 1085-1090.

Carter, D. B., & Levy, G. D. (1991). Gender schemas and the salience of gender: Individual differences in nonreversal discrimination learning. *Sex Roles, 25,* 555-567.

Carter, D. B., & Patterson, C. J. (1982). Sex roles as social conventions: The development of children's conceptions of sex role stereotypes. *Developmental Psychology, 18,* 812-824.

Cheshire, J. (1982). *Variations in an English dialect.* Cambridge, England: Cambridge University Press.

Coates, J. (1986). *Men, women, and language.* London: Longman.

Cordua, G. D., McGraw, K. O., & Drabman, R. S. (1979). Doctor or nurse: Children's perceptions of sex typed occupations. *Child Development, 50,* 590-593.

Damon, W. (1977). *The social world of the child.* San Fransicso: Jossey-Bass.

De Klerk, V. (1990) Sland: A male domain? *Sex Roles, 22,* 589-606.

Drabman, R. S., Robertson, S. J., Patterson, J. N., Jarvie, G., Hammer, D., & Cordua, C. (1981). Children's perceptions of media-portrayed sex roles. *Sex Roles, 7,* 379-389.

Eaton, W. O., VonBargen, D., & Keats, J. G. (1981). Gender understanding and dimensions of preschooler activity choice: Sex stereotypes versus activity level. *Canadian Journal of Behavioral Science, 13,* 203-209.

Edelsky, C. (1977). Acquisition of an aspect of communicative competence: Learning what it means to talk like a lady. In S. Ervin-Tripp & C. Mitchell-Kernan (Eds.) *Gender discourse* (pp. 225-243). New York: Academic Press.

Edwards, J. R. (1979). Social class differences and the identification of sex in children's speech. *Journal of Child Language, 6,* 121-127.

Eisenberg, N., Murray, E., & Hite, T. (1982). Children's reasoning regarding sex typed toy choices. *Child Development, 53,* 81-86.

Emmerich, W. (1981). Non-monotonic development trends in social cognition: The case of gender constancy. In S. Strauss (Ed.), *U-shaped behavioral growth* (pp. 249-269). New York: Academic Press.

Emmerich, W., & Shepard, K. (1984). Cognitive factors in the development of sex-typed preferences, *Sex Roles, 11,* 997-1007.

Fagan, J. F. (1979). The origins of facial pattern perception. In M. H. Bornstein & W. Kessen (Eds.), *Psychology development from infancy: Image to retention* (pp.83-113). Hillsdale, NJ: Erlbaum.

Fagot, B. I. (1985a). Beyond the reinforcement principle: Another step toward understanding sex role development. *Developmental Psychology, 21,* 1097-1104.

Fagot, B. I. (1985b). Changes in thinking about early sex role development. *Developmental Review, 5,* 83-98.

Fagot, B. I., & Leinbach, M. D. (1989). The young child's gender schema: Environmental input, internal organization. *Child Development, 60,* 663-672.

Fein, G., Johnson, D., Kosson, N., Stork, L., & Wasserman, L. (1975). Sex stereotypes and preferences in the toy choices of 20-month old boys and girls. *Developmental Psychology, 11,* 527-528.

Frey, K. S., & Ruble, D. N. (1992). Gender constancy and the "cost" of sex-typed behavior: A test of the conflict hypothesis. *Developmental Psychology, 28,* 714-721.

Gelman, S. A., Collman, P., & Maccoby, E. E., (1986). Inferring properties from categories versus inferring categories from properties: The case of gender. *Child Development, 57,* 396-404.

Gouze, K. R., & Nadelman, L. (1980). Constancy of gender identity for self and others in children between the ages of three and seven. *Child Development, 51,* 275-278.

Graddol, D., & Swann, J. (1989*). Gender voices.* Oxford, England: Basil Blackwell.

Hort, B. E., Leinbach, M. D., & Fagot, B. I. (1991). Is there coherence among the cognitive components of gender acquisition? *Sex Roles, 24,* 195-207.

Jennings, S. A. (1975). Effects of sex typing in children's stories on preference and recall. *Child Development, 46,* 220-223.

Kagan, J., Henker, B. A., Hen-Tov, A., Levine, J., & Lewis, M. (1966) Infants' differential reactions to familiar and distorted faces. *Child Development, 37,* 519-532.

Kleinke, C. L. & Nicholson, T. A. (1979). Black and white children's awareness of de facto race and sex differences. *Developmental Psychology, 15,* 84-86.

Koblinsky, S.G., Cruse, D. F., & Sugawara, A. I. (1978). Sex role stereotypes and children's memory for story content. *Child Development, 49,* 452-458.

Kohlberg, L. (1966). A cognitive-developmental analysis of children's sex role concepts and attitudes. In E. E. Maccoby (Ed.), *The development of sex differences* (pp. 82-173). Stanford. CA: Standford University Press.

Kuhn, D., Nash, S. C., & Brucken, L. (1978) Sex role concepts of two and three year olds. *Child Development, 49,* 445-451.

Langlois, J. H., & Downs, C. (1980). Mothers, fathers, and peers as socialization agents of sex-typed play behavior in young children. *Child Development, 51,*1217-1247.

Langlois, J. H., Ritter, J. M., Roggman, L. A., & Vaughn, L. S. (1991). Facial diversity and infant preferences for attractive faces. *Developmental Psychology, 27,* 79-84.

Leinbach. M. D. (1991, April). *The beginnings of gender: What's happening before age 2?* Paper presented at the biennial meeting of the Society for Research in Child Development, Seattle, WA.

Leinbach, M. D., & Hort, B. E. (1989). *Bears are for boys: "Metaphorical" associations in the young child's gender schemata.* Paper presented at the biennial meeting of the Society for Research in Child Development, Kansas City, MO.

Levy, G. D. (1991, April). *Effects of gender constancy understanding, perception of figure's sex and size, and gender schematization on preschoolers' gender typing.* Paper presented at the biennial meeting of the Society for Research in Child Development, Seattle, WA.

Lewis, M. (1969). Infants' responses to facial stimuli during the first year of life. *Developmental Psychology, 1,* 75-86.

Lewis, M., & Brooks-Gunn, J. (1979). *Social cognition and the acquisition of self.* New York: Plenum Press.

Lewis, M., & Weinraub, M. (1979). Origins of early sex role development. *Sex Roles, 5,* 135-153.

Liben, L. S., & Signorella, M. L. (1980). Gender related schemata and constructive memory in children. *Child Development, 51,* 11-18.

Liebert, R. M., McCall, R. B., & Hanratty, M. S. (1971). Effects of sex typed information on children's toy preferences. *Journal of Genetic Psychology, 119,* 133-136.

List, J. A., Collins, W. A., & Westby, S. D. (1983). Comprehension and inferences from traditional and nontraditional sex role portrayals on television. *Child Development, 54,* 1579-1587.

Loveday, L. (1981). Pitch, politeness and sexual role: An exploratory investigation. *Language and Speech, 24,* 71-88.

Luecke, D., & Anderson, D. (1993, March) Gender constancy and attention to television. Paper presented at the biennial meeting of the Society for Research in Child Development, New Orleans.

Maccoby, E. E. (1980). *Social development: Psychological growth and the parent-child relationship.* New York: Harcourt, Brace, Jovanovich.

Marcus, D. E., & Overton, W. F. (1978). The development of cognitive gender constancy and sex role preferences. *Child Development, 49,* 434-444.

Martin, C. L. (1985, April) *The influence of sex stereotypes on children's impression formation.* Paper presented at the biennial meeting of the Society for Research in Child Development, Toronto.

Martin, C. L., & Halverson, C. F. (1981). A schematic processing model of sex typing and stereotyping in children. *Child Development, 52,* 1119-1134.

Martin, C. L., & Halverson, C. F. (1983a). The effects of sex-typing schemas on young children's memory. *Child Development, 54,* 563-574.

Martin, C. L., & Halverson, C. F. (1983b). Gender constancy: A methodological and theoretical analysis. *Sex roles, 9,* 775-790.

Martin, C. L., & Little, J. K. (1990). The relation of gender understanding to children's sex-typed preferences and gender stereotypes. *Child Development, 61,* 1427-1439.

Martin, C. L., & Wood, C. H. (1987, April). *Children's sex-typed interest attributions.* Paper presented at the biennial meeting of the Society for Research in Child Development, Baltimore, MD.

McConaghy, M. J. (1979). Gender permanence and the genital basis of gender: Stages in the development of constancy of gender identity. *Child Development, 50,* 1223-1226.

Meehan, A. M., & Janik, L. M. (1990). Illusory correlation and the maintenance of sex role stereotypes in children. *Sex Roles, 22,* 83-95.

Meltz, B. F. (1991, May 25). Round I in the battle of the sexes. *Boston Globe,* p. 64.

Miller, C. L., (1983). Developmental changes in male/female voice classification by infacnts. *Infant Behavior and Development, 6,* 313-330.

Montemayor, R. (1974). Children's performance in a game and their attraction to it as a function of sex-typed labels. Child *Development, 45,* 152-156.

Moss, H. A., & Robson, K. S. (1968). Maternal influences in early social visual behavior. *Child Development, 39,* 401-408.

Mullen, M. K. (1990). Children's classification of nature and artifact pictures into female and male categories. *Sex Roles, 23,* 577-587.

Munroe, R. H., Shimmin, H. S., & Munroe, R. L. (1984). Gender understanding and sex role preference in four cultures. *Developmental Psychology, 20.* 673-682.

Perry, D. G., & Perry, L. C. (1975). Observational learning in children: Effect of sex of model and subject's sex role behavior. *Journal of Personality and Social Psychology, 31,* 1084-1088.

Picariello, M. L., Greenberg, D. J., & Pillemer, D. B. (1990). Children's sex stereotyping of colors. *Child Development, 61,* 1453-1460.

Poulin-Dubois, D., Serbin, Lk A., Kenyon, B., & Derbyshire, A. (1991, April). *Intermodal gender concepts in 12-month-old infants.* Paper presented at the biennial meeting of the Society for Research in Child Development, Seattle, WA.

Reis, H. T., & Wright, S. (1982). Knowledge of sex role stereotypes in children aged 3 to 5. *Sex Roles, 8,* 1049-1056.

Romaine, S. (1984). *The language of children and adolescents.* Oxford, England: Basil Blackwell.

Rosenthal, D. A., & Chapman, D. C. (1982). The lady spaceman: Children's perception of sex typed occupations. *Sex roles, 8,* 959-965.

Ruble, D. N., Balaban, T., & Cooper, J. (1981). Gender constancy and the effects of sex typed televised toy commercials. *Child Development, 52,* 667-673.

Rudolph, E. (1991, September). Women's Talk. *New York Times Sunday Magazine,* p.8.

Signorella, M. L., & Jamison, W. (1984). Recall and reconstruction of gender related pictures: Effects of attitude, task difficulty, and age. *Child Development, 55,* 393-405.

Slaby, R. C., & Frey, K. S. (1985). Development of gender constancy and selective attention to same sex models. *Child Development, 46,* 849-856.

Smetana, J. G., & Letourneau, K. J. (1984). Development of gender constancy and children's sex-typed free play behavior. *Child Development, 20,* 691-696.

Smith, J., & Russell, G. (1984). Why do males and females differ? Children's beliefs about sex differences. *Sex Roles, 11,* 1111-1120.

Stangor, C., & Ruble, D. N. (1987). Development of gender role knowledge and gender constancy. In L. D. Liben & M. L. Signorella (Eds.), *Children's gender schemata* (pp. 5-22). San Francisco: Jossey-Bass.

Stangor, C., & Ruble, D. N. (1989). Stereotype development and memory: What we remember depends on how much we know. *Journal of Experimental Social Psychology, 25,* 18-35.

Statham, J. (1986). *Daughters and sons: Experiences of nonsexist childraising.* Oxford, England: Basil Blackwell.

Stein, A., Pohly, S., & Mueller, E. (1971). The influence of masculine, feminine, and neutral tasks on children's achievement behavior, expectancies of success, and attainment values. *Child Development, 42,* 195-207.

Stoddart, T., & Turiel, E. (1985). Children's concepts of cross-gender activities. *Child Development, 56,* 1241-1252.

Tavris, C., & Wade, C. (1984). *The longest war: Sex differences in perspective* (2nd ed.). San Diego: Harcourt, Brace, Jovanovich.

Taylor, M. C., & Gelman, S. A. (1991, April). *Children's beliefs about sex differences: The role of nature vs nurture.* Paper presented at the biennial meeting of the Society for Research in Child Development, Seattle, WA.

Thompson, S. K. (1975). Gender labels and early sex role development. *Child Development, 46,* 339-347.

Thompson, S. K. & Bentler, P. M. (1971). The priority of cues in sex discrimination by children and adults. *Developmental Psychology, 5,* 181-185.

Trepanier-Street, M. L., & Knopp, J. J. (1986). Children's recall and recognition of sex role stereotyped and discrepant information. *Sex Roles, 16,* 237-249.

Turnbull, A., (1988). Woman enough for the Games? *New Scientist, 131,* 61-64.

Ullian, D. Z. (1976). The development of conceptions of masculinity and femininity. In B. Lloyd & J. Ascher (Eds.). *Exploring sex differences* (pp. 25-47). London: Academic Press.

Urberg, K. A. (1982). The development of the concepts of masculinity and femininity in young children. *Sex Roles, 8,* 659-668.

Walsh, P. V., Katz, P. A., & Downey, E. P. (1991, April). *A longitudinal perspective on race and gender socialization in infants and toddlers.* . Paper presented at the biennial meeting of the Society for Research in Child Development, Seattle, WA.

Wehren, A., & De Lisi, R. (1983). The development of gender understanding: Judgments and explanations. *Child Development, 54,* 1568-1578.

Weinraub, M., Clemens, L. P., Sockloff, A., Ethridge, T., Gracely, E., & Myers, B. (1984). The development of sex role stereotypes in the third year: Relationships to gender labeling, gender identity, sex-typed toy preference, and family characteristics. *Child Development, 55,* 1493-1503.

Williams, J. E., Bennett, S. M., & Best, D. L. (1975). Awareness and expression of sex stereotypes in young children. *Developmental Psychology, 11,* 635-642.

Wyche, K. F. (1991). *The development of concepts of race, ethnicity, and gender in children from diverse racial ethnic groups.* Paper presented at the biennial meeting of the Society for Research in Child Development, Seattle, WA.

Chapter 8

The Media. *Julia Wood looks critically at how media depict roles and responsibilities of women and men. She says media portray an array of unrealistic ideals in which men are the dominant majority and women are passive, domestic, and supportive.*

Chapter 8 *Julia T. Wood,* Gendered Lives: Communication, Gender, and Culture

Gendered Media: The Influence of Media on Views of Gender

From newspapers to MTV, media interact with cultural images of gender and with individual identities in three ways. First, media reflect cultural values and ideals about gender. They portray women, men, and relationships between the sexes in ways that mirror widely shared understandings and ideals. Second, media reproduce cultural views of gender in individuals. By defining "normal" women, men, and relationships, media suggest how we should be as women and men. Third, media are gatekeepers of information and images. To a significant extent, they control what we see and know by deciding what programs to air, what news stories to feature, how to represent issues and events, and how to depict women and men. By selectively regulating what we see, media influence how we perceive gender issues, ourselves, and men women in general.

To launch our exploration of how media reflect and shape understandings of gender, we will first establish the significance of media in cultural life. Next, we will identify basic themes and trends in media's images of women, men, and relationships between sexes. Third, we will examine media's role in shaping our understanding of issues related to gender. Finally, we will ask how media's portrayals of gender issues and of men and women contribute to misconceptions of issues, violence against women, psychological and physical problems of men and women, and limited views of our human possibilities.

The Prevalence of Media in Cultural Life

How important are media in shaping our views of our world, ourselves, and gender? Consider what we know about the extent to which media are part of our lives. In a relatively short span of years, television has saturated American life. While only 9% of households owned televisions in 1950, by 1991 nearly all American households (98.3%) own a television, and two-thirds of households own more than one set (Television Bureau of Advertising, 1991, p. 2). Well over half of all households now own videocassette recorders (Edmondson, 1987), which suggests home film viewing is substantial. Cable penetration is now 60.2% (Television Bureau of Advertising, 1991, p. 2). The average household receives more than 28 stations (*American Demographics*, February 1990, p. 4), and at least one television is on more than 7 hours a day. Television reaches more people than any other medium, with 89% (18- to 54-year-olds) to 94% (those over 55 years old) watching television in a given day (Television Bureau of Advertising, 1990, p. 4). Children and adolescents are heavy viewers, averaging 2 to 31/2 hours daily (Television Bureau of Advertising, 1991, p. 7), and some watch as many as 7 hours in a single day (Gerbner & Gross, 1976; Nielsen Media Research, 1989).
By age 16, many adolescents have spent more time in front of a television than in school, and the amount of viewing is even higher for most African-Americans (Brown, Childers, Bauman, & Koch, 1990; Tangney & Feshbach, 1988).

Beyond television, media continue to pervade our lives. While walking or riding through any area, we take in a nearly endless procession of billboards that advertise various products, services, people, and companies. Magazines abound, and each one is full of stories that represent men and women and their relationships, thereby suggesting what is "normal." The hundreds of magazines available make it possible for just about anyone to select the kind of coverage she or he wants. In 1991, *Playboy* had 3,488,006 subscribers, while *Newsweek* had 3,211,958 and *Family Circle* had 5,431,779 ("Mediaworks," 1991, p. 37). Advertisements, which make up nearly half of some magazines, tell us what we need and where to buy it if we are to meet cultural standards for women and men. Radios, Walkmans, and stereo systems allow us to hear music as much of the time as we wish, while home videos are doing a record business as Americans see more films than ever. In 1991, 72.5% of homes had at least one VCR (Television Bureau of Advertising, 1991, p. 2). Newspapers, which circulate to over 62 million homes (Newsprint Information committee, 1992, p. 18), news programming, and talk shows provide us with a horizon on our world, contemporary issues, and the roles of various people in shaping cultural life. Popular advice books and gothic novels are top sellers, and pornographic print and visual media are readily available to anyone who is interested.

Themes in Media

Of the many influences on how we view men and women, media are the most pervasive and one of the most powerful. Woven throughout our daily lives, media insinuate their messages into our consciousness at every turn. All forms of media communicate images of the sexes, many of which perpetuate unrealistic, stereotypical, and limiting perceptions. Three themes describe how media represent gender. First, women are underrepresented, which falsely implies that men are the cultural standard and women are unimportant or invisible. Second, men and women are portrayed in stereotypical ways that reflect and sustain socially endorsed views of gender. Third, depictions of relationships between men and women emphasize traditional roles and normalize violence against women. We will consider each of these themes in this section.

Underrepresentation of Women

A primary way in which media distort reality is in underrepresenting women. Whether it is prime-time television, in which there are three times as many white men as women (Basow, 1992, p. 159), or children's programming, in which males outnumber females by two to one, or newscasts, in which women make up 16% of newscasters and in which stories about men are included 10 times more often than ones about women ("Study Reports Sex Bias," 1989), media misrepresent actual proportions of men and women in the population. This constant distortion tempts us to believe that there really are more men than women and, further, that men are the cultural standard.

Other myths about what is standard are similarly fortified by communication in media. Minorities are even less visible than women, with African-Americans appearing only rarely (Gray, 1986; Stroman, 1989) and other ethnic minorities being virtually nonexistent. In children's programming when African-Americans do appear, almost invariably they appear in supporting roles rather than as main characters (O'Connor, 1989). While more African-Americans are appearing in prime-time television, they are too often cast in stereotypical roles. In the 1992 season, for instance, 12 of the 74 series on commercial networks included large African-American casts, yet most featured them in stereotypical roles. Black men are presented as lazy and unable to handle authority, as lecherous, and/or as unlawful, while females are portrayed as domineering or as sex objects ("Sights, Sounds, and Stereotypes," 1992). Writing in 1993, David Evans (1993, p. 10) criticized television for stereotyping black males as athletes and entertainers. These roles, wrote Evans, mislead young black male viewers into thinking success "is only a dribble or dance step away," and blind them to other, more realistic ambitions. Hispanics and Asians are nearly absent, and when they are presented it is usually as villains or criminals (Lichter, Lichter, Rothman, & Amundson, 1987).

Also underrepresented is the single fastest growing group of Americans-older people. As a country, we are aging so that people over 60 make up a major part of our population; within this group, women significantly outnumber men (Wood, 1993c). Older people not only are underrepresented in media but also are represented inaccurately. In contrast to demographic realities, media consistently show fewer older women than men, presumably because our culture worships youth and beauty in women. Further, elderly individuals are frequently portrayed as sick, dependent, fumbling, and passive, images not borne out in real life. Distorted depictions of older people and especially older women in media, however, can delude us into thinking they are a small, sickly, and unimportant part of our population.

The lack of women in the media is paralleled by the scarcity of women in charge of media. Only about 5% of television writers, executives, and producers are women (Lichter, Lichter, & Rothman, 1986). Ironically, while two-thirds of journalism graduates are women, they make up less than 2% of those in corporate management of newspapers and only about 5% of newspapers publishers ("Women in Media," 1988). Female film directors are even more scarce, as are executives in charge of MTV. It is probably not coincidental that so few women are behind the scenes of an industry that so consistently portrays women negatively. Some media analysts (Mills, 1988) believe that if more women had positions of authority at executive levels, media would offer more positive portrayals of women.

Stereotypical Portrayals of Women and Men

In general, media continue to present both women and men in stereotyped ways that limit our perceptions of human possibilities. Typically men are portrayed as active, adventurous, powerful, sexually aggressive, and largely uninvolved in human relationships. Just as consistent with cultural views of gender are depictions of women as sex objects who are usually young, thin, beautiful, passive, dependent, and often incompetent and dumb. Female characters devote their primary energies to improving their appearances and taking care of homes and people. Because media pervade our lives, the ways they misrepresent genders may distort how we see ourselves and what we perceive as normal and desirable for men and women.

Stereotypical portrayals of men. According to J. A. Doyle (1989, p. 111), whose research focuses on masculinity, children's television typically shows males as "aggressive, dominant, and engaged in exciting activities from which they receive rewards from others for their 'masculine' accomplishments." Relatedly, recent studies reveal that the majority of men on prime-time television are independent, aggressive, and in charge (McCauley, Thangavelu, & Rozin, 1988). Television programming for all ages disproportionately depicts men as serious, confident, competent, powerful, and in high-status positions. Gentleness in men, which was briefly evident in the 1970s, has receded as established male characters are redrawn to be more tough and distanced from others (Boyer, 1986). Highly popular films such as *Lethal Weapon, Predator, Days of Thunder, Total Recall, Robocop, Die Hard, and Die Harder* star men who embody the stereotype of extreme masculinity. Media, then, reinforce long-standing cultural ideals of masculinity: Men are presented as hard, tough, independent, sexually aggressive, unafraid, violent, totally in control of all emotions, and -- above all -- in no way feminine.

Equally interesting is how males are not presented. J.D. Brown and K. Campbell (1986) report that men are seldom shown doing housework. Doyle (1989) notes that boys and men are rarely presented caring for others. B. Horovitz (1989) points out they are typically represented as uninterested in and incompetent at homemaking, cooking, and child care. Each season's new ads for cooking and cleaning supplies include several that caricature men as incompetent buffoons, who are klutzes in the kitchen and no better at taking care of children. While children's books have made a limited attempt to depict women engaged in activities outside of the home, there has been little parallel effort to show men involved in family and home life. When someone is shown taking care of a child, it is usually the mother, not the father. This perpetuates a negative stereotype of men as uncaring and uninvolved in family life.

Stereotypical portrayals of women. Media's images of women also reflect cultural stereotypes that depart markedly from reality. As we have already seen, girls and women are dramatically underrepresented. In prime-time television in 1987, fully two-thirds of the speaking parts were for men. Women are portrayed as significantly younger and thinner than women in the population as a whole, and most are depicted as passive, dependent on men, and enmeshed in relationships or housework (Davis, 1990). The requirements of youth and beauty in women even influence news shows, where female newscasters are expected to be younger, more physically attractive, and less outspoken than males (Craft, 1988; Sanders & Rock, 1988). Despite educators' criticism of self-fulfilling prophesies that discourage girls from success in math and science, that stereotype was dramatically reiterated in 1992 when Mattel offered a new talking Barbie doll. What did she say? "Math class is tough," a message that reinforces the stereotype that women cannot do math ("Mattel Offers Trade-In," 1992). From children's programming, in which the few existing female characters typically spend their time watching males do things (Feldman & Brown, 1984; Woodman, 1991), to MTV, which routinely pictures women satisfying men's sexual fantasies (Pareles, 1990; Texier, 1990), media reiterate the cultural image of women as dependent, ornamental objects whose primary functions are to look good, please men, and stay quietly on the periphery of life.

Media have created two images of women: good women and bad ones. These polar opposites are often juxtaposed against each other to dramatize differences in the consequences that befall good and bad women. Good women are pretty, deferential, and focused on home, family, and caring for others. Subordinate to men, they are usually cast as victims, angels, martyrs, and loyal wives and helpmates. Occasionally, women who depart from traditional roles are portrayed positively, but this is done either by making their career lives invisible, as with Claire Huxtable, or by softening and feminizing working women to make them more consistent with traditional views of femininity. For instance, in the original script, Cagney and Lacey were conceived as strong, mature, independent women who took their work seriously and did it well. It took 6 years for writers Barbara Corday and Barbara Avedon to sell the script to CBS, and even they had to agree to subdue Cagney's and Lacey's abilities to placate producer Barney Rosenzweig, who complained, "These women aren't soft enough. These women aren't feminine enough" (Faludi, 1991, p. 150). While female viewers wrote thousands of letters praising the show, male executives at CBS continued to force writers to make the characters softer, more tender, and less sure of themselves (Faludi, 1991, p. 152). The remaking of Cagney and Lacey illustrates the media's bias in favor of women who are traditionally feminine and who are not too able, too powerful, or too confident. The rule seems to be that a women may be strong and successful if and only if she also exemplifies traditional stereotypes of femininity -- subservience, passivity, beauty, and an identity linked to one or more men.

The other image of women the media offer us is the evil sister of the good homebody. Versions of this image are the witch, bitch, whore, or nonwoman, who is represented as hard, cold, aggressive -- all of the things a good women is not supposed to be. Exemplifying the evil woman is Alex in *Fatal Attraction*, which grossed more than

$100 million in its first four months (Faludi, 1991, p. 113). Yet Alex was only an extreme version of how bad women are generally portrayed. In children's literature, we encounter witches and mean stepmothers as villains, with beautiful and passive females like Snow White and Sleeping Beauty as their good counterparts.

Prime-time television favorably portrays pretty, nurturing, other-focused women, such as Claire Huxtable on "The Cosby Show," whose career as an attorney never entered storylines as much as her engagement in family matters. Hope in "Thirtysomething" is an angel, committed to husband Michael and daughter Janey. In the biographies written for each of the characters when the show was in development, all male characters were defined in terms of their career goals, beliefs, and activities. Hope's biography consisted of one line: "Hope is married to Michael" (Faludi, 1991, p. 162). Hope epitomizes the traditional woman, so much so in fact that in one episode she refers to herself as June Cleaver and calls Michael "Ward," thus reprising the traditional family of the 1950s as personified in "Leave It to Beaver" (Faludi, 1991, p. 161). Meanwhile, prime-time typically represents ambitious, independent women as lonely, embittered spinsters who are counterpoints to "good" women.

Stereotypical Images of Relationships Between Men and Women

Given media's stereotypical portrayals of women and men, we shouldn't be surprised to find that relationships between women and men are similarly depicted in ways that reinforce stereotypes. Four themes demonstrate how media reflect and promote traditional arrangements between the sexes.

Women's dependence/men's independence. Walt Disney's award-winning animated film *The Little Mermaid* vividly embodies females' dependence on males for identity. In this feature film, the mermaid quite literally gives up her identity as a mermaid in order to become acceptable to her human lover. In this children's story, we see a particularly obvious illustration of the asymmetrical relationship between women and men that is more subtly conveyed in other media productions. Even the Smurfs, formless little beings who have no obvious sex, reflect the male-female, dominant-submissive roles. The female smurf, unlike her male companions, who have names, is called only Smurfette, making her sole identity a dimunitive relation to male smurfs. The male dominance/female subservience pattern that permeates mediated representations of relationships is no accident. Beginning in 1991, television executives deliberately and consciously adopted a policy of having dominant male characters in all Saturday morning children's programming (Carter, 1991).

Women, as well as minorities, are cast in support roles rather than leading ones in both children's shows and the commercials interspersed within them (O'Connor, 1989). Analyses of MTV revealed that it portrays females as passive and waiting for men's attention, while males are shown ignoring, exploiting, or directing women (Brown, Campbell, & Fisher, 1986). In rap music videos, where African-American men and women star, men dominate women, whose primary role is as objects of male desires (Pareles, 1990; Texier, 1990). News programs that have male and female hosts routinely cast the female as deferential to her male colleague (Craft, 1988; Sanders & Rock, 1988). Commercials, too, manifest power cues that echo the male dominance/female subservience pattern. For instance, men are usually shown positioned above women, and women are more frequently pictured in varying degrees of undress (Masse & Rosenblum, 1988; Nigro, Hill, Gelbein, & Clark, 1988). Such nonverbal cues represent women as vulnerable and more submissive while men stay in control.

In a brief departure from this pattern, films and television beginning in the 1970s responded to the second wave of feminism by showing women who were independent without being hard, embittered, or without close relationships. Films such as *Alice Doesn't Live Here Anymore, Up the Sandbox, The Turning Point, Diary of a Mad Housewife*, and *An Unmarried Woman* offered realistic portraits of women who sought and found their own voices independent of men. Judy Davis's film, *My Brilliant Career*, particularly embodied this focus by telling the story of a woman who chooses work over marriage. During this period, television followed suit, offering viewers prime-time fare such as "Maude" and "The Mary Tyler Moore Show," which starred women who were able and achieving in their own rights. "One Day at a Time," which premiered in 1974, was the first prime-time program about a divorced woman.

By the 1980s, however, traditionally gendered arrangements resurged as the backlash movement against feminism was embraced by media (Haskell, 1988; Maslin, 1990). Thus, film fare in the 1980s included *Pretty Woman*, the story of a prostitute who becomes a good woman when she is saved from her evil ways by a rigidly stereotypical man, complete with millions to prove his success. Meanwhile, *Tie Me Up, Tie Me Down* trivialized abuse of women and underlined women's dependence on men with a story of a woman who is bound by a man and colludes in sustaining her bondage. *Crossing Delancey* showed successful careerist Amy Irving talked into believing she needs a man to be complete, a theme reprised by Cher in *Moonstruck*.

Television, too, cooperated in returning women to their traditional roles with characters like Hope in "Thirtysomething," who minded house and baby as an ultratraditional wife, and even Murphy Brown found her career wasn't enough and had a baby. Against her protests, Cybill Shepherd, who played Maddie in "Moonlighting," was forced to marry briefly on screen, which Susan Faludi (1991, p. 157) refers to as part of a "campaign to cow this independent female figure." Popular music added its voice with hit songs like "Having My Baby," which glorified a woman who defined herself by motherhood and her relationship to a man. The point is not that having babies or committing to relationships is wrong; rather, it is that media virtually require this of women in order to present them positively. Media define a very narrow range for womanhood.

Joining the campaign to restore traditional dominant-subordinate patterns of male-female relationships were magazines, which reinvigorated their focus on women's role as the helpmate and supporter of husbands and families (Peirce, 1990). In 1988, that staple of Americana, *Good Housekeeping*, did its parts to revive women's traditional roles with a full-page ad ("The Best in the House," 1988) for its new demographic edition marketed to "the new traditionalist women." A month later, the magazine followed this up with a second full-page ad in national newspapers that saluted the "new traditionalist woman," with this copy ("The New Traditionalist," 1988): "She has made her commitment. Her mission: create a more meaningful life for herself and her family. She is the New Traditionalist -- a contemporary woman who finds her fulfillment in traditional values." The long-standing dominant-submissive model for male-female relationships was largely restored in the 1980s. With only rare exceptions, women are still portrayed as dependent on men and subservient to them. As B. Lott (1989, p. 64) points out, it is women who "do the laundry and are secretaries to men who own companies."

Men's authority/women's incompetence. A second recurrent theme in media representations of relationships is that men are the competent authorities who save women from their incompetence. Children's literature vividly implements this motif by casting females as helpless and males as coming to their rescue. Sleeping Beauty's resurrection depends on Prince Charming's kiss, a theme that appears in the increasing popular gothic romance novels for adults (Modleski, 1982).

One of the most pervasive ways in which media define males as authorities is in commercials. Women are routinely shown anguishing over dirty floors and bathroom fixtures only to be relieved of their distress when Mr. Clean shows up to tell them how to keep their homes spotless. Even when commercials are aimed at women, selling products intended for them, up to 90% of the time a man's voice is used to explain the value of what is being sold (Basow, 1992, p. 161; Bretl & Cantor, 1988). Using male voice-overs reinforces the cultural view that men are authorities and women depend on men to tell them what to do.

Television further communicates the message that men are authorities and women are not. One means of doing this is sheer numbers. As we have seen, men vastly outnumber women in television programming. In addition, the dominance of men as news anchors who inform us of happenings in the world underlines their authority ("Study Reports Sex Bias," 1989). Prime-time television contributes to this image by showing women who need to be rescued by men and by presenting women as incompetent more than twice as often as men (Boyer, 1986; Lichter et al., 1986).

Consider the characters in "The Jetsons," an animated television series set in the future. Daughter Judy Jetson is constantly complaining and waiting for others to help her, using ploys of helplessness and flattery to win men's attention. *The Rescuers*, a popular animated video of the 1990s, features Miss Bianca (whose voice is that of Zsa Zsa Gabor, fittingly enough), who splits her time evenly between being in trouble and being grateful to male characters for rescuing her. These stereotypical representations of males and females reinforce a number of harmful beliefs. They suggest, first, that men are more competent than women. Compounding this is the message that a woman's power lies in her looks and conventional femininity, since that is how females from Sleeping Beauty to Judy Jetson get males to assist them with their dilemmas (McCauley, Thangavelu, & Rozin, 1988). Third, these stereotypes underline the requirement that men must perform, succeed, and conquer in order to be worthy.

Women as primary caregivers/men as breadwinners. A third perennial theme in media is that women are caregivers and men are providers. Since the backlash of the 1980s, in fact, this gendered arrangement has been promulgated with renewed vigor. Once again, as in the 1950s, we see women devoting themselves to getting rings off of collars, gray out of their hair, and meals on the table. Corresponding to this is the restatement of men's inability in domestic and nurturing roles. Horovitz (1989), for instance, reports that in commercials men are regularly the butt of jokes for their ignorance about nutrition, child care, and housework.

116

When media portray women who work outside of the home, their career lives typically receive little or no attention. Although these characters have titles such as lawyer or doctor, they are shown predominantly in their roles as homemakers, mothers, and wives. We see them involved in caring conversations with family and friends and doing things for others, all of which never seem to conflict with their professional responsibilities. This has the potential to cultivate unrealistic expectations of being "superwoman," who does it all without ever getting a hair out of place or being late to a conference.

Magazines play a key role in promoting pleasing others as a primary focus of women's lives. K. Peirce's (1990) study found that magazines aimed at women stress looking good and doing things to please others. Thus, advertising tells women how to be "me, only better" by dyeing their hair to look younger; how to lose weight so "you'll still be attractive to him"; and how to prepare gourmet meals so "he's always glad to come home." Constantly, these advertisements emphasize pleasing others, especially men, as central to being a woman, and the message is fortified with the thinly veiled warning that if a women woman fails to look good and please, her man might leave (Rakow, 1992).

There is a second, less known way in which advertisements contribute to stereotypes of women as focused on others and men as focused on work. Writing in 1990, Gloria Steinem, editor of *Ms.*, revealed that advertisers control some to most of the *content* in magazines. In exchange for placing an ad, a company receives "complimentary copy," which is one or more articles that increase the market appeal of its product. So a soup company that takes out an ad might be given a three-page story on how to prepare meals using that brand of soup; likewise, an ad for hair coloring products might be accompanied by interviews with famous women who choose to dye their hair. Thus, the message of advertising is multiplied by magazines content, which readers often mistakenly assume is independent of advertising.

Advertisers support media, and they exert powerful influence on what is presented. To understand the prevalence of traditional gender roles in programming, magazine copy, and other media, we need to only ask what is in the best interests of advertisers. They want to sponsor shows that create or expand markets for their products. Media images of women as sex objects, devoted homemakers, and mothers buttress the very roles in which the majority of consuming takes place. To live up to these images, women have to buy cosmetics and other personal care products, diet aids, food, household cleaners, utensils and appliances, clothes and toys for children, and so on. In short, it is in advertisers' interests to support programming and copy that feature women in traditional roles. In a recent analysis, Lana Rakow (1992) demonstrated that much advertising is oppressive to women and is very difficult to resist, even when one is a committed feminist.

Women's role in the home and men's role outside of it are reinforced by newspapers and news programming. Both emphasize men's independent activities and, in fact, define news almost entirely as stories about and by men ("Study Reports Sex Bias," 1989). Even stories about women who are in the news because of achievements and professional activities typically dwell on marriage, family life, and other aspects of women's traditional role (Foreit et al., 1980).

Women as victims and sex objects/men as aggressors. A final theme in mediated representations of relationships between women and men is representation of women as subject to men's sexual desires. The irony of this representation is that the very qualities women are encouraged to develop (beauty, sexiness, passivity, and powerlessness) in order to meet cultural ideals of femininity contribute to their victimization. Also, the qualities that men are urged to exemplify (aggressiveness, dominance, sexuality, and strength) are identical to those linked to abuse of women. It is no coincidence that all but one of the women nominated for Best Actress in the 1988 Academy Awards played a victim (Faludi, 1991, p.138). Women are portrayed alternatively either as decorative objects, who must attract a man to be valuable, or as victims of men's sexual impulses. Either way, women are defined by their bodies and how men treat them. Their independent identities and endeavors are irrelevant to how they are represented in media, and their abilities to resist exploitation by others are obscured.

This theme, which was somewhat toned down during the 1970s, returned with vigor in the 1980s as the backlash permeated media. According to S. A. Basow (1992, p.160), since 1987 there has been a "resurgence of male prominence, pretty female sidekicks, female homemakers." Advertising in magazines also communicates the message that women are sexual objects. While men are seldom pictured nude or even partially unclothed, women habitually are. Advertisements for makeup, colognes, hair products, and clothes often show women attracting men because they got the right products and made themselves irresistible. Stars on prime-time and films, who are beautiful and dangerously thin, perpetuate the idea that women must literally starve themselves to death to win men's interest (Silverstein et al., 1986).

Perhaps the most glaring examples of portrayals of women as sex objects and men as sexual aggressors occur in music videos as shown on MTV and many other stations. Typically, females are shown dancing provocatively in scant and/or revealing clothing as they try to gain men's attention (Texier, 1990). Frequently, men are seen coercing women into sexual activities and/or physically abusing them. Violence against women is also condoned in many recent films. R. Warshaw (1991) reported that cinematic presentations of rapes, especially acquaintance rapes, are not presented as power-motivated violations of women but rather as strictly sexual encounters. Similarly, others (Cowan, Lee, & Snyder, 1988; Cowan & O'Brien, 1990) have found that male dominance and sexual exploitation of women are themes in virtually all R- and X-rated films, which almost anyone may now rent for home viewing. These media images carry to extremes long-standing cultural views of masculinity as aggressive and femininity as passive. They also make violence seem sexy (D. Russel, 1993). In so doing, they recreate these limited and limiting perceptions in the thinking of another generation of women and men.

In sum, we have identified basic stereotypes and themes in media's representations of women, men, and relationships between the two. Individually and in combination these images sustain and reinforce socially constructed views of the genders, views that have restricted both men and women and that appear to legitimize destructive behaviors ranging from anorexia to battering. Later in this chapter, we will probe more closely how media versions of gender are linked to problems such as these.

Bias in News Coverage

Television is the primary source of news for at least two-thirds of Americans (Baslow, 1992, p. 160), with newspapers ranking second. This suggests that our understanding of issues, events, and people is shaped substantially by what television and newspapers define as news and the manner in which they present it. As gatekeepers of information, news reporting selectively shapes our perceptions of issues related to gender.

Beginning with the second wave of American feminism in the 1960's, media have consistently misrepresented the goals, activities, and members of women's movements. Because most editors and media executives are men, they have not experienced the daily frustrations women face in society where they lack rights, opportunities, and status equal to those of men. Some men may feel threatened by women's demands for more prerogatives and for equal treatment. Their lack of personal acquaintance with inequities and their apprehension about women who step out of familiar roles probably account for much of the distortion in coverage of feminism and women.

In the early days of radical feminism, media portrayed feminists as manhating, bra-burning extremists. The famous bra-burning, in fact, never happened, but was erroneously reported by a journalist who misunderstood the facts (Faludi, 1991, p. 75). This was no isolated effort to discredit the women's movement, since many stories caricatured feminists and undermined women's efforts to gain rights. In the early 1970's, an editor at *Newsday* gave these instructions to a reporter he assigned to research and write a story on the women's movement (Faludi, 1991, pp. 75-76): "Get out there and find an authority who'll say it's all a crock of shit." Little wonder that the story that later appeared reported that the women's movement was a minor ripple without much validity or support.

One of the most famous--or infamous--media stunts of the 1980's was another manifestation of the backlash movement against feminism, which consistently received more favorable press than the women's movement itself. The cover story for the June 21, 1986, issue of *Newsweek* was about the so-called man shortage. With dramatic charts showing that chances for marrying plunge precipitously as a working woman ages, *Newsweek* proclaimed that after age 40, a woman was more likely to be killed by a terrorist than to marry, a comment that led one wit to declare that was the best rationale she'd ever heard for terrorism! Behind the headlines, the facts were shaky. The predications of women's opportunities to marry were based on a study by researchers at Harvard and Yale, but the data of the study were discredited and the study was withdrawn from publication. Did the flaws in the study and its withdrawal get headlines? No way. When the accurate U.S. Census Bureau's figures were released some months later and disproved the bogus study, *Newsweek* relegated that information to a mere two paragraphs in a minor column (Faludi, 1991, pp. 98-100).

Another incident illustrative of media's distortion of feminism came in 1989, when Felice Schwartz, a management consultant, published an article in the prestigious *Harvard Business Review*, in which she argued that women who want to have children cost businesses too much money and should be placed on a separate track in which they do not get the opportunities for advancement that go to men and women who are career oriented. Dubbing this "the mommy track," newspapers and magazines took Schwartz's article as occasion to reassert the viewpoint that women's place really is in the home and that they are lesser players in professional life. Once again, though, facts to support the claim were scant. Schwarz's article was speculative, as was her opinion that most women would willingly trade promotions and opportunities for more time with their families. When the annual Virginia Slims Poll (1990) directly asked women working outside of the home whether they favored mommy tracks, nearly three-fourths thought such a policy was regressive and discriminatory. Schwartz later retracted her suggestions, saying she had erred in claiming women were more expensive as employees than men. Her retraction, however, got little coverage, since Schwartz's revised point of view did not support the media's bias regarding women's roles. Because there was virtually no coverage of Schwartz's change of opinion (Faludi, 1991, p. 92), many people read only the first article and continue to believe it is credible.

Other gender issues have been similarly transformed to fit media's biases. Two instances of bending events to fit stereotypes of gender occurred in the 1990 Gulf War. As substantial numbers of women joined men in fighting, traditional values were shaken. Throughout the war, newspapers and magazines featured melodramatic pictures of children watching mothers go to war, while talk shows asked the question "Should a woman leave her baby to go to war?" (Flanders, 1990). Surely, this is a reasonable question to ask about any parent, but it was rarely applied to fathers. In focusing on women's roles as mothers, the media communicated two gender messages. First, they implied that women--real women--don't leave their children. The second gender message was that fathers are not primary parents. In dismissing fathers' abilities to take care of children while mothers were overseas, media reinforced men's marginality in family life.

The second gender issue out of the Gulf War came when an American woman in the military, along with several men, was taken as a prisoner of war. Rather than presenting this as straightforward news, however, media focused on her femininity rather than on her military role. Newspapers showing photographs of all P.O.W.s featured the male ones in military uniform and the female in a glamour shot from her school yearbook. In highlighting her femininity, media ignited powerful public sentiment about women's fragility, vulnerability, and, therefore, inappropriateness in positions of danger. All attention focused, as the media directed it to, on possibilities of sexual assault of women P.O.W.s, thereby reinforcing images of women as sex objects. Only a year later, we learned of the Tailhook scandal in which numerous male naval personnel sexually harassed female personnel. This made it clear that women are at least as likely to suffer sexual assault from male peers in the service as from enemies who capture them.

When Geraldine Ferraro ran for vice president and Pat Schroeder ran for president in the late 1980s, morning talk shows focused on whether women's hormonal swings disqualified them for leadership. A thorough review of all research on the effects of hormonal cycles on women's abilities (Golub, 1988) somehow never made the airwaves, perhaps because it demonstrated conclusively that women's cycles do not consistently impair their performance. This issue resurfaces virtually every time a woman runs for high office, yet media have yet to cover James Dabbs and Robin Morris's (1990) finding that male hormonal cycles do affect behavior. A few years later when it was revealed that President Bush was taking Halcion, a drug demonstrated to affect judgment and sometimes to cause hallucinations, scant attention was paid. Facts and fairness were sacrificed in the media's quest to reinforce views of women as irrational, emotional, and frail and men as in control, competent, and able.

Do media representations of events shape our perceptions? To find out, I asked students to answer five questions. First, I asked whether feminists had burned bras to protest inequalities; second, whether women who have children cost more to employ than men; third, whether men have hormonal cycles that affect their behavior; fourth, whether women's hormonal swings affect their behavior; and fifth, whether there is a shortage of men for women who want to marry. In every case, the majority of students believed the myths created by media, with nearly all students thinking that women are more expensive to employ and are subject to severe hormonal swings but that men either do not have hormonal cycles or are not affected by them. Too often the messages media create misinform us about issues that affect our lives and perceptions.

Implications of Media Representations of Gender

We have seen that media passes along gendered themes and skews coverage of gender issues. Acting as the announcer of cultural values, media reinforce traditional stereotypes of men and women and of relationships between them. Media encourage us to perceive women as dependent, decorative, passive, and subservient and men as independent, powerful, active, and superior. Besieging us from childhood through adult life, media messages reinforce and reproduce gendered identities.

In this final section of the chapter, we want to probe the consequences of media communication about gender. As we will see, media potentially hamper our understandings of ourselves as women and men in three ways. First, media perpetuate unrealistic ideals of what each gender should be, implying that normal people are inadequate by comparison. Simultaneously, because cultural ideals promoted by media are rigid, they limit views of each gender's abilities and opportunities, which may discourage us from venturing into areas outside of those that media defines for our sex. Second, media pathologize the bodies of men and especially of women, prompting us to consider normal physical qualities and functions as abnormal and requiring corrective measures. Third, media contribute significantly to normalizing violence against women, making it possible for men to believe they are entitled to abuse or force women to engage in sex and for women to consider such violations acceptable.

Fostering Unrealistic and Limited Gender Ideals

Many of the images dispensed by media are unrealistic. Most men are not as strong, bold, and successful as males on the screen. Few women are as slender, gorgeous, and well dressed as stars and models, whose photographs are airbrushed and retouched to create their artificial beauty. Most people will not reach executive positions by the age of 35, and those who do are unlikely to be as glamorous, stress-free, and joyous as the atypical few featured in magazines like *Savvy, Business Week, Fortune,* and *Working Woman.* Further, no woman who is healthy can avoid crossing 40, which is the age at which women virtually disappear from media ("Women on TV," 1990). The relationships depicted in media also defy realistic possibilities, since most of us will encounter problems that cannot be solved in 30 minutes (minus 4 ½ minutes for commercial interruptions), and most of you will not be able to pursue a demanding career and still be as relaxed and available to family and friends as media characters.

Do idealized images in media really affect us? You might reasonably assume that we all know the difference between fantasy and reality, so we don't accept media images as models for our own lives and identities. Research, however, suggests that the unrealistic ideals in popular media do influence how we feel about ourselves and our relationships. Mediated images seem to function at a less than conscious level as implicit models for our own lives. In Chapter 7, we noted that modeling contributes to development of gender identity. We look to others--including mediated others--to define how we are supposed to be. Especially during the early years when children often do not clearly distinguish reality form fantasy, they seem susceptible to confusing media characters with real people (Woodman, 1991). In one interesting study, M. M. Kimball (1986) compared the sex-stereotypical attitudes of children who lived in areas without television and those in similar areas who watched television. He found that children who watched television had more stereotyped views of the sexes; further, when television was introduced into communities that had not had it, the children's beliefs became more sex typed. Other research confirms the finding that television is linked to sex-typed attitudes in children and adolescents (Morgan, 1987), especially ones in working-class families (Nikken & Peeters, 1988). One exception is programming that presents nonstereotypical portrayals of males and females, which tends to decrease, not fortify, sex stereotypes (Eisenstock, 1984; Rosenwasser, Lingenfelter, & Harrington, 1989).

The effects of media are not limited to childhood. For adolescents, radio is a major influence, with the average listening time being 5 hours a day--slightly less for Caucasians and slightly more for African-Americans, especially African-American females (Brown et al., 1990). While most popular music reflects sex stereotypes (Lont, 1990), this is less true of work composed and/or sung by women (Groce & Cooper, 1990). However, because most songs are written and sung by males, rock and rap music generally reflects a male point of view (Brown &Campbell, 1986) in which women are depicted sexually and negatively (St. Lawrence & Joynder, 1991). Other media stereotypes have similar distorting effects on our identities. For instance, popularized images of men as independent and women as nurturing and as relationship experts encourage women to feel responsible for others and men to regard caring as peripheral in their lives.

A study by J. Shapiro and L. Kroeger (1991) suggests that mediated myths or relationships contribute to socializing people into unrealistic views of what a normal relationship is. In particular, they found that MTV's and rock music's emphasis on eroticism and sublime sex is linked to an expectation of sexual perfectionism in real relationships. Further, Shapiro and Kroeger reported that readers of self-help books tended to have more unrealistic ideals for relationships than did nonreaders. Consequently, those who read self-help books experienced more than typical amounts of frustration and disappointment when their relationships failed to meet the ideals promoted by media.

Of the many influences on how we feel about ourselves and what we expect in our relationships, media are substantial. Clinicians such as A.T. Beck (1988) as well as researchers (Adelmann, 1989; McCormick & Jordan, 1988; Wadsworth, 1989) maintain that unrealistic images of what we and our relationships should be contribute significantly to dissatisfaction and its consequences, including feelings of inadequacy, anorexia, cosmetic surgery, and emotional difficulties. Media's images of women, men, and relationships are ideals--they are not real, and few of us can even approximate the standards they establish. Yet when we are constantly besieged with ideals of how we should look, feel, act, and be, it's difficult not to feel inadequate. Men as well as women may feel woefully deficient if they rely on media characters as models. If we use media as a reference point for what is normal and desirable, we may find ourselves constantly feeling that we and our relationships are inferior by comparison. To the extent that we let ourselves be influenced by the unreal and unreasonable images presented by media, we may be hindered in our ability to enjoy real people and real relationships.

References

Adelmann, R. (1989, May). Marital myths: What we "know" hurts. *Psychology Today, 23,* 68-69.

American Demographics. (1990, February). P.4.

Basow, S. A. (1992). *Gender: Stereotypes and roles.* (3re Ed.). Pacific Grove, CA: Brooks/Cole.

Beck, A. T., (1988). *Love is never enough.* New York: Harper and Row.

The best in the house. (1988, October 19). *New York Times,* p. 52Y.

Boyer, P. J., (1986, February 16). TV turns to the hard-boiled male. *New York Times,* pp. Hi, H29.

Bretl, D., & Canton, J. (1988). The portrayal of men and women in U. S. commercials: A recent content analysis and trend over 15 years. *Sex roles, 18,* 595-609.

Brown, J. D., & Campbell, K. (1986). Race and gender in music video: The same beat but a different drummer. *Journal of Communication, 36,* 94-106.

Brown, J. D., Childers, K. W., Bauman, K. E., & Koch, G. G. (1990). The influence of new media and family structure on young adolescents' television and radio use. *Communication Research, 17,* 65-82.

Carter, B. (1991, May 1) Children's TV, where boys are king. *New York times,* pp. A1, C18.

Cowan, G., Lee, C., Levy, D., & Snyder, D. (1988). Dominance and inequality in X-rated videocassettes. *Psychology of Women Quarterly, 12,* 299-311.

Cowan, G., & O'Brien, M. (1990). Gender and survuval vs. death in slasher films: A content analysis. *Sex roles, 23,* 187-196.

Craft, C. (1988). *Too old, too ugly, and not deferential to men: An anchor-woman's courageous battle against sex discrimination.* Rockland, CA: Prima.

Dabbs, J. M., Jr., & Morris, R. (1990). Testosterone, social class, and antisocial behavior in a sample of 4,452 men. *Psychological Science, 1,* 209-211.

Davis, S. (1990) Men as success objects and women as sex objects: A study of personal advertisements. *Sex Roles, 23,* 43-50.

Doyle, J. A., (1989). The male experience (2nd Ed.). Dubuque, IA: William C. Brown.

Edmondson, B. (1987, August). Reality on screen. *American Demographics, 9,* 21.

Eisenstock. G. (1984). Sex role differences in children's identification with counter-stereotypical televised portrayals. *Sex roles, 10,* 417-430.

Evans, D. (1993), March 1). The wrong examples. *Newsweek,* p. 10.

Faludi, S. (1991). *Backlash: The undeclared war against American women.* New York: Crown.

Feldman, N. S., & Brown, E. (1984, April). *Male vs. female differences in control strategies: What children learn from Saturday morning television.* Paper presented at the meeting of the Eastern Psychological Association, Baltimore, MD. (Cited in Basow, 1992).

Flanders, L. (1990, November/December). Military women and the media. *New directions for women,* pp. 1,9.

Foreit, K. G., Argor, T., Byers, J., Larue, J., Lokey, H., Palazzini, M., Patterson, M., & Smith, L. (1980). Sex bias in the newspaper treatment of male-centered and female-centered news stories. *Sex Roles, 6,* 475-480.

Golub, S. (1988). A developmental perspective. In L. H. Gise (Ed.), *The premenstrual syndromes.* New York: Churchill Livingstone.

Gray, H. (1986). Television and the new black man: Black male images in prime-time situation comedies. *Media, Culture, and Society, 8,* 223-242.

Groce, S. B., & Cooper, M. (1990). Just me and the boys? Women in local-level rock and roll. *Gender and Society, 4,* 220-229.

Haskell, M. (1988, May). Hollywood Madonnas. *Ms.,* pp. 84, 86, 88.

Horovitz, B. (1989, August 10). In TV commercials, men are often the butt of the jokes. *Philadelphia Inquirer,* pp. 5b, 6b.

Kimball, M. M. (1986). Television and sex role attitudes. In T. M. Williams (Ed.), The impact of Television: A natural experiment in three communities (pp. 265-301). Orlando, FL:Academic Press.

Lichter, S. R., Lichter, L. S. & Rothman, S. (1986, September/October). From Lucy to Lacey: TV dream girls. *Public Opinion,* pp. 16-19.

Lichter, S. R., Lichter, L. S., Rothman, S., & Amundson, D. (1987, July/August). Prime-time prejudice: TV's images of blacks and Hispanics. *Public Opinion,* pp.13-16.

Lont, C. M. (1990). The roles assigned to females and males in non-music radio porgramming. *Sex Roles, 22,* 661-668.

Lott, B. (1989). Sexist deiscrimination as distancing behavior: II. Prime-time television. *Psychology of women Quarterly, 13,* 341-355.

Mattel offers trade-in for "Teen Talk" Barbie. (1992), October 13). *Raleigh News and Observer,* p. A3.

McCauley, C. Thangavelu, K., & Rozin, P. (1988). Sex stereotyping of occupations in relation to television representations and census facts. *Basic and Applied Social Psychology, 9,* 197-212.

McCormick, N., & Jordan, T. (1988). Thoughts that destroy intimacy: Irrational beliefs about relationships and sexuality. In W. Dryden & P. Trower (Eds.) *Developments in rational emotive therapy.* Philadelphia, PA: Open University Press.

Mediaworks. (1991, February 18). *Advertising Age,* p. 37.

Mills, K. (1988). *A place in the news: From the women's pages to the front page.* New York: Dodd, Mead.

Modleski, T. (1982). *Loving with a vengence: Mass-produced fantasies for women.* New York: Methuen.

Morgan, M. (1987). Television, sex-role attitudes and sex-role behavior. *Journal of Early Adolescence, 7,* 269-282.

Newsprint Information Committee. (1992) *Newspaper and newsprint facts at a glance 1991-92* (33rd Ed.). New York: Author.

The new traditionalist. (1988, November 17). *New YorkTimes* p. Y46.

Neilsen Media Research. (1989). *'89 Nielsen report on television.* Northbrook, IL:Author.

Nigro, G. N., Hill. D. E., Gelbein, M. E., & Clark, C. L. (1988). Changes in facial prominence of women and men over the last decade. *Psychology of Women Quarterly, 12,* 225-235.

Nikken, P., & Peeters, A. L. (1988). Children's perceptions of television reality. *Journal of Broadcasting and Electronic Media, 32,* 441-452.

O'Connor, J. J. (1989, June 6). What are commercials selling to children? *New York Times,* p. 28.

Pareles, J. (1990, October 21). The women who talk back in rap. *New York Times,* pp. H33, H36.

Peirce, K. (1990). A feminist theoretical perspective on the socialization of teenage girls through *Seventeen* magazine. *Sex Roles, 23,* 491-500.

Rakow, L. F. (1992). "Don't hate me because I'm beautiful": Feminist resistance to advertising irresistible meanings. *Southern Communication Journal, 36,* 132-141.

Rosenwasser, S. M., Lingenfelter, M., & Harringrton, A. F. (1989). Nontraditional gender role portrayals on television and children's gender role perceptions. *Journal of Applied Developmental Psychology, 10,* 97-105.

Russell. D. E. H. (Ed.). (1993). *Feminist views on pornography.* Cholchester, VT: Teacher College Press.

St. Lawrence, J. S., & Joynder, D. J. (1991). The effects of sexually violent rock music on males' acceptance of violence against women. *Psychology of Women Quarterly, 15,* 49-63

Sanders, M., & Rock, M. (1988). *Waiting for prime time: The women of television news.* Urbana, IL: University of Illinois Press.

Shapiro, J., & Kroeger, L. (1991). Is life just a romantic novel? The relationship between attitudes about intimate relationships and the popular media. *American Journal of Family Therapy, 19,* 226-236.

Sights, sounds, and stereotypes. (1992, October 11). *Raleigh News and Observer,* pp. G1, G10.

Silverstein, B., Perdue, L., Peterson, B., & Kelly, E. (1986). The role of the mass media in promoting a thin standard of bodily attractiveness for women. *Sex Roles, 14,* 519-532.

Steinem, G. (1990, July/August). Sex, lies, and advertising. *Ms.,* pp. 18-28.

Stroman, C. A. (1989). To be young, male and black on prime-time television. *Urban Research Review, 12,* 9-10.

Study reports sex bias in news organizations. (1989, April 11). *New York Times,* p. C22.

Tangney, J. P., & Feshbach, S. (1988). Children's television viewing frequency: Individual differences and demographic correlations. *Personality and Social Psychology Bulletin, 14,* 145-158.

Television Bureau of Advertising. (1990). *Media comparisons* (SRI Rep. A 9055-4). New York: Author.

Television Bureau of Advertising. (1991). *Media comparisons* (SRI Rep. A 9055-4). New York: Author.

Texier, C. (1990, April 22). Have women surrendered in MTV's battle of the sexes? *New York Times,* pp. H29, H31.

The Virgina Slims Opinion Poll. (1990), pp. 79-81. (Cited in Faludi, 1991, p. 91.)

Wadsworth, A. J. (1989). The uses and effects of mass communication during childhood. In J. Nussbaum (Ed.), *Life-span communication* (pp. 93-116). Hillsdale, NJ: Lawrence Erlbaum.

Warshaw, R. (1991, May 5). Ugly truths of date rape elude the screen. *New York Times,* pp. H17, H22.

Women in media say careers hit "glass ceiling." (1988, March 2). *Easton Express,* p. A9.

Women on TV: The picture will need some tuning, study says. (1990, October 20). *Charlotte Observer,* pp. B1, B2.

Wood, J. T. (1993c). *Who cares: Women, care, and culture.* Carbondale, IL: Sounthern Illinois University Press.

Woodman, S. (1991, May). How super are heros? *Health,* pp. 40, 49, 82.

Chapter 9

Men on Rape. *Tim Beneke explains how the widespread threat of rape affects the lives of women. He also mentions some ways in which men try to blame the women they raped for the rape. Beneke, a writer in the San Francisco Bay Area, is the author of Men on Rape, (New York: NY: St. Martin's Press, 1982). His book is an important contribution for insight into the conditions that women endure, often unconsciously, and the reflections of one man in a case study explaining his outlook on the women he works with.*

Chapter 9 *Tim Beneke,* Men on Rape

Rape may be America's fastest growing violent crime; no one can be certain because it is not clear whether more rapes are being committed or reported. It *is* clear that violence against women is widespread and fundamentally alters the meaning of life for women; that sexual violence is encouraged in a variety of ways in American culture; and that women are often blamed for rape. Consider some statistics:

- In a random sample of 930 women, sociologist Diana Russell found that 44 percent had survived either rape or attempted rape. Rape was defined as sexual intercourse physically forced upon the woman, or coerced by threat of bodily harm, or forced upon the woman when she was helpless (asleep, for example). The survey included rape and attempted rape in marriage in its calculations (Personal communication).
- In a September 1980 survey conducted by *Cosmopolitan* magazine to which over 106,000 women anonymously responded, 24 percent had been raped at least once. Of these, 51 percent had been raped by friends, 37 percent by strangers, 18 percent by relatives, and 3 percent by husbands. Ten (10) percent of the women in the survey had been victims of incest. Seventy-five (75) percent of the women had been "bullied

into making love." Writer Linda Wolfe, who reported on the survey, wrote in reference to such bullying: "Though such harassment stops short of rape, readers reported that it was nearly as distressing."

- An estimated 2-3 percent of all men who rape outside of marriage go to prison for their crimes.[1]
- The F.B.I. estimates that if current trends continue, one woman in four will be sexually assaulted in her lifetime.[2]
- An estimated 1.8 million women are battered by their spouses each year.[3] In extensive interviews with 430 battered women, clinical psychologist Lenore Walker, author of *The Battered Woman*, found that 59.9 percent had also been raped (defined as above) by their spouses. Given the difficulties many women had in admitting they had been raped, Walker estimates the figure may well be as high as 80 or 85 percent. (Personal communication.) If 59.9 percent of the 1.8 million women battered each year are also raped, then a million women may be raped in marriage each year. And a significant number are raped in marriage without being battered.
- Between one in two and one in ten of all rapes are reported to the police.[4]
- Between 300,000 and 500,000 women are raped each year outside of marriage.[5]

What is often missed when people contemplate statistics on rape is the effect of the *threat* of sexual violence on women. I have asked women repeatedly, "How would your life be different if rape were suddenly to end? (Men may learn a lot by asking this question of women to whom they are close.) The threat of rape is an assault upon the meaning of the world; it alters the feel of the human condition. Surely any attempt to comprehend the lives of women that fails to take issues of violence against women into account is misguided.

Through talking to women, I learned: *The threat of rape alters the meaning and feel of the night.* Observe how your body feels, how the night feels, when you're in fear. The constriction in your chest, the vigilance in your eyes, the rubber in your legs. What do the stars look like? How does the moon present itself? What is the difference between walking late at night in the dangerous part of a city and walking late at night in the country, or safe suburbs? When I try to imagine what the threat of rape must do to the night, I think of the stalked, adrenalated feeling I get walking late at night in parts of certain American cities. Only, I remind myself, it is a fear different from any I have known, a fear of being raped.

It is night half the time. If the threat of rape alters the meaning of the night, it must alter the meaning and pace of the day, one's relation to the passing and organization of time itself. For some women, the threat of rape at night turns their cars into armored tanks, their solitude into isolation. And what must the space inside a car or apartment feel like if the space outside is menacing?

I was running late one night with a close woman friend through a path in the woods on the outskirts of a small university town. We had run several miles and were feeling a warm, energized serenity.

"How would you feel if you were alone?" I asked.

"Terrified!" she said instantly.

"Terrified that there might be a man out there?" I asked, pointing to the surrounding moonlit forest, which had suddenly been transformed into a source of terror.

"Yes."

Another woman said, "I know what I can't do and I've completely internalized what I can't do. I've built a viable life that basically involves never leaving my apartment at night unless I'm directly going some place to meet somebody. It's unconsciously built into what it occurs to women to do." When one is raised without freedom, one may not recognize its absence.

The threat of rape alters the meaning and feel of nature. Everyone has felt the psychic nurturance of nature. Many women are being deprived of that nurturance, especially in wooded areas near cities. They are deprived either because they cannot experience nature in solitude because of threat, or because, when they do choose solitude in nature, they must cope with a certain subtle but nettlesome fear.

Women need more money because of rape and the threat of rape makes it harder for women to earn money. It's simple: if you don't feel safe walking at night, or riding public transportation, you need a car. And it is less practicable to live in cheaper, less secure, and thus more dangerous neighborhoods, if the ordinary threat of violence that men experience, being mugged, say, is compounded by the threat of rape. By limiting mobility at night, the threat of rape limits where and when one is able to work, thus making it more difficult to earn money. An obvious bind: women need more money because of rape, and have fewer job opportunities because of it.

The threat of rape makes women more dependent on men (or other women). One woman said: "If there were no rape I wouldn't have to play games with men for their protection." The threat of rape falsifies, mystifies, and confuses relations between men and women. If there were no rape, women would simply not need men as much, wouldn't need them to go places with at night, to feel safe in their homes, for protection in nature.

The threat of rape makes solitude less possible for women. Solitude, drawing strength from being alone, is difficult if being alone means being afraid. To be afraid is to be in need, to experience a lack; the threat of rape creates a lack. Solitude requires relaxation; if you're afraid, you can't relax.

The threat of rape inhibits a woman's expressiveness. "If there were not rape," said one woman, "I could dress the way I wanted and walk the way I wanted and not feel self-conscious about the responses of men. I could be friendly to people. I wouldn't have to wish I was ugly. I wouldn't have to make myself small when I got on the bus. I wouldn't have to respond to verbal abuse from men by remaining silent. I could respond in kind."

If a woman's basic expressiveness is inhibited, her sexuality, creativity, and delight in life must surely be deminished.

The threat of rape inhibits the freedom of the eye. I know a married couple who live in Manhattan. They are both artists, both acutely sensitive and responsive to the visual world. When they walk separately in the city, he has more freedom to look than she does. She must control her eye movements lest they inadvertently meet the glare of some importunate man. What, who, and how she sees are restricted by the threat of rape.

The following exercise is recommended for men.

Walk down a city street. Pay a lot of attention to your clothing; make sure your pants are zipped, shirt tucked in, buttons done. Look straight ahead. Every time a man walks past you, avert your eyes and make your face expressionless. Most women learn to go through this act each time we leave our houses. It's a way to avoid at least some of the encounters we've all had with strange men who decided we looked available.[6]

To relate aesthetically to the visual world involves a certain playfulness, spirit of spontaneous exploration. The tense vigilance that accompanies fear inhibits that spontaneity. The world is no longer yours to look at when you're afraid.

I am aware that all culture is, in part, restriction, that there are places in America where hardly anyone is safe (though men are safer than women virtually everywhere), that there are many ways to enjoy life, that some women may not be so restricted, that there exist havens, whether psychic, geographical, economic, or class. But they are *havens*, and as such, defined by threat.

Above all, I trust my experience: no woman could have lived the life I've lived the last few years. If suddenly I were restricted by the threat of rape, I would feel a deep, inexorable depression. And it's not just rape; it's harassment, battery, Peeping Toms, anonymous phone calls, exhibitionism, intrusive stares, fondlings--all contributing to an atmosphere of intimidation in women's lives. And I have only scratched the surface; it would take many carefully crafted short stories to begin to express what I have only hinted at in the last few pages. I have not even touched upon what it might mean for a woman to be sexually assaulted. Only women can speak to that. Nor have I suggested how the threat of rape affects marriage.

Rape and the threat of rape pervades the lives of women, as reflected in some popular images of our culture.

"She Asked for It"--Blaming the Victim[7]

Many things may be happening when a man blames a woman for rape.

First, in all cases where a woman is said to have asked for it, her appearance and behavior are taken as a form of speech. "Actions speak louder than words" is a widely held belief; the woman's actions--her appearance may be taken as action--are given greater emphasis than her words; an interpretation alien to the woman's intentions is given to her actions. A logical extension of "she asked for it" is the idea that she wanted what happened to happen; if she wanted it to happen, she *deserved* for it to happen. Therefore, the man is not to be blamed. "She asked for it" can mean either that she was consenting to have sex and was not really raped, or that she was in fact raped but somehow she really deserved it. "If you ask for it, you deserve it," is a widely held notion. If I ask you to beat me up and you beat me up, I still don't deserve to be beaten up. So even if the notion that women asked to be raped had some basis in reality, which it doesn't, on its own terms it makes no sense.

Second, a mentality exists that says: a woman who assumes freedoms normally restricted to a man (like going out alone at night) and is raped is doing the same thing as a woman who goes out in the rain without an umbrella and catches a cold. Both are considered responsible for what happens to them. That men will rape is taken to be a legitimized given, part of nature, like rain or snow. The view reflects a massive abdication of responsibility for rape on the part of men. It is so much easier to think of rape as natural than to acknowledge one's part in it. So long as rape is regarded as natural, women will be blamed for rape.

A third point. The view that it is natural for men to rape is closely connected to the view of women as commodities. If a woman's body is regarded as a valued commodity by men, then of course, if you leave a valued commodity where it can be taken, it's just human nature for men to take it. If you left your stereo out on the sidewalk, you'd be asking for it to get stolen. Someone will just take it. (And how often men speak of rape as "going out and *taking* it.") If a woman walks the streets at night, she's leaving a valued commodity, her body, where it can be taken. So long as women are regarded as commodities, they will be blamed for rape.

Which brings us to a fourth point. "She asked for it" is inseparable from a more general "psychology of the dupe." If I use bad judgment and fail to read the small print in a contract and later get taken advantage of, "screwed" (or "fucked over") then I deserve what I get; bad judgment makes me liable. Analogously, if a woman trusts a man and goes to his apartment, or accepts a ride hitchhiking, or goes out on a date and is raped, she's a dupe and deserves what she gets. "He didn't *really* rape her" goes the mentality-- "he merely took advantage of her." And in America it's okay for people to take advantage of each other, even expected and praised. In fact, you're considered dumb and foolish if you don't take advantage of other people's bad judgment. And so, again, by treating them as dupes, rape will be blamed on women.

Fifth, if a woman who is raped is judged attractive by men, and particularly if she dresses to look attractive, then the mentality exists that she attacked him with her weapon so, of course, he counter-attacked with his. The preview to a popular movie states: "She was the victim of her own *provocative beauty*." Provocation: "There is a line which, if crossed, will *set me off* and I will lose control and no longer be responsible for my behavior. If you punch me in the nose then, of course, I will not be responsible for what happens: you will have provoked a fight. If you dress, talk, move, or act a certain way, you will have provoked me to rape. If your appearance *stuns* me, *strikes* me, *ravishes* me, *knocks me out*, etc., then I will not be held responsible for what happens; you will have asked for it." The notion that sexual feeling makes one helpless is part of a cultural abdication of responsibility for sexuality. So long as a woman's appearance is viewed as a weapon and sexual feeling is believed to make one helpless, women will be blamed for rape.

Sixth, I have suggested that men sometimes become obsessed with images of women, that images become a substitute for sexual feeling, that sexual feeling becomes externalized and out of control and is given an undifferentiated identity in the appearance of women's bodies. It is a process of projection in which one blurs one's own desire with her imagined, projected desire. If a woman's attractiveness is taken to signify one's own lust and a woman's lust, then when an "attractive" woman is raped, some men may think she wanted sex. Since they perceive their own lust in part projected onto the woman, they disbelieve women who've been raped. So long as men project their own sexual desires onto women, they will blame women for rape.

And seventh, what are we to make of the contention that women in dating situations say "no" initially to sexual overtures from men as a kind of pose, only to give in later, thus revealing their true intentions? And that men are thus confused and incredulous when women are raped because in their sexual experience women can't be believed? I doubt that this has much to do with men's perceptions of rape. I don't know to what extent women actually "say no and mean yes"; certainly it is a common theme in male folklore. I have spoken to a couple of women who went through periods when they wanted to be sexual but were afraid to be, and often rebuffed initial sexual advances only to give in later. One point is clear: the ambivalence women may feel about having sex is closely tied to the inability of men to fully accept them as sexual beings. Women have been traditionally punished for being openly and freely sexual; men are praised for it. And if many men think of sex as achievement of possession of a valued commodity, or aggressive degradation, then women have every reason to feel and act ambivalent.

These themes are illustrated in an interview I conducted with a 23-year-old man who grew up in Pittsburgh and works as a file clerk in the financial district of San Francisco. Here's what he said:

"Where I work it's probably no different from any other major city in the U.S. The women dress up in high heels, and they wear a lot of makeup, and they just look really *hot* and really sexy, and how can somebody who has a healthy sex drive not feel lust for them when you see them? I feel lust for them, but I don't think I could find it in me to overpower someone and rape them. But I definitely get the feeling that I'd like to rape a girl. I don't know if the actual act of rape would be satisfying, but the *feeling* is satisfying.

"These women look so good, and they kiss ass of the men in the three-piece suits who are *big* in the corporation, and most of them relate to me like "Who are *you*? Who are *you* to even *look* at?" They're snobby and they condescend to me, and I resent it. It would take me a lot longer to get to first base than it would somebody with a three-piece suit who had money. And to me a lot of the men they go out with are superficial assholes who have no real feelings or substance, and are just trying to get ahead and make a lot of money. Another thing that makes me resent these women is thinking "How could she want to hang out with somebody like that? What does that make her?"

"I'm a file clerk, which makes me feel like a nebbish, a nerd, like I'm not making it, I'm a failure. But I don't really believe I'm a failure because I know it's just a phase, and I'm just doing it for the money, just to make it through this phase. I catch myself feeling like a failure, but I realize that's ridiculous."

What exactly do you go through when you see these sexy, unavailable women?

"Let's say I see a woman and she looks really pretty and really clean and sexy, and she's giving off very feminine, sexy vibes. I think, 'Wow, I would love to make love to her,' but I know she's not really interested. It's a tease. A lot of times a woman knows that she's looking really good and she'll use that and flaunt it, and it makes me feel like she's laughing at me and I feel *degraded*.

"I also feel dehumanized because when I'm being teased I just turn off, I cease to be human. Because if I go with my human emotions I'm going to want to put my arms around her and kiss her, and to do that would be unacceptable. I don't like the feeling that I'm supposed to stand there and take it, and not be able to hug her or kiss her; so I just turn off my emotions. It's a feeling of humiliation, because the woman has forced me to turn off my feelings and react in a way that I really don't want to.

"If I were actually desperate enough to rape somebody, it would be from wanting the person, but it would be a very spiteful thing, just being able to say, 'I have power over you and I can do anything I want with you,' because really I feel that *they* have power over *me* just by their presence. Just the fact that they can come up to me and just melt me and make me feel like a dummy makes me want revenge. They have power over me so I want power over them...."

"Society says that you have to have a lot of sex with a lot of different women to be a real man. Well, what happens if you don't? Then what are you? Are you half a man? Are you still a boy? It's ridiculous. You see a whiskey ad with a guy and two women on his arm. The implication is that real men don't have any trouble getting women."

How does it make you feel toward women to see all these sexy women in media and advertising using their looks to try to get you to buy something?

"It makes me hate them. As a man you're taught that men are more powerful than women, and that men always have the upper hand, and that is it's a man's society; but then you see all these women and it makes you think "Jesus Christ, if we have all the power how come all the beautiful women are telling us what to buy?" And to be honest, it just makes me hate beautiful women because they're using their power over me. I realize they're being used themselves, and they're doing it for money. In *Playboy* you see all these beautiful women who look so sexy and they'll be giving you all these looks like they want to have sex so bad; but then in reality you know that except for a few nymphomaniacs, they're doing it for the money; so I hate them for being used and using their bodies in that way.

"In this society, if you ever sit down and realize how manipulated you really are it makes you pissed off--it makes you want to take control. And you've been manipulated by women, and they're a very easy target because they're out walking along the streets, so you can just grab one and say, "Listen, you're going to do what I want you to do,' and it's an act of revenge against the way you've been manipulated.

"I know a girl who was working down the street by her house, when this guy jumped her and beat her up and raped her, and she was black and blue and had to go to the hospital. That's beyond me. I can't understand how somebody could do that. If I were going to rape a girl, I wouldn't hurt her. I might *restrain* her, but I wouldn't *hurt* her....

"The whole dating game between men and women also makes me feel degraded. I hate being put in the position of having to initiate a relationship. I've been taught that if you're not aggressive with a woman,

133

then you've blown it. She's not going to jump on *you*, so *you've* got to jump on *her*. I've heard all kinds of stories where the woman says, 'No! No! No!' and they end up making great love. I get confused as hell if a woman pushes me away. Does it mean she's trying to be a nice girl and wants to put up a good appearance, or does it mean she doesn't want anything to do with you? You don't know. Probably a lot of men think that women don't feel like real women unless a man tries to force himself on her, unless she brings out the 'real man,' so to speak, and probably too much of it goes on. It goes on in my head that you're complimenting a woman by actually staring at her or by trying to get into her pants. Lately, I'm realizing that when I stare at women lustfully, they often feel more threatened than flattered."

Notes

[1] Such estimates recur in the rape literature. See *Sexual Assault* by Nancy Gager and Cathleen Schurr, Grosset & Dunlap, 1976, or *The Price of Coercive Sexuality* by Clark and Lewis, The Women's Press, 1977.

[2] *Uniform Crime Reports*, 1980.

[3] See *Behind Closed Doors* by Murray J. Strauss and Richard Gelles, Doubleday, 1979.

[4] See Gager and Schurr (above) or virtually any book on the subject.

[5] Again, see Gager and Schurr, or Carol V. Horos, *Rape*, Banbury Books, 1981.

[6] From "Willamette Bridge," in *Body Politics* by Nancy Henley, Prentice-Hall, 1977, p. 144.

[7] I would like to thank George Lakoff for this insight.

Chapter 10

Domestic Violence. This article from Time Magazine in 1993 represents the ultimate gender conflict: a physical battle between a man and a woman that involves serious injury or death to one partner or both. Courts, law officers and community service organizations alike struggle to understand these conflicts and intervene or preside over the individuals caught up in domestic violence in a fair and humane way. Nancy Gibbs helps us understand two big issues in this pursui: the battered woman's syndrome and the clemency movement. With the conclusion of this article, we leave our coverage of gender-related problems and the social symptoms that result. After this, we turn to a process of problem resolution and begin to construct a process to help correct or avoid these difficulties.

Chapter 10 Nancy Gibbs, 'Til Death Do Us Part

The law has always made rooms for killers. Solders kill the nation's enemies, executioners kill its killers, police officers under fire may fire back. Even a murder is measured in degrees, depending on the mind of the criminal and the character of the crime. And sometime this spring, in a triumph of pity over punishment, the law may just find room for Rita Collins.

"They all cried, didn't they? But not me," she starts out, to distinguish herself from her fellow inmates in a Florida prison, who also have stories to tell. "No one will help me. No one will write about me. I don't have a dirty story. I wasn't abused as a child. I was a respectable government employee, employed by the Navy in a high position in Washington."

Her husband John was a military recruiter, a solid man who had a way with words. "He said I was old, fat, crazy and had no friends that were real friends. He said I needed him and he would take care of me." She says his care included threats with a knife, punches, a kick to the stomach that caused a hemorrhage. Navy doctors treated her for injuries to her neck and arm. "He'd slam me up against doors. He gave me black eyes, bruises. Winter and summer, I'd go to work like a Puritan, with long sleeves. Afterward he'd soothe me, and I'd think, He's a good man. What did I do wrong?"

The bravado dissolves, and she starts to cry.

"I was envied by other wives. I felt ashamed because I didn't appreciate him." After each beating came apologies and offerings, gifts, a trip. "It's like blackmail. You think it's going to stop, but it doesn't." Collins never told anyone--not her friends in the church choir, not even a son by her first marriage. "I should have, but it was the humiliation of it all. I didn't want people to think I was crazy." But some of them knew anyway; they had seen the bruises, the black eye behind the dark glasses.

She tried to get out. She filed for divorce, got a restraining order, filed an assault-and-battery charge against him, forced him from the house they had bought with a large chunk of her money when they retired to Florida. But still, she says, he came, night after night, banging on windows and doors, trying to break the locks.

It wasn't her idea to buy a weapon. "The police did all they could, but they had no control. They felt sorry for me. They told me to get a gun." She still doesn't remember firing it. She says she remembers her husband's face, the glassy eyes, a knife in his hands. "To this day, I don't remember pulling the trigger."

The jury couldn't figure it out either. At Collins' first trial, for first-degree murder, her friends, a minister, her doctors, and several experts testified about her character and the violence she had suffered. The prosecution played tapes of her threatening her husband over the phone and portrayed her as a bitter, unstable woman who had bought a gun, lured him to the house, and murdered him out of jealousy and anger over the divorce. That trial ended with a hung jury. At her second, nine men and three women debated just two hours before finding her guilty of the lesser charge, second-degree murder. Collins' appeals were denied, and the parole board last year recommended against clemency. Orlando prosecutor Dorothy Sedgwick is certain that justice was done. "Rita Collins is a classic example of how a woman can decide to kill her husband and use the battered woman's syndrome as a fake defense," she says. "She lured him to his death. He was trying to escape her." Collins says her lawyers got everything: the $125,000 three-bedroom house with a pool, $98,000 in cash. "I've worked since I was 15, and I have nothing," she says. "The Bible says, 'Thou shalt not kill,' and everybody figures if you're in here, you're guilty. But I'm not a criminal. Nobody cares if I die in here, but if I live, I tell you one thing: I'm not going to keep quiet."

If, in the next round of clemency hearings on March 10, Governor Lawton Chiles grants Collins or any other battered woman clemency, Florida will join 26 other states in a national movement to take another look at the cases of abuse victims who kill their abusers. Just before Christmas, Missouri's conservative Republican Governor John Ashcroft commuted the life sentences of two women who claimed they had killed their husbands in self defense. After 20 years of trying, these women have made a Darwinian claim for mercy: Victims of perpetual violence should be forgiven if they turn violent themselves.

More American women--rich and poor alike--are injured by the men in their life than by car accidents, muggings, and rape combined. Advocates and experts liken the effect over time to a slow-acting poison. "Most battered women aren't killing to protect themselves from being killed that very moment," observes Charles Ewing, a law professor at Suny Buffalo. "What they're protecting themselves from is slow but certain destruction, psychologically and physically. There's no place in the law for that."

As the clemency movement grows, it challenges a legal system that does not always distinguish between a crime and a tragedy. What special claims should victims of fate, poverty, violence, addiction be able to make upon the sympathies of juries and the boundaries of the law? In cases of domestic assaults, some women who suffered terrible abuse resorted to terrible means to escape it. Now the juries, and ultimately the society they speak for, have to find some way to express outrage at the brutality that women and children face every day, without accepting murder as a reasonable response to it.

But until America finds a better way to keep people safe in their own homes or offers them some means of surviving if they flee, it will be hard to answer the defendants who ask their judges, "What choice did I really have?"

Home is where the hurt is

Last year the A.M.A., backed by the Surgeon General, declared that violent men constitute a major threat to women's health. The National League of Cities estimates that as many as half of all women will experience violence at some time in their marriage. Between 22 and 35 percent of all visits by females to emergency rooms are for injuries from domestic assaults. Though some studies have found that women are just as likely to start a fight as men, others indicate they are six times as likely to be seriously injured in one. Especially grotesque is the brutality reserved for pregnant women: the March of Dimes has concluded that the battering of women during pregnancy causes more birth defects than all the diseases put together for which children are usually immunized. Anywhere from one-third to as many as half of all female murder victims are killed by their spouses or lovers, compared with 4 percent of male victims.

"Male violence against women is at least as old as the institution of marriage," says clinical psychologist Gus Kaufman Jr., cofounder of Men Stopping Violence, an Atlanta clinic established to help men face their battering problems. So long as a woman was considered her husband's legal property, police and the courts were unable to prevent--and unwilling to punish--domestic assaults. Notes N.Y.U. law professor Holly Maguigan: "We talk about the notion of the rule of thumb, forgetting that it had to do with the restriction on a man's right to use a weapon against his wife: he couldn't use a rod that was thicker than his thumb." In 1874 North Carolina became one of the first states to limit a man's right to beat his wife, but lawmakers noted that unless he beat her nearly to death "it is better to draw the curtain, shut out the public gaze, and leave the parties to forget and forgive."

Out of that old reluctance grew the modern double standard. Until the first wave of legal reform in the 1970s, an aggravated assault against a stranger was a felony, but assaulting a spouse was considered a misdemeanor, which rarely landed the attacker in court, much less in jail. That distinction, which still exists in most states, does not reflect the danger involved: a study by the Boston Bar Association found that the domestic attacks were at least as dangerous as 90 percent of felony assaults. "Police seldom arrest, even when there are injuries serious enough to require hospitalization of the victim," declared the Florida Supreme Court in a 1990 gender-bias study, which also noted the tendency of prosecutors to drop domestic-violence cases.

Police have always hated answering complaints about domestic disputes. Experts acknowledge that such situations are often particularly dangerous, but suspect that there are other reasons for holding back. "This issue pushes buttons, summons up personal emotions, that almost no other issue does for police and judges," says Linda Osmundson, who co-chairs a battered wives' task force for the National Coalition Against Domestic Violence. "Domestic violence is not seen as a crime. A man's home is still his castle. There is a system that really believes that women should be passive in every circumstance." And it persists despite a 20-year effort by advocates to transform attitudes toward domestic violence.

While most of the effort has been directed at helping women survive, and escape, abusive homes, much of the publicity has fallen on those rare cases when women resort to violence themselves. Researcher and author Angela Browne points out that a woman is much more likely to be killed by her partner than to kill him. In 1991, when some 4 million women were beaten and 1,320 murdered in domestic attacks, 622 women killed their husbands or boyfriends. Yet the women have become the lightening rods for debate, since their circumstances, and their response, were most extreme.

What choice did she have?

"There is an appropriate means to deal with one's marital problems -- legal recourse. Not a .357 magnum," argues former Florida prosecutor Bill Catto. "If you choose to use a gun to end a problem, then you must suffer the consequences of your act." Defense lawyers call it legitimate self-protection when a victim of abuse fights back -- even if she shoots her husband in his sleep. Prosecutors call it an act of vengeance, and in the past, juries have usually agreed and sent the killer to jail. Michael Dowd, director of the Pace University Battered Women's Justice Center, has found that the average sentence for a woman who kills her mate is 15 to 20 years: for a man, 2 to 6.

The punishment is not surprising, since many judges insist that evidence of past abuse, even if it went on for years, is not relevant in court unless it occurred around the time of the killing. It is not the dead husband who is on trial, they note, but the wife who pulled the trigger.

"Frankly, I feel changing the law would be authorizing preventive murder," argued Los Angeles Superior Court Judge Lillian Stevens in the *Los Angeles Times*. "The only thing that really matters is, was there an immediate danger? There can't be an old grievance." And even if a woman is allowed to testify about past violence, the jury may still condemn her response to it. If he was really so savage, the prosecutor typically asks, why didn't she leave, seek shelter, call the police, file a complaint?

"The question presumes she has good options," says Julie Blackman, a New Jersey-based social psychologist who has testified as an expert witness in abuse and murder cases. "Sometimes, they don't leave because they have young children and no other way to support them, or because they grow up in cultures that are so immersed in violence that they don't figure there's any place better to go, or because they can't get apartments." The shelter facilities around the country are uniformly inadequate: New York has about 1,300 beds for a state with 18 million people. In 1990 the Baltimore zoo spent twice as much money to care for animals as the state of Maryland spent on shelters for victims of domestic violence.

Last July, even as reports of violence continued to multiply, the National Domestic Violence Hotline was disconnected. The 800 number had received as many as

10,000 calls a month from across the country. Now, says Mary Ann Bohrer, founder of the New York City-based Council for Safe Families, "There is no number, no national resource, for people seeking information about domestic violence."

The other reason women don't flee is because, ironically, they are afraid for their life. Law-enforcement experts agree that running away greatly increases danger a woman faces. Angered at the loss of power and control, violent men often try to track down their wives and threaten them, or their children, if they don't come home. James Cox III, an unemployed dishwasher in Jacksonville, Florida, was determined to find his ex-girlfriend, despite a court order to stay away from her. Two weeks ago, he forced her mother at gunpoint to tell him the location of the battered women's shelter where her daughter had fled, and stormed the building, firing a shotgun. Police shot him dead. "This case illustrates the extent to which men go to pursue their victims," said executive director Rita DeYoung. "It creates a catch-22 for all battered women. Some will choose to return to their abusers, thinking they can control their behavior."

"After the law turns you away, society closes its doors on you, and you find yourself trapped in a life with someone capable of homicide. What choice in the end was I given?," asks Shalanda Burt, 21, who is serving 17 years for shooting her boyfriend James Fairley two years ago in Bradenton, Florida. She was three months pregnant at the time. A week after she delivered their first baby, James raped her and ripped her stitches. Several times she tried to leave or get help. "I would have a bloody mouth and a swollen face. All the police would do is give me a card with a deputy's name on it and tell me it was a 'lovers' quarrel. The battered women's shelter was full. All they could offer was a phone counselor."

Two weeks before the shooting, the police arrested them both: him for aggravated assault because she was pregnant, her for assault with a deadly missile and violently resisting arrest. She had thrown a bottle at his truck. Her bail was $10,000; his was $3,000. He was back home before she was, so she sent the baby to stay with relatives while she tried to raise bail. The end came on a Christmas weekend. After a particularly vicious beating, he followed her to her aunt's house. When he came at her again, she shot him. "They say I'm a violent person, but I'm not. I didn't want revenge. I just wanted out." Facing 25 years, she was told by a female public defender to take a plea bargain and 17 years. "I wanted to fight. But she said I'd get life or the electric chair. I was in a no-win situation."

It is hard for juries to understand why women like Burt do not turn to the courts for orders of protection. But these are a makeshift shield at best, often violated and hard to enforce. Olympic skier Patricia Kastle had a restraining order when her former husband shot her. Lisa Bianco in Indiana remained terrified of her husband even after he was sent to jail for eight years. When prison official granted Alan Matheney an eight-hour pass in March 1989, he drove directly to Bianco's home, broke in and beat her to death with the butt of a shotgun. Last March, Shirley Lowery, a grandmother of 11, was stabbed 19 times with a butcher knife by her former boyfriend in the hallway of the courthouse where she had gone to get an order of protection.

The mind of the victim

Defense lawyers have a hard time explaining to juries the shame, isolation and emotional dependency that bind victims to their abusers. Many women are too proud to admit to their family or friends that their marriage is not working and blame themselves

139

for its failure even as they cling to the faith that their violent lover will change. "People confuse the woman's love for the man with love of abuse," says Pace's Dowd. "It's not the same thing. Which of us hasn't been involved in a romantic relationship where people say this is no good for you?"

It was Denver psychologist Lenore Walker, writing in 1984, who coined the term battered-woman syndrome to explain the behavior of abuse victims. Her study discussed the cycle of violence in battering households: first a period of growing tension: then a violent explosion, often unleashed by drugs or alcohol: and finally a stage of remorse and kindness. A violent man, she argues, typically acts out of a powerful need for control -- physical, emotional, even financial. He may keep his wife under close surveillance, isolating her from family and friends, forbidding her to work or calling constantly to check on her whereabouts. Woven into the scrutiny are insults and threats that in the end can destroy a woman's confidence and leave her feeling trapped between her fear of staying in a violent home -- and her fear of fleeing it.

Many lawyers say it is virtually impossible to defend a battered woman without some expert testimony about the effect of that syndrome over time. Such testimony allows attorneys to stretch the rules governing self-defense, which were designed to deal with two men caught in a bar fight, not a woman caught in a violent relationship with a stronger man.

In a traditional case of self-defense, a jury is presented a "snapshot" of a crime: the mugger threatens a subway rider with a knife; the rider pulls a gun and shoots his attacker. It is up to the jurors to decide whether the danger was real and immediate or whether the response was reasonable. A woman who shoots her husband while he lunges at her with a knife should have little trouble claiming that she acted in self-defense. Yet lawyers still find jurors to be very uncomfortable with female violence under any circumstances, especially violence directed at a man she may have lived with for years.

Given that bias, it is even harder for a lawyer to call it self-defense when a woman shoots a sleeping husband. The danger was hardly immediate, prosecutors argue, nor was the lethal response reasonable. Evidence about battered-woman syndrome may be the only way to persuade a jury to identity with a killer. "Battered women are extraordinarily sensitive to cues of danger, and that's how they survive," says Walker. "That's is why many battered women kill, not during what looks like the middle of the fight, but when the man is more vulnerable or the violence is just beginning."

A classic self-defense plea also demands a fair fight. A person who is punched can punch back, but if he shoots, he runs the risk of being charged with murder or manslaughter. This leaves women and children, who are almost always smaller and weaker than their attackers, in a bind. They often see no way to escape an assault without using a weapon and the element of surprise -- arguing, in essence, that their best hope of self-defense was a pre-emptive strike. "Morally and legally a woman should not be expected to wait until his hands are around her neck," argues Los Angeles defense attorney Leslie Abramson. "Say a husband says, 'When I get up tomorrow morning, I'm going to beat the living daylights out of you,'" says Joshua Dressler, a law professor at Wayne State University who specializes in criminal procedures. "If you use the word imminent, the woman would have to wait until the next morning and, just as he's about to kill her, then use self-defense."

That argument, prosecutors retort, is an invitation to anarchy. If a woman has survived past beatings, what persuaded her that this time was different, that she had no choice but to kill or be killed? The real catalyst, they suggest, was not her fear but her fury. Prosecutors often turn a woman's history of abuse into a motive for murder. "What some clemency advocates are really saying is that the s.o.b. deserved to die and why should she be punished for what she did," argues Dressler. Unless the killing came in the midst of a violent attack, it amounts to a personal death-penalty sentence. "I find it very hard to say that killing the most rotten human being in the world when he's not currently threatening the individual is the right thing to do."

Those who oppose changes in the laws points out that many domestic disputes are much more complicated than the clemency movement would suggest. "We've got to stop perpetuating the myth that men are all vicious and that women are all Snow White," says Sonny Burmeister, a divorced father of three children who, president of the Georgia Council for Children's Rights in Marietta, lobbies for equal treatment of men involved in custody battles. He recently sheltered a husband whose wife had pulled a gun on him. When police were called, their response was "So?" Says Burmeister: "We perpetuate this macho, chauvinistic, paternalistic attitude for men. We are taught to be protective of the weaker sex. We encourage women to report domestic violence. We believe men are guilty. But women are just as guilty."

He charges that feminists are trying to write a customized set of laws. "If Mom gets mad and shoots Dad, we call it PMS and point out that he hit her six months ago," he complains. "If Dad gets mad and shoots Mom, we call it domestic violence and charge him with murder. We paint men as violent and we paint women as victims, removing them from the social and legal consequences of their actions. I don't care how oppressed a woman is; should we condone premeditated murder?"

Only twenty-two states have passed laws permitting expert testimony on battered-woman syndrome and spousal violence. In most cases it remains a matter of judicial discretion. One Pennsylvania judge ruled that testimony presented by a prosecutor showed that the defendant had not been beaten badly enough to qualify as a battered woman and therefore could not have that standard applied to her case. President Bush signed legislation in October urging states to accept expert testimony in criminal cases involving battered women. The law calls for development of training materials to assist defendants and their attorneys in using such testimony in appropriate cases.

Judge Lillian Stevens instructed the jury on the rules governing self-defense at the 1983 trial of Brenda Clubine, who claimed that she killed her police-informant husband because he was going to kill her. Clubine says that during an 11-year relationship, she was kicked, punched, stabbed, had the skin on one side of her face torn off, a lung pierced, ribs broken. She had a judge's order protecting her and had pressed charges to have her husband arrested for felony battery. But six weeks later, she agreed to meet him in a motel, where Clubine alleges that she felt her life was in danger and hit him over the head with a wine bottle, causing a fatal brain hemorrhage. "I didn't mean to kill him," she says. "He had hit me several times. Something inside me snapped; I grabbed the bottle and swung." The jury found Clubine guilty of second-degree manslaughter, and Judge Stevens sentenced her to 15 years to life. She says Clubine drugged her husband into lethargy before fatally hitting him. "It seemed to me (the beatings) were some time ago,"

Stevens told the *Los Angeles Times*. Furthermore, she added, "there was evidence that a lot of it was mutual."

It is interesting that within the legal community there are eloquent opponents of battered-woman syndrome -- on feminist grounds -- who dislike the label's implication that all battered women are helpless victims of some shared mental disability that prevents them from acting rationally. Social liberals, says N.Y.U.'s Marguigan, typically explain male violence in terms of social or economic pressures. Female violence, on the other hand, is examined in psychological terms. "They look to what's wrong with her and reinforce a notion that women who use violence are, per se, unreasonable, that something must be wrong with her because she's not acting like a good woman, in the way that women are socialized to behave."

Researcher Charles Ewing compared a group of 100 battered women who had killed their partners with 100 battered women who hadn't taken that fatal step. Women who resorted to violence were usually those who were most isolated, socially and economically; they had been the most badly beaten, their children had been abused, and their husbands were drug or alcohol abusers. That is, the common bond was circumstantial, not psychological. "They're not pathological," says social psychologist Blackman. "They don't have personality disorders. They're just beat up worse."

Women who have endured years of beatings without fighting back may reach the breaking point once the abuse spreads to others they love. Arlene Caris is serving a 25-year sentence in New York for killing her husband. He had tormented her for years, both physically and psychologically. Then she reportedly learned that he was sexually abusing her granddaughter. On the night she finally decided to leave him, he came at her in a rage. She took a rifle, shot him, wrapped him in bedsheets and then hid the body in the attic for five months.

Offering such women clemency, the advocates note, is not precisely the same as amnesty; the punishment is reduced, though the act is not excused. Clemency may be most appropriate in cases where all the circumstances of the crime were not heard in court. The higher courts have certainly sent the message that justice is not uniform in domestic-violence cases. One study found that 40 percent of women who appeal their murder convictions get the sentence thrown out, compared with an 8.5 percent reversal rate for homicides as a whole. "I've worked on cases involving battered women who have talked only briefly to their lawyers in the courtroom for 15 or 20 minutes and then they take a plea and do 15 to life," recalls Blackman. "I see women who are Hispanic and don't speak English well, or women who are very quickly moved through the system, who take pleas and do substantial chunks of time, often without getting any real attention paid to the circumstances of their case."

The first mass release in the U.S. came at Christmas in 1990, when Ohio Governor Richard Celeste commuted the sentences of 27 battered women serving time for killing or assaulting male companions. His initiative was born of longheld convictions. As a legislator in the early '70s, he and his wife helped open a women's center in Cleveland and held hearings on domestic violence. When he became lieutenant governor in 1974 and moved to Columbus, he and his wife rented out their home in Cleveland as emergency shelter for battered women. He and the parole board reviewed 107 cases, looking at evidence of past abuse, criminal record, adjustment to prison life and participation in postrelease programs before granting the clemencies. "The system of justice had not really worked in their cases," he says. "They had not had the opportunity for a fair trail because vitally important evidence affecting their circumstances and the terrible things done to them was not presented to the jury."

The impending reviews in other states have caused some prosecutors and judges to sound an alarm. They are worried that Governors' second-guessing the courts undermines the judicial system and invites manipulation by prisoners. "Anybody in the penitentiary, if they see a possible out, will be claiming. 'Oh, I was a battered woman,'" says Dallas assistant district attorney Norman Kinne. "They can't take every female who says she's a battered woman and say, 'Oh, we're sorry, we'll let you out.' If they're going to do it right, it's an exhaustive study."

Clemency critics point to one woman released in Maryland who soon afterward boasted about having committed the crime. Especially controversial are women who have been granted clemency for crimes that were undeniably premeditated. Delia Alaniz hired a contract killer to pretend to rob her home and murder her husband in the process. He had beaten her and their children for years, sexually abusing their 14-year-old daughter. The prosecutor from Skagit County, Washington, was sufficiently impressed by the evidence of abuse that he reduced the charge from first-degree murder and life imprisonment to second-degree manslaughter with a sentence of 10 to 14 years. In October 1989, Governor Booth Gardner granted her clemency, "Delia was driven to extremes. The situation was desperate, and she viewed it that way," says Skagit County public defender Robert Jones. "The harm to those kids having a mom in prison was too much considering the suffering they went through. As a state, we don't condone what she did, but we understand and have compassion."

The alternatives to murder

There is always a risk that the debate over clemency will continue to obscure the missing debate over violence. "I grew up in a society that really tolerated a lot of injustice when it came to women," says Pace University's Dowd. "It was ingrained as a part of society. This isn't a woman's issue. It's a human-rights issue. Men should have as much to offer fighting sexism as they do racism because the reality is that it's our hands that strike the blows." The best way to keep battered women out of jail is to keep them from being battered in the first place.

In a sense, a society's priorities can be measured by whom it punishes. A survey of the population of a typical prison suggests that violent husbands and fathers are still not viewed as criminals. In New York State about half the inmates are drug offenders, the result of a decade-long War on Drugs that demanded mandatory sentences. A War on Violence would send the same message, that society genuinely abhors parents who beat children and spouses who batter each other, and is willing to punish the behavior rather than dismiss it.

Minnesota serves as a model for other states. In 1981 Duluth was the first U.S. city to institute mandatory arrests in domestic disputes. Since then about half the states have done the same, which means that even if a victim does not wish to press charges, the police are obliged to make an arrest if they see evidence of abuse. Advocates in some Minnesota jurisdictions track cases from the first call to the police through prosecution and sentencing, to try to spot where the system is failing. Prosecutors are increasingly reluctant to plea-bargain assault down to disorderly conduct. They have also found it helpful to use the arresting officer as complainant, so that their case does not depend on a frightened victim's testifying.

Better training of police officers, judges, emergency-room personnel, and other professionals is having an impact in many cities. "We used to train police to be counselors in domestic-abuse cases," says Osmundson. "No longer. We teach them to go make arrests." In Jacksonville, Florida, new procedures helped raise the arrest rate from 25 to 40 percent. "Arrests send a message to the woman that help is available and to men that abuse is not accepted," says shelter executive director DeYoung, who also serves as president of the Florida Coalition Against Domestic Violence. "Children, too, see that it's not accepted and are more likely to grow up not accepting abuse in the home."

Since 1990 at least 28 states have passed "stalking laws" that make it a crime to threaten, follow or harass someone. Congress this month may take up the Violence Against Women bill, which would increase penalties for federal sex crimes, provide $300 million to police, prosecutors, and courts to combat violent crimes against women, and reinforce state domestic-violence laws. Most women, of course, are not looking to put their partners in jail; they just want the violence to stop.

A Minneapolis project was founded in 1979 at the prompting of women in shelters who said they wanted to go back to their partners if they would stop battering. Counselors have found that men resort to violence because they want to control their partners, and they know they can get away with it -- unlike in other relationships. "A lot of people experience low impulse control, fear of abandonment, alcohol and drug addiction, all the characteristics of a batterer," says Ellen Pence, training coordinator for the Domestic Abuse Intervention Project in Duluth. "However, the same guy is not beating up his boss."

Most men come to the program either by order of the courts or as a condition set by their partners. The counselors start with the assumption that battering is learned behavior. Eighty percent of the participants grew up in a home where they saw or were victims of physical, sexual or other abuse. Once imprinted with that model, they must be taught to recognize warning signs and redirect their anger. "We don't say, 'Never get angry,'" says Carol Arthur, the Minneapolis project's executive director. "Anger is a normal, healthy emotion. What we work with is a way to express it." Men describe to the group their most violent incident. One man told about throwing food in his wife's face at dinner and then beating her to the floor -- only to turn and see his two small children huddled terrified under the table. Arthur remembers his self-assessment at that moment: "My God, what must they be thinking about me? I didn't want to be like that."

If the police and the courts crack down on abusers, and programs exist to help change violent behavior, victims will be less likely to take--and less justified in taking--the law into their own hands. And once the cycle of violence winds down in this generation, it is less likely to poison the next. That would be a family value worth fighting for.

Chapter 11

Ecological Solutions. *In the traditional sense, conflicts are approached competitively; someone will win, someone will lose. Because of the potential seriousness of gender-based conflict, we want to develop a sound alternative to competitive battle. This process for solving gender-based dilemmas begins by shifting our attention to environmental variables for a more in-depth analysis of both the source of our problems and the site of resolution for our problems. This chapter will present a model to develop an ideology drawn from sociological microstructural theory paired with a strategy from psychology known as attribution theory. The two are compatible when, in combination, they construct a pragmatic approach that considers adults' relative position of influence over elements in their lives and applies a specific psychological component to common areas of conflict. At first, our alternative ideology is basically preventative. We will consider troublesome everyday struggles that are gender based. The reader is encouraged to test the following suggestions in hypothetical situations or simply use personal reflection to determine their appropriateness to each individual real-life dilemma.*

Chapter 11 *Barbara Collamer,* *The Ecological Paradigm*

Nature versus nurture

A long-standing controversy swirls around the question about the source of human behavior. Most often this argument takes the form of whether behavior can or should be attributed to forces of *nature* (genetic, biological, inherited or internalized psychological factors) or to the conditions of *nurture* (situational, experiential, or environmental factors). In many areas of study the issue has more or less been neutralized by the assumption that it is an interaction or combination of the two that explains the average person's actions. For us, applying the nature and nurture distinction to gender issues is more effective when viewed as two *belief systems* that, when one or the other is acted upon, leads a person to act in predictably different ways. When a person believes that gendered behavior is an innate or fixed entity (i.e., the nature of the individual) they will interact with others and direct their lives differently than a person who believes that gendered behavior is prompted by experiential factors (i.e., the nurture of the individual). The actions launched by each belief system can mean the difference between an indivdualist perspective or gender relations perspective, a passive or active approach, even an ineffective or effective conflict resolution. Up to this point we have a relatively comprehensive overview of the individualist (nature) perspective. This perspective has been with us longer as a cultural artifact and is more securely embedded in our general orientation toward each other and ourselves. We need now to more thoroughly explore the nurture perspective, especially as it applies to solving problems that occur in gendered interactions. We will determine how these interactions can be situated in our ecological world and construct a plan to interact with the ecology of gender.

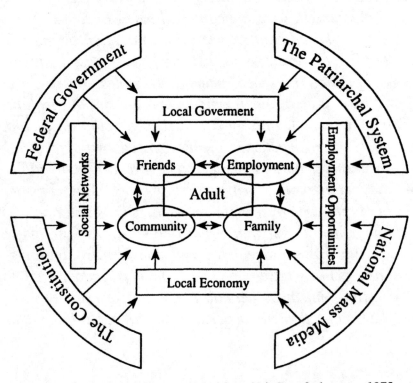

THE ECOLOGICAL SYSTEM. Adapted from Urie Bronfenbrenner, 1975, 1982, 1986.

The Ecological paradigm

The ecology of gender is described in terms of levels of influence. A diagram adapted from the work of Urie Bronfenbrenner illustrates the position of three distinct levels with arrows defining the direction of influence.[1] The individual is located at the very center of this model. The outer level consists of cultural institutions and governance at the most removed position from the individual. The direction of influence is shown as moving from the institutional level toward the individual but the arrows indicate that the individual does not have influence over the institutions themselves. (The common perception that the individual has influence over cultural and political institutions by voting and the democratic process is not addressed at this point.) This outer-most level is referred to as the macrosystem and for our ideological purpose is depicted as the most inaccessible of the three systems. The macrosystem is general, socially and culturally, and our interaction with it is often impersonal and indirect. The next level is the intermediate location called the mesosystem. This level combines the extended macrosystem above in the diagram and the microsystem located below. The mesosystem may include the individual's regional politics, ethnic membership, parental employment, parental friendship network, and other influences that are closer to the individual than the macrosystem. Lastly, the inner most circle of influence is the microsystem. It is within this system that the individual has the greatest amount of influence over their environment and from this system comes the strongest influence over the individual. This interaction is illustrated by the overlap of the center box (adult) and the four elements of the microsystem depicted at each corner (family, employment, friends, and community). From a contextual framework, this level is a powerful source of expectations directing individual behavior and also the most likely context for adaptable behavioral change. Using this model of ecological influence on behavior we can imagine our gender enactment occurring within the context of the microsystem. At these intimate levels we can reconstruct and redefine our gender performance according to contextual necessity. That is, we can exercise our variability and flexibility, our capacity to direct and adjust our lives, and to explore our adaptability and enhance our relations with others.

Ecological theory

The term *ecological* refers to environmental, social, situational, or circumstantial variables that help us explain or solve problems. When we look to the ecology of an event to explain the source of a problem we typically look for factors outside of ourselves. The first factor to consider is *role expectations*. The influence and force of expectations from other people guides us and may, in fact, override our intended behavior. For instance, we may be convinced we have elements of our personality that enhance some behaviors but interfer with other behaviors. We may believe that certain roles are difficult for us because we "just aren't wired that way", or we may think that we simply can't perform a task because we don't know how. Contrary to this belief, sociologists find that if those around us *expect* us to behave in a certain way, we are likely to begin behaving according to those expectations.[2] Most role expectations are subtle, non-coercive forms of social pressure, but can also include direct verbal communication, "We expect you to now carry on in the footsteps of your father." When we are expected to carry out a particular role, we will usually adapt and conform to those expectations. The flip side of this issue is that if we want to facilitate our adoption of a particular role in society (e.g., manage a large corporation, or teach the first grade), then we need to assure that those important individuals around us will at least *act out* expectations that are compatible with those goals. In sum, there is an immense capacity for role flexibility in human behavior if expectations are strong enough.

147

The second area of interest is *circumstance*. Circumstance is an ecological factor that can determine how an individual acts. The immediate conditions that determine why someone acts as they do, the events that lead up to a particular behavior, the status of the position that a person holds (either high or neutral or low) at any given time in the hierarchy of influence may explain, circumstantially, why someone behaves in what looks like a gender stereotypical way. It is an important aspect of problem-solving to consider the circumstances of behavior in addition to or in conjunction with personality characteristics.

The final area of ecology we will mention at this time is *context*. Whether it is social (community, friends, parents, romantic partners), or other than social (business or employment) the relationships in our lives direct our behavior within a context compounded by the characteristics of the other people. Hierarchical arrangements evolve as we interact with those around us. It is well known that people who find themselves in subordinate positions will put more effort into decoding the emotions and attitudes of the dominant figure.[3] The subordinate figure then adjusts their behavior to align with their position in the hierarchy. B. Puka demonstrated that women, minorities, and others who are often in subordinate positions decoded the expectations, moods, and feelings of the people who are superordinate in position *as an adaptive skill*.[4] The pattern of interaction is useful in ensuring acceptance, maintenance, and balance in the relationship. However, what might be viewed strictly as a survival skill behavior might simply be our natural response to the actions or intentions of the person we are dealing with. Because our society is hierarchical in structure, we are socialized to comply with many of our social interactions in a hierarchical way. For example, when working or living with a person who is acting passively, we may find ourselves acting more dominantly (or at least view ourselves as more dominant). In the course of the same week we may interact with someone who is domineering and we, in turn, may respond by being passive. That the behaviors we employ have this environmental motivation is not uncommon, but what complicates the process of solving the surrounding problems, is that we often erroneously assign the motivation to personality factors rather than contextual factors. To avoid this inclination, we should probe contextual motivations. Ecological approaches to problems solving depend on critical thinking skills and, additionally, an effort to avoid a view of human behavior that relies unduly on psychological characteristics. A clearer understanding of a problem-solver's tendency to favor personality factors can be illustrated by reviewing an area of study that psychologists call *attribution theory*.

Attribution theory

Humans have a drive, a motivation, to make sense of their own and others' behavior.[5] Interest in this motivation has focused on **attribution theory**. Researchers in this area have proposed two kinds of explanations or attributions for why we do the things we do. When we make a *situation attribution*, we regard an action as being caused by something in our environment: "Alicia tripped because the brick walkway was uneven". When we make a *person attribution*, we regard an action as being caused by some disposition or trait of the person: "Alicia tripped because she is clumsy."

Through experimental research, social psychologists have specified some of the conditions under which people prefer to attribute the cause of behavior. We have the tendency to explain someone else's behavior in terms of person variables and exclude

148

situation variables. That is, we tend to overestimate personality factors and personal characteristics and underestimate the influence of situations. In fact, its more complicated than that; we tend to attribute other people's bad behavior to their personalities and our own bad behavior to our situations. In other words, *they did it* because that is the way they are (he's a little devil) and *we did it* because someone or something *influenced* us (the devil made me do it). This tendency is called the **fundamental attribution error.**

When we are aware of this tendency, we should be able to avoid the pitfalls of this error. The fascinating thing is that many people persist in the fundamental attribution error even when they know a person's behavior is required by the situation.[6] In one experiment, students spent some time talking with a target person who was either friendly or unfriendly. In each case, students were told either that the target's behavior was spontaneous or that the target was specifically instructed to behave in that way. The students thought the friendly person was "truly friendly", even when they had been told the friendliness was forced. The students said that the unfriendly person was "truly unfriendly" even when they knew the unfriendliness was required.[7] The fundamental attribution error probably explains why we respond so favorably to smiling flight attendants, polite telephone operators, and charming salespeople. Even when we know their manner is "part of their job," we also believe it is "part of their personality."

The fundamental attribution error can be identified in more instances than mere attitudes or mental calculation about what caused a behavior in someone we observed. It is prevalent in important policy making decisions as well. To lock ourselves in to either one of these ideologies is to ignore our powers of critical thinking. The following example by Alfie Kohn from the Phi Delta Kappan magazine is on the topic of character education in public schools:[8]

> The Jefferson Center for Character Education in Pasadena, California, has produced a video that begins with some arresting images. Young people are shown being led away in handcuffs, the point being that crime can be explained on the basis of an "erosion of American core values," as the narrator intones ominously. The idea that social problems can be explained by the fact that traditional virtues are no longer taken seriously is offered by many proponents of character education as though it were just plain common sense. But if we are sensitive to the pervasiveness of the fundamental attribution error, we would caution the assumption that people steal or rape or kill solely because they possess bad values—that is, because of their personal characteristics. The implications of this reasoning would be that political and economic realities are irrelevant and need not be addressed. Never mind the staggering levels of unemployment in the inner cities or a system in which more and more of the nation's wealth is concentrated in fewer and fewer hands; just place the blame on individuals whose characters are deficient.[9]

Kohn continues with his example and uses attribution theory to explain why he thinks it may be harmful to ignore situational variables. He cites several landmark studies in the field of psychology that helped us understand this phenomenon.

If a program proceeds by trying to "fix the kids"—as do almost all brands of character education—it ignores the accumulated evidence from the field of social psychology demonstrating that much of how we act and who we are reflects the situation in which we find ourselves. Virtually all the landmark studies in this discipline have been variations on this theme. Set up children in an extended team competition at summer camp and you will elicit unprecedented levels of aggression.[10] Assign adults to the roles of prisoners or guards in a mock jail, and they will start to become their roles.[11] Put normal healthy adult experimental subjects into a mental hospital and they will be diagnosed with schizphrenia.[10] Move people into a small town and they will be more likely to rescue a stranger in need. So common is the tendency to attribute to an individual's personality or character what is actually a function of the social environment that a special effort needs to be made to recognize the presence and effects of the fundamental attribution error.[13]

As I mentioned previously, mainstream recognition of the phenomenon does not seem to reduce its prevalence or effect on our patterns of viewing other people's behavior. It is particularly troublesome in our personal relationships. Attribution theory can be critical when it comes to resolving conflict in close relationships.[14] Important differences were found in a study involving 22 happy couples and 22 unhappy couples. When the happy couples explained why their mates were irritable they found situational attributes or temporary environmental conditions responsible. ("He didn't get much sleep last night" or "She just had an argument with her sister"). Unhappy or distressed couples, however, find the reasons for their mate's irritability in inherent traits and personality. ("She's just lazy" or "He's a control freak").[15]

The benefits of critical thinking are clear. If attribution of behavior is flexible then couples are better able to find satisfying resolutions to their conflicts. Happy couples settle their disputes through discussion, compromise, and problem solving, the basic techniques of negotiation. They neither yield every point nor bully the other side into submission. They are able to identify their goals, identify short-term solutions for the sake of long-term gains.[16] Unhappy couples end up in repeated cycles of bickering and insults, blaming each other's personality traits ("He's lazy"; "She's a nag").

The foundation for attribution theory was set by the work of Fritz Heider[17] and was later expanded and refined by Julian Rotter [18], Bernard Weiner[19], and H. M. Lefcourt.[20] Attributions refer to people's interpretations of experience. Causal attribution refers to the analysis we make of observations and situations where we seek "why" answers. Research indicates that we are more likely to be generous in our opinions of another person if we see that they have been affected by situational or environmental events. For example, one of Weiner's earlier studies on causal attribution illustrates that college students are more likely to lend a stranger their class notes if they observe that the stranger has a valid excuse for not attending class (the stranger is wearing an eye patch). The college students were less likely to lend the stranger their class notes when the stranger told them he missed class because he was at the beach. The "beach" excuse would indicate that the stranger was responsible for the missed class problem. The "eye patch" would indicate that the stranger might not be personally to blame for missing class.[21]

The fundamental attribution error occurs more often when we have no observational clue as to why an individual has a problem. That is, without a clue, we tend to blame the person for their own problems. If this response becomes common in our close relationships, we may, in fact, create one of the elements described in the Pruitt & Rubin work: blaming each other's personality; a characteristic of unhappy relationships.[23]

Another consequence of the attribution error concerns the potential for resolving the problem through change. If the problem's source is perceived as a flawed personality, change is hard fought at best and probably unlikely. Ultimately, change can only occur if the person with the "flawed personality" agrees that they indeed have a flaw and then is also motivated to want to change. Changing traits, attitudes, and personality characteristics will involve plenty of stress, sweat, and tears. Although it may happen on a television program or in a movie within the course of 60 minutes, it rarely happens at all in the real world. Likewise, pushing a person to change has long been deemed futile and a likely source of more problems within a close relationship.

So, if we're assuming that attributing the source of a problem to a person-variable (i.e., a flawed personality), is bad for our relationships, then is attributing the source of a problem to an environmental variable good for our relationships? It appears to be better, but remember, attributing the source of an observed problem to environmental factors goes against our natural tendency to attribute the cause to personality factors (that we will make the fundamental attribution error). What this implies is that avoiding the fundamental attribution error is going to involve a **strategy**.

Studies indicate that some couples (e.g., the happy couples in the Pruitt & Rubin study) avoid the fundamental attribution error by habitually looking for environmental reasons when a problem occurs involving the behavior of their mate. They may ask themselves "What caused my partner to act in an angry way?"; "Why is my partner acting so lazy today?" The assumption here is that this is a temporary condition or that there is a situational solution to the problem. If the problem is perceived as temporary then perhaps just sympathy or understanding is all that will be necessary to alleviate the stress or facilitate the wait until time resolves the problem. If there is hope to resolve the problem through change, then the emphasis is on various situational options and away from the tendency to want to change a person's characteristics. Applying a strategy thus means we will routinely look for environmental explanations as to why someone has made a mistake or behaves poorly. When it is appropriate to go beyond explanations and attempt to solve the problem, we will focus on changing events, situations, or environments rather than people.

Case studies and sample solutions

"You can't change the people"

Here some examples of problems written as case studies by college students in a gender studies class

151

A friend of mine works in a public day care program. He is educated in early childhood development and is great with kids. Unfortunately, he has to put up with some attitudes about his gender and questions about why he wants to work with children. Some parents once commented that they would be more comfortable if he was working in the weekend program designed for adolescents. One parent came in to help out and my friend felt like she was watching his every move all morning long. She wouldn't speak to him and acted as though she were angry with him. This hurts his feelings and causes him to feel self-conscious on the job. I suggested he find a way to tell these parents not to worry about his presence around their children. He thinks he should find another day care program where the parents are not so hostile.

It goes with the natural inclination to work on opinions and attitudes to consider how we can change a person's mind. But what would be an alternative to this inclination if we want to consider a situational solution to this problem? The environmental explanation is may be a more effective plan than finding fault with the parents who bring their children to this day care facility. Consider this. Anytime a person engages in a non-traditional role or work, male or female, they can expect to experience some social pressure to conform to the norm. In this case, a man is involved in professional child care; a role very much outside the norm for the typical male. In addition to being outside the normal role for men, he can expect suspicious looks and questions about his intentions. By recognizing this as a possible condition of his choice of employment, (i.e., situational rather than personal) he can build necessary auxiliary skills to deal with the public opinion he is bound to face. Some parents simply will not be comfortable with a day care facility that employs a male teacher and they can be expected (or encouraged) to take their child somewhere else. He knows he will not be accepted by every parent who come in contact with him. On the other hand, by knowing the subsequent collateral of being in a non-tradition field, he now knows the reality of his situation and may choose to shift goals or direction. In either case, he will probably be more successful with a "circumstantial fix" than a "people fix" to his problem. The issue here is to recognize the complexity of the off-norm situation and avoid emotional confrontations that increase conflict rather than resolve conflict.

"Let's fix the situation first"

The following case study was written by a student responding to a topic presented in one of my gender studies classes:

This weekend I saw a great example of the ecological paradigm. Although this is not a gender situation, it typified the inherent problems of the fundamental attribution error and illustrates the advantages of ecological solutions.

On a CNN news report, a lengthy story was presented depicting the plight of homeless families with children. The report contained distressing scenes of young children living in shelters with graphic views of overcrowded rooms filled with sleeping mats, piles of clothes and personal belongings. The story explained that these children suffered from more than the apparent economic deprivations. In addition to learning disabilities, the children experienced severe depression, loss of appetite, suicidal fantasies, and profoundly low self-worth.

The report concluded with Dr. J. Zim, who emphasized the imperative need to provide counseling for these children. It appears that these professional social workers viewed the solution to the "deviant" behavior of depression was to "fix" the children. The Ecological approach would attempt to change the environment and very likely, provide stability through permanent housing.

This news report also revealed how deeply entrenched our society is in the individualist paradigm. Children without homes has become an accepted reality. The only perceived "viable" solution is to "counsel" the victimized children. Improving their environment was never presented or investigated as an alternative.

In conclusion, I believe this example gave me a startling understanding of ecological and individualist ideologies. In retrospect, "counseling" would be costly, time consuming, and ineffective as compared to the immediate relief and joy children might feel to simply learn they were going "home."

This student recognized the futility in attempting a solely psychological intervention for a problem that has it roots in a situational problem.

"Isn't this sex discrimination?"

Even when it is hard to deny that traits, attitudes and personality are factors determining a person's behavior, there is an alternative strategy to solving the dilemma by attempting to change the situation rather than the person. The following is one such case study written by a college female..

This case study is in regards to my work environment. An answer to this situation alludes me and, most of the time, I feel that it would be better to leave it alone. This might be because I will not be at this job for too much longer and it would be better not to raise a fuss.

My superior supervisor is an older man from the East Coast. This man demands respect even though many fellow workers don't believe he deserves it. I have been working for him for a year. I began to take a closer look at him, as well as question other workers, to see what was going on.

I noticed little things about his attitude and actions that degraded females. If I were to try to explain it to somebody that does not know him it would be difficult. First of all, he favors the male workers. He teaches them more and explains things better than he does to the female workers. I sometimes get the feeling that he does not think we females will understand. He sends the females on menial errands like sharpening his pencil or copying a paper for him. He generally becomes infuriated with the females when they do not perform the job correctly, where he is usually pretty patient with the males.

My direct supervisor is a female. She is aware of this situation but explains to us that "this is just the way it is." She tells us, "We can't change an older man from the East Coast so try your best to work with him." Most times I agree with her and try to deal with it. I just think about how I could change a person's characteristics that seem so ingrained. Yet, there are times that I get so frustrated when I see he is eager to teach the guys something as such opportunity arises. Then, if I am in the same situation he treats it like I'm a waste of his precious time. Is there anything to be done to rectify this situation?

To analyze this situation and develop strategies one must first ask a few questions. Questions arise from our understanding of critical thinking, ecological strategies, and attribution theory. What is the problem behavior? What are the consequences of the problem behavior? What can be changed? What are the situational variables that are negotiable or flexible?

To avoid the fundamental attribution error, we will not focus on the person with the problem behavior. We can agree with the female supervisor that the male superior supervisor is not going to change and to expect him to change would only cause stress for everyone involved. We can, however, define the specific behavior that is the problem: the male superior supervisor trains and mentors male workers but dismisses as unimportant female workers. The consequence of this situation for the females is the lost potential and missed training needed to move forward in the company (or workforce in general). The situational factors involve mentoring and training in important aspects of operations of this company. One ecological approach would be to *redesign the entire interaction around the problem activity.* Possible solutions involve: (1) request for training and mentoring, probably not by this man, but someone else in a position to work equally with male and female workers; (2) assign someone to work just as effectively with the female employees as this superior supervisor works with the males; (3) arrange for training sessions that are open to all employees; (4) request company meetings in which advice on how to handle challenges is offered to all those interested (and other such variations on situational solutions). If these alternatives are resisted by the company officials, or considered impossible to implement, then an another situational solution is for the female workers who want mentoring and training to move on to another place of employment.

Modifying power and status difference

Some of the toughest problems to solve are those that are emotionally charged and as a natural response we tend to blame people rather than situations. How can we mediate the worst of our conflicts, those that concern power and control, ecologically? There are two common approaches that are considered situational. One involves the use of power to fight power. If subordinates find themselves overwhelmed by an imbalance of power, they can identify a source of auxiliary or institutional power to call into play. In many cases, this means making formal complaints to supervisors, filing charges or hiring an attorney to explore legal options. This approach, of course, is not without the strain and possible backlash of confrontation. The other approach is to negotiate a settlement directly with the other party involved in the conflict. This is the approach outlined above. Redesigning the activity around the problem is a viable and unemotional step to getting the job done with the least amount of interpersonal turmoil.

How can a pro-feminist man moderate male priviledge

The majority of men are interested in working amicably with others. At the same time, they are challenged by implicit advantages of being male. A part of being male is learning to construct the male identity. For most men it is connected in some way to real power through work, recognition, talent or other such status. For a few it is *power over* one or more other people with elements of coercion and force being substituted for real power. Our concern at the moment is with the more mainstream power achieved through work and recognition and includes the power and status afforded to males, in general, in the global patriarchal system. To diminish this power status once it is experienced is extremely challenging for the pro-feminist male. It may involve skillfully blending the masculine with the feminine in themselves. However, to enact a feminine role means performing a gendered activity of a lower value than the standard assignment of masculine gender role. The answer to this dilemma lies in the ideology of power. It has been constructed by society and can be reconstructed by any individual man. The way to encourage men to reconnect to the feminine in themselves and in others is to re-define power and status. Winning is the standard traditional proof of power. But the pro-feminist man knows there is power (value) in the ability to arbitrate or negotiate through a confrontation or conflict rather than win. There is power (status) in being able to get along with a subordinate on *their* terms. Without a doubt, there is power in role flexibility. And there is power in understanding that power is not finite.

The concept of egalitarian power

There is no loss of power or status if the ideology of masculinity diminishes hierarchical social order; there is just a shift of definition. Egalitarian social settings are only seen as a threat if power is viewed as finite. That is, if one believes that the reduction of personal power means that someone else gets more power. When the definition of power is **not finite**, then sharing power does not imply there is less power to the one who shares. In egalitarian social settings there is plenty of power and status for everyone. Hierarchy is not part of the definition of egalitarian power. Instead it is viewed an empowerment for all. Redefining power and status means rethinking hierarchical order, perhaps replacing hierarchy with something more cyclical.

In the official macrosystematic world of government and business, hierarchies serve a more global purpose, a purpose that goes beyond masculine ideology. The ideology of masculinity is redefinable primarily within an individual's microsystem. The hierarchy of power is shifted to egalitarian power in the context of friends, family, jobs, and community. Egalitarian power can exist in microsystems, first and foremost.

It is essential to understand that institutional power is not exclusive to white males, but is representative of status in a hierarchical system. Shifts in hierarchical systems can and do occur if the need is strong enough. More likely, the need to shift power will be evident in our personal relations with significant others where the need to moderate power to resolve conflict will be more immediate. Examples of how to shift power in the microsystem include striving to (1) decrease competitive behaviors, (2) increase sharing behaviors, (3) increase flexibility in thinking, (4) increase flexibility in role enactment, (5) understand the ecology of gender, and (6) apply attribution theory. The following chapters demonstrate each of these elements in practical detail and lively illustrations.

[1] Adapted from U. Bronfenbrenner, 1979, 1982, 1986

[2] L Beckhouse, J. Tanur, J. Weiler, & E. Weinstein, 1975, And some men have leadership thrust upon them, *Journal of Personality and Social Psychology*

[3] N. M Gebket, 1977, *Body Politics: Power, sex, and nonverbal communciation.*

[4] B. Puka, 1990, The liberation of caring: A different voice for Gilligan's different voice, *Hypatia.*

[5] M. Ross & J. O. Garth, 1985, Attribution and social perception, *Handbook of Social Psychology*, Vol. II

[6] E. Jones, 1979, The rocky road from acts to dispositions, *American Psychologist*

[7] D. Napolitan & G. Goethals, 1979, The attributions of friendliness, *Journal of Experimental Social Psychology*

[8] J. Kohn, 1997, How not to teach values: A critical look at character education, *Phi Delta Kappan*

[9] Ibid, pp. 430-431

[10] Kohn, from the above article, is citing M. Sherif, 1958, Superordinate goals in the reduction of intergroup conflicts, *American Journal of Sociology*

[11] Kohn, from the above article, is citing C. Haney, C. Banks, & P. Zimbardo. 1973, Interpersonal dynamics in a simulated prison, *International Journal of Criminology and Penology*

[10] Kohn, from the above article, is citing D. Rosenhan, 1973, Psychological abnormality and law, in Scheirer & Hammonds (eds.) *Psychology and the law: The APA Master Lecture Series*

[13] J. Kohn, 1997, *Phi Delta Kappan*

[14] C. Wade & C. Tavris, 1990, *Learning to think Critically: A case of close relationships*

[15] A. Holtzworth-Munroe, & N. Jacobson, 1985, Causal attributions of married couples: When do they search for causes? What do they conclude when they do? *Journal of Personality and Social Psychology*

[16] D. Pruitt, & J. Rubin, 1986, *Social Conflict: Escalation, stalemate, and settlement.*

[17] F. Heider, 1946, Attitudes and cognitive organization, *Journal of Psychology* and F. Heider, 1958, *The Psychology of Interpersonal Relations*

[18] J. Rotter, 1966, Generalized expectancies for internal versus external control of reinforcement, *Psychological Monographs.*

[19] Bernard Weiner, et al., did multiple publications on this topic from 1974 to the present. One most applicable to this context is a 1985 paper presented at the annual meeting to the American Psychological Association in Los Angeles, "Social psychology of emotions with some classroom implications"

[20] H. M. Lefcourt, 1986, *Humor and life stress: Antidote to adversity*

[21] B. Weiner, 1980

[23] D. Pruitt, & J. Rubin, 1986, *Social Conflict: Escalation, stalemate, and settlement.*

Notes

Chapter 12

The microstructural level. In the last chapter we identified the site for the shift to occur (the microsystem) and a psychological perspective we might apply (the situational side of attribution theory. As we build our <u>alternative</u> to the win/lose standard of conflict resolution we also need to consider specific sociological theory. Barbara Risman presents symbolic interaction theory under the gender lens. The foremost concept guiding this approach concerns ecological expectations. That is, how our behavior may be influenced by the expectations from those around us. As the process of discovering the meaning of each element of symbolic interaction theory--as it is applied to gender-based situations--unfolds, the reader is encouraged to extend the model to our previously established problem-solving ideology. For example, if network theory determines gender behavior, then how can problems with your "network" be handled microstructually and situationally?

Chapter 12 *Barbara J. Risman and Pepper Schwartz,* Being Gendered: A Microstructural View of Intimate Relationships

A few years ago a group of sociology professors and graduate students at the University of Washington met informally to study gender. The reason for the group, besides intellectual camaraderie, was a shared view that we needed to discuss gender as a sociological rather than psychological phenomenon. We felt then, as we do today, that too much of the literature on men's and women's roles explained each sex's conduct on biological or psychological disposition. Although we found the literature that advanced social learning and socialization hypotheses very useful, we felt they were inadequate and perhaps ultimately misleading about how male and female roles are truly constructed.

The more we read, the more convinced we became that an alternative explanation for gender in intimate relationships was necessary. What was needed was a *microstructural* theory of gender, a theory that took into account the impact of adult life experiences on men's and women's self-concept and actions. The theme of a microstructural theory is simple but powerful: men and women are not created all at once--at birth or during early socialization--but are continually re-created during the life cycle by the opportunities available to them and their interactions with others.

This strikes us as particularly true in male and female roles played in intimate relationships. We decided to gather together articles that would begin to explain intimacy by showing how microstructural forces help create men's and women's actions and beliefs. The articles that follow, show we hope, how the format of an institution (such as bridal shower), the expectations of others (such as parents), the options available (social mobility through either marriage or work) operate to form stereotypically male and female behavior, what we shall call gendered behavior. But before presenting each example, we begin by explaining our theory in more detail.

The predominant model of gender in interpersonal relationships is called "individualist" because it rests on a theory of relatively inflexible personalities, which once created, remain throughout life whatever other experiences or circumstances come about. This individualist paradigm posits that by adulthood men and women have developed sex-typed personalities that are quite different from one another. Females have become nurturant, person-oriented, and child-centered, and males have become competitive and work-oriented. Once formed, these core personality traits continue to influence behavior throughout life.

Researchers using such individualist perspectives are biased toward psychological explanations for sex differences and do not consider seriously enough how males and females are shaped by their immediate social settings. In an often-cited statement of the individualist perspective, Bem and Bem (1976) argue, for example, that a 21-year-old woman is not free to choose a nonsterotypical lifestyle because "society has controlled not only her alternatives, but her motivation to choose any but one of those alternatives."

The personality and socialization arguments are well stated, and many different kinds of individualist theories have been generated. Some of them have been extremely influential. For example, Chodorow's (1978) theory in the *Reproduction of Mothering* gave a great boost to feminist psychoanalytic explanations of how the earliest parent-child interaction (mothering) explains male and female personality differences. Individualist explanations are also expressed in differential reinforcement and socialization theory (for example, Bandura and Walters, 1963; Mischel, 1966; Weitzman 1979; and others) and cognitive development theory (Kohlberg, 1966; Gilligan, 1982). Even sociobiological theories (for example, Wilson, 1978; Symons, 1979; Van den Berghe, 1979) and bio-social theories (Rossi, 1984) that integrate evolutionary, genetic, hormonal, and social variables, ultimately focus on individuals' preferences rather than on the social systems that influence them.

The defining characteristic of various individualist paradigms, from Chodorow's (1978) feminist psychoanalytic approach to a more traditional sex-role socialization theory, is the presumption that gendered behavior is the result of *internalized* traits.

Although individualist theorists do not ignore the role of social structural influences on intimate behavior (see, especially, Chodorow), they focus on how culturally determined family patterns create gendered personalities, which then provide the motivations for individuals to fill their socially appropriate roles. All research within this tradition shares the central presumption that internalized psychological motivation is a more salient explanation for gendered behavior than immediate social relations.

We don't want to create a useless antagonism between an individualist and a microstructural explanation of gender and intimate conduct, but we do feel that sociological variables are given too little weight in individualist discussions of intimate relationships and that the more potent microstructural argument has been too often ignored. When individualist theorists assume relatively inflexible, internalized, gender-based personality traits, they are making incorrect assumptions that inevitably lead to wrong conclusions. An illustration may help explain our position. Individualist theories debate whether women desire to stay home with their children more than men because they have been mothered by same-sex parents and have therefore developed the desire for intense intimacy, or whether the social reinforcement girls receive for doll play and other nurturant behavior is a better explanation for exclusively female mothering. It is an interesting question -- except that by assuming internalized predispositions exist we are directed only to inquire about the consequences of the female predisposition to mother. We have a more basic question: Do such sex-based predispositions really exist? Or would the social conditions that promote full-time mothering also promote full-time parenting in men equally well? If fathers were not only actually given the option of remaining at home with their babies, but also expected to do so, would more men choose the role of primary caretaker? And what if these same men earned considerably less than their wives? Different assumptions lead to different problems and therefore, potentially, to different answers. Most of the questions that are currently explored in the realm of intimate relationships assume sex-typed preferences and the overwhelming importance of sex-role socialization.

This presumption that gender is internalized as a stable personality trait is the thread that weaves through all the individualist theories, though they may conflict and disagree otherwise. Motivation becomes a central research question in this paradigm. Researchers look for answers about why someone would *want* to behave a certain way rather than why they may be merely behaving like other actors with the same constraints or rewards.[1]

We believe that individualist paradigms posit an oversocialized conception of masculine men and feminine women. The "oversocialized conception of *man*," first identified by Wrong (1961), would have us believe that once we know what people are trained to think and do, everything else about their lives is only secondarily important. Ongoing social relations are reduced to postscripts rather than to determinants of social forces. Individualist paradigms have led to an oversocialized conception of men and women, of gender.

How a microstructural perspective helps explain interpersonal relations

Taken to its logical extreme, our microstructural theory predicts that men and women would behave *exactly* the same way if they were given identical expectations and positions in society. More realistically, the theory has to take certain biological conditions into account, such as the impact of childbirth on interpersonal relations and placement in society. Our position is that biology and psychology are going to be relatively unimportant in contemporary Western societies and thus, most of what we continue to believe are gender differences in intimacy are continually constructed during interaction (see Risman 1987). Social design has been mistaken for psychological reality. In other words, the over-representation of men at the top of Fortune 500 companies is less a consequence of greater male motivation and drive than the result of men's greater opportunities to join the right social networks and fulfill the expectations for the company. Our position, of course, is not to be taken on faith. This book is designed to support our thesis by comparing sex-based personality traits with the impact of social circumstances to see which best predicts male and female behavior.

Our microstructural theory assumes that the players in the game of life adapt to ongoing patterns of interaction that are themselves produced by a socially organized system. The factors at work are often called "structural," but sociologists have used this word in so many different ways that it is now too confused to be resuscitated with a nice, clear meaning. Classically, (Merton, 1975; Goode, 1960) structure has referred to the relationships between various economic historical forces and social institutions. The most restrictive definition (Mayhew, 1980) for structure is a macro-level one: relationships between societal forces. But others (Hewitt, 1979, and Stryker, 1980, 1981) have argued that structural forces also describe how social organization affects interactions between individuals. In this view, the "nature of situations" as people experience them helps shape behavior.

We will not debate here what is "true" structural theory--only to say that we are proceeding within the tradition of those who believe that situational interaction is necessarily a component of a structuralist approach. For clarity, when studying interpersonal relations we call this a microstructural theory. And it is in this link, the world experienced by the individual, that we wish to define better for a more complete understanding of how and why gender evolves as it does. The guiding vision behind each article is the desire to go beyond the notion of socially created sex-typed personalities toward a theory that focuses on how the day-to-day social relations of men and women create gendered behavior.

There are three sociological traditions useful for the reader to think about when trying to understand gender: symbolic interaction theory, status expectations theory, and network. All three traditions help us focus on different aspects of the experiences we face each day.

Symbolic Interaction Theory

Symbolic interaction research has shown for decades that situational factors influence behavior over and above individual factors such as training or biological predisposition. Even today gender remains a "master status," an organizing principle of everyday life (Hughes, 1945). We all hold implicit and explicit expectations that differ by sex. Men are not expected to assume a subordinate identity to women in marriage (that is, Mr. Helen Smith). Nor are employed married women considered unsuccessful if they alone cannot earn enough money to support their families well. These expectations, known to the participants of an interaction and to everyone in our society, exert powerful constraints on how men and women are likely to behave.

Symbolic interactionists use the term *altercasting* to show one process by which such roles are formed by expectations (Weinstein and Deutschberger, 1963). When people are confronted with expectations that differ from their self image, they look for cues about how to proceed (Beckhouse *et al.*, 1975). When the person they are dealing with shows them what he or she expects, they generally try to behave accordingly. No one likes the discomfort that can happen when we don't meet others' expectations. When we get mixed messages about who we are expected to be, we try to make sense of the conflicting transmissions so that interaction can continue smoothly. We all change our behavior in response to new or changing expectations. This inconsistency suggests that personality traits do not make us act only one way. Rather, behavior is often an attempt to meet expectations to do well at what we are *supposed* to do at any given moment.

We believe that understanding the process of social expectations and altercasting is important to the study of gender in two ways. First, even when men and women are in identical settings, they often face differential expectations. Second, men and women do not often even have access to identical settings or opportunities. For example, if ever there was a behavior supposed to be more biological and based more on feminine personality than sociological variables, it is mothering. From a symbolic interactionist perspective, however, it is the child's, the family's, and society's expectations of full-time mothering by females that may produce the behaviors we see in today's women. If expectations were changed (for example, if the child and society made it clear that "mothering" is expected from the father), the symbolic interactionist would predict that mothering behaviors would be produced in fathers.

We predict that males would respond to such changed expectations with mothering skills as they are altercast into the mothering role, if not right away then over time. At first they might find the child's expectations incongruent with their own self-images, but eventually fathers would become what the child expects and needs them to be (Risman, 1986). In fact, that does seem to happen when men become single fathers. Indeed, the same process of altercasting may be what turns many, though certainly not all, women into "good enough" mothers.

Many of the chapters illustrate how the expectations of others help create gendered behavior in intimate relationships. The research by LaRossa and LaRossa on infant care shows that mothers in our society are expected to lose more freedom to child care than are fathers. Interviews with new parents suggest that such expectations at least partly create the inequitable burden of childrearing that even employed mothers carry. Swain's study of male college students suggests that the societal constraints against men expressing their emotions shape the kind of intimacy possible within same-sex friendships. DiIorio's research on working-class youth suggests that even in a club with an expressed commitment to sexual equality, the norms and expectations attached to the status of boyfriend versus girlfriend vary so tremendously that girls remain subordinate.

Other chapters suggest not only that expectations differ for men and women, but also that the sexes rarely have access to similar experiences and opportunities. For example, Cancian suggests that when industrialization split the world of paid work from the hearth and home, women were for the first time expected to become specialists in love. Men had little option to devote themselves to the emotions of others; women had little option to do otherwise. Kimmel continues a historical analysis by suggesting that when the American frontier shrank, a definition of manhood based on physical prowess and bravery became unattainable. This created a crisis for the definition of masculinity. Such a crisis was irrelevant to femininity, which had never been defined in similar terms.

Lorber suggests that social institutions -- including family and sexual relationships -- need not categorize persons by gender; institutions should be developed to provide similar experiences and opportunities to men and to women.

Status Expectations Theory

Status expectations theory can also help us understand gendered behavior in intimate relationships. A large literature shows that expectations of individuals differ based on the status ranking of the group to which they belong -- even when that status is irrelevant to the task at hand (Berger *et al.*, 1972; Ridgeway, 1982; Wagner *et al.*, 1986). Lower-status groups have less influence. People who hold higher social status, white males in our society, tend to dominate groups even in small experimental settings (Meeker and Weitzel-O'Neill, 1977). Thus, men and women behave quite differently because responses to members of the higher-status male group are quite different than responses to lower-status females. For example, if you are a man, people tend to stop talking when you raise your voice just because you are a man. No matter what you say it is taken seriously, even if it is eventually repudiated. But if you are a woman you always have to fight to get the floor, and it is hard to be taken seriously even when you have a solution your colleagues may need. Experience has taught you that it is unlikely your proposal will be acted on. In this way sexual stratification organizes interaction even though the people may believe they are giving fair weight to the abilities of each person in the room.

Research has shown that if social status is experimentally manipulated, expectations based on sex can be subordinated to other status conditions. One study (Geis *et al.*, 1984) showed how student reaction to television commercials changed when the high-status person was male and when the high-status person was female. The results were supportive of status expectations theory: high-status males and females were rated as independent, rational, dominant, ambitious, and good leaders while low-status men and women were rated as dependent, irrational, submissive, unambiguous, and followers. Of course, in real life, males are more likely to be in the high-status position in commercials. But in this experiment, when sex was disassociated with social status, sexual stereotypes disappeared.

Network Theory

Symbolic interaction and status expectation theories independently suggest that actual social relations (expectations, opportunities, and altercasting during interaction) mold behavior that might otherwise be presumed motivated by gendered personality traits. Granovetter (1985) suggests we integrate the analysis of interaction and social status by studying how people are placed in or are embedded in social networks. They may be central actors, important and known to everyone else, or they may be peripheral to the social system, acquainted with only a few others and different from them in some fundamental way. We think that how people are embedded in social networks helps create gendered behavior, and such behavior is not merely the expression of personal gendered choices. Men and women have had different life options at least partly because of how they are differently embedded in social networks. For example, mothers with young children are unlikely to find themselves in social networks that expect and demand achievement outside the home. Men of any age, married or single, however, can hardly escape such expectations.

Network embeddedness has been used as a particularly effective variable explaining women's performance in the labor force. In 1977, Kanter critiqued studies on female labor force participation for their individualist presumptions. The literature of the time was full of descriptions about why women workers were different from male workers. Kanter showed that when an individual had access to powerful mentors, interaction with people like themselves, and the possibility for upward mobility, they behaved like others with similar advantages -- regardless of sex. These social network variables could explain work success far better than assumptions of masculine versus feminine work styles. Women were less often successful because they were more often blocked from network advantages. When they had such advantages, women behaved very much like their male colleagues. When men lacked such opportunities they did not advance, and they behaved with stereotypically female work styles. Other researchers (Thompson, 1981; Lorber, 1984; Geis *et al.*, 1984) also report findings supportive of such a network approach.

This network perspective can be transferred to domestic settings. For example, studies have found structural explanations for what had seemed to be gender-linked language patterns. Kollock *et al.* (1985) compared conversations between homosexual partners and heterosexual partners and found that power dynamics accounted for some of the privileges (for example, who can interrupt, who talks more) in conversation that other researchers had attributed to sex-linked personality traits. Past research had shown that men interrupted and talked more. By comparing homosexual and heterosexual couples, the authors demonstrated that it was really power that conferred conversational privilege and that gender almost disappeared as a factor once it was known who was the more powerful person in the relationship. Since men are more often the more powerful person in heterosexual relationships, sex had been confounded with power. We have mistakenly thought that certain interactional styles were male and others were specifically female, but these styles are actually tied to power, not only to sex.

The chapter by Gerson also supports the importance of microstructural factors. Instead of attributing women's desire to mother to sex-role socialization, Gerson shows that whether employed women choose to remain childless or become mothers depends on their social context. Neither feminine personality traits nor biological instincts propelled women toward motherhood. What did predict childbearing was access to a stable heterosexual relationship, the kinds of jobs available in the labor force, and the relative interest of male partners in fatherhood.

Other chapters also focus on how social networks help shape gendered behavior. Richardson illustrates the importance of social networks for the very definition of relationships, even those secret and forbidden. She suggests that some of the subordination of single women to married men in extramarital liaisons can be attributed to privileges based on marital status, rather than on gender per se. Being married seems to be an important determinant of interactional power. Marriage confers greater prestige and alternative avenues for social-psychological support upon the married partner in an extramarital liaison. Hertz illustrates the strength of social networks with her focus on how the demands of corporate careers shape new types of interpersonal relationships. Cheal also looks at contemporary marriage, but his focus is on how a bride's new position in a network of married women helps define her role as wife.

163

Microstructural theory and social change

Each chapter supports our basic argument: when the sociological traditions of symbolic interaction, status expectations, and social networks are integrated, we have a more powerful explanation for the continuing existence of gendered behavior in intimate relationships than if we continue to depend on individualist, oversocialized concepts of men and women. Until now, there really hasn't been much research that has avoided what we consider unjustified assumptions about the over-whelming influence sex-role socialization has on gender and intimacy. And so, we've collected what we consider to be the best new sociological work on gender and intimacy. The book is designed for use in classes on gender roles, sexual inequality, marriage and the family, and women's studies. It is organized into four sections. Part One, "Gender Relations and Historical Change: Past, Present, and Future," is designed to provide the reader with some understanding of the larger institutional forces that have created the conditions under which our current beliefs about gender have developed. The chapters in this first section illustrate how industrialization has helped to change the meaning and shape of our most intimate relationships. The rest of the book focuses more specifically on how the microstructural variables of social expectations and networks shape gendered behavior.

Part Two highlights the importance of social expectations, placement in social networks, and sexual inequality for relationships between friends and lovers. Part Three, "Becoming a Parent: Options and Realities," shows how microstructural variables help explain contemporary sex differences in parenting styles. The chapters in Part Four, "Interconnections Between Work and Family," illustrate that we can never study intimate relationships or gendered behavior isolated from the world of paid work. Economic needs and constraints set the context in which we experience our private desires.

Some of the chapters have been published before, others were written especially for this volume. We have not attempted to cover every kind of intimate relationship, nor every stage in the life cycle. Instead, each chapter was chosen to provide solid empirical evidence for our thesis, while helping the reader to better understand contemporary relationships in and outside the family.

We find the microstructural explanation convincing for ourselves and so we offer it to the reader. But we believe this book should do more than advance this perspective. We think this new approach to intimacy should have a profound impact on social policy about men and women in society today. If we adopt an individualist position, changing the relation of the sexes to one another, in the labor force or in the family is a long and laborious process. The individualist approach assumes that in order to end sexual inequality we must re-socialize everyone -- parents and children, husbands and wives, employers and employees. This laborious re-socialization process, plus the impediments of biology, will surely take a very long time to create an egalitarian society. Moreover, serious reluctance to re-socialization may resurface because many will fear that by changing the "essential" nature of men and women, we may lose those personality capacities we find socially necessary (for example, competitiveness in men for career advancement or nurturance in women for family strength).

If our microstructural approach is correct, however, the assumptions of necessarily slow change and the loss of desirable traits are not accurate. Change need not be so slow if it comes by changing situational experiences and economic conditions rather than by re-socializing individuals or teaching them new directives from birth.

Moreover, we will not lose valued personality traits if we keep the institutions that promote them. As long as we work in hierarchical institutions, we will maintain the competitive personalities and behaviors necessary to climb to the top. And if equal opportunities are truly available, competitiveness will be produced equally in both men and women. If we want to make sure that nurturance remains widely distributed (among women, or men for that matter), we will make sure that opportunities to "mother" and be involved in family systems are easy options to claim.

In other words, if the reader finds our theory of gender formation convincing, social change can be accomplished by restructuring the environment and designing new opportunities for men and women, not by re-training individuals. For example, social policy designed to reduce differences between men and women, based on our theory, would not only encourage but *expect* men to do substantial infant care, would provide parental leaves and flex-time for both men and women, and would reduce the wage differential between male and female workers. Our vision is not therapeutic; it is architectural. Rather than focus on assertiveness training programs we feel that female assertiveness will grow when the jobs women hold demand it, when women are accorded high status, and when institutional forces support female aggressiveness. We believe male nurturance will develop when men are held responsible for caring for others. If we are right, that gender is created by everyday life and everyday institutions, then escaping gender constraints is a matter of redesigning the social structure.

We do not mean to imply that macro- and microstructural social forces together are deterministic, or that free will does not exist. Social structural forces do not develop magically, or spring full-formed from some mysterious celestial space. Human beings, in our creative attempt to solve everyday problems, have -- over time -- created the social forces that direct our lives. A full understanding of the social structure must include -- not deny -- the two-way relationship between individuals and society. We focus heavily on how microstructural forces create gendered behavior in intimate relationships, but we must all remain aware that when individuals collectively choose to defy current expectations and to organize new agendas, they eventually change the social structure itself. Indeed, this is what we recommend.

When social structural forces are in flux -- when individuals face conflicting options, opportunities, and expectations -- their choices shape, mold, and create the structural forces that future generations will take for granted. The choices we make today between conflicting work and family roles will shape tomorrow's social structure. These readings concentrate on showing how intimate relationships are currently constrained by socially created gender. We do not cover every aspect of life that helps construct gender, but this is one place, close to our hearts, to begin.

References

Bandura, Albert, and Richard H. Walters. 1963. *Social Learning and Personality Development*. New York: Holt, Rinehart and Winston.

Beckhouse, Lawrence, Judith Tanur, John Weiler, and Eugene Weinstein. 1975. "And Some Men Have Leadership Thrust Upon Them," *Journal of Personality and Social Psychology, 31*(3): 557-566.

Bem, Sandra L. and Darby J. Bem. 1976. "Case Study of a Nonconscious Ideology: Training the Woman to Know Her Place," in Sue Cox (ed.), *Female Psychology: The Emerging Self.* Chicago: Science Research Associates, pp. 180-190.

Berger, Joseph, Bernard P. Cohen, and Morris Zelditch, Jr. 1972. "Status Characteristics and Social Interaction," *American Sociological Review 37*: 241-255.

Chodorow, Nancy. 1978. *The Reproduction of Mothering.* Berkeley: University of California Press.

Geis, F. L., V. Brown, J. Jennings, and D. Corrado-Taylor. 1984. "Sex vs. Status in Sex-Associated Stereotypes," *Sex Roles 11*(9/10): 771-785.

Gilligan, Carol. 1982. *In a Different Voice.* Cambridge, MA: Harvard University Press.

Goode, William J. 1960. "A Theory of Role Strain." *American Sociological Review 24*: 38-47.

Granovetter, Mark. 1985. "Economic Action, Social Structure, and Embeddedness," *American Journal of Sociology 91*(3): 481-510.

Hewitt, John P. 1979. *Self and Society: A Symbolic Interactionist Social Psychology.* Boston: Allyn and Bacon.

Hughes, Everett C. 1945. "Dilemmas and Contradictions of Status," *American Journal of Sociology 50*: 353-359.

Kanter, Rosabeth. 1977. *Men and Women of the Corporation.* New York: Harper and Row.

Kohlberg, Lawrence. 1966. "A Cognitive-Developmental Analysis of Children's Sex-Role Concepts and Attitudes," in Eleanor Maccoby (ed.), *The Development of Sex Differences.* Stanford: Stanford University Press, pp. 82-173.

Kollock, Peter, Philip Blumstein, and Pepper Schwartz. 1985. "Sex and Power in Interaction: Conversational Privileges and Duties," *American Sociological Review, 50*(1): 34-46.

Lorber, Judith. 1984. *Women Physicians: Careers, Status, and Power.* New York: Tavistock.

Mayhew, Bruce H. 1980. "Structuralism Versus Individuals: Part I, Shadow Boxing in the Dark," *Social Forces 59*(2): 335-375.

Meeker, B. F., and P. A. Weitzell-O'Neill. 1977. "Sex Roles and Interpersonal Behavior in Task-Oriented Groups," *American Sociological Review 42*: 91-105.

Merton, Robert K. 1975. "Structural Analysis in Sociology," in P. M. Blau (ed.), *Approaches to the Study of Social Structure.* New York: Free Press, pp. 21-52.

Mischel, Walter. 1966. "A Social Learning View of Sex Differences in Behavior," in Eleanor Maccoby (ed.), *The Development of Sex Differences.* Stanford: Stanford University Press.

Ridgeway, Cecilia L. 1982. "Status in Groups: The Importance of Motivation." *American Sociological Review 47*: 76-88.

Risman, Barbara J. 1987. "Intimate Relationships from a Microstructural Perspective: Men Who Mother," *Gender and Society 1*(1): 6-32.

_____. 1986. "Can Men Mother: Life as a Single Father," *Family Relations 35*(1): 95-102.

Risman, Barbara, and Kyung Park. 1988. "Just the Two of Us: Parent-Child Relationships in Single-Parent Homes," *Journal of Marriage and the Family.* Forthcoming.

Rossi, Alice S. 1984. "Gender and Parenthood," *American Sociological Review 49*: 1-19.

Stryker, Sheldon. 1981. "Symbolic Interactionism: Themes and Variations," in Morris Rosenberg and Ralph H. Turner (eds.), *Social Psychology: Sociological Perspectives*. New York: Basic Books.

_____. 1980. *Symbolic Interactionism: A Social Structural View*. Menlo Park, CA: Benjamin/Cummings.

Symons, Donald. 1979. *The Evolution of Human Sexuality*. New York: Oxford University Press.

Thompson, Martha E. 1981. "Sex Differences: Differential Access to Power or Sex Role Socialization?" *Sex Roles, 7*(4): 413-424.

Van den Berghe, Pierre L. 1979. *Human Family Systems: An Evolutionary View*. New York: Elsevier.

Wagner, David G., Rebecca S. Ford, and Thomas W. Ford. 1986. "Can Gender Inequalities Be Reduced?" *American Sociological Review 51*(1): 47-60.

Weinstein, Eugene, and Paul Deutschberger. 1963. "Some Divisions of Altercasting," *Sociometry 26*(4): 454-466.

Weitzman, Lenore J. 1979. *Sex Role Socialization*. Palo Alto, CA: Mayfield.

Wilson, Edward O. 1978. *On Human Nature*. Cambridge, MA: Harvard University Press.

Wrong, Dennis H. 1961. "The Oversocialized Conception of Man in Modern Sociology," *American Sociological Review 26*(2): 183-193.

Notes

[1] We are not suggesting that stable personality traits do not exist, only that gendered behavior is not primarily a consequence of gendered personality traits.

Chapter 13

Masculine style affection. In this essay, men's expressiveness is explored. Impirical evidence of larger samples supports this qualitative detailing of how men act out the style of expressiveness that is the norm for close friendships with other men. Swain reports, in verbatim narratives, how what he considers covert intimacy is communicated when a man interacts with another man that he considers a close friend. The covert style for men is different than the overt style that style that happens to be the more accepted definition of what intimacy is in our culture. Thus, sometimes, male expressiveness is misinterpreted as nonexpressiveness. The reader is encouraged to extend the ideas presented in this study to how men and women interpret covert expressions of intimacy differently. How much need is there for expressive role flexibility on the part of men? How much role flexibility (covert vs. overt) is expected of women?

Chapter 13 *Scott Swain,* Covert Intimacy: Closeness in Men's Friendships

This study is an analysis of college men's intimate behavior in same-sex friendships and their standards for assessing intimacy. It documents the development, causes, and manifestation of a covert style of intimate behavior in men's friendships. Covert intimacy is a private, often nonverbal, context-specific form of communication. The concept of covert intimacy is rooted in the behaviors that men reported as indicative of closeness and intimacy in their relationships with other men.

First, I trace differences in the development of men's and women's adolescent friendships that shape and promote differing styles of intimacy. Next, such contexts are linked to the emergence of the separate worlds of men and women and how such separate worlds and microstructural contexts continue into adulthood. I analyze these separate worlds for the specific behaviors and values that shape intimacy among same-sex friends, and then clarify the distinctive cues and nuances of men's intimate behavior by comparing them to behaviors in male-female platonic friendships and friendships among women. I conclude the study with an assessment of the strengths and limitations of men's covert style of intimacy with men friends and its relationship to the inexpressive male.

The Inexpressive Male, or Sex-Specific Styles of Intimacy

Sex-role theorists have characterized men as instrumental (Parsons and Bales, 1955), agentive (Bakan, 1966), and task-oriented (Komarovsky, 1964). Women have been characterized as expressive (Parsons and Bales, 1955), communal (Bakan, 1966), and empathic (Hoffman, 1977; Bem, 1976). Consistent with these theoretical formulations, researchers on the male role have interpreted men's interpersonal behavior as non-intimate and have stressed the restraints and limitations that cultural conceptions of masculinity impose on intimate expression. Examples of this *deficit approach* to men's intimate capabilities are Jack Balswick's "The Inexpressive Male" (1976) and Mirra Komarovsky's concept of men's "trained incapacity to share" (1964).

In recent years many of these generalizations, which were based on slight yet significant sex differences, have been reexamined. The majority of studies that measure interpersonal skills and relationship characteristics report nonsignificant sex differences (Maccoby and Jacklin, 1974; Pleck, 1981; Tavris and Wade, 1984). When studies report significant sex differences, the results have been mixed and sometimes conflicting. In support of the male deficit model, men are reported to be less likely than women to disclose sadness and fears (Rubin, 1983; Allen and Hacoun, 1976; Davidson and Duberman, 1982), less affective and spontaneous with friends than women (Booth, 1972), and less adept than women at nonverbal decoding skills (Henley, 1977). Men are also reported to be more homophobic than women, which may inhibit the use of certain interpersonal skills in men's friendships (Lehne, 1976; Morin and Garfinkle, 1978).

However, the majority of self-disclosure studies reveal nonsignificant sex differences (Cozby, 1973); and related analyses report that men score higher than women on nonverbal decoding skills (Hall and Halberstadt, 1981), rate their friendships as more trusting and spontaneous than do women (Davidson and Duberman, 1982), and value intimacy in friendship as much as do women (Caldwell and Peplau, 1982). In view of such findings and the conflicting results of other related studies, sex differences in interpersonal behavior appear to be minor or not adequately measured. However, notions of the "inexpressive male" continue to persist and guide research on men's interpersonal behavior.

Perhaps the most consistently reported difference in men's and women's friendships is men's preference for joint activities and women's preference for talking (Caldwell and Peplau, 1982; Cancian, 1985). Men's emphasis on instrumental action has been interpreted by past researchers as a less personal and less intimate form of interaction than verbal self-disclosure (Komarovsky, 1964; Rubin, 1983; Davidson and Duberman, 1982). This interpretation may be influenced by researchers' reliance on measuring feminine-type styles of behavior to assess topics involving love and interpersonal behavior. This bias has been critiqued by Cancian as the "feminization of love" (1986). Researchers concerned with intimacy have assumed that verbal self-disclosure is the definitive referent for intimacy, and have thus interpreted alternative styles that involve instrumental action as a less intimate, or nonintimate, behavior. [Previous definitions of intimacy relied primarily on verbal self-disclosure as an indicator of intimacy. But, the relationship between intimacy and self-disclosure is usually only implied and not specially defined.]

Caldwell and Peplau (1982) suggest that men and women may place the same value on intimacy in friendships, yet have different ways of assessing intimacy. Men are reported to express a wider range of intimate behaviors, including self-disclosure, while participating in gender-validating activities (Swain, 1984). Men may develop sex-specific contexts, cues, and meaning, which connote feelings and appraisals of intimacy similar to those connoted by self-disclosure for women.

Intimacy is defined in the present study as *behavior in the context of a friendship that connotes a positive and mutual sense of meaning and importance to the participants*. This definition allows respondents to determine what behaviors are meaningful and intimate, and assumes that there may be several avenues that may result in the experience of intimacy.

The results presented here are based on in-depth interview with fifteen men and five women. The college sample was young and white with a mean age of 22.5 years. This small sample was used to further explore sex-specific friendship behaviors, which have been significantly documented using larger samples of similar populations (Swain, 1984; Caldwell and Peplau, 1982).

The interview protocol was based on two empirical studies: the first was a pilot study (N=232) that measured the relative value of activities in men's and women's same-sex friendships, and the second (N=140) measured the relative importance and meaning that men and women attributed to those activities (Swain, 1984).

Interviews lasted an average of an hour and a half, with a female interviewer working with female subjects and a male interviewer (myself) working with the male subjects. For analysis, we then transcribed and organized the interviews by question and content. A disadvantage of such a focused sample is that the results may not generalize across age groups, or even represent this particular subgroup. However, we selected a private and personal interview setting to collect more detailed data about sensitive information concerning intimacy in friendships than would otherwise be possible when using larger samples and less personal data-collection techniques. Because of the college setting, we expected the sample to have more friends and contact with same-sex friends than men and women from the general population. The advantages of this sample of young adults are their temporal closeness to the development of adolescent friendships and their frequent interaction with friends because of the college environment. This should promote clarity in their recollections of the development of adolescent friendship behaviors and give them a sharpened and more sensitive vantage point from which to describe their current friendships with men and women.

The Development of Sex-Specific Styles of Intimacy: The Separate Worlds of Boys and Girls

Men and women grow up in overlapping, yet distinctly different worlds. Sex segregation begins at an early age when boys and girls are differently rewarded for various play activities. Boys are encouraged to actively participate in the outside environment by parental acceptance of the risks of physical injury and parents' flexible attitude toward personal hygiene and appearance. Torn clothes, skinned knees, and dirty hands are signs of the normal growth of healthy boys. If girls choose these same activities, they may be tolerated; however, they may be sanctioned differently. For example, the term tom-boy" is used to distinguish a girl with "boyish" behaviors, and to designate a stage of development that deviates from normative expectations of the female child. Several men attributed the distinctive friendship behaviors of men to this early segregation while growing up. Jim said:

> Well, you do different things. Little boys, they'll play in the dirt and things, whereas a guy and a girl they might play in the house or something. The guys like... they don't mind getting dirty. I don't want to stereotype or anything, but its' just the way I see it. The guys are more rugged and things.

Pete responded to the question, "How do you act just around the guys?"

> You'd talk about anything, do anything. You aren't as polite. You don't care as much how you look, how you dress, what you wear, things of that nature. Even if we're just platonic friends, for some reason when you're around girls you're different. In the United States men and women don't share bathrooms together in the public restrooms. That's a good example, right there -- obviously men and women are segregated then. That segregations exists in friendships, too.

Separate bathrooms are a concrete manifestations of the different realms experienced by boys and girls as they grow up and of the restrictions on crossing over into the other sex's domain. The curiosity that boys and girls experience about what the bathrooms are actually like for the other sex is evidence of this separateness. A boy who is teased and pushed into the girl's bathroom is called a "girl" as he hastily exits. Thus, children internalize sex-segregated boundaries and enforce these restrictions. Evidence of the long-term influence of this segregation is the humiliation and embarrassment an adult feels when accidentally entering the "wrong" bathroom. The association between gender and specific contexts is also suggested by men referring to a woman who is included in a men's poker game as being "just one of the guys." The separate contexts of men and women continue throughout the life cycle to shape the ways they express intimacy.

The male world is the outside environment of physical activity. Boys share and learn activities with male friends that involve an engagement with this outside world. Social encouragement is evident in such organizations as the Boy Scouts (Hantover, 1978), sports and recreation programs (Coleman, 1976; Stein and Hoffman, 1978), and a division of labor that often has boys doing home chores that are outdoors, such as mowing lawns. These outside activities have a shaping influence on their interests and values. Jack recalled his adolescence:

> I can remember only one friend that I had from years past. My friend Jim. Just the kind of all the fun we had, boyhood fun. We built a fort, lit firecrackers, and all that stuff.

He refers to "boyhood" rather than "childhood" fun, implying that these experiences tended to be shared with other males. Another man recalled:

172

The activities shared were a lot of outdoor-type things -- fishing, hunting, Tom Sawyer type things. It's a commonalty that we both shared that helped bring us together.

Men mentioned activities that ranged from dissecting lizards, riding bikes, and childhood sports to four-wheeling, lifting weights, playing practical jokes on friends, problem solving, and talking about relationships as they reached adulthood. By the time high school graduation arrives, most males have had more experiences and time with men friends than with women friends. Several men commented on this early division in their friendships. For instance, Rick replied:

Up to the sixth or seventh grade girls are "stay away from the girls!" So during that whole time you only associate with the guys, and you have all these guys friends. And after that you kind of, you know, the first time you go out, you're kind of shy with the girls, and you don't get to know them too well... I really didn't get over being shy with girls until my senior year.

His first contact with girls is in the dating context of "going out," which implies a heterosexual coupling dimension to the relationship in addition to friendship. The segregated contexts of men and women continue into adulthood, and shape the opportunities for expressing intimacy and the expectations of how that intimacy is to be expressed. As a result, men are more familiar with their men friends, and women are more familiar with their women friends.

Consequences of the Separate Worlds of Men and Women

Self-Disclosure: Profanity, Sameness, and Group Lingo

As boys move through adolescence surrounded and immersed in friendships with other boys, behavioral differences emerge that distinguish men's and women's friendships. Men develop language patterns that often rely on blunt, crude, and explicitly sexual terms. Bluntness, crudity, and profanity legitimize masculinity by tending to roughen the tone of any statement that a man may make. Swearing serves as a developmental credential in an adolescent boy's maturation process, much as do smoking, drinking, and getting one's driver's license. The "rugged" and "dirty" environment that boys share is translated into a coarser language during adolescence, which is also labeled as "dirty." Men felt that this language was more appropriate around other men, and then often related this sex-specific language to all-male contexts such as military service and sports. Greg responded:

Well (laugh), not that I cuss a lot, but when I, you know, get around the baseball field and stuff like that... They [women] don't like that. I try to stay away from the crude or harsh humor as much as I can (laugh).

Greg's laughing suggested a tense recognition that men's use of language in "harsh humor" does not easily translate in the company of women.

Men's harsh language and sexual explicitness in joking behavior are censored and muted when interacting with women friends. The censoring of humor to avoid offending women friends testifies to the different meaning and value men and women attribute to the same behaviors. Mike related:

Around girls you act more of a gentleman. You don't cuss. You watch what you say. Because you don't want to say anything that will offend them.

Men felt more at ease with close men friends, partially from a perception of "sameness." Men assume that male friends will be more empathetic concerning sexual matters since they have similar bodies. Jack related:

I find it much easier to talk about sexual things with guys, which makes sense.

A majority of the men said it was easier to talk to men about sexual matters than to women. Another man responded to the question, "What are some of the things that would be easier to talk over with a guy?"

Anything from financial problems to problems with relationships. That's a big thing I really don't like talking to girls about. For some reason I just... I don't know... I get.... usually because what I'm saying is from a male's point of view. And I know this is all sounding really sexist. But you know, there are certain things that I view that girls don't necessarily view the same way. And it's just easier talking to guys about that. Well, lately sex is one of those. I mean you can talk about certain sexual things; there are certain things. I had a conversation the other day, and he was talking to me about a sexual act that his girlfriend, his new girlfriend, wanted to do. And he really doesn't care to do it. There's no way I could talk to a girl about what he's talking about.

The men appeared to generalize a common world view to other men that fostered a feeling of comfort. Frank commented:

I'm more relaxed around guys. You don't have to watch what you say. Around friends like that [men] I wouldn't... what could you say? I wouldn't be careful I shouldn't say something like this, or I shouldn't do this. That's because with the guys, they're just like you.

Men friends used the degree of comfort and relaxation experienced with men friends as an indicator of closeness. Matt described this feeling when asked about the meaningful times he has shared with men friends.

Last week some really good friends of mine in my suite... one guy plays the guitar. And so he was just sitting around playing the guitar and we were making up tunes. We were making up songs to this, and that was really a lot of fun. The fun things come to mind. We rented a VCR and some movies and watched those, and just all the laughing together comes to mind as most remarkable. As to the most meaningful, those also come pretty close to being the most meaningful, because there was just total relaxation, there. That I felt no need to worry. There's no need to worry about anyone making conversation. The conversation will come. And we can laugh at each other, and you can laugh at yourself, which is handy.

Men were asked to compare their friendships with men to their platonic friendships with women. Generally, men felt more at ease and relaxed when with close men friends than with women friends. John answered the question, "Are there any differences between your friendships with men and your friendships with women?"

> You don't have to worry about the situation you're in. If you have to go to the bathroom, you just run up and go. You don't have to worry about "please excuse me" or anything. And it's a lot more relaxed. A lot more. Like in Jack's house we just go into the kitchen and make ourselves something to eat, you know, part of the family.

The "situation" is comfortable because the men's shared assumptions, cues, and meanings of behavior allow them "not to have to worry" whether they are acting appropriately. The formality associated with women friends is suggestive of Irving Goffman's concept of "frontstage" behavior, which is more rule-bound and distanced, while the "backstage" behavior with men friends is more intimate because of the lack of censoring and the feeling of informality associated with being "part of the family." The shared history, activities, and perception that other men are "just like you" gave a predictable familiarity to men's interactions. Women also felt that their similarity to each other produced an empathy unique between women friends. A woman responded to a question about the differences between her men and women friends:

> There are some things about a woman's feelings that I don't think a man, having never been in a woman's mind, could ever really understand. Because I think most women are a little more sensitive than men.

Men also developed unique terms with their close friends that expressed their history and connectedness. These terms acknowledged the particular experiences shared between friends and underlined their special relationship. When asked about his most meaningful experiences with his men friends, Tim related:

> The best thing, well the thing is, Rick, Mike, and me kind of have our own lingo. I haven't seen other people use them, like "Bonzo" is one of them. Like "go for Bonzo," and anybody else would just go "Well, whatever."

The "lingo" was derived from activities experienced by the group. The private meaning of the language served as a boundary separating friends from people outside the group.

Doing Versus Talking: The Intimacy of Shared Action

The men were asked, "What was the most meaningful occasion spent with a same-sex friend, and why was it meaningful?" The men mentioned a total of 26 meaningful occasions with men friends, and several men mentioned more than one meaningful experience. We analyzed the responses to clarify the link between sharing an activity and feeling close to a friend. Of those occasions, 20 meaningful times were spent in an activity other than talking. Men related a wide range of meaningful experiences from "flirting with disaster" in an out-of-control car and winning a court case to being with a close friend the night that the friend found out his sister had committed suicide. Activities such as fishing, playing guitars, diving, backpacking, drinking, and weightlifting were central to men's meaningful experiences.

Nine meaningful experiences directly referenced the sharing of skills and accomplishments. These meaningful times involved the shared enjoyment of learning and mastering skills and accomplishing goals ranging from a sexual experience with a woman to staying up all night on a weeknight. The essential ingredients in these experiences seemed to be comfort with a competitive challenge and a sense of shared accomplishment. A man responded to the question of what was the most meaningful experience he had shared with a male friend, and later a group of male friends:

> I've always been extremely shy with women, and one of my friends in between, after high school... women were always chasing after him like crazy -- and I'm defensive and stuff with women when one time we went to the river. And a couple of girls picked us up and we got laid and everything. And it was kind of, this is going to sound like the standard male thing, but we all kind of went, after, we went and had a few beers and compared notes. You know, and I felt totally accepted because I had just as many good things to say as they did, and I could relate. I knew what they were talking about, because most of my life I've never known what these guys were talking about sexually.

Although this quote might imply sexual exploitation, several aspects should be considered. First, this man admits he is shy with women, and furthermore he indicates that the women initiated the interaction. He was able to discuss with his men friends a new experience that had been alien to him until this occasion. The argument here is not that his sexual experience was exploitive or intimate; it appears to have been a purely physical encounter between strangers. However, the commonality gained from a shared life experience did provide meaningful interaction among the men.

We further examined the influence of men's active emphasis and women's verbal emphasis on intimate friendship behavior by asking men to compare their friendships with men to their friendships with women. Tim responded to the questions, ""What part of you do your share with your men friends and what part of you do you share with your women friends? How would you characterize those two different parts of you?"

> I think that the men characteristics would be the whole thing, would be just the whole thing about being a man. You know, you go out and play sports with your brothers, and have a good time with them. You just... you're doing that. And there are some things that you can experience, as far as emotional, [with] your best friends that are men... you experience both. And that's what makes it so good is that. With most of the girls you're not going to go out and drink beer and have fun with them. Well, you can, but it's different. I mean it's like a different kind of emotion. It's like with the guys you can have all of it...

Tim says that you can have "the whole thing" with men, suggesting that he can do things and talk about things with his close men friends. With women friends doing things is "different." Tim refers to a "different kind of emotion" and speaks of a "good time" when he is with his men friends. This good feeling may result from the ease and comfort of interacting with close friends who have developed a familiar style of communication from sharing activities.

The value of doing things is apparent in Matt's response, which described his most meaningful times with men friends:

It was like we were doing a lot of things together. It just seemed like we just grew on each other. Can't think of just one thing that stood out in my mind. It was more like a push-pull type thing. Like I'd pull him through things and he'd pull me through things. It wasn't like there was just one thing I can just think of right now, just a lot of things he did, whatever. Just the things we like to do, we just did them together, and just had a good time.

The closeness is in the "doing" -- the sharing of interests and activities. When Matt was asked about his meaningful times with his women friends, he responded:

It's like the things that you'd talk -- it's really just like "talk" with them. It's not so much like you'd go out and do something with them, or go out and maybe be with them.

Several men said that with women friends it's "just talking" and referred to interaction with women as "the lighter side of things." For men, it appears that actions speak louder than words and carry greater interpersonal value.

Women were also aware of a difference in men's style of expressing caring. A women commented on the differences in how her men and women friends let her know that they like her:

Women talk more about feelings than men do. A man might let me know that he likes me because when he was in New York, he saw a book I'd been looking for and he brought it to me. And so I know that he likes me because he did that. Where a woman might say, twelve days in a row, "I've been looking all over for that book, but I can't find it."

Her male friend expressed his caring through a direct action, while her female friend expressed her caring verbally.

The emphasis on activities in men's friendship shapes their communication of closeness and caring. The significance of the doing/talking emphases in men's and women's styles of intimacy is apparent in the following response of a man to the question, "Why do you think they'd [women friends] be more verbal than your guy friends [in showing that they like you]?

I don't know why. I think there's just more ways to... I think there's more ways for the males to show me their appreciation that's nonverbal. I don't know why. I just think that if, in the way that they respond to things we do together and stuff like that. There's more ways to show it. Like if we're, I make a good shot in a game or something, just give me a high-five or something like that. You don't have to say anything with the guys. That's just an example, it doesn't have to be just sports. But the same type of things, off the field or whatever, just a thumbs-up type thing from a guy or whatever. There's just more ways to show being around [each other]. Where with the girls, you know, what can they do? You know, run up and just give you a kiss or something. I know girls who would do that in high school. So it -- I think their options are just less -- so they opt for the verbal type of thing.

He views talking as one option or style of expressing caring. From his activity-oriented perspective, he actually views women as restricted by a lack of alternatives to verbal expressiveness. These expressive alternatives are available to men through cues developed by sharing and understanding common activities. Nonverbal cues, expressed in active settings, contribute to private, covert, and in general, sex-specific styles of intimacy. This suggests that each sex tends to overlook, devalue, and not fully comprehend the other sex's style of expressing care.

Men and women have different styles of intimacy that reflect the often-separate realms in which they express it. The activities and contexts that men share provide a common general experience from which emerge certain values, gestures, and ways of talking about things that show intimacy. Both men and women are restricted in crossing over into each other's realm by early sex segregation, which results in a lack of experience with the meanings and contexts of the other sex. Researchers often underestimate this segregation because of an emphasis on the loosening of sex-related boundaries in the past several decades. Despite such changes, sex segregation still influences men and women, especially during the development of friendships in adolescence.

Covert Intimacy in Sports and Competition

Sports are the primary format for rewarding the attainment and demonstration of physical and emotional skills among adolescent boys. A man stated:

> I would have rather taken my basketball out than I would a girl... you
> know how young men are in the seventh, eighth, and ninth grade... if I had
> the choice I'd play basketball with the guys instead of going out that night.

Researchers have documented detrimental interpersonal consequences that may result from sports participation (Stein and Hoffman, 1978; Coleman, 1976). However, the productive aspects of the sports context have received less attention from researchers. For men, the giving and receiving of help and assistance in a challenge context demonstrates trust and caring in a friendship. Engaging in the risk and drama of performing in a competitive activity provides the glue that secures the men in an intimate process of accomplishing shared goals. Jim responded to the question, "What situations or activities would you choose or would you feel most comfortable in with your close men friends?"

> I'm very comfortable, like playing racquetball. A lot of one-on-one things
> where you're actually doing something. Playing backgammon. Now being
> competitive makes it a little easier, because it's like a small battle going
> on. Not that you're out to show who's best, but it gives you something
> more that you two have in common in the situation.

The competition provides a structured context where friends can use their skills to create "something more" than they previously had in common. Each friend brings his own experiences and talents to join the other friend in the common arena of a competitive activity. The competition provides an overt and practical meaning; the covert goal, however, is not to "show who's best" but to give "something more that you two have in common."

The sports context provides a common experience whereby men can implicitly demonstrate closeness without directly verbalizing the relationship. Nonverbal communication skills, which are essential for achieving goals in the fast moving sports context, also provide avenues for communicating intimacy. Greg responded to the question, "What were the most meaningful times that you spent with your men friends?"

> In athletics, the majority of these friends that are close to me were on teams of mine. We played together. We were on the same team, me playing first and him catcher, or at times he played third. You know, first and third looking across the infield at each other. Knowing that we were close friends, and winning the CIF championship. I could just see that it meant a lot to me in terms of friendship too. As soon as that last pitch was made, we just clinched the title, to see the first person that he looked for to give, you know, to hug or congratulate, or whatever, was me. And the same for me to him. That was a big, another emotional thing for the two of us. Because I could just... it's just... you could just see how close your friends really are, or something like that. When there's twenty-five guys on the team and they're all going crazy, you're just trying to rejoice together, or whatever, for the victory. And the first, the main thing you wanted to do was run across the diamond and get to each other, and just congratulate each other first. And that meant a lot to me emotionally as well as far as friendship is concerned. It was only a split second, because after it was just a mob.

The two friends had grown up playing baseball together. Sharing the accomplishment of winning the championship provided a context where a close friendship could be affirmed and acknowledged nonverbally in "only a split second." Other members of the team, and perhaps even family members, may not have been aware of the intimacy that took place. The nonverbal nature of the glance and the context of excitement in the team's rejoicing after the victory allowed the intimacy to be expressed privately in a covert fashion. Both the intimate style and the context in which the intimacy was expressed contributed to an environment that was relatively safe from ridicule.

How Do I Know You Like Me: Intimacy and Affection in Men's Friendships

When asked, "How do you know that your men friends like you?" only one man responded that his friend tells him directly that he likes him. If men do not tend to self-disclose to each other the closeness of their friendship, how do they evaluate closeness and intimacy with a man friend? In men's friendships with other men, doing something together and choosing a friend and asking him if he wants to participate in an activity demonstrate that they like one another and enjoy being together. These acts have a meaning similar to a boy who asks a girl to a dance; it's assumed that he likes her by the nature of the action. Mike responded to the question, "How do you know or get the idea that they [men friends] like you?"

> When I suggest that we do something I can tell in their voice or the way their actions are that they want to do it. Like hey! they really want to do it. Like, "Anyone want to go to the baseball game?" "Yeah, great! That's exactly what I want to do." That's a good feeling to know that you can make some sort of a suggestion that fits. Laughter, the joking, the noise.

Knowing that they like to do the things that I like to do and that I like to do the things that they like to do. And it's the same in reverse, and basically I want to do it as well, me agreeing with them. As far as that goes, you'd say, I like it when they show me by asking me, if they want to do it with me.

Men mentioned physical gestures, laughing at jokes, doing one another favors, keeping in touch, "doing stuff," teasing, and just being around friends as ways they know that men friends like each other. The most common responses to the question of how their men friends let them know that they liked them were "doing things together" and "initiating contact." John responded:

I think it's just something you can sense, that you feel by... obviously if you continue to go out and do things with them.

Mike responded:

Well, they'll call me up and ask me to do stuff, if they have nothing to do, or if they do have something to do and they want me to be a part of it.

Men feel liked by other men as a result of being asked to spend time in activities of common interest. Within such active contexts, reciprocated assistance, physical gestures, language patterns, and joking behaviors all had distinctive meanings that indicated intimacy between male friends.

Reciprocity of Assistance. Men mentioned doing favors, which included mailing a letter, fixing a car, loaning money, and talking about problems relating to heterosexual relationships. The men emphasized a reciprocity of assistance and a goal orientation to both problem solving and situations that involved self-disclosure. This reciprocity demonstrated mutual interest and also was a means to achieve a balanced dependency. Pete responded to the question, "How do your friends let you know that they like you?"

We help each other out, just like doing favors for someone. Like right now, me and my roommate were going to class, and he was asking me questions because he slept in and didn't study. So I go "what's this -- OK, here, just have my notes." Even though I'm going to need them for my thing at three. You know, just little stuff like that.

Matt referred to the assistance given between his closest male friend and himself as a "barter" arrangement.

Jack and I had a good relationship about this. He's a very good mechanic, and I would ask him. And I would develop something that I do that was rewarding for him. Like I could pull strings and get free boat trips and stuff like that when I was an [diving] instructor. And he would work on my car and I would turn him on to the Islands and dives and stuff. It was sort of a barter situation.

The sharing of their skills and access to opportunities fostered interdependency, yet also maintained their independence through a mutual give-and-take.

Physical Gestures. Men also reported physically demonstrating affection to each other. However, the physical gestures had a distinctively masculine style that protected them from the fear of an interpretation of a homosexual preference. Men mentioned handshakes, bear hugs, slaps on the back, and an arm on the shoulder as ways that friends demonstrated affection.

Handshakes were the most frequently mentioned. Handshakes offer controlled physical contact between men and are often considered an indicator of strength and manliness. A strong, crisp, and forthright grip is a sign of "respectable" masculinity while a limp and less robust handshake may be associated with femininity and a homosexual orientation. A bear hug also offers a demonstration of strength, often with one friend lifting another off the ground. Gary described an occasion in his response to the question, "How do your men friends let you know that they like you?"

> I came back from a swim meet in Arkansas last week, and I hadn't seen Mike for two weeks. When I came back he came right at me and gave me a big old bear hug, you know, stuff like that. And my mom and dad were in the room, and they're going, "Hey, put my son down!" and we were all laughing.

Men give the affectionate hug a "rugged," nonfeminine veneer by feigning playful aggression through the demonstration of physical strength. The garb and trappings of roughness allow a man to express affection while reducing the risks of making his friend uncomfortable or having his sexual identity ridiculed. A slap on the back is much less risky for a man than a caress on the cheek, although they may have a similar message in the communication of closeness.

Joking Behavior. Men develop joking behaviors that communicate closeness and similar ways of viewing the world. Ken responded to the question, "How do you get the idea that they [men friends] are close friends?"

> Laughter is one of them. I'll admit, when I'm around anybody really, not just them, I try to be the world's best comic. Like I said, humor is just important and I love it. I'd rather... I just like to laugh. And when they laugh, and they get along with me, and we joke with each other, and not get personal, they don't take it too harshly.

Although Ken says he attempts to be a comic "when I'm around anybody," he goes on to elaborate about the differences in joking when around men or around women:

> For the girls, not so much the laughter because you can't, with the comedian atmosphere, or whatever, you can't tell with the women... Because, you know, if you get together with some girl or someone that likes you a little bit, or whatever -- you can tell them that your dog just died, and they'll laugh. You know what I mean, you know how it goes. It's just, they'll laugh at anything, just to... I don't know why it is. But you get together with certain girls and they'll just laugh no matter what you say. So it's kind of hard to base it on that. Because the guys, you know, they'll say it's a crappy joke or something like that, or say that was a terrible thing.

181

Women friends did not respond to his humor in as straightforward and rigorous a manner as did his men friends. This appears to be a result of a covert sexual agenda between the cross-sex friends and a misunderstanding of the cues and nuances of male joking behavior by his women friends. Joking behaviors often are rooted in the contexts of men's shared experience, an experience that women may have little access to. Joking relationships are used by men to show caring and to establish trust in the midst of competitive activities. The following response to the question, "What are the most meaningful occasions that you spent with a male friend?" demonstrated a context where joking behavior expressed intimacy in the midst of competitive action. First, Greg describes the context in which the joking took place.

> The first time I'd been waterskiing was last summer. And among these guys I was really athletic, maybe more so than them even. And he knew how to waterski and I didn't. And we got there, and I tried maybe six or eight times, and couldn't do it, just couldn't do it. I don't know what the deal was because I'm really an athletic person and I figure it wouldn't be that tough, and it was tough. As far as the friendship goes, for Mark, for him to sit there and have the patience to teach me what to do, what was going on, it must have taken an hour or so or more of just intense teaching. Like he was the coach and I was the player, and we got done with that and I did it. And the next time we went I was on one ski, thanks to him. It was that much of an improvement. And to know that we could communicate that well around something that I love, sports, and to know that we could communicate that well in something that we both like a lot, athletics, that meant a lot to our friendship.

Mark provided assistance that altered a potential traumatic experience into a positive success. Specifically, Mark used a joking relationship to reduce the pressure on Greg and allowed him to perform while in a vulnerable position. Mark did not exploit his superior capabilities, but shared them and empowered his friends. Greg explains:

> We were just able to make jokes about it, and we laughed at each other all day. And it finally worked out. I mean it was great for me to be that frustrated and that up-tight about it and know the only thing he was going to do was laugh at me. That may seem bad to some people. They'd have gotten more upset. But for me that was good... It really put things in perspective.

The joking cues expressed acceptance and communicated to Greg that it was okay to fail, and that failing would not jeopardize continuing the lesson. Mark's acceptance of a friend's failures reduced the performance pressure on Greg, and thus released him to concentrate on learning to water-ski.

Joking behavior is important to me because it offers a style of communication that consists of implicit meanings not readily accessible to people outside the group. "In" jokes between friends demand attentiveness to an individual's thinking, emotional states and reactions, and nuances of behavior. They provide a format where a man can be meticulously attentive to the feelings and tastes of another man. An elaborate reciprocation of jokes can be a proxy for more overt forms of caring. Yet, because joking behavior is often used as a distancing gesture and hostile act, joking behavior is not interpreted as an expression of attachment. This adds to the covert nature of the act and further protects men from possible ridicule. The tenuous line between aggression and affection is demonstrated by Tim's response to the question, "Can you think of any other qualities that would be important to a close friendship?"

> Basically that they'll understand you. Like if you do something wrong and they go, "Oh, what a jerk." I mean they can say it, but they'll say it in a different way than some guy who shoots his mouth off, "What a jerk, you fell off your bicycle."

Tim was questioned further, "How would it be different -- I know what you mean -- but can you describe it?"

> You know, they'll poke fun at you but they'll say it in a friendly way. Where someone else will just laugh. "What an idiot," and they'll mean it. Where your friend will say... you know, just make fun of you and stuff. I don't know if I explained it too well.

The same words used by two different men are interpreted and reacted to in very different ways. The tone of voice and social distance between the two men are essential factors in the determination of an understanding friend as opposed to an aggressive enemy. Tim's reactions to both cues reveal the different meanings. The question was asked, "Okay, maybe if I ask another question to get at it, say you fell off your bike, how would you feel when your friend joked about you as opposed to...?"

> I would just start laughing, you know. I mean he'd start laughing at me and I'd just look and he'd go, "You jerk," and I'll start laughing. We know each other and stuff. Some guy off the street -- I'll just cuss at him and flip him off, you know. So it's a little different.

Such discriminations are difficult for men to explain and describe. This would suggest that the discriminating task may be even more difficult for women, who have not had the experience in the contexts from which men's friendships have developed. Matt explained how he lets his closest male friend know that he likes him.

> I'll have a tendency to say, "Well, why don't you write?" in a teasing way, and "Okay, when are we going to get together?... and this bullshit of you being up there in Stockton."

Coarse language is injected into the teasing to legitimize the implicit meaning that he misses his friend and wishes that they were together. Joking relationships provide men with an implicit form of expressing affection, which is an alternative to explicit forms such as hugging and telling people that they care about them. Joking also may be more personal, since it often relies on a knowledge and sensitivity to a friend's attitudes and tastes, thus recognizing and affirming a unique part of him. The following portion of an interview demonstrates this masculine style. Jim responds to the question, "Why do you think [women are more likely than men to come out and tell you that they like you] that is?"

> Oh, it's just the way you were raised. It's society. You might hug a girl and say, "See you later and good luck on your test tomorrow." Whereas you'll joke around with a guy about it.

"Why would you joke around with a guy?"

It's just a... it's just a different relationship, you know. I think society would accept two girls hugging each other and a guy hugging a girl, but it's a little different when you're two guys. I don't know if you saw the movie *Grease* where there, like Danny and that other guy who's driving the car, they do it, well like they hug each other right? After they pull out of the shop, it's kind of like that, they stop, they realize what they did. You might even want to, you might wanna say, "Hey, thanks a lot." You do stuff like that. But you don't act silly. You might shake their hand.

Jim was asked if he hugged his closest male friend, to which he responded, "No, I don't do that." He was then asked, "How would it feel if you went up to hug Fred [closest male friend]? How do you think he would react?"

Well, I can remember a couple of times that we had... after a football game when you're real excited and things. It all depends on the situation. If I just did it, you know, out of the clear blue sky, he'd probably look at me and, you know. I could do it jokingly. It might even be pretty funny. I might try that. But I don't think he'd like it. He'd probably think it was a little strange.

Jim was able to hug his friend after a football game, when emotions ran high, and the men's masculinity had just been validated by participating in, and presumably wining, the game. The football context insulated the hugging from being interpreted as unmanly or gay. Jim says, "It depends on the situation." At one point when Jim was asked what it would be like to hug his friend, he interpreted it as a challenge or a dare. "I could do that." However, he translates the act into a joking behavior, "I could do it jokingly," in an effort to stylize the hug as masculine. Men's styles of intimacy attempt to minimize the risks taken when overtly expressing affection. These risks are summed up best by Jim when asked why he would feel strange if he hugged his best male friend. Jim said:

The guys are more rugged and things, and it wouldn't be rugged to hug another man. That's not a masculine act, where it could be, you know, there's nothing unmasculine about it. But somebody might not see it as masculine and you don't want somebody else to think that you're not, you know -- masculine or... but you still don't want to be outcast. Nobody I think wants to be outcast.

Thus Jim could not hug his friend "out of the clear blue sky," overtly and without a gender-validating context. The styles of male intimacy attempt to limit these risks. Joking behavior camouflages the hidden agenda of closeness by combining elements of a private awareness of a friend's history and personal nuances with a public tone of aggression and humiliation. A man describes his most meaningful times with men friends.

The conversation will come and we can kind of laugh at each other. And you can laugh at yourself, which is really handy.

Much as the slap on the back covers an affectionate greeting with an aggressive movement, joking behavior provides a covert avenue in which to express caring and intimacy.

Conclusions

These findings suggest that microstructrual variables, particularly interactional expectations, are powerful explanations for male intimacy styles. Intimacy between men is influenced by their awareness of the restrictive sanctions that are often imposed on men who express certain emotions, such as sadness or fear. Men's intimate verbal style is partially shaped by the fear of sanctions that may be imposed on emotional behaviors deemed culturally unacceptable. Homophobia and the difficulty men have disclosing weaknesses testify to the limitations they experience when attempting to explore certain aspects of their selves. These limitations of male intimacy may distance men from all but their closest men friends, and may also create a premium on privacy and trust in close friendships. Such limitations may be more detrimental later in life where structural settings are less conducive and supportive to maintaining active friendships. A college environment fosters casual access to friendships, and friendships may also be integral and functional for the successful completion of a degree. Thus, the sample in the present study may be experiencing an intimacy that is more difficult for men to maintain in job and career settings.

The interview data show that although constraints in the masculine role limit men in certain situations and in verbal intimacy, men do develop intimate friendship behavior that is based on shared action. Men's intimacy often depends on nonverbal cues that are developed in contexts of active engagement. Men expressed intimacy with close friends by exchanging favors, engaging in competitive action, joking, touching, sharing accomplishments, and including one another in activities. The strengths of men's active style of intimacy involve sharing and empowering each other with the skills necessary for problem solving, and gaining a sense of engagement and control of their lives by sharing resources and accomplishments. Nonverbal cues offered an intimacy based on a private affirmation and exchange of the special history that two men share. This unique form of intimacy cannot be replicated solely by self-disclosure.

In addition to the men's active style of intimacy, they also reported self-disclosure to friends. Contrary to previous research, most men reported that they were more comfortable expressing themselves to a close male friend than to female friends. These men assumed that close male friends would be more understanding because of their shared experiences. Men said that self-disclosure and hugging "depended on the situation," and were more likely to self-disclose in a gender-validating context. Thus, men overcome cultural prohibitions against intimacy with this gender-validating strategy.

There are advantages and disadvantages to both feminine and masculine styles of intimacy. Feminine intimacy is productive for acknowledging fears and weaknesses that comprise a person's vulnerability. Admitting and expressing an emotional problem are enhanced by verbal self-disclosure skills. Masculine styles of intimacy are productive for confronting a fear or weakness with alternative strategies that empower them to creatively deal with a difficulty. Both styles appear necessary for a balanced approach to self-realization and the challenge of integrating that realization into a healthy and productive life.

Although this study focused on generalized sex differences to document a previously unrecognized active style of intimacy, women also demonstrated active styles of intimacy and men demonstrated verbal styles of intimacy. Thus, although the results are based on generalized tendencies, the data also support the flexibility of gender-based behavior and the ability of men and women to cross over and use both active and verbal styles of intimacy.

The documentation of active styles of intimacy sharpens the understanding of intimate male behavior, and it provides a more accurate and useful interpretation of the "inexpressive male." The deficit model of male expressiveness does not recognize men's active style of intimacy, and stresses men's need to be taught feminine-typed skills to foster intimacy in their relationships. This negation or denial of men's active style of intimacy may alienate and threaten men who then assume that intimacy is a challenge they will fail. An awareness of the strengths in men's covert style of intimacy provides a substantive basis from which to address and augment changes in restrictive and debilitating aspects of masculinity. The finding that gender-validating activities foster male self-disclosure suggests that strategies for developing more intimate capabilities in men would be most successful when accompanied by a gender-validating setting that acknowledges, enhances, and expands the use of the intimate skills that men have previously acquired.

The data suggest the influence that sex-segregated worlds exert on the ways women and men choose, and are most comfortable in expressing, intimacy. The separate adult social worlds that women and men often experience shape the opportunities and forms of intimacy shared between friends. These structural opportunities and the styles of intimacy that become integral to specific opportunities become familiar, expected, and assumed between friends of the same sex, and often are bewildering, inaccessible, and misinterpreted by cross-sex friends or partners.

The implications are clear: men and women will have to be integrated in similar microstructrual realms in the private and public spheres if we are to expect men and women to develop fluency in what are not termed "male" and "female" styles of intimacy. If such integration does indeed take place, the reduction of misunderstanding, frustration, and abuse in cross-sex relationships could be profound.

References

Allen, J., and Haccoun, D. "Sex Differences in Emotionality: A Multidimensional Approach." *Human Relations 29* (1976): 711-722.

Bakan, D. *The Duality of Human Existence*. Chicago: Rand McNally, 1966.

Balswick, J. "The Inexpressive Male: A Tragedy of American Society." In D. David and R. Brannon (eds.), *The Forty-Nine Percent Majority*. Reading, MA: Addison-Wesley, 1976: 55-67.

Bem, S.; Martyna, W.; and Watson, C. "Sex Typing and Androgyny: Further Explorations of the Expressive Domain." *Journal of Personality and Social Psychology 34* (1976): 1016-1023.

Booth, A. "Sex and Social Participation." *American Sociological Review* 37 *(*1972): 183-192.

Caldwell, R., and Peplau, L. "Sex Differences in Same-Sex Friendship." *Sex Roles 8* (1982): 721-732.

Cancian, F. M. "Marital Conflict Over Intimacy." In A. Rossi (ed.), *Gender and the Life Course*. Hawthorne, NY: Aldine, 1985.

_____. "The Feminization of Love." *Signs 11* (1986): 692-709.

Coleman, J. "Athletics in High School." In D. David and R. Brannon (eds.), *The Forty-Nine Percent Majority*. Reading, MA: Addison-Wesley, 1976: 264-269.

Cozby, P. "Self-Disclosure: A Literature Review." *Psychological Bulletin 79* (1973): 73-91.

Davidson, J., and Duberman, L. "Same-Sex Friendships: A Gender Comparison of Dyads." *Sex Roles 8* (1982): 809-822.

Goffman, Irving. *Presentation of Self*. Garden City, NY: Doubleday, 1959.

Hall, J. and Halberstadt, A. "Sex Roles and Nonverbal Communication Skills." *Sex Roles 7* (1981): 273-287.

Hantover, J. "Boy Scouts and the Validation of Masculinity." *Journal of Social Issues 34* (1978): 184-195.

Henley, N. *Body Politic, Power, Sex, and Nonverbal Communication*. Englewood Cliffs, NJ: Prentice-Hall, 1977.

Hoffman, M. "Sex Differences in Empathy and Related Behaviors." *Psychological Bulletin 84* (1977): 712-722.

Komarovsky, M. *Blue-Collar Marriage*. New York: Vintage, 1964.

_____. *Dilemmas of Masculinity: A Study of College Youth*. New York: Norton, 1976.

Lehne, G. "Homophobia Among Men." D. David and R. Brannon (eds.), *The Forty Nine Percent Majority*. Reading, MA: Addison-Wesley, 1976: 66-88.

Maccoby, E. and Jacklin, C. *The Psychology of Sex Differences*. Stanford: Stanford University Press, 1974.

Morin, S., and Garfinkle, E. "Male Homophobia." *Journal of Social Issues 34* (1978): 29-47.

Parsons, T., and Bales, R. *Family, Socialization, and Interaction Process*. New York: Free Press, 1955.

Pleck, J. *The Myth of Masculinity*. Cambridge, MA: MIT Press, 1981.

Rubin, L. *Intimate Strangers*. San Francisco: Harper and Row, 1983.

Stein, P., and Hoffman, S. "Sports and Male Role Strain." *Journal of Social Issues 34* (1978): 136-150.

Swain, S. "Male Intimacy in Same-Sex Friendships: The Influence of Gender-Validating Activities." Conference paper presented at the American Sociological Association Annual Meetings, San Antonio, 1984.

Tavris, C., and Wade, C. *The Longest War: Sex Differences in Perspective* (Second Edition). San Diego: Harcourt Brace Jovanovich, 1984.

Chapter 14

Attribution theory. Critical and creative thinking are positive features of any problem-solving plan. We must be aware of the running assumptions in our beliefs about people and society. Most importantly, resolving conflicts and reducing strain on relationships requires the gathering of evidence about the assumptions we make. Using data from impirical work such as the Boston Couples Study, we will explore both the assumptions and the realities of common interactions within the context of relationships. In this material, how many times can you detect the preference for solving problems through situational factors over personality factors? In other words, how much attribution theory is applied to critical thinking?

Chapter 14 *Carole Wade and Carol Tavris,* **Learning to Think Critically:**

The Case of Close Relationships

Do you think critically? Chances are you do. Every day, each of us makes judgments and decisions based on information. The process of examining this information and reaching a judgment or decision is at the heart of critical thinking. In this handbook, we will show you some critical thinking strategies that will make you a better consumer of information. We will apply critical thinking to a sphere of life that all of us care about very much, the sphere of close relationships.

What is critical and creative thinking?

If you ever have been in a rousing quarrel with your friends, parents, or strangers, you have probably encountered the following styles of argument -- all of which illustrate failures of critical thinking:

- "Just shut up about this, OK? You don't know what you're talking about."

- "I don't care what your so-called evidence is. Anybody can find any survey to support anything they want it to."
- "Don't argue with me. I'm older than you are and I know from personal experience that I'm right."
- "My feelings are very strong on this point, so don't try to change them."
- "I was raised to believe that..."

In critical thinking, a person finds *reasons* to support or reject an argument or belief. Feelings aren't enough, personal experience or anecdotes aren't enough, and shouting down the opposition isn't enough. Critical thinkers are willing to question received wisdom and ask why things are as they are: and they are willing to think creatively about alternative ways of doing things or explaining them. They understand that it is important to be able to define terms, examine the evidence for all sides of a problem, and analyze assumptions and biases. They try to avoid emotional reasoning (as in "I feel uncomfortable with that argument, so therefore it must be wrong") and oversimplification (as in "All the evil in the world is due to that small group of loathsome people"). And they tolerate uncertainty, for no one can ever know all the answers to every problem -- and even when we think we have some answers, we must be prepared for them to change when new information or new circumstances appear.

In this handbook, we will demonstrate how psychologists have used critical thinking strategies in their studies of close relationships and suggest ways that you can apply these strategies to your own experience. The subject of love and intimacy has produced many "common sense" notions and barrels of folklore, but how much of it is true? Do opposites attract? Is passionate love the key to a happy marriage? Do breakups occur primarily because of "incompatibility"? Are men more likely to be bullies and women more likely to be manipulative in getting their way?

We will show how psychologists have gathered information about such questions, and tested and evaluated possible answers -- in short, how they have applied critical thinking to what, for most people, is an emotional topic. In addition to practicing your critical thinking skills, you may find some surprising answers to your questions about what attracts people to each other, keeps them together, and causes them to break up.

Guidelines for thinking critically and creatively

1. *Ask questions; be willing to wonder.* To think critically you must be willing to think creatively -- that is, to be curious about the puzzles of human behavior, to wonder why people act the way they do, and to question received explanations and examine new ones.

2. *Define the problem.* Identify the issues involved in clear and concrete terms, rather than vague generalities such as "happiness," "potential," or "meaningfulness." What does meaningfulness mean, exactly?

3. *Examine the evidence.* Consider the nature of the evidence that supports all aspects of the problem under examination. Is it reliable? Valid? Is it someone's personal assertion or speculation? Does the evidence come from one or two narrow studies, or from repeated research?

4. *Analyze biases and assumptions* -- your own and those of others. What prejudices, deeply held values, and other personal biases do you bring to your evaluation of a problem? Are you willing to consider evidence that contradicts your beliefs? Be sure you can identify the biases of others, in order to evaluate their arguments as well.

5. *Avoid emotional reasoning* ("If I feel this way, it must be true"). Remember that everyone holds convictions and ideas about how the world should operate -- and that your opponents are as serious about their convictions as you are about yours. Feelings are important, but they should not substitute for careful appraisal of arguments and evidence.

6. *Don't oversimplify.* Look beyond the obvious. Reject simplistic, either-or thinking. Look for logical contradictions in arguments. Be wary of "argument by anecdote."

7. *Consider other interpretations.* Before you leap to conclusions, think about other explanations. Be especially careful about assertions of cause and effect.

8. *Tolerate uncertainty.* This may be the hardest step in becoming a critical thinker, for it requires the ability to accept some guiding ideas and beliefs -- yet the willingness to give them up when evidence and experience contradict them.

Getting to know you: The dynamics of attraction

Critical thinking begins with a willingness to ask creative questions about human experience. For example, we all meet thousands of people during a lifetime. Have you ever wondered why some become central characters in our lives while others remain bit players, or stay offstage altogether?

Common assumption: We are attracted to people for their special qualities. We seek out those who are witty, wise, kind, or attractive, and our excellent judgment recognizes their good qualities.

Thinking critically: Your text points out that most of us concentrate on personal qualities and dispositions when we are trying to explain our own or someone else's behavior, and ignore the effects of the situation and the environment. *Critical thinking demands that we overcome this bias, and consider the external as well as internal influences on attraction.* Certainly not everyone is compatible with everyone else. But there are five billion people on this earth, and for any one individual, there are many others who would qualify as an appealing partner. What must happen before two individuals actually get together?

In the process of *gathering evidence* on this question, psychologists have established that people are often drawn to each other for a most mundane reason: simple proximity. That is, they happen to be in the same place at the same time. They may live in the same neighborhood, attend the same classes, take the same bus every morning, or work for the same company. Spatial proximity makes people available and reduces the costs of pursuit, in terms of time and effort. If the person lives too far away, becoming better acquainted is not worth the effort -- which is why students in some parts of the country talk about a potential date as being "G. U." geographically undesirable.

Proximity also makes people more familiar, and, according to research, familiarity breeds comfort more often than contempt. In a classic study of proximity, researchers plotted the development of friendships in a new housing project for married students (Festinger, Schachter, & Back, 1950). The students, who were initially strangers, lived in two-story buildings with five apartments to a floor. The closer students lived to one another, the better friends they became.

Think critically about this finding, though; do not just passively absorb the information. If mere physical closeness were the whole answer to attraction, neighbors separated by a hedge, or office workers separated by a partition, would be as likely to become friends as two people not so separated. Does that seem reasonable? In fact, researchers have also discovered that geographical distance is less important than frequency and ease of contact. People who live near stairways, courtyards, and entrances, where people are always going in and out, have more friends than people who live in the same building but outside the flow of traffic (Monge & Kirste, 1980; Newcomb, 1961).

To apply critical thinking you should also *look for the implications of research.* One implication of the proximity principle is that if you live in an isolated room, house, or apartment, and you want to meet more people, you should consider ways to get yourself in the flow of traffic. If you can't move your living quarters, you might move yourself to more populated environments. It makes no sense to be angry that the world isn't beating a path to your door; this is human nature. How often do you go out of your way to visit distant friends?

Before going on, can you think of any other implications of the research on proximity?

Common assumption: Opposites attract.

Thinking critically: Critical thinking includes *looking for logical contradictions.* Is the notion that opposites attract consistent with the principle we have just discussed, the proximity principle? Think about it: people find themselves in physical proximity because they do the same work, have chosen the same sort of neighborhood to live in, or share some common hobbies or ambitions. Thus people who bump into each other all the time are likely to have interests, activities, and backgrounds in common. This is inconsistent with the notion that opposites attract.

Psychologists have called the "opposites attract" idea the *complementarity principle*. (To *complement* means to balance or make whole.) The complementarity principle predicts that people will seek friends or spouses who have some quality that they lack or that balances the qualities they have (Winch, 1958). However, the evidence has not supported the complementarity principle. In a study of 321 dating couples in Boston (henceforth referred to as the "Boston Couples study"), those who eventually broke up were less well-matched in age, educational ambitions, intelligence, and physical attractiveness than those who stayed together (Rubin, Peplau, & Hill, 1981). Another study, of 108 married couples, tested the common belief that traditionally masculine husbands (aggressive, individualistic, ambitious, decisive, and dominant) are happiest with traditionally feminine wives (cheerful, sympathetic, warm, tender, and nurturant toward children), and that such wives are happiest with traditionally masculine husbands (Antill, 1983). The researcher found no support for the "opposites attract" idea. Instead, the happiest couples were those in which *both* spouses scored high on "feminine" traits, qualities that are especially useful in marriage and child rearing.

An alternative to the complementarity principle is the *matching principle*, which predicts that people will seek out and be attracted to those who are similar to them in looks, interests, intelligence, education, age, family background, religion, attitudes, and values (Burgess & Wallin, 1943; Byrne, 1971; Murstein, 1982). This principle has been confirmed by scores of studies. Birds of a feather really do flock together, whether they are mating, dating, or just out for a lark.

Why should like attract like? One reason is that similar people belong to the same *field of eligibles*, or pool of potential intimates, in terms of the socially "correct" religion, class, education, and age (Winch, 1958). The field of eligibles for an individual is defined by social norms and may change over time. For example, interracial and interreligious marriages are no longer as taboo as they once were, and their numbers are growing (Murstein, 1982). So are marriages between older women and younger men.

If you are thinking critically, you might be asking yourself why some people you know have partners who are not from the same "field of eligibles," who, everyone keeps telling them, "aren't right for you." Indeed, research finds that the very fact of opposition by friends and parents to a "wrong choice" may produce the "Romeo and Juliet Effect": The lovers become even more steadfast in their desire for each other. (This response is an example of *reactance* discussed elsewhere in your text. Reactance leads people to react against the perception of loss of freedom to do what they want.) In a study of dating and married couples, researchers found that the greater the parents' interference, the greater the young couple's love. Several months after the initial interviews, those couples whose parents had stepped up their opposition were even more deeply in love, while those whose parents were becoming resigned had started to cool off (Driscoll, Davis, & Lipetz, 1972). What are the implications of this study?

If you are thinking critically, you might ask yourself whether psychologists have overlooked certain areas in which complementarity *does* apply. *The critical-thinking approach rejects simplistic either-or thinking and calls for a continual refining of hypotheses*. It is reasonable to speculate that in such fundamental areas as class, education, and values, similarity matters a great deal, but that in daily living, complementarity in certain personality traits may sometimes be useful. For example, two extremely ambitious people may find it more complicated and stressful to live together than a couple in which one person is professionally ambitious and the other is not. Or it may help when one likes to cook and another to eat, or when one likes to garden and the other to vacuum. In science, questions are never closed, and new discoveries often depend on admitting some uncertainty. Further research may find that similarity and complementarity both operate in successful relationships, but in different ways.

Common assumption: "You can't judge a book by its cover" because "beauty is only skin deep."

Thinking critically: Folk sayings, which are supposed to reflect the common wisdom, may hide as well as reflect the truth about human behavior. "Money isn't everything" and "The best things in life are free" are two bits of popular wisdom, yet in our culture people are often so busy trying to accumulate wealth that they have no time for all of those free "best things." Could the denial of beauty's importance in folk sayings similarly mask an anxious concern about it? Why do we idolize glamorous celebrities and portray the unattractive as villainous or pitiful?

As psychologists have gathered evidence from field and laboratory studies, they have discovered that physical appearance influences the reactions of others literally from the moment an infant emerges from the womb ("Look at that gorgeous head of hair!" "Oh dear, he's as homely as a plucked chicken"). Parents, teachers, and playmates tend to give more attention and praise to children who are good-looking than to plainer children, and this bias continues into adulthood (Berscheid, 1985). It may be unfair and undemocratic, but physical attractiveness is one of the strongest determinants of attraction. It is so strong, in fact, that when the "book" has an unattractive cover, other people may not bother turning to the first page of a relationship.

The importance of beauty in their choices of friends and lovers is hard for many people to admit. *But if we think critically, we will be cautious about using people's self-reports of their attitudes as a valid guide to how they really feel.* When college students are asked to rank the attributes that are important to them in a potential date, they almost never put looks at the top of the list. But what they *say* is not always related to what they *do*. Elaine Hatfield and her associates randomly matched 752 college students for a "computer dance." The researchers had assessed each student's intelligence, aptitudes, social skills, personality traits, and physical attractiveness. During an intermission at the dance, and again a few months later, the students were asked in private how much they liked their dates. The *only* variable that predicted their answers was attractiveness. The researchers, thinking that looks would be only one aspect of the date's desirability, diligently examined every possible factor. But they could not argue with the data: No matter how they analyzed the results, looks mattered most (Walster *et al.*, 1966).

One reason that looks count so much with both sexes is the *physical attractiveness stereotype*. Those who hold this stereotype do not really believe that beauty is only skin deep; they believe it reflects the whole person. When people are asked to judge attractive and unattractive individuals whom they have never me, they assume the attractive ones are kinder, more sensitive, more interesting, stronger, more poised, more outgoing, more sexually responsive, happier, and on and on (Berscheid, 1985; Cash & Janda, 1984; Dion, Berscheid, & Walster, 1972).

Sometimes stereotypes have a kernel of truth. Attractiveness is correlated with a good self-concept, good mental health, self-confidence, and other positive traits (Adams, 1981; Dion & Stein, 1978). Why should this be so? In this case, a self-fulfilling prophecy may explain the positive qualities often found in attractive people. Perhaps when adults expect attractive individuals to have nice qualities, they treat them especially nicely, thereby fostering the development of nice qualities. Laboratory research supports this conclusion. In one study, men talked on the telephone with a woman they had been led to believe was either attractive or unattractive. When they thought they were talking to a beauty, they were friendlier, funnier, and more animated than when they thought they were talking to an unattractive woman. Their behavior, in turn, affected the friendliness and animation of the woman they spoke to (Snyder, Tanke, & Berscheid, 1977).

These findings about physical attractiveness may seem discouraging for the majority of us who are ordinary-looking. But *critical thinking requires us to examine all sides of an issue.* When we do so, we see that, first, the beautiful have problems too. The physical attractiveness stereotype is not completely positive: Very attractive people are sometimes assumed to be vain, egocentric, less intelligent, or snobbish (Dermer & Thiel, 1975). Second, the beautiful are sometimes assumed to be unavailable when they are not. Finally, almost everyone does find friends and a mate. Based on what you have read so far, can you find reasons why this should be so? Remember the matching principle. It predicts that people will tend to select friends and lovers whose attractiveness roughly matches their own, and indeed, they do (Feingold, 1988). In the real world, people minimize the chances of rejection by choosing partners who are like themselves in attractiveness. [It is also possible that good-looking people get "first pick," selecting one another as mates and leaving less attractive people to choose from the remaining field of eligibles (Kalick & Hamilton, 1986)].

You can apply critical thinking in your own life by being wary of the physical attractiveness stereotype. It may be limiting your choice of friends or blinding you to people's real qualities. *If you are thinking critically, you are questioning assumptions*, in this case, the very definition of beauty. Just who is defining what is beautiful, anyhow? This country is made up of many racial and ethnic groups -- blacks, Swedes, Native Americans, Asians, and Hispanics, just for starters -- and how many of *them* end up in psychological studies? Indeed, members of different races and cultures have differing ideas about what physical attributes qualify as "beautiful": which skin color, hair texture, shape of eyes, degree of plumpness (and where it is located). The cultural practices that define a "beautiful look" are enormously varied, from piercing the earlobe to piercing the nose.

In every culture, the majority that has power is the group the defines the standards of attractiveness, and those standards become widely shared. For example, it is often difficult for minorities to accept their own attributes if these are not considered "beautiful" by the majority. *Critical thinking, therefore, requires us to consider that the origin of our feelings sometimes lies in social norms and outside circumstances, not in individual failings or preferences.*

Common assumption: True love means being selfless, and always placing your partner's needs above your own.

Thinking critically: Does this common assumption jibe with the law of human behavior? Elsewhere we learned that reinforcements, or rewards, are powerful controllers of behavior. Rewarded behavior is likely to continue; unrewarded behavior is likely to disappear, or be "extinguished." In light of this fact, is it reasonable to assume that people "truly in love" can continue a relationship with no thought of reward? The evidence reveals that, in fact, good relationships depend on a two-way, or *reciprocal*, exchange of rewards and punishments (Homans, 1961; Thibaut & Kelley, 1959). People do not enter or stay in relationships without any thought of what they will be getting from them.

Other people have the power to bestow all sorts of rewards: praise, affection, sexual pleasure, entertainment, help, good company, and insurance against loneliness. They can also bestow punishments: They can be demanding, irritable, intrusive, and financially burdensome. According to *social exchange theory*, when two people embark on a relationship or consider whether to stay in one, they mentally compute what they can get from each other and what they have to offer in return.

Sometimes, of course, people begin or stay in relationships that others see as unrewarding. These cases do not necessarily contradict social exchange theory, though. If you stop to *define your terms*, in this case the meaning of a reward, you will find that "reward" is a relative term. A drop of water is extremely rewarding if you have been lost in the desert for three days, but not so rewarding if you've been camped by a spring. A job transfer that increases your pay but reduces your free time is rewarding if you are low on funds, but not so rewarding if you are rich. Similarly, an offer of friendship will mean more to someone who is lonely than to someone whose social calendar is always full.

The exchange that people compute when deciding whether to begin or stay in a relationship, then, is not selfless; it is something like an economic transaction. The "bottom line" of the balance sheet is affected by your *comparison level*, the standard against which you evaluate the costs and rewards of the relationship (Thibaut & Kelley, 1959). That standard, in turn, depends on what you expect from a relationship and what you think you deserve. If the other person gives you more than you expect or feel you deserve, you will be attracted to that person (if you're starting out) or satisfied with what you have (if you're in a relationship). If the other person gives you less than you expect or feel you deserve, you will not pursue the relationship or you will feel dissatisfied with an existing one.

Attraction to others also depends on your *comparison level for alternatives*. This is the lowest standard you will accept in light of what you believe is possible in other relationships. People often remain in relationships that they know are unsatisfactory, continuing to live with people they find unpleasant and difficult, because they believe they have no better alternative. Teresa may be surly and critical, yet Tom may stay with her if he thinks he cannot do better and doesn't want to be alone.

Popular songs and stories often equate "true love" with selflessness, self-sacrifice, and even suffering. But if you are thinking critically, you will distinguish the cultural ideal from what really is. The evidence shows that it is normal to want to receive as well as give in a love relationship. This is why the *principle of reciprocity*, which holds that we tend to like those who like us, may be the strongest principle of all in explaining attraction (Berscheid & Walster, 1978). By looking for signs that another person thinks well of you, you minimize the chances of being hurt by rejection, and you enhance your self-esteem.

Can you think of a way to apply the principle of reciprocity? One application might benefit lonely people, who tend to focus their attention on themselves and their unhappiness. When they meet a new person, they are so worried about the impression they are making that they become self-absorbed. This is not the best way to make a new friend! Lonely people often assume in advance that the new person won't like them, even when this isn't true. To avoid the pain of rejection, they have a pattern of "rejecting others first" (Jones, 1982). Naturally, this creates another self-fulfilling prophecy. How might the lonely person break out of this cycle? One way is to give to others what he or she hopes to get: attention, interest, support.

As you were reading about the principles and rules of attraction, perhaps you found yourself quarreling with some of the conclusions in this section. You may know a Beauty who married an adoring Beast. You may know a commuting couple who defy the laws of proximity, maintaining a relationship across many miles. You may know an extrovert who has been happily married for 42 years to an introvert. If you are questioning the generalizations in the preceding section, that's good; it means you are actively evaluating what you are reading, which is what this booklet is all about.

However, apparent exceptions to the rules of attraction do not necessarily invalidate them. Why not? First, when people make choices about which relationships to pursue, they don't necessarily count every factor equally (Berscheid, 1985). The importance of any one influence depends on a person's needs. A person may decide that looks are nice, but less important than a kind nature, or power, or money. A commuting couple may put up with the inconvenience of distance, because his ability to play the tuba and hers to play the flute allows them to make beautiful music together.

Second, the general determinants of attraction interact with individual personality traits. One such trait is *self-monitoring*, the self-conscious need to observe and control one's image in social situations (Snyder, 1987). In one study, young men were given the choice of going out with one of two dates. "Kristen" was described as plain-looking but friendly and outgoing. "Jennifer" was described as good-looking but self-centered and moody. Most high self-monitoring men chose Jennifer, despite her grumpy personality. But most low self-monitoring men chose Kristen (Snyder, Berscheid, & Glick, 1985). Apparently men who are concerned about their own social image are also concerned with a date's. Men who do not shift their images to suit the occasion are more interested in a date's   inner qualities.

Remember, then, as you apply general principles of attraction in your own life, that *critical thinking avoids oversimplification*. The influence of any principle depends both on the situation and on an individual's needs and beliefs.

Growing Closer: The Dynamics of Intimacy

As two people grow closer, certain changes occur in their relationship. Chief among them are the establishment of equity, an increase in self-disclosure, and a strengthening of commitment.

Common assumption: in a modern relationship, all benefits and obligations should be shared.

Thinking critically: In everyday life, "fairness" or "equity" is often confused with a strict 50-50 division of benefits and obligations (paying half the rent, doing half the chores, giving equal gifts, and so forth). If you analyze the concept of equity carefully, however, you will see that it is not that simple. As we have noted, social exchange theory predicts that people will try to maximize the rewards they receive in a relationship. But they will judge those rewards in light of what they, themselves, can offer a partner. Thus fairness does not always mean that two partners must receive exactly equal benefits.

According to *equity theory*, in order to see a relationship as fair, two partners must believe that each person's benefits are proportional to what he or she contributes to the relationship (Walster, Walster, & Berscheid, 1978). Equity results when the *ratio* of costs to benefits is perceived to be the same for two people -- when the more a person puts in, the more he or she gets out. Suppose we can measure costs and benefits on a scale of one to ten. Norma's contribution to a relationship may be worth only a two and her rewards only a four, while Nat's contributions may earn a five and his benefits a ten. But since the ratio for each of them is the same ($2/4 = 5/10$), both will feel that the relationship is equitable.

Research finds that people in equitable relationships are happier and more content than those in inequitable ones (Hatfield *et al.*, 1985; Sprecher, 1986). Partners who are "underbenefited," who feel they are getting less than they deserve, are apt to feel angry or depressed. (For most people, it seems, too much selflessness quickly leads to feelings of resentful martyrdom.) Some studies have found that people don't like being "overbenefited" either, and that when they think they are getting more than they deserve, they may feel guilty or depressed (McElfresh, 1982; Schafer & Keith, 1980). Women seem especially likely to feel uncomfortable with being overbenefited. Other studies, though, find that overbenefited partners are as happy and satisfied with their relationships as equitable partners are (Traupmann *et al.*, 1981). *When there is a conflict like this in the data, critical thinking requires us to wait for more evidence before drawing any conclusions.*

Again, you may be able to think of some apparently happy relationships that are not equitable. Does that invalidate equity theory? Before you decide that the theory is no good, *consider some alternative explanations.* First, in long-term relationships, the goal is not usually immediate repayment for everything one does, but fairness over the long haul. A spouse, for instance, may be willing to live with an inequitable balance during a specific phase of life (say, when rearing young children or staring a new career), in the confidence that equity will eventually be restored (Traupmann & Hatfield, 1983). Second, it is the *perception* of equity that matters, rather than the objective state of affairs. Partner A may decide that partner B deserves the greater benefits, because he or she is "special" and A is merely ordinary (Brehm, 1985). Or partner A may have a comparison level for alternatives that makes A feel well treated compared to others of the same gender, even if B doesn't really deserve all those extra benefits. Moreover, in long-term relationships, fulfilling the other person's needs may be experienced as rewarding, even when doing so entails considerable "costs" (Clark & Reis, 1988).

There is, however, another problem with equity theory. *Thinking critically prevents us from drawing conclusions about causation from findings that are correlational.* The finding that "the most happily married couples have the most equitable relationships" is correlational. Equity may cause happiness, but it is also possible that happiness causes equity -- or the perception of equity. That is, happy couples may be especially likely to emphasize the fair aspects of their relationships. Once a couple becomes dissatisfied, they may begin to attend to issues of unfairness that were previously swept under the rug. At present, then, we cannot be sure that equity *causes* happiness, or that inequity brings discontent, though we suspect that is true (Hatfield *et al.*, 1982).

Common assumption: Women are the "intimacy experts"; men are afraid of intimacy.

Thinking critically: In order to evaluate an assumption critically, we must examine the way we define our terms. The truth of this particular assumption depends on what we mean by *intimacy.*

If we equate intimacy with verbal disclosure of personal feelings, thoughts, and weaknesses, then there is some truth to this common assumption. When men talk to each other or to women, they tend to talk about relatively impersonal matters, such as cars, sports, work, and politics. When they reveal anything about themselves, it tends to be their strengths and achievements. Women are more likely to talk about personal matters, such as their feelings and relationships, and are more willing to reveal weaknesses, fears, and worries (Cozby, 1973; Hacker, 1981).

There are other ways to define intimacy, though. It turns out that both men and women want intimacy, but they often have different ideas about self-disclosure as a way of achieving it. By and large, men are more apt to be *doers*, and women to be *talkers*. As noted previously, men tend to want "side-by-side" relationships, in which intimacy means sharing the same activity. Women tend to prefer "face-to-face" relationships, in which intimacy means revealing ideas and emotions (Brehm, 1985). This sex difference begins early. A study of 300 eighth-graders found that boys expressed intimacy with other boys through shared experiences, typically group activities such as football. The girls, however, preferred one-to-one conversations. The researchers found that shared experiences were just as effective as self-disclosure in engendering feelings of closeness (Camerena & Sarigiani, 1985).

These differences in male and female styles of intimacy reflect traditional gender roles in American culture. Men are as able as women to have "intimate" conversations when the situation makes it desirable to them to do so (Reis, Senchak, & Solomon, 1985). Both sexes are equally likely to report wanting intimate friends, and the same men who fear self-disclosure with their male friends are often happy to disclose to their romantic partners. Social norms, however, can be hard on the man or woman who breaks out of the traditional role. Most people like women who freely disclose their feelings, especially if these are feelings of love, weakness, or concern. Yet, studies find, the man who does the same thing is often disliked by other men or women. Conversely, most Americans admire men who boldly reveal their feelings of competitiveness and achievement. But the woman who does the same thing is often considered "pushy" and "aggressive" (Brehm, 1985; Petty & Mirels, 1981). [And an American man who does the same thing in Europe, say in England or Germany, will be considered immodest and immature (Hall & Hall, 1986).]

Differences between men and women in styles of intimacy are often a source of tension between them. "Why doesn't he talk more?" the woman laments. "Why doesn't she shut up?" the man wonders. In one study, husbands were instructed to increase the frequency of expressions of love toward their wives, and the wives were asked to keep track of such demonstrations. One husband, asked by the researcher why he hadn't complied with the instructions, replied huffily that he certainly *had* complied -- by *washing his wife's car*. The husband thought that was a perfectly good way to communicate love for his wife, but she hadn't a clue to his intentions (Wills, Weiss, & Patterson, 1974).

To think critically, we must examine and evaluate our own values and judgments. Critical thinking leads us to recognize that the same behavior can be regarded as good or bad, depending on your point of view. In her book *Intimate Relationships*, Sharon Brehm (1985) observes that a man who is emotionally inexpressive may be regarded as calm and steady *or* cold and selfish. A woman who is emotionally expressive may be regarded as warm and responsible *or* as hysterical and irrational. When people talk about sex differences in intimacy, their biases often get in the way. Each sex, of course, thinks that its way of doing things is the best way.

If we can *overcome our biases and the temptation to reason emotionally*, we may find that there are positive and negative aspects to each gender's preferred form of intimacy. As noted previously, social support is an important element in mental and physical health, and women have more sources of social support than men do. In part, this is because women are more likely than men to seek and to give emotional comfort (both to men and to other women). Both sexes feel better after talking things over with a woman (Burda, Vaux, & Schill, 1984; Wheeler, Reis, & Nezlek, 1983). Disclosing one's feelings often helps the discloser to feel understood, validated, and cared for (Reis & Shaver, 1988).

However, the female emphasis on self-disclosure also has disadvantages. The constant ventilation of an emotion often rehearses the feeling instead of getting rid of it. Could this fact be related to the finding that emotional disorders, such as anxiety and depression, are more common among women than among men? Perhaps when women endlessly discuss their fears and worries, they make themselves more fearful and anxious. Men, by suppressing their fears and forcing themselves to act, may conquer their anxiety - a sort of self-imposed "exposure therapy" (Chambless, 1986). Perhaps, too, dwelling on the problems in their relationships allows women to avoid taking action to improve them.

"Intimacy" is one of those nice warm words that sounds good, but *critical thinking requires us to avoid oversimplification.* As Elaine Hatfield (1984) observes, there are certain dangers in too much self-revelation and certain pleasures in privacy. When people reveal their weaknesses and wants, they risk being abandoned, having their revelations betrayed to others, provoking anger or contempt in their partners, and losing their individuality. If men sacrifice intimacy (in the sense of self-revelation) because they fear loss of independence, women may sacrifice independence because they fear loss of intimacy.

You can see that critical thinking leads us far from the simple-minded notion that one sex has the edge on intimacy.

Common assumption: All you need is love.

Thinking critically: The truth of this assumption, like the truth of the previous one, depends on how you define your terms. For many people in our culture, *love* is largely synonymous with romantic passion. The secret of a lasting relationship is thought to be keeping passion alive. Yet in almost every culture, proverbs recognize and lament the inevitable death of passion. "A dish of married love grows soon cold," say the Scots. "Love makes the time pass. Time makes love pass," say the French. "Love and eggs are best when they are fresh," says the Russians.

In this case, research confirms what proverbs observe: No intense emotion lasts forever. Tempers cool, elation ebbs, hurt evaporates, and romantic passion fades (Berscheid, 1985; Botwin, 1985). As two people become familiar with each other, their relationship loses the element of novelty and surprise. As a result, the physiological arousal they once felt in each other's presence declines. This is probably necessary for survival. A constant state of romantic excitement would produce enormous wear and tear on the body, to say nothing of making it difficult to read, work, or wash the dishes.

Consider the practical implications of this finding. In many cultures, marriage is viewed as a contractual arrangement between two families; love has nothing to do with it. But in our culture, marriage has been largely divorced (so to speak) from its economic purposes, and people are free to marry for love. Most couples expect romance not only to precede the wedding but to continue for a lifetime afterwards. Yet passion is bound to subside. When that happens, a couple may be disappointed and disillusioned. "The divorce rate is so high," says Robert Sternberg (1985), "not because people make foolish choices, but because they are drawn together for reasons that matter less as time goes on."

Clearly, if you want your relationship to survive, love, or at least romantic passion, is not enough. The forces that bring a couple together have little to do with the forces that keep them together. Grand passion, it seems, is like fireworks on the Fourth of July: spectacular but fleeting. According to Sternberg (1988), love in the fullest sense includes not only passion, but *intimacy* and *commitment*. Passion is an emotional element, involving high arousal and energy. Intimacy involves the motivation to be close to the loved one. Commitment is a cognitive element, consisting of the judgment that one is in love, the decision to become committed, and attitudes about the other person. The *amount* of love we feel, in Sternberg's view, depends on the strength of these three components. The *kind* of love we feel depends on the strengths of each relative to the others. Thus you might have a commitment to a lover -- an intention to maintain the relationship -- but feel little passion. Or you might have intense emotions toward a lover, but not be mentally prepared for commitment.

For lovers and spouses in our culture, commitment usually means an agreement not to "shop around" for another relationship. Committed partners save the time, money, and effort they would otherwise spend on "shopping," and gain in turn emotional security and a confidence that the relationship will continue. (Are you reading actively? Can you tie in this claim with social exchange theory?) A commitment may be expressed publicly, which is what weddings are for, or it may be a private decision.

Considering the importance of commitment, it is surprising how little research has been done on it; however, psychologists are starting to investigate this important element of successful relationships. In one recent study, 351 couples who had been married for at least 15 years (most of them happily) were asked what had kept their unions alive and well. Husbands and wives put the belief that marriage is a long-term commitment near the top of the list. These couples expressed a determination to work through their problems, and to endure some temporary unhappiness while they were doing it. As one man, married for 20 years, said, "I wouldn't go on for years and years being wretched in my marriage. But you can't avoid troubled times. You're not going to be happy with each other all the time. That's when commitment is really important" (Lauer & Lauer, 1986).

We still do not know all the factors that allow some people to make a commitment and others not. However, commitment seems to be tied more closely to trust than to romantic love. In interviews with dozens of couples happily married for many years, Francine Klagsbrun (1985) found that trust came up over and over again. "Feelings of love may wax and wane in the course of a marriage," she observed, "... but trust is a constant: without it there is no true marriage." Each partner must trust that the other will be there, will protect confidences, and will offer support and safety. In a sample of 47 couples (married, cohabiting, or dating, with an average age of 30), researchers found that the most important aspect of trust was *faith*, the belief that one's partner will act in loving and caring ways, whatever happens in the future (Rempel, Holmes, & Zanna, 1985).

These findings on love and trust should cause you to think about the implications in your own life. Are many grand passions worth the stability of one trustworthy one? Do people in our culture overvalue romance? Perhaps there is a kind of love psychologists have so far overlooked, one that is more intense than mere affection but more permanent that a brief, whirlwind passion. Perhaps people in successful long-term relationships experience what we might call "romantic sentiment," an ability to seek and enjoy novelty in each other, and to maintain a sense of courtship and surprise.

Troubled Waters: The Dynamics of Conflict

What do you think makes a relationship "close"? Psychologists have come up with many answers to this question, but when you boil them all down, what's left at the bottom of the definitional pot is *interdependence* (Kelley & Thibaut, 1978). Interdependence refers to the ability of two people to influence each other's plans, thoughts, actions, and emotions. The degree of closeness depends on how often the participants influence each other, how many areas of their lives are affected, and how intensely they are affected.

Yes, you say, but what about all those warm fuzzy feelings we've just discussed, feelings of intimacy, trust, respect, and love? To be sure, close relationships usually do involve positive emotions, but not all the time. In ongoing relationships, people have the power to affect each there in negative as well as positive ways, sometimes simultaneously. The more time two people spend together, the more they have to disagree about, and the more opportunities there are for disappointment, hurt feelings, and conflict. As Elaine Hatfield (1984) notes, "The opposite of love is not hate, but indifference."

The way a couple resolves their differences affects the quality of their relationship and its chances of survival. Let's examine some common assumptions about how people deal with differences, and about what happens when their efforts fail.

Common assumption: As Carl Jung said, "Where love rules, there is no will to power; and where power predominates, there love is lacking."

Thinking critically: This common assumption is a charming one, but unfortunately it isn't true. Like the assumption that love is always selfless, it describes an ideal rather than an actual state. *Power* is the ability to influence decisions, and get over people to do what you want. By that definition, lovers are as likely as anyone else to use and abuse their power. In the Boston Couples study, 95 percent of the women and 87 percent of the men thought that both partners should have exactly equal say. Yet fewer than half thought that their relationship were equal. When one person had more say, it was the man in 40 percent of the cases and the woman in only 15 percent (Peplau, 1984).

Why do you think men tend to have more power in a relationship? A first guess might be that men understand power better, or are trained to exercise power, and that women are trained to be more submissive or cooperative. But remember, *critical thinking requires that we consider other less obvious explanations, such as factors external to personality, when explaining behavior*. One such factor is a person's resources. In general, the greater a person's resources, the greater his or her power. A *resource* is anything that can be used to satisfy or frustrate the needs of others, or move them toward or away from their goals (Huston, 1983). Resources include education, income, skills, occupational prestige, and physical strength. In all these areas, husbands have traditionally had the edge, and the greater a husband's resources, the more power he has in the family. When a couple's resources are more balanced, so is the distribution of power.

When wives are employed and contributing directly to the family's standard of living, their resources and power rises. For decades, this finding has turned up consistently in studies of families (Blood & Wolfe, 1960; Blumstein & Schwartz, 1983). But why do full-time homemakers, who contribute to the family by caring for children, organizing the housework, and providing emotional support, have so much less power than spouses who bring in money? To understand this issue, we must *go beyond simplistic notions*, such as "men are male chauvinists" or "women want to be dominated." Such explanations don't tell us much. A more illuminating analysis may be that in the United States, people's value is measured by their economic worth (Crosby, 1986). Most people do not recognize the financial value of work performed in the home. (This is true despite the fact that insurance companies in 1983 estimated the value of a homemaker's yearly services -- as cook, babysitter, decoration, housekeeper, dishwasher, and chauffeur -- at $25,000.) Another popular misconception is that the goal of equity actually diminishes a homemaker's power. As we said earlier, what people feel entitled to in a relationship depends on what they are contributing. In many families, economic contributions count heavily in the equity equation. The result is a sadly modern version of the Golden Rule: Those that have the gold make the rules.

Consider the implications of these arguments. If power is related to resources, and particularly financial ones, then there is nothing inherently female about lack of power or inherently male about having it. That hypothesis is borne out by evidence. When men are "househusbands," staying home to raise the children while their wives earn the family income, the wives have greater power (Beer, 1984). Among homosexual couples, there is no expectation based on gender that one partner will be "the boss," yet power in gay relationships is often lopsided. As in heterosexual relationships, it is the partner who has more resources, and in particular a higher income, who tends to have more power (Blumstein & Schwartz, 1983).

Of course, money isn't the only determinant of power. According to the *principle of least interest*, the person with the least need to continue a relationship has the greatest influence and control in it (Waller, 1938). The degree of interest depends in part on how attracted the two partners are to each other and how emotionally dependent they are. HE may be a millionaire oil magnate and she a struggling secretary, but if he is wildly in love with her and she is merely mildly interested in him, she will have the greater power (though his millions may last longer than his feelings).

The degree of interest in a relationship depends not just on who loves more, but on who needs more. Women who are completely dependent financially on their husbands often report that they love their husbands more than their husbands love them, and they have lower self-esteem than employed wives (Hochschild, 1975). Again, this is not special to women. In working couples in which the wife has the greater income, many husbands react like traditional housewives. Their self-esteem drops, and they lament that they love their wives more than their wives love them (Rubenstein, 1982).

If you are actively considering the implications of these findings, you may be wondering how power is related to satisfaction. A few studies find that satisfaction is high when the husband has more power. Most, however, find that a high degree of marital satisfaction and stability are associated with roughly equal power in decision making (Gray-Little & Burks, 1983). When either spouse has most of the power, arguments and even violence are more frequent than in families in which both spouses feel they have influence (McElfresh, 1982; Yllo, 1983). Both sexes are particularly uncomfortable and dissatisfied when the woman has the greater power. Why might this be so? One factor is the cultural expectation that men should be dominant. Another is that many of the wives who assume authority do so by default rather than by mutual agreement. That is, they pick up the reins of power when their husbands are physically ill, unemployed, or unwilling to be involved in family life.

It would be nice to believe that "love can conquer all," but *critical thinking requires us to question cherished ideas when the evidence contradicts them*. In this case, the evidence suggests that emotional involvement cannot be separated from financial realities.

Common assumption: To get their way, men shout or give orders and women cry or give hints.

Thinking critically: There is some truth to this assumption. Men are more likely than women to give orders directly ("Lock the door"), women to give them indirectly (Would you mind locking the door?") (Lakoff, 1975). And in dating and marriage, the sexes do tend to use different strategies for getting their way. Influence strategies may be *direct* (saying what you want) or *indirect* (dropping hints). They may also be *bilateral* (requiring interaction with your partner) or *unilateral* (requiring only your own action). Psychologists have found that men are more likely than women to use strategies that are direct and bilateral, such as reasoning and bargaining. Women are more likely than men to use strategies that are indirect and unilateral, such as pouting, crying, or withdrawing (Falbo & Peplau, 1980). Men are also more likely to use what some researchers call "hard" strategies (demanding, shouting, being assertive), whereas women are more likely to use "soft" strategies (acting nice, flattering the other person) (Kipnis & Schmidt, 1985).

These findings jibe with stereotypes about men and women. Both sexes expect women to cry, sulk, be "nice," be "emotional," and use flattery or manipulation if necessity. Both sexes expect men to show anger, call of logic and reason, be "rational," and use force if necessary. But, as we have shown in previous sections, an apparent sex difference may be due to something other than gender itself. *To think critically, we must always look beyond the obvious to find the forces that actually account for some phenomenon.* Failure to do this is a common weakness in people's thinking.

Given our preceding discussion, you might already have some idea of what lies behind sex differences in strategies of influence. Research has found that these differences are related less to gender than to power. Lesbians and gay men do not differ from each other in the techniques they favor (Falbo & Peplau, 1980). Bilateral strategies are used by people who have the greater power and status in a relationship, whatever their gender or sexual preference. Powerless people prefer indirect strategies in order to avoid angering their partners by direct confrontation.

People who share decisions and power tend to bargain rationally and to make compromises. These couples tend to be the most satisfied with their relationships. Unlike users of hard tactics, they do not alienate their partners and create hostility or fear. Unlike users of soft tactics, they do not lose self-respect (Kipnis & Schmidt, 1985).

Common assumption: Most couples break up because of incompatibility. They just "didn't get along" because they had mismatched personalities.

Thinking critically: This assumption is an example of what logicians call a *tautology*, a statement that is true by definition but doesn't really say anything. All the assumption says is that when couples don't get along it's because... they don't get along. It tells us nothing about *why* people fail to get along.

Research finds that happy couples and distressed couples do not differ in the number of conflicts they have, or even in what they fight about. Indeed, they differ in *how* they argue and in how they think about conflict. In a previous section we discussed the effects on behavior of *attributions*, the explanations people make of their own and others' behavior. Attributions are critical in how people approach conflict. A study of 22 contented couples and 22 unhappy ones found significant differences between these couples in their attributions about their spouses (Holzworth-Munroe & Jacobson, 1985). When contented people are irritated by their mates, they find reasons in the mate's temporary situation ("He's under a lot of pressure"). Distressed spouses, though, find reasons in the mate's personality ("He's thoughtless"). When people explain their mates' *good* behavior, though, their attributions reverse! Now happy couples look for reasons within the person ("She's so thoughtful to make my favorite meal"), and unhappy couples give credit to the situation ("She only makes a decent dinner when her mother pressures her to"). (See also Grigg, Fletcher, & Fitness, 1989).

Happy and unhappy couples also differ in how they resolve their conflicts. Happy couples settle their disputes through discussion, compromise, and problem solving, the basic techniques of negotiation. They neither yield every point nor bully the other side into submission. They are able to identify their goals, identify common interests, separate issues from personalities, and make short-term compromises for the sake of long-term gains (Pruitt & Rubin, 1986). Unhappy couples end up in repeated cycles of bickering and insults, blaming each other's faulty personality traits ("He's lazy"; "She's a nag").

You should not have too much difficulty recognizing the implications of findings on power, attributions, and negotiation in everyday life. Chances are you may have found yourself in this sort of situation: You watch your relationship with someone begin to deteriorate and it seems that everything you do only makes things worse. The findings we have been discussing suggest the following strategies to help pull your relationship out of its downward spiral:

- *Evaluate the explanations (attributions) you make of your partner's behavior.* Are you quick to blame him or her for some personality defect, while rarely crediting your partner with a personality strength? Do you consider how the situation might be influencing your partner's (and your own) behavior?
- *Analyze the relationship to find out whether inequity or an imbalance of power exists.* If you are feeling underloved, unappreciated, and underbenefited, you are likely to be feeling vaguely depressed or irritable. Does one of you make most of the decisions affecting you both? Does one of you have a financial advantage? Is one of you more invested emotionally in the relationship?
- *Examine whether you and your partner have different strategies for "getting your way."* A clash of methods may make communication difficult. If one of your is direct and assertive in expressing your preferences, while the other withdraws and sulks, the

two of you may end up quarreling over how to quarrel ("Lee's a bully": "Chris is a sniveler"). Before you leap to conclusions about the entire opposite sex, though, consider whether your differences are due to a lopsided distribution of power. One clue might be whether you get your way differently with different people. Are you forthright with your sister but cowardly with your sweetheart? Do you wheedle your way around your father but yell at your mother? If so, chances are that you feel less powerful with your sweetheart than your sister, and less with your father than your mother.

- *Negotiate your differences instead of resorting to bullying or blind submission.* As negotiation researcher Jeffrey Rubin once told us, "Negotiation requires patience and good will, but it is a pathway of hope, an alternative to brutality, coercion, and submission. And it can also be a great deal of fun."

Common assumption: Women suffer more than men do at the end of a relationship.

Thinking critically: Breakups are rarely easy for anyone, even when a person wants the breakup and even when both parties agree that the relationship wasn't very good (Berscheid, 1985). One reason lies in the nature of human attachment. Attachment grows out of familiarity; it confers a feeling of connectedness with another. Although we usually associate attachment with committed, affectionate relationships, it also occurs in punishing, abusive ones. (Mistreated children, spouses, and even pets may be strongly attached to those who abuse them.) Couples may be emotionally attached to each other even when the emotions in question are negative ones, such as anger or anxiety. Such individuals are often surprised to find, on separation, more emotional attachment than they had anticipated (Berscheid, 1985; Mandler, 1984).

Even so, studies find that men, contrary to stereotype, suffer somewhat more on the average than women. In the Boston Couples study, men reported longer-lasting grief after separation than the women did, even when the women had been more emotionally involved (Hill, Rubin, & Peplau, 1976). In another study, divorced women said that the worst time for them was before the separation, while divorced men said the worst time was *after* the separation (Hagestad & Smyer, 1982).

In general, men seem to suffer more than they expect to after a separation. The fact provides a clue to why separating is somewhat harder on men. Sharon Brehm (1985) suggests that the explanation lies in the difference between recognized and unrecognized dependency. Women, she maintains, are aware of their financial and emotional dependency on their husbands or partners. Husbands, though, do not invest much time or energy in thinking about their marriages until something goes wrong (Holtzworth-Munroe & Jacobson, 1985). As a result, they may not be aware of how dependent they have become on their wives for emotional and domestic support.

If you are thinking critically, though, you may notice that men and women have different problems after a divorce or separation -- once again, differences not based on gender, but on power and income. That is, most wives have more to lose economically after divorce that most husbands do. After "no-fault" divorce, women's disposable income falls 72 percent on the average while men's income rises 42 percent (Weitzman, 1985). How can this be? One reason is that women earn less than men in general.

Another is that after divorce, most wives retain custody of the children and continue to have child-rearing expenses. Their former husbands, "freed" of family expenses, have more income to spend on themselves. Think critically about what you read or hear in the news. In spite of sensational divorce cases, only 15 percent of all divorced women are awarded alimony (and only half of those actually get it), and the great majority of divorced fathers pay no child support. The result is that the "new poor" in America consist chiefly of divorced women with children. Can you think of constructive ways to solve this growing problem?

As you can see, *critical thinking requires that we reject glib generalizations*, such as the common notion that one sex is dependent and the other independent. Apparent independence may mask unrecognized dependence. Just as we are unaware of our dependency on oxygen until we can't get any air, we may be unaware of how dependent we are on a relationship -- and for what reason -- until we lose it.

Common assumption: Legal reforms and the fact that divorce is now so widespread have made divorce less traumatic than it used to be.

Thinking critically: Legal reforms do not necessarily affect the distress of separation, and the fact that separations are common does not necessarily make them easier to endure (Wallerstein & Blakeslee, 1989). As mentioned previously, attachment is a profound human need, and people do not react casually to the breakups of major attachments -- even when they choose the breakup or no longer feel close to the other person.

Recently we heard an exchange between a "radio psychologist" and a man who called in with this problem: He loved his wife, but he also was "in love" with another woman. How could he love two women, he wanted to know, and what should he do about it? In about 45 seconds, the radio psychologist got him to admit a preference for his woman friend. "No problem, then," she said. "Now that you know what you want, all you have to do is leave your wife."

The radio psychologist did not offer this man any information to help him think critically about his feelings and make an informed, if difficult, choice. She did not discuss research on romantic love, emotional attachments, the difficulty of separation, or (as described previously) the effects of divorce on children. She did not assess the man's own values about commitment or trust, though clearly he felt both toward his wife. For her, the answer was easy: If you want to leave a relationship, do it, and never mind the consequences.

It is not for us -- or the radio psychologist -- to say whether the man should or shouldn't leave his marriage. Ultimately, the man's decision must be based on his values and aspirations, and no amount of research can tell him what to do. But psychology -- and critical thinking -- can offer new perspectives on old problems. For example, it may be that our culture's emphasis on romantic passion has tended to obscure the need for commitment and to underemphasize the strength of emotional attachments.

Relationships crumble for all sorts of reasons, including incompatible interests, boredom, extramarital sex (or love), abuse and violence, or the emotional problems of one or both partners. Outside factors also affect the personal decision to part. Social as well as legal barriers to divorce have fallen in the last 20 years; more women are working and do not depend on their husbands for support, and religious opposition to divorce has diminished. Divorce has enabled many people to escape from painful, abusive, or deadening relationships. Yet divorce also produces much pain and unhappiness for all members of the family, at least in the short run and sometimes in the long run.

Ellen Berscheid and Bruce Campbell (1981) argue that easy divorce has affected marriage in ways that are subtle but profound. As the cost of parting declines, people feel entitled to get more if they stay. As more and more marriages dissolve, the number of available partners increases, adding further pressure on a relationship to justify itself. "The freedom to stay or go has a price," say Berscheid and Campbell. "To have a perpetual choice means that one must choose -- not once, but over and over again. And to do so, one must continually expend time and energy in evaluating and re-evaluating the wisdom of the choice."

Of course, if you have a choice, so does your partner. Knowing this may prevent a couple from taking their relationship for granted and behaving in thoughtless ways. But, say Berscheid and Campbell, it also requires them to continually take the temperature of the relationship and worry about its health. Ironically, paying too much attention to its health may help kill it.

The Future of Close Relationships

People often regard their close relationships as a safe haven in a stormy world. But the winds of change rock even the sturdiest boats. Attitudes about close relationships, and the roles we play in them can change with dizzying speed. For example, at one time no "self-respecting" middle-class white man wanted his wife to work. Then, in the 1970s, when wives' incomes became economically necessary, it was fine for a wife to work as long as she didn't earn too much money. Soon it became desirable for a wife to work, so the man wouldn't have to bear all the burden. Today, many men find it difficult to accept a wife's earning more than they do, but this too may change. The point is that attitudes and the nature of relationships are affected by shifting economic conditions and social norms (Bernard, 1981).

In this handbook, we have encouraged you to challenge prevailing assumptions about close relationships, and to look beyond obvious and oversimplified explanations of why they do or do not succeed. We have pointed out how factors external to personality, from proximity to power, can affect relationships. You can use this information, along with your own ability to reason and draw conclusions, to speculate about the relationships of tomorrow. To get you started, we offer these possibilities:

Similar interests draw people together and increase satisfaction in relationships. As gender roles have become more alike, men's and women's interests have converged -- on the job, in sports, in hobbies, in rearing children. If this trend continues, it should foster increased closeness between the sexes. But we are beginning to see a renewed emphasis on traditional gender roles, which suggests that we could see some return to separate spheres of influence and interest.

Power relationships depends on each partner's resources. As women become more financially independent, male-female relationships may approach the balance of power that most people say they want. Yet women's financial independence depends on the availability of jobs (and

208

of husbands) and on the nation's need for female labor. Economic changes could produce a return to traditional divisions of labor and therefore of power.

Physical attractiveness has a strong impact on people's impressions of strangers and choices of friends. In the United States, where people make frequent changes in jobs, cities, friends, and families, individuals are often assessed quickly on the basis of how they look rather than on their record of behavior or their personal qualities. But perhaps, as the baby-boom generation (now in its thirties and forties) ages, youth may become less valued and standards of beauty may change.

One thing is certain. In whatever form it occurs, intimacy with others will continue to offer both giant headaches and giant satisfactions. We hope that applied critical thinking will help you minimize the headaches and increase the satisfactions in your own close relationships.

References

Adams, G. R. (1981). The effects of physical attractiveness on the socialization process. In G. W. Lucker, K. A. Ribbens, & J. A. McNamara, Jr. (eds.) *Psychological aspects of facial form.* Ann Arbor, Mich.: Center for Human Growth and Development.

Antill, John K. (1983). Sex role complementarity versus similarity in married couples. *Journal of Personality and Social Psychology, 45,* 145-155.

Beer, William R. (1984). *Househusbands: Men and housework in American families.* South Hadley, Mass.: J. F. Bergin.

Bernard, Jessie (1981). The good-provider role: Its rise and fall. *American Psychologist, 36,* 1-12.

Berscheid, Ellen (1985). Interpersonal attraction. In G. Lindzey & E. Aronson (eds.), *Handbook of social psychology*, Vol. II. New York: Random House/Erlbaum.

Berscheid, Ellen, & Campbell, Bruce (1981). The changing longevity of heterosexual close relationships: A commentary and forecast. In M. Lerner (ed.), *The justice motive in times of scarcity and change.* New York: Plenum.

Berscheid, Ellen, and Walster, Elaine (1978). *Interpersonal attraction* (2nd edition). Reading, Mass.: Addison-Wesley.

Blood, Robert O., Jr., & Wolfe, Donald M. (1960). *Husbands and wives: The dynamics of married living.* New York: Free Press.

Blumstein, Philip, & Schwartz, Pepper (1983). *American couples.* New York: Morrow.

Botwin, Carol (1985). *Is there sex after marriage?* Boston, Mass.: Little, Brown.

Brehm, Sharon (1985). *Intimate relationships.* New York: Random House.

Burda, Philip C., Jr.; Vaux, Alan; & Schill, Thomas (1984). Social support resources: Variation across sex and sex-role. *Personality and Social Psychology Bulletin, 10,* 119-126.

Burgess, Ernest W., & Wallin, Paul W. (1943). Homogamy in social characteristics. *American Journal of Sociology, 48,* 109-124.

Byme, Donn (1971). *The attraction paradigm.* New York: Academic Press.

Camarena, Phame, & Sarigiani, Pamela (1985). Gender influences on intimacy development in early adolescence. Paper presented at the American Psychological Association, Los Angeles, California.

Cash, Thomas F., & Janda, Louis H. (1984). The eye of the beholder. *Psychology Today, 18*(12), December, 46-52.

Chambless, Diane (1986). Fears and anxieties. In C. Tavris (ed.), *EveryWoman's emotional well-being.* New York: Doubleday.

Clark, Margaret S., & Reis, Harry T. (1988). Interpersonal processes in close relationships. *Annual Review of Psychology, 39*, 609-672.

Cozby, Paul (1973). Self-disclosure: A literature review. *Psychological Bulletin, 70*, 73-91.

Crosby, Faye (1986). Work. In C. Tavris (ed.), *EveryWoman's emotional well-being.* New York: Doubleday.

Dermer, Marshall, & Thiel, Darrel (1975). When beauty may fail. *Journal of Personality and Social Psychology, 31*, 1168-1176.

Dion, Karen K.; Berscheid, Ellen; & Walster, Elaine (1972). What is beautiful is good. *Journal of Personality and Social Psychology, 24*, 285-290.

Dion, Karen K., & Stein, Steven (1978). Physical attractiveness and interpersonal influence. *Journal of Experimental Social Psychology, 14*, 97-108.

Driscoll, Richard; Davis, Keith; & Lipetz, Milton (1972). Parental interference and romantic love. *Journal of Personality and Social Psychology, 24*, 1-10.

Falbo, Toni, & Peplau, Letitia A. (1980). Power strategies in intimate relationships. *Journal of Personality and Social Psychology, 38*, 618-628.

Feingold, Alan (1988). Matching for attractiveness in romantic partners and same-sex friends: A meta-analysis and theoretical critique. *Psychological Bulletin, 104*, 226-235.

Festinger, Leon; Schachter, Stanley; & Back, Kurt (1950). *Social pressures in informal groups: A study of human factors in housing.* New York: Harper & Brothers.

Gray-Little, Bernadette, & Burks, Nancy (1983). Power and satisfaction in marriage: A review and critique. *Psychological Bulletin, 93*, 513-538.

Grigg, Faye; Fletcher, Garth J. O.; & Fitness, Julie (1989). Spontaneous attributions in happy and unhappy dating relationships. *Journal of Social and Personal Relationships, 6*, 61-68.

Hacker, Helen M. (1981). Blabbermouths and clams: Sex differences in self-disclosure in same-sex and cross-sex friendship dyads. *Psychology of Women Quarterly, 5*, 385-401.

Hagestad, Gunhild, & Smyer, Michael (1982). Dissolving long-term relationships: Patterns of divorcing in middle age. In S. Duck (ed.), *Personal relationships. 4: Dissolving relationships.* New York: Academic Press.

Hall, Edward T., & Hall, Mildred, R. (1986). *Hidden differences: How to communicate with the Germans.* Hamburg, West Germany: Gruner & Jahr.

Hatfield, Elaine (1984). The dangers of intimacy. In V. J. Derlega (ed.), *Communication, intimacy, and close relationships.* Orlando, FL: Academic Press.

Hatfield, Elaine; Greenberger, David; Traupmann, Jane, & Lambert, Philip (1982). Equity and sexual satisfaction in recently married couples. *Journal of Sex Research, 18*, 18-32.

Hatfield, Elaine; Traupmann, Jane; Sprecher, Susan; Utne, Mary; & Hay, Julia (1985). Equity and intimate relations: Recent research. In W. Ickes (ed.), *Compatible and incompatible relationships.* New York: Springer-Verlag.

Hill, Charles T.; Rubin, Zick; & Peplau, Letitia A. (1976). Breakups before marriage: The end of 103 affairs. *Journal of Social Issues, 32,* 147-168.

Hochschild, Arlie (1975). The sociology of feeling and emotion. In M. Millman & R. M. Kanter (eds.), *Another voice.* Garden City, NY: Anchor/Doubleday.

Holtzworth-Munroe, Amy & Jacobson, Neil S. (1985). Causal attributions of married couples: When do they search for causes? What do they conclude when they do? *Journal of Personality and Social Psychology, 48,* 1398-1412.

Homans, George C. (1961). *Social behavior: Its elementary forms.* New York: Harcourt.

Huston, Ted L. (1983). Power. In H. H. Kelley, E. Berscheid *et al.* (eds.), *Close relationships.* New York: Freeman.

Jones, Warren H. (1982). Loneliness and social behavior. In L. A. Peplau & D. Perlman (eds.), *Loneliness: A source book of current theory, research, and therapy.* New York: Wiley-Interscience.

Kalick, S. Michael, & Hamilton, Thomas E. (1986). The matching hypothesis reexamined. *Journal of Personality and Social Psychology, 51,* 673-682.

Kelley, Harold H., & Thibaut, John W. (1978). *Interpersonal relations: A theory of interdependence.* New York: Wiley-Interscience.

Kipnis, David, & Schmidt, Stuart (1985). The language of persuasion. *Psychology Today, 19*(4), April, 40-46.

Klagsbrun, Francine (1985). *Married people: Staying together in the age of divorce.* Toronto and New York: Bantam.

Lakoff, Robin (1975). *Language and women's place.* New York: Colophon.

Lauer, Jeanette, & Lauer, Robert (1986). *Til death do us part: How couples stay together.* New York: Haworth Press.

McElfresh, Stephen B. (1982). Conjugal power and legitimating norms: A new perspective on resource theory. Paper presented at annual meeting of the American Psychological Association, Washington, D. C..

Mandler, George (1984). *Mind and body: Psychology of emotion and stress.* New York: W. W. Norton & Company.

Monge, Peter, & Kirste, Kenneth (1980). Meaning proximity in human organization. *Social Psychology Quarterly, 43,* 110-115.

Murstein, Bernard L. (1982). Marital choice. In B. B. Wolman (ed.), *Handbook of developmental psychology.* Englewood Cliffs, NJ: Prentice-Hall.

Newcomb, Theodore (1961). *The acquaintance process.* New York: Hold, Rinehart, & Winston.

Peplau, Letitia A. (1984). Power in dating relationships. In J. Freedman (ed.), *Women: A feminist perspective* (3rd edition). Palo Alto, CA: Mayfield.

Petty, Richard E., & Mirels, Herbert L. (1981). Intimacy and scarcity of self-disclosure: Effects on interpersonal attraction for males and females. *Personality and Social Psychology Bulletin, 7,* 493-503.

Pruitt, Dean, & Rubin, Jeffrey Z. (1986). *Social conflict: Escalation, stalemate, and settlement.* New York: Random House.

Reis, Harry T.; Senchak, Marilyn; & Solomon, Beth (1985). Sex differences in the intimacy of social interaction: Further examination of potential explanations. *Journal of Personality and Social Psychology, 48*, 1204-1217.

Reis, Harry T., & Shaver, Phillip (1988). Intimacy as an interpersonal process. In S. Duck (ed.), *Handbook of personal relationships: Theory, relationships, and interventions.* New York: Wiley.

Rempel, John K.; Holmes, John G.; & Zanna, Mark P. (1985). Trust in close relationships: *Journal of Personality and Social Psychology, 49*, 95-112.

Rubenstein, Carin (1982). Real men don't earn less than their wives. *Psychology Today, 16*(11), November, 36-41.

Rubin, Zick; Peplau, Letitia A.; & Hill, Charles (1981). Loving and leaving: Sex differences in romantic attachments. *Sex Roles, 7*, 821-835.

Schafer, Robert B., & Keith, Patricia M. (1980). Equity and depression among married couples. *Social Psychology Quarterly, 43*, 430-435.

Snyder, Mark (1987). *Public appearances and private realities: The psychology of self-monitoring.* New York: W. H. Freeman.

Snyder, Mark; Berscheid, Ellen; & Glick, Peter (1985). Focusing on the exterior and the interior: Two investigations of the initiation of personal relationships. *Journal of Personality and Social Psychology, 48*, 1427-1439.

Snyder, Mark; Tanke, Elizabeth; & Berscheid, Ellen (1977). Social perception and interpersonal behavior: On the self-fulfilling nature of social stereotypes. *Journal of Personality and Social Psychology, 35*, 656-666.

Sprecher, Susan (1986). The relation between inequity and emotions in close relationships. *Social Psychology Quarterly, 49*, 309-321.

Sternberg, Robert J. (1985). A triangular theory of love. Paper presented at the American Psychological Association, Los Angeles, California.

Sternberg, Robert J. (1988). *The triangle of love: Intimacy, passion, commitment.* New York: Basic Books.

Thibaut, John W., & Kelley, Harold H. (1959). *The social psychology of groups.* New York: Wiley.

Traupmann, Jane, & Hatfield, Elaine (1983). How important is marital fairness over the lifespan? *International Journal of Aging and Human Development, 17*, 89-101.

Traupmann, Jane; Petersen, R.; Utne, Mary; & Hatfield, Elaine (1981). Measuring equity in intimate relations. *Applied Psychological Measurement, 5*, 467-480.

Waller, Willard (1938). *The family: A dynamic interpretation.* New York: Dryden.

Wallerstein, Judith, & Blakeslee, Sandra (1989). *Second chances: Men, women, & children a decade after divorce.* New York: Ticknor & Fields.

Walster, Elaine; Aronson, Vera; Abrahams, Darcy; & Rottmann, Leon (1966). Importance of physical attractiveness in dating behavior. *Journal of Personality and Social Psychology, 4*, 508-516.

Walster, Elaine; Walster, George W.; & Berscheid, Ellen (1978). *Equity: Theory and Research.* Boston, Mass.: Allyn & Bacon.

Weitzman, Lenore (1985). *The divorce revolution: The unexpected social and economic consequences for women and children in America.* New York: The Free Press.

Wheeler, Ladd; Reis, Harry T.; & Nezlek, John (1983). Loneliness, social interaction, and sex roles. *Journal of Personality and Social Psychology, 45*, 843-853.

Wills, Thomas A.; Weiss, Robert L.; & Patterson, Gerald R. (1974). A behavioral analysis of the determinants of marital satisfaction. *Journal of Consulting and Clinical Psychology, 42*, 802-811.

Winch, Robert (1958). Mate-selection. *A study of complemntary needs.* New York: Harper.

Yllo, Kersti (1983). Sexual equality and violence against wives in American states. *Journal of Comparative Family Studies, 14,* 67-86.

Chapter 15

Baby care: fathers versus mothers. Through this work, the LaRossas convey the meaning of aligning actions and illuminate role expectations that guide new parents. In this look at issues fundamental to the division of labor, we are introduced to how traditionalization of partners' roles can restrict healthy relationships by using assumptions of fixed or inflexible role enactment. The LaRossas point out that as competition builds between the mother and father of a new baby, the tendency to shift to traditional roles can negatively affect both parents. The shift can place role strain on fathers to increase focus on work and mothers to provide all the primary child care. Too much of one thing consequently leaves a person burnt out and isolated. What are the remedies to traditionalization of this type? How can we avoid using aligning actions to justify our unmet plans and goals? Why are these classic role expectations so strong?

Chapter 15 *Ralph LaRossa and Maureen Mulligan LaRossa,* Baby Care: Fathers vs. Mothers

How do husbands' and wives' everyday lives change when they become parents? By "everyday life" we mean their daily routines -- their eating, sleeping, working, and playing routines. Also, how is the everyday life of a new father different from that of a new mother? These are the questions we set out to answer when we began our study of the transition to parenthood.

As studies of the transition to parenthood go, ours is unique in several respects. First, it is a study of parenthood as parents see it. Each interview was essentially open-ended and free-flowing, which is to say that the men and women in the study were encouraged to talk about what was important to them, not what we presumed to be important. Second, it is a participant-informed study. Married in 1970, we had our first child in 1979 which, coincidentally enough, happened to be the point at which we started to analyze the interviews. Thus, we were in the unusual position of experiencing our own transition to parenthood at the same time we were trying to understand the experiences of others. Third, it is a study of change. Each of the twenty couples in the study was interviewed not once but three times, during the third, sixth, and ninth months postpartum. Fourth, it is a study of both first- and second-time parenthood. Whereas most studies of the transition to parenthood focus only on the first birth, we thought it important to view the transition to parenthood as a continuum that, in principle, can extend the length of the childbearing phase. Last but not least, it is a study of social patterns, social processes, and sociohistorical conditions surrounding the transition to parenthood. All too often, researchers look only at whether or not new parents are "coping with" or "adjusting to" the transition to parenthood, while ignoring the transition to parenthood itself. As a result, we know very little about *what actually happens* when people become parents; and we know even less about how what happens is linked to larger sociohistorical realities. (For a detailed description of the methodology used in the study, see LaRossa and LaRossa, 1981).

In our efforts to make sense of the transcripts, we found ourselves increasingly relying on three conceptual frameworks: the conflict framework, the choice and exchange framework, and the symbolic interactionist framework.

The *conflict framework*, of which the major premise is "when confronted with a choice under conditions of real or perceived scarcity, humans will be inclined to choose themselves over others" (Sprey, 1979: 132), proved to be the overarching orientation because of how central the "problem of continuous coverage" is to understanding the transition to parenthood.

A newborn child cannot survive on its own, but is dependent on adults to feed it, protect it from the elements, and teach it to use symbols (most importantly language) so that it can become a functioning member of society. The helplessness of the human infant places a family that is in the midst of a transition to parenthood within the class of social arrangements that have as their primary function "coverage." For example, a medical hospital in the United States is a "continuous coverage social system"; there is always someone who is on call, ready to respond to the needs of the patients at a moment's notice (Zerubavel, 1979b). The same kind of coverage characterizes new parenthood. Having a baby launches a couple into the responsibilities of continuous coverage for that baby; someone, either the couple themselves or their representative (for example, a babysitter), must always be on call.

The obligation of having to be ready and able to care for their infant son or daughter tends to reduce the father's and mother's free time, the time when they can do what they want to do rather than what someone else (the baby) wants them to do. Indeed, it is the loss of free time accompanying parenthood that surprises and bothers new parents more than anything else (Harriman, 1983; Hobbs, 1965; Hobbs and Wimbish, 1977; LaRossa, 1983). The scarcity of this valued resource creates a conflict of interest between the husband and wife. No matter how much they may try to avoid it, periodically there will arise zero-sum-game-like situations in which one partner's "winning" (being free to pursue his or her own interests) means that the other must "lose" (forgo his or her own interests for the sake of the baby). Conflicts of interest generally result in conflict behavior, tactics, and strategies which theoretically extend from verbal persuasion to the use of force, as both parties in the encounter pursue their own short- and long-term interests, often at the expense of the other.

It is this basic pattern -- child dependency resulting in continuous coverage, which means a scarcity of free time, which leads to conflicts of interest and often conflict behavior -- that cuts across the experiences of all the couples in our sample; and it is this basic pattern that explains why the conflict framework became the linchpin in our analysis.

Closely tied to the conflict framework is the *choice and exchange framework*, which operates on the assumption that "humans avoid costly behavior and seek rewarding statuses, relationships, interaction, and feeling states to the end that their profits [or outcomes] are maximized" (Nye, 1979: 2). The choice and exchange framework was found to be useful in understanding the organization of men's and women's commitments to activities, like infant care, outside employment, and recreation. The choice and exchange framework also helped us to understand how power relations in families are directly tied to institutionalized sexism and, more specifically, to the dependency of women on men. One reason that the marital power structure in the United States tends to be patriarchal is that women often have to rely on men for economic support.

Not as often associated with the conflict framework but just as important to our argument is the *symbolic interactionist framework*. The basic insight derived from this framework is that "humans live in a symbolic [conventional sign] environment as well as a physical environment," and that "the best way to understand humans is to deal with the mentalistic meanings and values [the symbols] that occur in the minds of the people, because that is the most direct cause of their behavior" (Burr *et al.*, 1979: 46, 49). The inability of infants at birth to use symbols, the different levels of value that fathers and mothers attribute to free time, the definitions of social structures as legitimate or illegitimate, and, finally, the symbolic or ideological aspects of conflict behavior are all crucial to our analysis and, indirectly, to the conflict framework which supports that analysis.

By accentuating the part that sociocultural forces and interactional contexts play during the transition to parenthood, the three frameworks, taken together, form the basis for a sociological -- or structural -- approach to the transition to parenthood. Up to now, transition-to-parenthood researchers have relied almost exclusively on an individualistic approach, an approach that focuses on biological or psychological explanations for parental behavior. Rossi (1977, 1984), for example, talks about the effect of biologically based gender differences on parenting, while Chodorow (1978) offers a psychoanalytic theory that locates the roots of fathering and mothering in the personality differences between men and women. In contrast, we hypothesize that sociological variables, such as social time, power, commitment, and ideology, do as good a job -- if not better job -- of explaining the conduct of fathers and mothers *vis-à-vis* their children; and we believe that any theory of parenthood that strives to be comprehensive must include sociological as well as biological and psychological factors.

Work and Play, Primary and Secondary Time

The continuous coverage of infants is somewhat unique in that it entails both work and play. Not only is it important to feed, clothe, and carry the baby, it is also important to play with the baby, since it is through play (and especially games) that the child develops a concept of self, which is indispensable to becoming a full-fledged member of society (Mead, 1934).

In his 1965-66 study, Robinson (1977) discovered several things about child work and child play that we think are highly significant. First of all, he found that not only did housewives spend seven times as much time as employed men in child-care activities, and employed women twice as much time, but that while less than a tenth of women's child care was play, half of all men's child care was play (1977: 64-65). When one considers the range of activities that constitute "baby care," it is indeed remarkable that fathers are able to limit their own activities to such a degree. In their study of the content and organization of housework, Berk and Berk (1979) identify approximately sixty discrete tasks that can be categorized as baby care (1979: 265-275). However, only six of these tasks fall under the heading of play. Combining Robinson's and the Berks' surveys thus suggests that fathers are devoting 50 percent of their baby care time to 10 percent of the baby care. We also found that it was not uncommon for new fathers to define short bursts of play with their infants (often immediately upon coming home from work, or after dinner) as efforts which made up for the fact that they were absent all day or which balanced out their inability or unwillingness to take a more active part in the so-called "dirty work" (for example, diaper changing, feeding). The fact that playing is generally "cleaner" than other kinds of baby care and thus more desirable may only partially explain why fathers tend to prefer this form of contact with their children. The other, perhaps more important, factor in the equation is that play requires less *attention* than custodial responsibilities.

Here is what we mean: With the express purpose of measuring different levels of attention, Robinson's research was based on having families keep a log or a diary of their activities over a specified time, usually a twenty-four hour period. Looking somewhat like a bookkeeper's ledger sheet, a time-diary lists the hours of the day down the left-hand side of the page, and the following seven questions across the top (thus creating seven columns): "What did you do [at this time]? Time began? Time ended? Where? With whom? Doing anything else? Remarks?" (Robinson, 1977: 7). The first question ("What did you do [at this time]?") tapped into the subject's *primary* activity. The next-to-last question ("Doing anything else?") recorded the subject's *secondary* activity, which by definition was anything done secondarily and in addition to the primary activity. Robinson found that the comparisons between men and women with respect to primary child care were exactly the same as the comparisons for child care in general; that is, housewives spend seven times as much time in primary child care, and employed women spend twice as much time in primary child care as men (1977: 72). The principal reason for the similar figures can be traced to the correlation between the kind of child-care activity and the amount of attention devoted to that activity. In a footnote, Robinson reports that (1977: 70):

> While over two-thirds of primary activity child care in the 1965-1966
> study was "custodial" (feeding, clothing, chauffeuring, etc.) rather than

"interactional" (reading, playing, etc.) in nature, the bulk of secondary activity child care consisted of interactional activities.

When we look at our data in light of Robinson's findings, we came up with another factor that may help explain why fathers devote a greater proportion of their child-care time to play than do mothers. Not only is play cleaner than many other forms of child-care activity, but play also has the advantage of being less demanding in terms of the amount of attention that one must give to that activity. *Fathers, in other words, may choose play over work because play "eats" less into their own free time.*

How does play "consume" less free time? Think of play and work as ideal-typical poles of a hypothetical continuum. Toward the play end of the continuum one would include activities such as piggy-back riding, tickling, and hide-and-seek. Toward the work end of the continuum one would include feeding, diaper changing, putting to sleep, and so forth. In the middle would be those activities that fall between play and work, the borderline cases: reading a story, giving a bath (with toys, of course), going on nature walks. Generally speaking, activities that are toward the play end of the continuum require less parental attention than the other activities. First, these activities are often shorter in duration. A piggy-back ride, for example, may last only two or three minutes. Yet at the end of the ride, the parent can legitimately terminate contact with the baby, often with the assistance of the other parent (for example, "Come on now, give Daddy a break, you tired him out"). Second, play activities are typically not as scheduled or as urgently required as work activities. The parent can usually decide when and how long to play ("Not now, later, but only for a few minutes"), whereas activities such as feeding and diaper changing are more on demand; letting one's child go hungry or remain dirty is frowned upon. Third, play activities are less bounded spatially than work activities. Roughhousing can take place anywhere in the house -- in front of the television, in the backyard -- which means that the parent can more easily integrate personal activities with play. Feeding and diaper changing, on the other hand, are usually done in specific locales, severely restricting the kinds of activities that a parent can perform in addition to child work.

Getting "Down Time"

Primary and secondary are not the only levels of attention. There is logically a third level of activity, *tertiary* activity, which can be defined as time during which there is no social contact whatsoever. Of course, as with primary and secondary activity, tertiary activity must be operationalized in terms of some referent or referents. Thus, for example, a mother at work would be at a tertiary level with respect to her children, while being primarily and secondarily involved with her job. If, on the other hand, her child happens to call her at her office, then during the phone call she would be primarily attending to her child, and secondarily attending to her work.

Rather than think of attention, one may think of social accessibility (Zerubavel, 1979a). In the primary mode one is most accessible to a referent, and in the tertiary mode least accessible to a referent. Hence, primary, secondary, and tertiary time actually represents points on a continuum that extends from being totally attuned or accessible to a referent (total connection) to being totally neglectful or inaccessible to a referent (total separation).

When adults interact with each other, they generally have the freedom to move, within specified parameters and rules, across all three levels. A husband and wife can, for example, be involved in a very intense conversation one moment (primary status), then shift their attention to the television while still maintaining contact with each other (secondary status), and finally move to separate corners of their house to work on their individual hobbies (tertiary status). (Some husbands and wives might define this third move as secondary status because, as far as they are concerned, being in the same house means that they are *with* each other. But let us assume, for the sake of simplicity, that the husband and wife do not define their situation in this way, but believe that any time that they are not in face-to-face contact with each other, they are in a no-contact status.) The advantage of being able to move across all three levels is that husbands and wives can give each other their undivided attention at one moment, and then withdraw completely from each other the next. They can, in other words, coordinate a system of connectedness and separateness such that at one moment they are concentrating on each other, and the next they are essentially removed from each other.

This is very different from what it is like to interact with an infant. If a mother, for example, is alone with an infant at home, she can never move to a tertiary level, but must always be "up" or "ready" to attend to her child's needs. This is indeed one of the biggest surprises for new parents. They soon learn that infants are not only very dependent on them, but that the demands of infants are also nonnegotiable. The simple phrase "I'll be with you in a moment," which works so well in the adult world to delay moving to a primary or secondary level, is useless with someone who does not understand language. ("Infant" is derived from the Latin word *infans* which means incapable of speech.)

We do not mean to suggest that primary contact with one's child is unrewarding, or that some parents do not find pleasure in having an individual who is totally depending on them. But as the couples in our study suggested over and over again, what can be unrewarding and unpleasant is the *repetitiveness* of that level of contact. No matter how much we love someone or something, satiation (too much of a good thing) reduces the reward value of that person or object (Homans, 1974: 29). Also the *pace* of parent-infant interaction can take its toll. As with assembly-line work (see Blauner, 1964) and air traffic control work, the most alienating and most distressing aspect of baby care is its pace. It is the baby and not the parent who generally controls when shifts from one level to the next will occur. The parents' job is to "keep track" of the child, who, if mobile (crawling or toddling), must be "plotted" in terms of direction, speed, and altitude (height).

It is perhaps worth noting that people who work in situations from which they cannot voluntarily withdraw, from which they cannot take "time-outs" when they want to but must wait to be relieved, have been found to be more prone to "burn-out," the symptoms of which include not only physical and emotional exhaustion, but social exhaustion as well as, involving "the loss of concern for the people with whom one is working," taking a "very cynical and dehumanized perception of these people," and treating them accordingly (Maslach and Pines, 1977: 101; also Maslach, 1976). Thus, we suspect that there are parents who develop dehumanized views of their own children as a result of the constant attention they are giving to them, and that the parents who are probably most likely to undergo this experience are those who "cannot do enough for their kids," the supermoms and superdads.

Even when the baby is sleeping, an adult left alone in the house cannot move to a tertiary level. Although the parent will probably not be in the same room as the baby during nap time, the parent is still monitoring the infant, still standing watch. This is not to say that the parent will not feel restored by having an hour or two "off." In reality, however, the "ah" feeling experienced by the parent when he or she carefully closes the door to the nursery after having just rocked the baby to sleep is because now there is time to be primarily involved in his or her own needs while secondarily involved with the baby's needs, rather than vice versa. In short, after a hectic morning of being "up" for the baby -- feeding, changing, amusing, watching, consoling, and so forth -- the parent can now enjoy a long awaited *semi*-attentiveness.

If there are two adults in the house, the picture can change dramatically. Now each adult can slip into periodic "down times" while the other remains on a secondary level. Sometimes responsibility for the baby is formally arranged, as in those cases where fathers and mothers alternate who gets up in the morning with the baby and who sleeps late. However, more often than not, we suspect, the movement from one level to the next is informal and emergent, a procedure which can sometimes court disaster (He: "I thought *you* were watching the baby!" She: "And I thought *you* were watching the baby!")

If one of the adults refuses to share responsibility for the baby, then the other must always be "up" or "ready." Thus, while one parent watches television, reads a book, works in the den -- essentially oblivious to the needs of the baby -- the other must be continuously on guard. Again the formal/informal distinction applies. One husband in the sample formally announced to his wife that, as far as he was concerned, she was always on duty -- seven days a week, twenty-four hours a day. With other husbands, the results were still the same -- the wife always attending to the baby -- but the means were more subtle and more informal. Thus, a husband may claim that he, too, is in a secondary status with respect to the baby, but in reality he is technically in second while functionally in third; if the baby starts to cry or moves too close to the house plants, he will not feel any compulsion to intervene, but will let his wife take care of it. Even more subtle is the strategy of arranging his activities so that he precludes his having to share in the baby work. The father who decides to pay the bills or perhaps clean the kitchen just when the baby needs to be fed or changed has effectively preserved a tertiary level of contact with his child.

The significance of negotiating protectiveness becomes clear at this point. It is quite common for fathers and mothers to debate over how protective they should be with their babies (for example, "Should we let her cry?"). Although the manifest function of these discussions is to decide what is best for the child, the hidden agenda is often what is best for the husband and wife. Should a father conclude that his wife is too protective ("You are spoiling her"), he can then justify his refusal to respond to the baby's demands. However sincere he may be, the results are still the same -- "down time" for the father, often at the expense of the wife. For example, one of the fathers went out virtually every night of the week, despite his wife's protests that he should stay home with her and the baby. One of his responses to her protests was that if she were willing to hire a babysitter, she could join him. Since she refused (she felt that as a working mother it was bad enough that she had to leave her baby during the day; she was not going to leave her at night too), it was, in his opinion, basically *her* fault that the two of them did not spend more time together.

Helping Versus Sharing

The father who refuses, either formally or informally, to do anything is the exception, to the rule. What is the rule -- as suggested by our data and other studies -- is that fathers will periodically move to a primary or secondary attention level with their infants, thus enabling their wives to get tertiary ("down") time, but that when they do take over, they almost always assume that they are "helping" their wives rather than "sharing" the parental responsibilities.

Mothers are also likely to see fathers as surrogate parents, and, like their husbands, will use words such as "helping" and "babysitting" to denote the father's contribution. It is interesting to note that in the 1701 pages of transcripts, *every* couple would, at least once in their interviews, refer to the husband as "helping" the wife with the baby, whereas not a single couple defined the wife's parental responsibilities in these terms.

There are a variety of ways that a "helping" role can be performed. The first signs that the father will be less involved than the mother in child care can be seen before the baby arrives, during the pregnancy. More often than not, the wife will be the one to think first about and eventually buy several of the how-to books on parenting. If the father does read any of the books, either in whole or in part, it is likely to be as a result of the mother's coaxing. Clearly, from the start, the mother is the one who is "in charge" of the baby. Her purchase of the books reflects what is generally accepted: Babies are "women's work." The fact that she will read the books more thoroughly than her husband directs what is to come: since the father is not as informed about what it means to be a parent, both parents will assume that Mom is the one to orchestrate and implement the child's care. When and if the father does participate, it is presumed to be under the mother's direction.

After the baby is born, performances which reflect and direct the father and mother's separate roles become more sophisticated. Perhaps the most easily recognized is the behavior that ensues the first few times the father holds the baby. Upon being handed his infant son or daughter, he will often say something to the effect that he hopes he does not drop the baby. Then, while he is cradling the baby in his arms, the father will stiffen up, demonstrating both to himself and to everyone in the room (including the baby) that this is not his accustomed role. Often, the coactors in this drama will reinforce the father's definition of the situation by standing very close, as if to be ready to catch the baby should he or she actually fall out of the father's arms. Another typical maneuver is to encourage the father to sit down, preferably in a stuffed chair, so that his arms can be supported. Throughout the scene, the father will ask for and the other performers will readily offer instructions on how to position the arms; where to hold the baby's head, and so forth. Additional touches may include having someone gather everyone in the house so that they can see Daddy holding Junior or, even better, grabbing a camera to capture a "rare" moment for posterity.

In sociological terms, this scene is a perfect example of what Goffman (1961) refers to as *role distance*. The mock or comedic aspects of the performance indicate an attempt by the father to deny "not the role but the virtual self that is implied in the role" (1961: 108). In other words, the father is distancing or disassociating his self from the parental role.

222

The father's performance stands in stark contrast to the mother's actions when she holds the baby. Even if she does fear that she will drop the baby during those first few days of parenthood, it is considered poor form for her to display that fear. Rather, she is likely to try to appear as if holding the baby is well within her abilities. And the other performers in the room are likely to communicate to the mother than she does indeed look "natural" for the job.

The mother's performance is the flip side of the role distance. What she is doing is *embracing* the parental role -- disappearing, as it were, "into the virtual self available in the situation," confirming "expressively [her] acceptance of it" (Goffman, 1961: 106).

The role distance/role embracement distinction is actually a continuum, one that may be useful for understanding a puzzling set of findings. Studies indicate that most husbands and wives do not believe that men should do more family work than they are doing now. And among the minority who do feel that men should contribute more, a greater proportion of men than women express an interest in expanding the man's family role (Pleck, 1976). Women, in other words, generally "want" to remain chiefly responsible for the house and for the children.

One explanation -- perhaps the most popular -- is that women have a psychological investment in their family roles, and become threatened if they cannot count on housework and baby care as their domain. For example, one of the case-study wives was very proud to be a full-time housewife and mother, feeling that these roles constituted her "career" in life. If her husband had decided one day that from then on he would take over a substantial part of homemaking duties, we have no doubt that this particular woman would have indeed felt threatened.

In terms of what we have been saying, the psychological investment explanation focuses on the role embracement of the mother. Because her self is so closely tied to motherhood, reducing her role performances would undermine her identity. This is probably true for many women, but it does not seem to us to be the whole story. Also operating, we suspect, are the consequences of the father's role distance. To continue our discussion of the variety of ways that helping behavior may manifest itself once the baby comes, consider these role-distancing performances disclosed by the couples: A father "forgets" to change the baby's diaper for the whole time (about six hours) that he is "babysitting" while his wife has gone shopping; he claimed that he was just about to do it. A father just "gives up" trying to feed his infant son and concludes that he is just not "as good at it" as his wife is. A mother reports that her husband did such a terrible job of cleaning their daughter that she finally decided that it was easier for her if she just did it herself. And finally, a mother notes that when her husband did care for the baby he would always ask for her assistance, which meant that she ended up doing most of the work anyway. Thus, another explanation for why mothers do not want more cooperation is that they may not trust their husbands to do a good job, or they have learned that their husband's assistance is more trouble than it is worth.

What about the fathers? Although fathers are more inclined to "want" to increase their participation more than mothers "want" them to, the number of fathers who advocate change is still small. Role embracement and role distance can still apply. While the mother embraces parenthood, the father is embracing the traditional male role, which means he sees himself more as the breadwinner than the caretaker. His job, as some of our husbands said, is to "put the food on the table and pay for the kid's college education." Thus, many fathers take exception to the claim that they do not care for or about their children. They point out that although they may not be involved in the day-to-day feeding and cleaning of the baby, they are very much involved in the day-to-day responsibility of providing financial support. Indeed, they argue, because their responsibilities in this realm are so time consuming and energy exhausting, they cannot possibly help their wives more, nor should they be expected to. Even if the wives themselves are employed, many fathers still insist that their jobs are more pressure-laden than their wives' jobs are, and that they still, therefore, should not be expected to help more around the house. (Studies have found that the wife's employment has a negligible impact on the husband's housework and child-care responsibilities [Berk and Berk, 1979; Pleck and Rustad, 1980; Robinson, 1977].) One father in the sample resented the whole idea that men in this society must hold a job, while women can presumably take off when they have to have a baby. The implication was that although men may be "helpers" at home, women are "helpers" in the economic world.

Related, of course, to the father's embracement of the traditional role is the fact that some men have a psychological investment in *not* helping more at home. In their minds, husbands who do too much housework and baby care are not "real men."

The fact that fewer mothers than fathers advocate change is, however, the real puzzle, the solution to which may be linked to the use of the word "help" to denote the father's parental performances. If the wife believes that her husband's contribution to child care is an act of charity, a "gift" from him to her, then each time the husband helps with the baby, he alters the social exchange balance in the marriage. Having done his wife a "favor," both he and she expect that the favor will be returned (*quid pro quo*). The form of the repayment may not be known. It can itself, be an act of charity (for example, helping the husband pay the bills), or simply an immediate response to a request (for example, sex even though she is tired). The norm of reciprocity (Gouldner, 1960), nevertheless, dictates that over time role partners will strive for a balanced exchange (Blau, 1964).

Thus, the reason that more mothers than fathers may not be too keen on the idea of having men help more (and significantly, it is in terms of "help" that the surveys are sometimes phrased; see Robinson, 1977, for example) is that mothers may not want to "pay the price." They may not be comfortable with the deferential stance they are expected to take to offset their husband's gratuities (cf. Bell and Newby, 1976).

Of course, the choice may not be theirs to make. The few studies that have examined whether the marital power structure changes after the birth of a child have found that marriages typically become more patriarchal during the transition to parenthood (Cowan *et al.*, 1978; Meyerowitz and Feldman, 1966). Speculation on why this shift occurs has generally centered on the fact that many women quit work when they have their first baby (see Hoffman, 1978, for example). Since power is inversely related to dependency (Emerson, 1962), the increased financial reliance of the wife on the husband is presumed to decrease her power in the relationship, all other things being equal (cf. Blood and Wolfe, 1960). We would hypothesize that the wife's power will typically decrease, regardless of whether there is a change in her employment status. The unrelenting demands of an infant increase the wife's dependency on the husband for "down time." Though she may not like the fact that when she does get relief from her husband it is defined as a gift for which she will be beholden, she is not likely to cut

224

herself off from his aid. Nor is the husband likely to stop contributing care, particularly if he begins to sense that his wife is indeed grateful for his support. Some husbands in our sample, in fact, tried to increase their wives' dependency not by doing more baby work, but by demanding that their wives acknowledge that since they did a lot more than most of their male friends, they should be appreciated more than they are now. In short, we suspect that marriages tend to become more patriarchal after the birth of the first child because of the socially defined character of baby care.

As might be expected, there are always exceptions to the rule. Women can and do increase their power in a relationship by using their children to increase their demands on their husbands (LaRossa, 1977: 45-46). Also, husbands and wives who do not see the husband's contribution as "helping" are less likely to have the power dependency balance in their marriages dramatically altered.

One final point of helping: One of the few studies to examine how (rather than whether) the marital power structure changes after the first birth found that couples use more "coercive tactics" (power plays, guilt induction, disparagement) with each other when they become parents (Raush et al., 1974). These tactics may very well be related to the power-dependence imbalances that are created by helping behavior during the transition to parenthood. If so, then having a baby could, for some couples, precipitate a cycle of mutual coercion escalating ultimately to the use of physical force. The existence of a relationship between parenthood and marital violence is not unheard of. Gelles (1975) found that a disproportionate number of women are hit by their husbands while they are pregnant. And Straus et al. (1980) recently reported that the most likely conflict to lead to blows between a husband and wife is conflict over children.

The Reification of Infants

After reading the transcripts only once, we realized that the value of parenthood was different for the fathers and mothers in our sample. What we did not immediately realize, but what became more apparent with each successive reading, was the way in which the fathers' and mothers' value differences influenced their interactions with their children. In a nutshell, because of the configuration of the fathers' values, they were more likely to act toward their infants as if they, the infants, were *things* (reifications).

One of the fathers, for example, said that his mind would often wander while he was talking with people. His wife, in particular, would become annoyed when, in the middle of a conversation, she would sense that he had "left." The father said that he was working very hard to break this habit with his wife, but that when he did it with his new son, he did not feel that guilty. Since his son was too young to sense that he was not getting his undivided attention, he could, as he put it, "fink [out]" on his kid. Critical to this father's attitude was his disappointment with very young babies. As far as he was concerned, they could not "interact." When the father made this remark, his wife immediately disagreed, saying that their son, and indeed all infants, could interact, but on a different level. The mother, in other words, seemed more sensitive to the fact that infants may not be able to use symbols, but they can communicate through signs (for example, crying means "I want something"). In general, the mothers in the sample were more sensitive to their infant's abilities than the fathers were.

Another way of describing the different attributions that fathers and mothers gave to their infants is to say that mothers were likely to see their infants as more "interpersonally competent" than fathers saw them. The more interpersonal competence that one imputes to other actors in a relationship, the more satisfied one is with the relationship (Burr *et al.*, 1979). Thus, we would hypothesize that mothers generally enjoy the relationship with their infants more than fathers do.

All of this is not to say that fathers do not want their children, that they do not think they are rewarding. Nor do we mean to suggest that there are not moments when mothers would just as soon hide from their kids, or that mothers do not have other reasons, besides simple enjoyment, for wanting to be mothers. Rather, the point is that the socially determined configuration of values for fathers and mothers is different. To explain what we mean by this, we will apply the often-used intrinsic/extrinsic distinction to parental values.

A *value* "is the position of anything in a preference ordering" (Kuhn, 1974: 107). All social objects, including people, have some value -- and often a complex of values -- attached to them by others. Essentially, there are two kinds of values -- intrinsic and extrinsic. The *intrinsic value* of something or someone is the amount of sheer pleasure or enjoyment that one gets from experiencing that object or person. The *extrinsic value* of something or someone is the amount of social rewards (for example, money, power, prestige, approval, positive self-image, avoidance of stigma or physical pain) associated with having or being with that object or person.

If, for the sake of simplicity, we divide both intrinsic value and extrinsic value into "high" and "low," we arrive at the following ideal types:

A. High Intrinsic Value, High Extrinsic Value
B. High Intrinsic Value, Low Extrinsic Value
C. Low Intrinsic Value, High Extrinsic Value
D. Low Intrinsic Value, Low Extrinsic Value

Configurations "A" and "D" in their most extreme forms would include "love" and "hate," respectively. Thinking in interpersonal terms, an "A" type would be the parent who very much enjoys interacting with his or her child, and who derives prestige and social approval from being a parent. An example of a "D" type would be the parent who has decided not to keep his or her baby because of the lack of both enjoyment and perceived social rewards accompanying the transition to parenthood. Category "B" would, in its extreme form, include fathers and mothers who get a thrill just from being in contact with their kids but who have never seen their children as assets to be displayed or bartered. And finally, category "C" would, in its extreme form, include fathers and mothers who see their children only in utilitarian terms, as commodities in the interpersonal marketplace. Though presented here as dichotomous variables (high/low), intrinsic value and extrinsic value are, in reality, continuous variables (highest...midpoint...lowest). Hence, whereas it may be difficult to conceive of the four types in their most extreme forms, the chances are that all of us have directly or indirectly known people who more or less conform to one type or another. We may not know, for example, a parent who derives only intrinsic benefits from being a parent, but we can perhaps think of fathers and mothers who just seem to get "a charge" out of being parents, and who seem to be relatively uninterested in the extrinsic payoffs.

The relevance of the typology to understanding the reification of infants is that category "C" is a reified relationship. To see a baby largely in terms of the social rewards which he or she provides is to dehumanize the baby. We recognize that this statement is itself a value judgment, but we believe that "thing-like relationships" is an accurate description of some of the interactions that were described during the interviews. To be more specific, and to return to the central point about father-child relationships, our data suggest that there are many fathers who could be said to, more or less, fall into category "C," many fathers who certainly want and treasure their children, but who do not really enjoy being with their kids. Sure, they will roughhouse with their toddlers on the living-room floor, and will blush when hugged or kissed by their one-year-olds, but when you really get down to it, they just do not have that much fun when they are with their children. If they had their druthers, they would be working at the office or drinking at the local pub -- and quite often they are doing precisely that either in fact or in fantasy -- but they commit themselves to their kids out of a sense of responsibility.

Relationships which are perceived as primarily obligatory take on a very different character than intrinsically valued relationships. First, obligation relationships operate at lower levels of attention than intrinsically valued relationships, which is to say that there would be more divided attention, more secondly activity in these relationships. Also, obligatory relationships are generally more routinized, so as to facilitate the addition of other activities (and other people) when enacting the obligatory relationship. Thus, we would hypothesize that low intrinsic/high intrinsic parent-child relationships would be marked by more multiple activities and, because they can be easily routinized, more play activities than High Intrinsic/High Extrinsic parent-child relationships.

The best example of this was provided by the father who complained that his son could not interact and who said that the had developed a series of "tricks" which helped him get through any extended contact with his son. Basically, the tricks were toys and events which kept the baby distracted, and which thus decreased the father's level of attention. The father had also learned what particular sequence of introducing the tricks worked best for distracting the baby the longest. Thus, the father would initiate a routinized series of distractions when his son started to get too demanding.

Reification of children can spiral. Parents who, from the start, assume that their infants are not interpersonally competent may conclude that they do not enjoy being with their children, which can result in a lowering of their attention and routinization of their interaction with their kids. This strategy can prevent the parents from effectively discovering that their children (1) may be more interpersonally competent than they originally thought they were, and (2) are becoming more interpersonally competent with each passing day (because of developmental changes). Not being receptive to these changes may contribute further to the parents' low level of enjoyment when they are with their children, which may mean that they will withdraw even more so, and so on. The significance of this hypothetical pattern is that it suggests that child-care differences between couples and between fathers and mothers are not simply a function of internalized value differences being "played out," but are a consequence of *interactional processes* that take place during the transition to parenthood itself.

Aligning Actions and Traditional Divisions of Labor

It is clear from the above analysis that during the transition to parenthood, the probability of misunderstandings, screw-ups, snafus, conflicts of interest, and unplanned consequences is quite high. In a word, things can "get out of line" quite easily. Generally, these misalignments take two forms. *Interpersonal misalignments* are those situations in which there is a misunderstanding or basic conflict of interest between people. *Culture-conduct misalignments* are those situations in which there is a perceived discrepancy between the cultural ideals and expectations of the participants in a social system and their actual or intended conduct; they say one thing and do another (Stokes and Hewitt, 1976).

When people are confronted with either an interpersonal misalignment or a culture-conduct misalignment, they will engage in what are called (reasonably enough) aligning actions (Stokes and Hewitt, 1976). *Aligning actions* are principally verbal activities and include, among other things, *motives* ("answers to questions interrupting acts or programs" [Mills, 1940: 473]), *remedial interchanges* ("corrective readings calculated to show that a possible offender actually had a right relationship to the rules, or if he seemed not to a moment ago, he can be counted on to have such a relationship henceforth" [Goffman, 1971: 108]), and *accounts* ("a statement made by a social actor to explain unanticipated or untoward behavior" [Scott and Lyman, 1968: 46]).

Aligning actions are central to a sociological perspective because they help us to understand a central sociological problem, namely, the existence of continuity and change in social life. Given instances of culture-conduct misalignment (the second of the two forms of misalignment), the major functions of aligning actions are to (1) "maintain culture in the face of conduct that is at variance with it," and (2) "provide a social lubricant that simultaneously permits a social change and yet allows conduct to be linked to recognized cultural boundaries" (Stokes and Hewitt, 1976: 848).

With respect to the first function, aligning actions explain how a couple can believe that they have a role-sharing (nontraditional) system when their conduct clearly indicates that they have a role-segregated (traditional) system. The aligning actions in this case define role-segregated conduct as nothing more than a legitimate exception to the rule. Thus, for example, the couple who very much wants to institute an androgynous parental arrangement but who finds it virtually impossible to carry out, given the existing societal constraints, may conduct themselves on a traditional plane but continue to believe that they are "into androgyny" by defining their deviance from their beliefs as "excusable," "justifiable," and so forth. In other words, aligning actions are a form of situational ethics which allows people to hold on to their absolute standards. Of course, aligning actions need not be used conjointly by a couple. A husband may, through aligning actions, continue to genuinely believe that he is sharing the load despite evidence to the contrary. A wife may, through aligning actions, continue to honestly believe that she wants to be with her kids more than anything else in the world despite her efforts to disassociate from them.

The second function of aligning actions -- the change function -- is perhaps even more important than the continuity function, in that the change function provides a sociological explanation for traditionalization during the transition to parenthood. Several studies have found that traditional marital behavior *increases* during the months following the birth of a first child (Cowan *et al.*, 1978; Entwisle, and Doering, 1981; Meyerowitz and Feldman, 1966; Raush *et al.*, 1974). Explanations for why these changes occur have typically centered on either physiological or personality factors which are supposedly triggered by parenthood (Chodorow, 1978; Rossi, 1977, 1984).

We cannot test the relative validity of the physiological and personality explanations with our data. And this is not the place to embark on a review of studies which have attempted to test these two theories. We can, however, say this: The existing evidence indicates that physiological and personality factors are *not sufficient* to explain traditionalization after birth. As important as these variables may be, no one has yet conclusively demonstrated that physiology or personality, or some combination of the two, is all that is needed to understand why couples shift to a traditional family system during the transition to parenthood.

The inability of physiological and personality theories to explain everything points to the importance of including sociological variables in models of traditionalization. But we must be careful here; in principle, a sociological approach does not mean simply paying homage to societal factors impacting on couples after they become parents. Contending that society "forces" couples into traditional roles is to conceive of a society that is separate from, rather than integrated with, individuals. This approach is nothing more than deterministic reasoning disguised as sociological reasoning. Substituting societal determinism for physiological or personality determinism is *not* in keeping with a sociological perspective.

Thus, for example, when Michael Lamb, a psychologist by training, attempts to explain traditionalization by arguing that "the insistent and undeniable dependency of the baby makes equivocation or ambiguity about role demands more difficult to sustain than in the preparental phase, and our society's expectations regarding nurturant maternal roles are more clearly defined than any other" (Lamb, 1978: 146), he falls short of offering a truly sociological explanation because he leaves open the question of exactly how societal expectations translate into marital behavior. Where Lamb's proposition actually fails is in his implicit assertion that traditional behavior is nothing more than cultural programming. As noted earlier, however, the relationship between culture and conduct is not as smooth as Lamb suggests. Whereas in earlier times traditionalization may indeed have been a puppet-like process, postindustrial society does not provide couples with a "clearly defined" script for how to act when a baby arrives. To the contrary, parental expectations in modern society are extremely complex and highly ambiguous (LeMasters, 1970).

The part of Lamb's statement that, in our opinion, should have been developed more is the beginning, where he says that "the insistent and undeniable dependency of the baby" poses special problems for new parents. Here he is suggesting some social interactional process operating to move the couple toward traditional role behavior. Our data suggest that the dependency of the baby on the parents is indeed an important factor in traditionalization, but that it is not simply a matter of making "equivocation or ambiguity about role demands more difficult to sustain." Rather it is the dependency of the baby which creates a scarcity of free time, and which places the couple in a more competitive stance toward the other.

Before the transition to parenthood, it is relatively easy for couples (and especially men) to believe that they are nontraditional in the same way that it is easy, during times of economic growth and prosperity, for the middle class to believe that it is not racist. In both situations, valued resources (time in one case, money in the other) are not immediately threatened. However, history has shown that when it becomes apparent that strict adherence to sexual or racial equality can mean personal losses, then the basic axiom of the conflict orientation applies: When resources are scarce, people tend to choose themselves over others. Put simply, under conditions of scarcity, whites become more racist and men become more sexist. But in choosing themselves over others, both the middle-class white and the husband-father are faced with their own culture-conduct misalignments. In all likelihood, their behavior in the economic or temporal "squeeze" is at odds with their stated beliefs before the scarcity. This is where aligning actions come into play. By blaming others (their parents, their bosses, the government, and even the people they are competing with -- blacks and women) and/or by justifying their conduct, they try their best to symbolically (but not behaviorally) mend their broken promises. Initially, these aligning actions serve as stopgap measures, helping the people in the system (both the "haves" and the "have-nots") cope with the transition, helping them maintain a consistent and orderly reality to their lives. Over time, the aligning actions help to transform the reality of the system itself.

In order to make our point clear, we should more precisely define what we mean by "traditionalization." Up to now, we have used the term to refer to increases in traditional behavior. This is because the existing studies on the transition to parenthood have employed the term in this way, and because it would not have been meaningful to question their approach until after we had introduced the change function of aligning actions. In truth, limiting traditionalization to behavioral shifts is theoretically vacuous. To know simply that a couple exhibits traditional behavior tells us nothing about whether the husband or wife "have their hearts in it" (role embracement), or whether they are mechanically "going through the motions." In other words, the meaning which the couple inputes to their activity is lost. We are not talking about whether the couple is "bothered" or "gratified" by their behavior. Rather, we are referring to the couple's total way of looking at what they are doing, their world view, their *Weltanschauung*. Although the studies which have focused on the transition to parenthood have equated traditionalization with behavioral change, there are other studies which have attempted to access the impact of parenthood by comparing couples with and without children, and which indicate that , in addition to changing their behavior, couples may also shift to traditional ways of thinking (Hoffman and Manis, 1978). If both culture and the conduct of a marriage traditionalize, then *traditionalization is an organizational transformation rather than simply a behavioral change*. This is how we prefer to use the term, and for good reason. Our data suggest more often than not, the transition to parenthood initiates a systemic level change in marriage toward a more traditional social organization.

The key to the difference between the continuity and the change function of aligning actions is time. On a short-term basis, aligning actions serve a preservative function, allowing beliefs to persist despite contradictory evidence. But on a long-term basis, aligning actions serve a morphogenic function, allowing beliefs to drift, ever so gradually, in the direction of the misaligned conduct. The presumption being made here is that over extended periods of time "culture follows conduct" (Stokes and Hewitt, 1976: 848). Thus, on a short-term basis, the couple whose conduct after the birth of their child is more traditional than their beliefs can use aligning actions to preserve those beliefs. But on a long-term basis, their willingness to excuse and justify their behavior rather than actually make it conform to their beliefs will result in an adjustment of their beliefs to their conduct. They will, in other words, begin to develop a marital culture that is closer to (but not necessarily in exact correspondence with) their actual conduct. Thus, aligning actions serve as a "social lubricant" for traditionalization in that they allow misalignments to be explained away rather than seriously examined.

The legitimacy of aligning actions is also important. Not all aligning actions are honored -- that is, accepted -- by the "offended" party as a legitimate explanation for the misalignment. Whether or not an aligning action is deemed legitimate is a function of the social structural and symbolic universe of the people in the interaction. For example, while it is generally considered socially acceptable for a father to say that his career is keeping him from his children, it is not as acceptable for mothers to use this excuse. It is also not as acceptable for mothers to say that they have less patience with their newborns than their husbands do, or that they are not as skilled in feeding, changing, or quieting the baby. If any of these aligning actions were offered by a mother, there is a fairly good chance that they would be disallowed by her husband, her family, her friends, and others. Thus, crucial to the traditionalization process is the availability of aligning actions that legitimate the father's withdrawal from baby care, and the corresponding absence of aligning actions that legitimate the mother's withdrawal from baby care.

The legitimacy of the aligning action is, however, not a given, which is to say that social factors cannot assume that an aligning action will be accepted when it is offered. The critical stage in the "life" of an aligning action is when the aligning action is presented and accepted or not accepted by the other party. Up until this point, the validity of an aligning action for any particular relationship is an open question. Only after the aligning action is presented *and* accepted does it become part of the social reality of the relationship. For example, when a husband says for the first time (perhaps just after he has had difficulty giving the baby breakfast) that he feels that he is inept at feeding his son or daughter, the wife's immediate response to the husband's assertion is critical. If at this point she does not challenge her husband's definition of the situation, or if she takes over responsibility for feeding the baby because of what he has just said, she has effectively endorsed the aligning action, accepting it, at least for the moment, as part of the consensual world. *Thus, the theory proposed here for the traditionalization process is both sociohistorical and interactional. As much as the aligning actions may appear to the husband and wife as realities that are "out there," programming their every move, the fact is that they are part and parcel of the negotiation process itself, intrinsic to the whole idea of social interaction.*

Conclusion

Our objective in this chapter has been to present a sociological view of the transition to parenthood. We believe that the transition to parenthood offers the student of social life a unique opportunity to see in action what Mills (1959) meant by "the sociological imagination." Few family experiences provide so vivid a picture of how biography and history are dialectically related. Few family experiences are so close to the cornerstone of a society.

The picture of parenthood that we have presented may not be as "beautiful" as some people would like. Nonetheless, we think that it will be ultimately beneficial. By laying bare some of the social patterns, social processes, and sociohistorical linkages underlying conflict and sexism during the transition to parenthood, we have at least provided a clue into how we might go about improving the social world of fathers and mothers.

References

Bell, C. and H. Newby (1976). "Husbands and wives: the dynamics of the deferential dialectic." Pp. 152-168 in D. Barker and S. Allen (eds.) *Dependence and Exploitation in Work and Marriage.* London: Longman.

Berk, R. A., and S. F. Berk (1979). *Labor and Leisure at Home.* Beverly Hills, CA: Sage Publications.

Blau, P. M. (1964). *Exchange and Power in Social Life.* New York: John Wiley.

Blauner, R. (1964). *Alienation and Freedom: The Factory Worker and His Industry.* Chicago: University of Chicago Press.

Blood, R. O., Jr., and D. M. Wolfe (1960). *Husbands and Wives: The Dynamics of Married Living.* New York: Free Press.

Burr, W. R., G. K. Leigh, R. D. Day, and J. Constantine (1979). "Symbolic interaction and the family." Pp. 42-111 in W. R. Burr, R. Hill, F. I. Nye, and I. L. Reiss (eds.) *Contemporary Theories about the Family,* Vol. 2: *General Theories/Theoretical Orientations.* New York: Free Press.

Chodorow, N. (1978). *The Reproduction of Mothering: Psychoanalysis and the Sociology of Gender.* Berkeley: University of California Press.

Cowan, C. P., P. A. Cowan, L. Coie, and J. D. Coie (1978). "Becoming a family: the impact of a first child's birth on the couple's relationship." Pp. 296-324 in W. B. Miller and L. F. Newman (eds.) *The First Child and Family Formation.* Chapel Hill: Carolina Population Center, University of North Carolina.

Emerson, R. M. (1962). "Power-dependence relations." *American Sociological Review 27* (February): 31-41.

Entwisle, D. R., and S. G. Doering (1981). *The First Birth.* Baltimore, MD: John Hopkins University Press.

Gelles, R. J. (1975). "Violence and pregnancy: A note on the extent of the problem and needed services." *Family Coordinator 24* (January): 81-86.

Goffman, E. (1961). *Encounters: Two Studies in the Sociology of Interaction.* Indianapolis: Bobbs-Merrill.

_____. (1971). *Relations in Public.* New York: Harper & Row.

Gouldner, A. W. (1960). "The norm of reciprocity: A preliminary statement." *American Sociological Review 25,* (April): 161-178.

Harriman, L. C. (1983). "Personal and marital changes accompanying parenthood." *Family Relations 32* (July): 387-394.

Hobbs, D. E. Jr. (1965). "Parenthood as crisis: A third study." *Journal of Marriage and the Family 27* (August): 367-372.

Hobbs, D. E. Jr., and J. M. Wimbish (1977). "Transition to parenthood by black couples." *Journal of Marriage and the Family 39* (November): 677-689.

Hoffman, W. (1978). "Effects of the first child on the woman's role." Pp. 340-367 in W. B. Miller and L. F. Newman (eds.) *The First Child and Family Formation.* Chapel Hill: Carolina Population Center, University of North Carolina.

Hoffman, W. and J. D. Manis (1978). "Influences of children on marital interaction and parental satisfaction and dissatisfactions." Pp. 165-214 in R. M. Lerner and G. B. Spanier (eds.) *Child Influences on Marital and Family Interaction: A Life-Span Perspective.* New York: Academic Press.

Homans, G. (1974). *Social Behavior: Its Elementary Forms.* New York: Harcourt Brace Jovanovich.

Kuhn, A. (1974). *The Logic of Social Systems.* San Francisco: Jossey-Bass.

Lamb, M. (1978). "Influences of the child on marital quality an family interaction during the prenatal, perinatial and infancy periods." Pp. 137-164 in R. M. Lerner and G.

B. Spanier (eds.) *Child Influences on Marital and Family Interaction: A Life-Span Perspective*. New York: Academic Press.

LaRossa, R. (1977). *Conflict and Power in Marriage: Expecting the First Child*. Beverly Hills, CA: Sage Publications.

_____. (1983). "The transition to parenthood and the social reality of time." *Journal of Marriage and the Family 45* (August): 579-589.

LaRossa, R. and M. Mulligan LaRossa (1981). *Transition to Parenthood: How Infants Change Families*. Beverly Hills, CA: Sage Publications.

LeMasters, E. E. (1970). *Parents in Modern America*. Homewood, IL: Dorsey Press.

Maslach, C. (1976). "Burned Out." *Human Behavior 59* (September): 16-22.

Maslach, C. and A. Pines (1977). "The burn-out syndrome in the day care setting." *Child Care Quarterly 6* (Summer): 100-113.

Mead, G. H. (1934). *Mind, Self, and Society from the Standpoint of a Social Behaviorist* (Edited by C. W. Morris). Chicago: University of Chicago Press.

Meyerowitz, J. H. and H. Feldman (1966). "Transition to parenthood." *Psychiatrist Research Report 20* (February): 78-84.

Mills, C. W. (1940). "Situated actions and vocabularies of motive." *American Sociological Review 5 (*December): 904-913.

_____. (1959). *The Sociological Imagination*. London: Oxford University Press.

Nye, F. L. (1979). "Choice, exchange, and the family." Pp. 1-41 in W. R. Burr, R. Hill, F. I. Nye, and I. L. Reiss (eds.) *Contemporary Theories about the Family.* Vol. 2: *General Theories/Theoretical Orientations*. New York: Free Press.

Pleck, J. H. (1976). "Men's new roles in the family: Housework and child care." Working paper. Wellesley, MA: Wellesley College Center for Research on Women.

Pleck, J. H., and M. Rustad (1980). "Husbands' and wives' time in family work and paid work in the 1975-76 study of time use." Working paper. Wellesley, MA: Wellesley College Center for Research on Women.

Raush, H. L., W. A. Barry, R. K. Hertel, and M. A. Swain (1974). *Communication, Conflict, and Marriage*. San Francisco: Jossey-Bass.

Robinson, J. P. (1977). *How Americans Use Time: A Social-Psychological Analysis of Everyday Behavior*. New York: Praeger.

Rossi, A. S. (1977). "A biosocial perspective on parenting." *Daedalus 106* (Spring): 1-31.

_____. (1984). "Gender and parenthood: American Sociological Association, 1983 presidential address." *American Sociological Review 49* (February): 1-19.

Scott, M. B. and S. M. Lyman (1968). "Accounts." *American Sociological Review 33* (February): 46-62.

Sprey, J. (1979). "Conflict theory and the study of marriage and the family." Pp. 130-159 in W. R. Burr, R. Hill, F. I. Nye, and I. L. Reiss (eds.) *Contemporary Theories about the Family,* Vol. 2: *General Theories/Theoretical Orientations*. New York: Free Press.

Stokes, R. and P. Hewitt (1976). "Aligning actions." *American Sociological Review 41* (October): 838-849.

Straus, M. A., R. J. Gelles, and S. K. Steinmetz (1980). *Behind Closed Doors: Violence in the American Family*. New York: Doubleday/Anchor.

Zerubavel, E. (1979a) "Private time and public time: The temporal structure of social accessibility and professional commitments." *Social Forces 58* (September): 38-58.

_____. (1979b). *Patterns of Time in Hospital Life: A Sociological Perspective.* Chicago: University of Chicago Press.

Chapter 16

Can men mother? Some of the assumptions we have about men's skill at being the sole caretaker of a child have provided great material for film and television comedies. This chapter shows just how flexible and competent men can be when they find themselves in a single parent role. In terms of symbolic interaction theory, this study demonstrates altercasting. What does it take to altercast to the extent that the men in this study have done? Can women altercast to the same degree when they are faced with work or career responsibilities?

Chapter 16 *Barbara J. Risman,* **Can Men "Mother"? Life as a Single Father**

Research on single fathers is vital because more children than ever before are living -- at least part of the time -- with divorced fathers (Katz, 1979: Orthner, Brown & Ferguson, 1976; Rosenthal & Keshet, 1981). Judges, counselors, teachers, social workers, policy specialists and single parent families themselves all need accurate and verifiable information as to how this emerging family form operates. Single fathers must often fill social roles for which they have not been trained. Do they feel competent to nurture their children, or had their male sex role socialization been so overwhelmingly consistent (e.g., Bandura & Walters, 1963; Chodorow, 1978; Stockard & Johnson, 1980) that by adulthood fathers have neither the inclination nor aptitude to provide primary care for young children?

Individualist and microstructural theorists would give different answers to the question of whether single fathers can be viable primary caretakers for young children. This paper begins with a discussion of these two theoretical perspectives. An assessment of previous literature follows the theoretical discussion. New research which differs from past work in two ways is then presented. The sample used for these analyses is diverse enough to identify what demographic and life-style factors may affect satisfaction with single fatherhood. In addition, the conclusions suggest that microstructuralist theory provides a better explanation than does individualist theory for the experiences of single fathers. The implications of a microstructuralist perspective for professionals who work with single fathers and their children are discussed.

Theory

Most writing about gender differences and parenting (e.g. Chodorow, 1978; Gilligan, 1982; Rossi, 1984; Stockard & Johnson, 1980; Van den Berghe, 1979) is clearly individualist. Authors suggest that by adulthood men and women have developed very different individual personality characteristics. Females have become more nurturant, person oriented and child centered, and males have become more competitive and work oriented. In an articulate and influential statement of this individualistic perspective, Linton (1945) argued that personality develops from habitualized attitudes and as a result of repeated experiences. Intensely held emotions, values and predispositions develop during childhood and coalesce into a person's core identity, which has limited flexibility once formed. Most of the literature on parenting attributes the observed sex differences between mothers and fathers to internalized psychic predispositions: women desire to mother their children while men do not.

Although individualist theorists (e.g., Chodorow, 1978; Gilligan, 1982; Stockard & Johnson, 1980; Van den Berghe, 1979) identify differing social and/or biological determinants for sex differences in parental behavior, they all take for granted the *consequences* of sex role acquisition and focus their debate on *how* sex role acquisition occurs. In particular, individualist theorists often assume that women make better caretakers than do men. They debate whether this is true because women have themselves been mothered by same-sex parents and have therefore developed the desire for intense intimacy or whether the social reinforcement girls receive for doll play and other nurturant behavior is a better explanation for exclusively female mothering.

Although there are as many varieties of structuralism (see review by Mayhew, 1980) as of individualism, all structuralists dispute the assumption that individual motivations, learned through whatever processes, can explain human behavior. When applied to the study of gender (Kanter, 1977; Lorber, 1981; Risman, 1987), microstructuralism rejects the assumption that sex roles are internalized as personality traits. Because behavior is not viewed as immutably fixed by childhood experiences and biological preconditions, the differing parental behaviors of men and women must be explained as adaptive to ongoing interaction, the product of more immediate situational demands.

Individualist and structural theories make very different predictions about the possibility for successful single father households. Individualist theories would predict that single fathers lack both the internal motivation and the expressive skills to provide the intense intimacy necessary for nurturing young children. In contrast, structural theories suggest that human behavior, including family roles, is determined by the social context in which people live. Although mothers are currently expected to shoulder primary responsibility for childrearing, microstructrual theory suggests that when that responsibility is shifted to fathers, men will adopt those behaviors which have traditionally been considered mothering.

The present research was designed to test whether individualist or microstructrual theories are more accurate predictors of single fathers' lives. Such a theoretical debate is vital to those who work with single parents and their children because social policies, including those which affect single parents, are based on implicit theoretical perspectives. Assumption based on these contrasting theories will lead to very different social policies. For example, an individualist theory suggests that single fathers, and other men interested in primary caretaking, need to be taught to parent. Social workers implicitly using an individualist perspective might suggest the development of special courses or individual counseling for fathers before they be allowed to shoulder primary caretaking responsibility. In contrast, microstructrual theory suggests that instead of retraining individuals, social policies designed to aid single parents, men or women, need to focus on restructuring paid work so that it does not create conflict for those persons who also shoulder primary responsibility for young children.

Review of the Literature

Research on single fathers began in the late 1960s in the United States, Canada, England, and Australia. The research thus far has been primarily descriptive. Because the methods, samples and therefore results differ dramatically by geographical region, this review focuses mostly on American (i.e., U.S. and Canadian) single fathers[1] The American studies (Ambert, 1982; Defrain & Eirich, 1981; Gasser & Taylor, 1976; Greenberg, 1979; Hanson, 1979; Mendes, 1979; Orthner *et al.*, 1976; Rosenthal & Keshet, 1981; Santrock & Warshack, 1979) have small samples of predominantly white, middle-class fathers. These men were identified from single parent organizations, by answering media advertisements, or by referrals. Greif's (1985) research on American single fathers is conceptually sophisticated and based on a large sample. But like most other studies, it is based entirely on men who join support groups (e.g., Parents Without Partners), and the data are presented descriptively.

The descriptive findings about American single fathers appear remarkably consistent. Few single fathers (Ambert, 1982; Defrain & Eirich, 1981; Gasser & Taylor, 1976; Greenberg, 1979; Hanson, 1979; Mendes, 1979; Orthner *et al.*, 1976; Rosenthal & Keshet, 1981; Grief, 1985; Santrock & Warshack, 1979) recruit either female kin or paid help to perform the "female" tasks of housekeeping. Homemaking does not appear to be a particular problem for single fathers. Another consistent finding is that although American single fathers do report some problems, such as worry that their daughters lack a female role model, most respondents generally feel satisfied with their perceived competence as single parents and single adults.

With such consistent results, it may appear that the theoretical questions raised here have already been answered: despite their male sex role socialization, today's single fathers believe themselves successful. Unfortunately, there is a major weakness in past research. Most studies have been exploratory, with samples that are small and homogeneous on factors which may affect role performances -- income and reason for custody. No previous American study has a large and diverse enough sample to identify respondents in various economic statuses and with a variety of reasons for father custody.

It is important that research on American single fathers includes more diverse samples because the English and Australian studies (e.g., Ferri, 1973; George & Wilding,

237

1972; Hipgrave, 1982; Katz, 1979; Murch, 1973; O'Brien, 1982), which include more economically deprived families, suggest that financial status is a key factor in men's performance and satisfaction as single fathers. Within one large sample (George & Wilding), those fathers who reported financial problems also felt less competent as parents. An analogous situation exists between samples. Researchers whose samples include many financially deprived families (e.g., Katz, O'Brien) tend to report more serious problems in both father/child relationships and the father's role satisfaction. A single father's economic standing may be an important determinant of his satisfaction with lone parenthood.

One other recent British study provides direction for research on American families. O'Brien (1982) found that the reason for father custody influences the adaptation and success of single fathers. O'Brien categorized single fathers into three groups by the reason for custody: conciliatory negotiators, hostile seekers, and passive acceptors. Conciliatory negotiators had been partners in dual career marriages and gained custody of their children as a result of amicable discussions and joint decisions. Hostile seekers fought for custody, often to punish ex-wives for extra-marital affairs. Finally, passive acceptors had been deserted by their wives.

O'Brien found that conciliatory negotiators were considerably more successful single parents than passive acceptors or hostile seekers. Unfortunately, social class was confounded with reason for custody in this study. When custody was amicably negotiated, both parents were usually professionals, and comfortably middle-class. Hostile seekers had lived in more traditional one paycheck households, while passive acceptors were most often from the lower-middle class and reported severe financial stress. It may be that the reason for father custody is merely one indication of difference in the lifestyle of each social class. If, however, reason for custody and economic status have independent effects on custodial fathers' adjustment, no research thus far can differentiate such effects.

Methodology

The present study was designed so that the sample was large and diverse enough to disentangle the independent effects of economic status from reasons for father custody on father's perceptions of their role in life as single parents. Do all kinds of men, for whatever reason they became single fathers, adopt the behaviors usually considered mothering? Do fathers who face economic insecurity have more problems adopting the role of primary caretaker? In this section, the data collection techniques and resultant sample characteristics are discussed in detail. The dependent variables are then described, followed by a brief presentation of the statistical techniques used in the analysis.

To locate single fathers, advertisements appeared in national single parent magazines and newsletters. In addition, referrals were solicited from social service agencies in Washington state and Boston, Massachusetts. To avoid sampling only respondents who were identifiable via social service agencies or parenting associations, press releases were distributed to Washington and the national media. These press releases attracted the interest of talk show hosts and radio public service departments across the country. Word of mouth referrals were also thoroughly investigated. Two hundred eighty-one questionnaires were distributed between 1981 and 1983 and 141 completed surveys returned. This 54 percent response rate considerably underestimates the proportion of eligible single fathers who participated once contacted; questionnaires were often distributed unknowingly to ineligible referrals.[2] A detailed discussion of sampling strategies is available elsewhere (Risman, 1983).

To meet eligibility requirements, at least one child under 14 years of age had to live as a full-time resident in each home. Ninety percent of the respondents reported that their youngest resident child was a pre-teen. This study was designed to measure the relationship between a father and his youngest child. In over three-quarters of these families, at least one child lives with the father all of the time, in the other 23 percent, the children visit their mother for up to 3 months per year.

Over half (62 percent, n=87) of the respondents had little choice in adopting the single parent role,[3] because they had been deserted, widowed, or their wives had refused custody. These men, passive acceptors, had become single fathers through no active effort of their own. The rest were split evenly between having negotiated for custody while still married (n=26), conciliatory negotiators, and having obtained custody by forceful action against the mother's wish (n=28), or hostile seekers. The mean length of time these men have been in their current marital status is between 1 and 2 years; over half have been single for over 2 years.

Ninety percent of the single fathers in this study were white. About half these fathers had not graduated from college, one-third were graduates, and the rest had advanced degrees. Over half were employed in professional, managerial, or other white collar jobs, while approximately one-quarter of these fathers work in blue collar jobs. The men in this study were more likely to work in white collar jobs and less likely to work in blue collar jobs than a sample actually representative of the 1981 male labor force (U.S. Census, Statistical Abstract, 1982-1983). Eighty percent of these fathers worked full-time, the rest worked part-time or were currently unemployed. Seventeen percent of these respondents reported an annual income less than $15,000, and almost half (45.5 percent) earn between $15,000 and $29,999 per year. Nearly one-quarter of the sample reported yearly incomes between $30,000 and $50,000, while 14 percent reported incomes above annually. Given the mean yearly income of $20,000 to $25,000, these single fathers earned somewhat more money than the average white single father who supported a family in 1980 on approximately $18,731 annually (U.S. Census, 1982).

Reason for father custody and economic status were not related in this study. Although fathers who negotiated custody were more likely than other respondents to work in white collar jobs (*tau* $b=0.18$, $p=0.02$) they did not earn significantly more money.

Religion did not seem to play a major role in most of these men's lives. Nearly a third reported "no religious preference." Thirty-nine percent were Protestant and almost 20 percent were Catholic. Only 4 percent were Jewish, and the rest reported "other" religions. On a 9 point religiosity scale (1=not at all; 9=very religious), the group mean was nearly at 5, indicating less than orthodox religious attitudes.

Previous research has identified three issues as central to the role of single father: (1) the father's experience and skill with the instrumental tasks of homemaking; (2) the nature of the father/child relationship, or the expressive function of parenting; and (3) the father's overall role satisfaction. The present research was designed to address each of these issues systematically, measures for each dimension were created from items on a 20 page self-administered questionnaire; all measures were based entirely upon the fathers' perception.

The analysis proceeds very simply. Descriptive information on each dimension is presented briefly. Next, the impact of economic status and reason for custody are assessed for each dimension. For a more detailed discussion of methodology see Risman (1986).

Results

The Instrumental Tasks of Childrearing: Fathers as Homemakers

Four out of five single fathers in this study had no outside housekeeping help, either paid or volunteer. Most men did not depend on mother, girlfriend or housekeeper to perform the stereotypically female tasks of cooking or cleaning. Over 80 percent of all fathers reported that they were personally responsible for the varied tasks of housekeeping: grocery shopping, food preparation, house cleaning, and yard work. On the average, fathers ate dinner at home with their children from five to six times per week.

The fathers in this study showed a concern for making their homes child centered. Ninety-two percent of the respondents have children's first aid supplies on hand, and 83 percent have an average of three emergency phone numbers posted for children or sitter's use. When only 8 men in a sample of 141 respondents reported that friends or relatives routinely performed either child care or housework, it is safe to conclude that single fathers manage their households by themselves. They do not find female housekeepers to take responsibility for tasks usually assigned to wives (e.g., Nye, 1976).

Not only do fathers take responsibility for housecleaning and other mundane tasks, but they also report spending considerable time with their children in both household chores and recreational activities. On the average, single fathers and their children do joint household chores at least weekly. They watch TV together weekly, and play sports together more than once a month. These fathers take their children on an educational outing (e.g., museum) or watch spectator sports together monthly. In addition, respondents chauffeur their youngest child to some activity at least once every week.

The custodial fathers in this study are concerned that their children receive adequate health care. Nine out of 10 fathers have a family physician or clinic. Nearly all the children in this study visit a dentist at least once every once every year (91.4 percent) and half of them visit a dentist twice a year. The vast majority (89.9 percent) of the children do not have any serious health problems.

To measure less obvious aspects of child care, fathers were queried about involvement with their children outside of family activities. Nine out of 10 fathers with children enrolled in school organized by homerooms knew the homeroom teacher's name. Eighty-eight percent of the respondents could name at least 3 of their youngest child's friends, and only 4.5 percent of these fathers did not know any of their children's friends.

The Expressive Tasks of Childrearing: The Father/Child Relationship

Although the instrumental tasks of homemaking are surely important, the tenor and quality of the father/child relationships are perhaps the most central issue in research on single fathers. Psychoanalytic theorists (e.g., Chodorow, 1978) often suggest that a core attribute of mothering, but not fathering, is the ability and desire to develop intensely intimate relationships with young children. It is essential to ask whether single fathers develop intimate relationships with their young children, or whether children living alone with fathers lack the intense bonds they might have developed with mothers.

In this study, these relationships are measured by the fathers' perceptions of dyadic intimacy between themselves and their youngest child. First, fathers report the extent to which they believe the child discloses his or her feelings. Other measures of dyadic intimacy include frequency of physical affection, questions on closeness, and satisfaction with the relationship.

In general, these men believe their children share almost all of their emotions. Children are more likely to share positive feelings, such as being happy, excited, proud, and smart, than negative feelings such as being worried or lonely.

In addition to reporting a great deal of self-disclosure from child to parent, these fathers report considerable physical contact with their children. When asked how often they were physically affectionate with their children, including cuddling and body wrestling, the mean response was at least once every day. Similarly, when explicitly queried on how often they hugged their youngest child, the mean response was between every day and more than once a day.

Overall, the lone fathers in this study feel very close to (X=8.33 on a 9 point scale), and very affectionate toward (X=7.41), their youngest child. They also generally approve of their children's behavior (X=6.96). Indeed, the fathers are very satisfied (X=7.71) with the relationships they have developed as primary parents.

Fathers' Role Satisfaction

The fathers in this study are generally satisfied with the relationships described above, a satisfaction not a function of their integration into particularly supportive extended kin networks. Although half these men live in the same city as their own parents, they see their relatives either monthly or a few times yearly. Under one-third of these respondents (29 percent) can depend on either relatives or friends as usual babysitters. On the average, relatives care for the children only a few times a year.

Although relatives do not provide routine child care, they do provide emotional support and practical help during a crisis. When a child is ill, 37 percent of all respondents call a relative for emotional support. Another third call a friend or current dating partner, while the rest depend on other sources for support. About one-half of the fathers stay home from work with a sick child, one-quarter report that relatives help care for a sick child during the work week and the rest either pay a sitter or make other arrangements. Single fathers have support networks composed both of kin and friends, but do not depend on others to shoulder routine child-care responsibilities.

Although most respondents do hope to remarry eventually (90 percent), they do not claim to seek a woman to relieve them as primary parent. While a large minority (38 percent) intend to retain primary responsibility, the rest hope to share child care equally. Not one respondent wants a new wife to take the major responsibility for childrearing. Although these men are not searching for a replacement mother, they are concerned with the relationship between a hypothetical spouse and their children. Every respondent feels affection between children and possible wife is at least somewhat important, and almost all (80 percent) felt such affection to be very important or necessary.

The desire to continue intense involvement with their children, even after remarriage, is very strong evidence that these men feel comfortable with the role of primary parent. For example, when asked how often they would rather be childless the mean response is 1.68 on a 9 point scale (1=never). Despite their statistically deviant lifestyle, these men are glad to be fathers.

The Impact of Social Class

Thus far, this research supports previous findings: single fathers appear to have little trouble fulfilling either the instrumental or expressive functions of single parenthood. Indeed, the respondents in this study report a good deal of satisfaction with their lives. It is now appropriate to turn attention to the impact of financial status on the respondents' perceptions of their lives.

Overall, a father's economic status affects his role as a single parent primarily on instrumental tasks. Not surprisingly, income was positively related to having outside help come into the home (*tau b*=0.21, *p*=0.004). This relationship is not, however, strictly linear. Although the respondents are categorized into four income levels, it is those men with incomes over $50,000 annually who are different from the rest. Over half of the most wealthy men (57.6 percent) hire outside help for housekeeping versus 13 percent to 19 percent of men in the three other income categories. These high income single fathers are more likely to hire help for the following tasks: cooking dinner (*tau b*=0.15, *p*=0.05); housecleaning (*tau b*=0.27, *p*=0.001); and preparing lunches (*tau b*=0.17, *p*=0.01). There were no differences by income level in who fixed the families' breakfast, shopped for groceries or children's clothing, performed yard work, or how often the family ate dinner together.

As might be expected, there is also a positive relationship between expensive activities and father's income. For example, there is a positive relationship between the number of yearly visits to a dentist and father's income (*tau b*=0.20, *p*=0.002), but 92 percent of all children see a dentist at least once a year. There was also a weak positive relationship between having an established relationship with a family doctor or clinic and economic status (*tau b*=0.13, *p*=0.05); 80 percent of fathers who earn under $15,000 annually report such a relationship versus approximately 95 percent of fathers in all other income categories. Father's income is also positively related to the frequency of attendance at spectator sports (*r*=0.22, *p*=0.01) and the frequency of father chauffeuring a child to an activity (*r*=0.27, *p*=0.001). These findings make intuitive sense, as medical care, children's activities, and spectator sports are expensive. There were no differences by economic status for less expensive activities such as the frequency of family TV viewing, playing sports together, or going on educational outings.

On measures of paternal concern with creating an environment safe for children -- the number and types of first aid in the home and whether emergency phone numbers are posted for children or sitters -- there are absolutely no differences by economic status. In sum, the wealthiest fathers buy somewhat more housekeeping services and spend more money on recreational activities than do others, but there is no evidence that they are more safety conscious or concerned with their performance on other instrumental tasks.

Fathers' economic status is even less important for the tenor and ambiance or parent/child relations -- the expressive dimension of parenting. Only one difference related to social class emerged on the expressive dimension: an inverse relationship exists between income and fathers' rating of disclosure from their children about negative feelings. Children whose fathers earned more money were less likely to reveal when they were sad (*r*=-0.19, *p*=0.01), lonely (*r*=-0.22, *p*=0.01), or worried (*r*=-0.20, *p*=0.01). This cannot be attributed to children in poorer homes having more negative experiences, because when descriptions of children's personalities were analyzed no differences emerged by parental economic status.

The finding that income is inversely related to children's disclosure of negative emotions is surprising, as past research suggests that men who face economic uncertainty have more trouble adjusting to the role of primary parent than do middle-class men. Perhaps this finding can be interpreted by realizing that only *negative* emotions are disclosed more to low income fathers. Past research (e.g., Kerckhoff, 1972) suggests that because middle-class parents have higher expectations for their children's behavior than do poor ones, children may withhold some negative feelings to meet such performance expectations. Therefore, it may be that children of more middle-class, single fathers are withholding feelings to avoid disappointing their fathers.

A cautionary note is necessary. Despite the relationship between income and child's self-disclosure, most fathers in this study report both intimate relationships with their children and satisfaction with those relationships. In fact, there were no differences in role satisfaction based on social class. Although wealthier men were more likely to date frequently ($r=0.24$, $p=0.01$), they were no more likely to be seeking a wife. Men with higher incomes are, however, more likely to feel it essential for children and potential spouses to get along ($r=0.14$, $p=0.05$).

Despite these slight differences between respondents based on income, the substantive variation between the mean responses in each group is not impressive. Unlike the research conducted in other countries, social class does not seem to be a particularly important determinant of an American man's satisfaction with single fatherhood.

The Impact of Reason for Custody

Although instrumental tasks are not at all related to reason for custody, there seems to be one major difference in the respondents' perceptions of their relationships with children based on why they have custody. Fathers who fought for custody report better relationships with their youngest child than do other respondents. Men who received custody over ex-wives' objections believe their children are more likely to disclose feelings of loneliness ($F=_{(2.136)}4.26$, $p=0.02$) than are either fathers who negotiated for custody or passive acceptors. Similarly, although all fathers find childrearing a chore less than half the time, men who fought for custody report feeling that childrearing is a chore less often ($X=3.11$ on a 9 point scale, 9=always) than do negotiators ($X=4.15$) or passive acceptors ($X=4.13$; $F=_{(2.135)}3.25$, $p=0.04$). In addition, although not statistically significant, there is a trend for passive acceptors to more often wish they were childless ($X=1.84$ on a 9 point scale, 9=always) than do negotiators ($X=1.43$) or hostile seekers ($X=1.43$).

These results are not readily interpreted. It may be that fathers are more likely to want custody of children when they have previously developed intimate relationships. Another explanation, however, is that positive perceptions of the father/child relationship are justifications for the father's decision to pursue custody against the wishes of the mother. Fathers who fought for custody may be particularly likely to ignore negative experiences to avoid cognitive dissonance over their own actions. Whatever the reason for these findings, it is important to remember that the differences based on the reason for custody are not dramatic.

Conclusions: Theoretical and Practical Implications

These results support past research which suggested that, at least in their own perceptions, custodial fathers are competent as primary parents. However, these findings also differ from past research. Economic status seems to be less important as a determinant of life satisfaction among American single fathers than among those in England or Australia. An even more striking difference is that in this research, men who have fought for custody believe they have developed as, if not more, intimate relationships with their children than do other single fathers.

Despite the differences between fathers based on reason for custody and economic status, these findings suggest that men believe they can be competent custodial parents. With this conclusion, based on a large and diverse sample of fathers, it is now possible to assess the usefulness of microstructrual and individualist theories for understanding single fatherhood. The ability of men to provide primary care for pre-teenage children challenges currently popular individualist theories which suggest that the personality traits needed to mother are internalized as psychic predispositions, so that by adulthood males have neither the inclination nor skill to care for young children.

This research suggests that childhood experiences and sex role socialization do not create inflexible gender typed behavioral patterns. Instead, as microstructrual theory suggests, the situational demands of role requirements influenced adult behavior and lead men to mother when they have no wives to depend upon. Perhaps gender differences in our society are based as much on the differential expectations and role requirements males and females face throughout their lives as upon internalized personality characteristics. This study suggests that when males take full responsibility for child care, when they meet expectations usually confided to females, they develop intimate and affectionate relationships with their children. Despite male sex role training, fathers respond to the nontraditional role of single parent with strategies stereotypically considered feminine.

What are the practical implications of this structural perspective on single fathers? The implications for social policy are clear; the traditional assumption that children belong with their mothers after divorce needs to be reexamined. When judges decide what is in a child's best interest, they need to not always assume mothers are better primary caretakers than are fathers. Similarly, social workers and counselors employed in Family Court should be aware that females do not necessarily make better mothers. It may be in the arena of child custody men stand to gain -- and women stand to lose -- by the removal of gender-based societal and judicial inequity.

References

Ambert, A. (1982). "Differences in children's behavior toward custodial mothers and custodial fathers." *Journal of Marriage and the Family 44*(1): 73-86.

Bandura, A. and R. H. Walters (1963) *Social Learning and Personality Development.* New York: Holt, Rinehart and Winston.

Chodorow, N. (1978). *The Reproduction of Mothering.* Berkeley, University of California Press.

Defrain, J. and R. Eirich (1981). "Coping as single parents: A comparative study of fathers and mothers." *Family Relations.* 265-273.

Ferri, E. (1973). "Characteristics of motherless families." *British Journal of Social Work 3*(1): 91-100.

Gasser, R. D., and C. H. Taylor (1976). "Role adjustment of single fathers with dependent children." *Family Coordinator 25*(4): 397-402.

George, V., and P. Wilding (1972). *Motherless Families.* London: Routlege and Kegan Paul.

Gilligan, C. (1982). *In a Different Voice: Psychological Theory and Women's Development.* Cambridge: Harvard University Press.

Greenberg, J. B. (1979). "Single-parenting and intimacy: A comparison of mothers and fathers." *Alternative Lifestyles 2*(3): 308-330.

Greif, G. (1985). *Single Fathers.* Lexington, MA: Lexington Books.

Hanson, S. (1979). "Characteristics of single custodial fathers and the parent-child relationship." Doctoral dissertation, University of Washington. *Dissertation Abstracts International, 40*(12), 6438-A.

Hipgrave, T. (1982). "Lone fatherhood: A problematic status. Pp. 171-183 in L. McKee and M. O'Brien (eds.), *The Father Figure.* London: Tavistock Publications.

Kanter, R. M. (1977). *Men and Women of the Corporation.* New York: Harper Books.

Katz, A. J. (1979). "Lone fathers: Perspectives and implications for family policy." *Family Coordinator 28*(4): 521-528.

Kerckhoff, A. C. (1972). *Socialization and Social Class*. Englewood Cliffs, NJ: Prentice-Hall.

Linton, R. (1945). *The Cultural Background of Personality*. New York: D. Appleton-Century.

Lorber, J. (1981). "On the reproduction of mothering: A methodological debate." *Signs 6* 482-486.

Mayhew, B. (1980). "Structuralism versus individuals: Part 1, Shadow boxing in the dark." *Social Forces 42*: 91-105.

Mendes, H. A. (1979). "Single-parent families -- A typology of lifestyles." *Social Work 24*(3): 193-200.

Murch, M. (1973). "Motherless families project: Bristol council of social service report on first year's work." *British Journal of Social Work 3*(3): 365-376.

Nye, I. F. (1976). *Role Structure and Analysis of the Family* Beverly Hills, CA: Sage Publications.

O'Brien, M. (1982). "Becoming a lone father: Differential patterns and experiences." Pp. 184-207 in L. McKee and M. O'Brien (eds.), *The Father Figure*. London: Tavistock Publications.

Orthner, D. K., T. Brown, & D. Ferguson (1976). "Single-parenthood: An emerging life style." *Family Coordinator 25*(4): 429-437.

Risman, B. J. (1983). "Necessity and the invention of mothering: A test of individual versus structural explanations for gender roles." Doctoral dissertation, University of Washington, *Dissertation Abstracts International, 44*(11), 3510-A.

Risman, B. J. (1987). "Intimate relationships from a microstructrual perspective: Men who mother." *Gender and Society 1*(1): 6-32.

Rosenthal, K. and H. F. Keshet (1981). *Fathers without Partners*. Totowa, NJ: Rowman and Littlefield.

Rossi, A. S. (1984). "Gender and parenthood." *American Sociological Review 49* (February): 1-19.

Santrock, J. W. and R. A. Warshak (1979). "Father custody and social development in boys and girls." *Journal of Social Issues 35*(4): 112-125.

Stockard, J. and M. M. Johnson (1980). *Sex Role Inequality and Sex Role Development*. Englewood Cliffs, NJ: Prentice-Hall.

U.S. Department of Commerce, Bureau of the Census (1982). "Changing family composition and income differentials." *Special Demographic Analyses*. CDS-80-87.

U.S. Department of Commerce, Bureau of the Census (1982-1983). *Statistical Abstracts: National Data Book and Guide to Sources*. Washington, D. C.: U.S. Government Printing Office.

Van den Berghe, P. L. (1979) *Human Family Systems: An Evolutionary View*. New York: Elsevier.

Notes

[1] The early British studies (George & Wilding, 1972; Ferri, 1973; Murch, 1973) were based on much larger samples and commissioned because "motherless" families came to be considered a social problem. Poor fathers were over-represented in these studies because the sampling technique tended to identify those families who used social service agencies. The respondents in recent British and Australian studies (Hipgrave, 1982; Katz, 1979; O'Brien, 1982) more closely resemble American samples, but still

include more economically deprived families.

[2]   Because social service agencies insisted upon anonymity for the clients they referred and contacted, the percentage of no response due to intelligibility cannot be traced.

[3]   The over-representation of fathers with little choice in adopting the single parent role is a result of sampling techniques designed for a larger study of which these data are but one part. I have no information as to the actual proportion of American single fathers who had no choice, who negotiated or who fought for custody.

Chapter 17

Dual career couples. In this last chapter we consider the effort and complexity of designing a relationship or marriage to custom fit the careers of both people. Under conditions where both partners have important careers, they cannot rely on traditional roles or scripts to determine the division of labor at home. Dual careers call for a completely unique and explicit set of assumptions and rules that support egalitarianism. Thus, there is no hierarchy, no power advantage, no dominant/subordinate pattern to these relationships. What determines who does what at home in dual career relationships? Why are so many dual career couples committed to resolving the problems rather than disturb the delicate balance of their equally important careers? Why don't these dual career couples traditionalize as did the parents of the new baby in Chapter 16?

Chapter 17 *Rosanna Hertz,* **Dual-Career Couples: Shaping Marriages Through Work**

The dual-career marriage challenges a number of principles of traditional marriage. Employment and its rewards still shape a couple's life chances: but instead of a single career or job-defining marital roles, there are two careers qualifying each spouse as a "breadwinner." Many dual-career couples live better than their more traditional counterparts, but ambiguity and confusion surround the marriage of two careers. No one partner in the household can claim authority based on "bringing home the bacon." Questions as to whose career and time commitments should take precedence are befuddled by similar (and competing) employer demands. Arriving at a division of labor for household tasks is complicated by both spouses' daytime absence from the home. Traditional corporate careers require the husband (as employee) and the wife (as his aide) to join forces in what

Papanek (1975) referred to as the "two-person career." Dual-career marriages have, in this sense, two husbands and no wife.

Ambiguity and confusion about social roles are common among people experiencing social change. New expectations about behavior are only dimly perceived as new practices emerge. Marital roles are no exception. In this regard marital roles are not viewed as "fixed" in early childhood socialization or biological conditioning. Instead, as the microstructural approach suggests (Risman, 1987), behavior of husbands and wives is adaptive to ongoing interaction. But simply resocializing individuals to believe that a gender division of labor does not produce marital equality is not enough; instead, as Lorber (1986) argues, social change depends on reorganizing the social world. What makes the experience of the couples in the study important is that their efforts to define a new set of roles did not precede the marriage but, rather, occurred only after the practical implications of change began to emerge. For example, wives' careers demanded long hours in the office making them unable to be at home cooking dinner. Husbands learned to cook not because of a broader ideology but out of necessity. Not unlike a picture slowly brought into focus, the practical implications of change in their situations took time to appear as something comprehensible: marriage as a relationship apart from, yet dependent on, their individual careers.

The dual-career marriage consolidates three careers: his, hers, and theirs. The marriage, the "third career," bears remarkable similarities to the career one makes in work, especially in a new industry. That is, everyone knows what the title "manager" is, but few have a clear sense when they embark on a career just where they will end up -- though, of course, everyone has plans. Career marriages are similar; but in addition to wanting to be a "husband" or "wife," each has to comprehend and work at that role as it emerges over time.

Without many models to use as benchmarks, couples tend to measure themselves against the traditional husband and wife roles, a model that provides insufficient and often contradictory advice. The third career (marriage) is "made," not imitated or created automatically, and therefore it involves confusion and uncertainty. Thus, their unease in dealing with an ambiguous situation leads to frustration in trying to make a new reality fit an old model. Far from being the avant-garde of a social movement with an articulate vision of something they wanted to create, they are struck by their lack of ideological prescriptions about equality of marital roles. Instead, they simply practice it. Though rough edges remain to be smoothed, marital roles have been shaped in the direction of the objectives espoused by many feminist theorists, but largely without prior indoctrination of either spouse in the ideology of equality. That is, microstructural conditions (their opportunities and rewards) are far more important in explaining changes in those couples' behavior than ideology. His and her careers are microstructurals cause that helped create the "third career," the marriage. In this article, I will discuss the process through which dual-career couples "make" their third career.

The Sample

Data were collected in semistructured, in-depth interviews with twenty-one dual career couples. Participants in this study were selected from a pool of couples identified by informants in corporations located in the Chicago metropolitan area. I located couples in which husbands and wives were similarly situated professionally and organizationally. This close "matching" to one another in terms of earnings and employer-work requirements was necessary in order to asses how the absence of clear inequalities in income or career status would effect relations between husbands and wives and their accommodations in the household division of labor, financial arrangements, child care, and career strategies. Prior studies tended not to distinguish between jobs and careers. As a result they focused on husbands and wives whose work locations and opportunities were not equally valued or rewarded. Thus, it is unclear if employment opportunities or gender beliefs shape these marriages. By matching husbands and wives as closely as possible, this study illuminates how social relations are negotiated.

Each husband and wife was individually interviewed about his or her attitudes regarding work and family. The median age for males was thirty-six and for females thirty-four. The median number of years married was nine; 65 percent of the couples had children. Because they were corporate dual-career couples, they were quite affluent: the median joint income was $90,250 in 1981-82. Wives' median income was $40,200; husbands' median income was $47,500. Seventy-one percent live in the city. (For a lengthier discussion of dual-career couples and methods used in this study, see Hertz, 1986.)

Career Beginnings: His Career

The men in this study grew up in the 1940s and early 1950s. For them working was expected, not a matter of choice. Their lives reflect the prototypical middle-class pattern: college, graduate training, and then a series of jobs. Their lives followed a neat, orderly sequence as they moved directly from one stage to the next. Fifty-two percent of the men went directly from college to graduate school. Another 24 percent of the men went to the military after college graduation before proceeding to graduate school. Many men prepared for careers by their choice of undergraduate majors. Unlike women, whose undergraduate majors are a bit more evenly distributed, almost two-thirds of the men majored in social science (specifically economics), and only one-quarter majored in the humanities (specifically history).

Forty-three percent of the men married when they graduated from college. In the majority of these cases, wives supported husbands while the latter earned advanced degrees. However, 48 percent of the men married after competing graduate education when their wives typically were just completing graduate education. In the former group, husbands and wives went through graduate school in turn-taking fashion, and in the latter group it was the husbands who supported their wives through advanced training. At the time of these interviews, thirteen men held corporate positions as managers or vice-presidents, eight men were either corporate lawyers or doctors, and three men were self-employed.

The early part of the men's careers did not involve a change in attitude about their role as breadwinners. Change took place more subtly as a result of their wives' entry into the labor market. Whereas the academic market has a limited number of universities in any geographical area, forcing academic couples to commute more often (Gerstel and Gross, 1984), in the 1980s employment opportunities in the Chicago area for these corporate couples are much more abundant. Therefore, these corporate husbands and wives could afford to limit their geographical mobility and choose between positions in the immediate area and in the process maintain a dual-career *locally*-based marriage. The issue of how men's careers developed in tandem with their wives' and how that altered the social roles of husbands and wife will be discussed.

Career Beginnings: Her Career

Caught in the middle -- between an old dream and a new reality -- best captures the story of the lives of these women. The last issue to emerge out of the turbulent sixties was the question of women's rights. Most of these women graduated from college before 1972, the year in which the Senate passed the Equal Rights Amendment: few really had plans or thoughts of careers. Rather, they dreamt of traditional roles as wives and mothers. Work was a way station to fulfilling that dream.

These women were neither visionaries nor activists in the women's movement, nor enthusiastic adherents to its ideology even when it became visible. It is possible that the reason these women were unaffected by changing women's roles can be attributed to a self-selection of early corporate women from pools of women not involved in the antiwar or student movements. This study asked questions only about present and past participation in the women's movement and beliefs about feminism. It is also possible that single women in the higher echelons of the corporate world might respond differently than these married women. As these women reconstructed their pasts from the vantage points to the 1980s, their feelings about how little the women's movement did to help them integrate their personal and professional lives appears to explain their present sentiments. Their views on feminism and the women's movement echo Hewlett's (1986) remarks about the lack of support the movement gave women who wanted families in addition to careers. Feminism in the 1980s was typically viewed as antifamily and antimale. Little had been done to guarantee these women maternity leaves and adequate child care. They saw themselves as "isolates." That is, each woman was alone in her respective corporation fighting for the ability to have (not even to integrate) a family with her career. The women with children were quick to tell me how they had paved the way for other managerial women to be granted maternity leaves.

> When I found out I was pregnant, I then told my boss, and he was shat-tered, even though he knew that I was trying to get pregnant. You know, a "You're doing this to me" kind of reaction. "How am I going to tell the other guys on the block that I've got a pregnant manager?" He started out by informing me that I had the same amount of maternity leave policy as the secretaries, which is essentially that you don't get paid. You are prom-ised a job of equivalent status if you return within approximately six months. I told him that was all very nice, and I told him I would call him.

> Now I was the first woman manager on corporate staff *at all*. And I was the first nonsecreterial person to get pregnant. This corporation had no ex-perience and the maternity policy was written at that time...

There were exceptions, of course. A few women worried about how their present decisions to have children would effect other women who were in lower corporate posi-tions. But even for this minority, feminism was not perceived as moving beyond achieve-ments in female employment. The following quote expresses the dilemmas of having children and the "situational factors" (Lorber, 1981; Gerson, 1985; Hertz, 1986) of corporate climbing that discourage women from having children.

> I think feminism has a lot to do with my concern about having a child, and that's one of the things that I had wrestled with. I am thought of as likely

to be the first woman in our firm who would be elected principal, and
there isn't one now... If I even have a child, then I've confirmed all sorts of
stereotypes -- "Oh my God, there's another one who just went out and had
a kid after we've put all these years into her. How are we ever to have any
women as principals if they all leave? -- and I may damage the
opportunity for women who come behind me.

Instead of ideology fueling career decisions in the 1970s, these women were the
beneficiaries of labor market openings. They were in the right place at the right time. For
many this meant that early job experiences after college provided them with sufficient
training to move into managerial positions. For others employment backgrounds allowed
them to join the first large group of women to enter advanced-degree programs and
obtain credentials that were later translated into corporate careers.

Although both groups of women drifted into the work force, at some point something changed that placed them in career tracks instead of more peripheral occupations.
At the time these interviews were conducted, these wives, as well as their husbands,
occupied a fairly varied array of management or managerial-level corporate positions.
For example, five women were vice presidents, two were directors, nine were managers,
three were professionals, and two were consultants. Each foresees a reasonable
probability of promotion. None sees herself locked into the position that she presently
occupies. However, some do foresee corporate moves (within Chicago) as critical for
their career advancement. Their dreams of career success today match those of their
husbands and their male colleagues.

How is it that these women came to acquire and invest in corporate careers at
variance with traditional expectations? To answer this question, it is necessary to analyze
the process through which they made career investments. The decision to work was eased
by the fact that most of these women had acquired college degrees in disciplines that
qualified them for salaried positions in corporate settings. Despite the apparent
applicability of many of these degrees to a white-collar job market, the majority of these
women did not consciously decide to major in fields that would qualify them for salaried
positions. Most thought that their degrees and college experience would transfer into
employment, but they had no initial goals for business careers of the sort for which they
saw men being trained. One woman, typical of this group, describes her thoughts about
her "career start."

So I was somewhat directionless and unfocused at that point. Chicago
seemed as good a place to be as any, and my boyfriend was here. In 1966
it was relatively easy for women with math and philosophy degrees to get
good-paying jobs in data processing. The whole career start was
accidental.

Moreover, fully two-thirds did not begin to pursue careers until some time after they were married. In order to avoid confusion over the process of career investment, I will analyze these two groups separately, drawing them together later to discuss general issues.

The women who married before beginning careers married either before they finished college or shortly after receiving their college degrees. They married under the middle-class "rules" of the old dream, thinking that once their grooms had completed their graduate studies, they would assume their place beside them as homemakers and wives. As one woman explained:

> At that point I really didn't have any long-term career goals. My goals had stopped when I graduated from college and I hadn't really thought through what I intended to do after that... Here I was with the thought that I was going to obviously get married and have children at a young age and do all those nice things my mother did.

The initial employment histories of these women are simply not based on long-term career goals for themselves; instead, they are directly linked to their husbands' future career prospects.

> We both had degrees in journalism but I followed him -- his career. Every six months they would send him someplace else. His first job was in Georgia, and I worked as a news editor for the *Dublin Herald*... Six months later he got transferred to Chicago, and I followed him here and I got a job as a secretary at a TV studio, and six months later he got transferred to Philadelphia... and I worked as an assistant director for an advertising agency... He was pursuing his career, and I was picking up whatever I could.

So although the majority of these women were not thinking in terms of careers or career goals, they were gaining job experience and skills as they followed their husbands' leads.

Until this point they are pursing one career -- his. How is it that these women came to have careers of their own? Even though they expressed satisfaction with their work and feelings of self-confidence about their early employment histories, it is unclear that labor force participation by itself explains a shift in thinking about careers. Similarly, even though these women recall their traditional aspirations prior to marriage, marriage itself allowed their career goals to take hold. Both employment opportunities and husbands' encouragement appear critical. However, it is difficult to assess the relative contributions of employment opportunities and the marital relationship, especially since these data were gathered in the context of reconstructing personal histories.

Once these women began to consider themselves in a career path, they sought to acquire the additional training or certification necessary to enhance their chances of promotion. Fully 71 percent of the women earned a postgraduate degree in a career-related field. The percentage of women who earned postgraduate degrees is the same for those married before and after they began their careers.

For the one-third of the women who married in their mid-to-late twenties, employment was an assumed part of their marital relationship. Although their lives did not include following a husband from one position to the next, career beginnings for half this group were incremental as well. Regardless of which route they took to their careers, women's career decisions became intertwined with their husbands'.

Changing Gender Roles: The Choice to Work Outside the Home

Although employment prior to marriage or at the beginning of marriage, to help husbands financially, has always been part of the traditional female role, all the women talked about having chosen to seek a job beyond these early years. There are two dimensions to this choice: a gender-role decision and an economic decision. One woman compared male and female expectations about employment:

> I made a choice to work and I like it. And I do it because I like it. I mean I wasn't socialized to think I'm a bad person if I didn't work, when most men never really had that choice. They've always known they were going to work. They were going to support a family, and they never were able to make a choice. But I did. It's very important to me, or I wouldn't have made the choice.

Although this may sound like a personal and idiosyncratic choice, it is in fact a gender-role decision. Implicit in the choice to work outside the home is not only a comparison of women's and men's roles but a confrontation between traditional values for women and their new desires. The choice to work outside the home constitutes a decision *not* to pursue a traditional role as homemaker. This decision has been eased by the fact that few encountered direct opposition in their choice -- for example, from a husband who insisted on his wife's occupying a traditional role.

Employment was conceived of as something they should do because "we had to have more money." Almost from the very beginning of their marriage, her earnings constituted a significant contribution to their shared lifestyle. They did not just live on his salary, banking hers. Instead, they lived on both incomes, and their lifestyles expanded accordingly -- including their rent or mortgage, their bills, the places they chose to go, an so on. They became dependent upon their dual earnings. Put differently, their joint earnings determine their standard of living, and at the same time, their standard of living determines how much money they need to earn. Both husbands and wives made comments like: "We could live on one salary. We could adjust. But we couldn't live today the way we live on two salaries."

These women cannot choose to opt out of the labor force and give up their "choice to work outside the home." Without planning to do so, they have accrued financial obligations and debts. Women, then, come to experience the same kind of career pressure as men.

At the time when many of these women took their jobs, no real decisions had to be made about *future* investments in careers. These women assumed that, in the early stages of a career, the opportunity costs were relatively low: since little investment had been made, little cost would be incurred if they left the workplace. Questions concerning her career only became salient when children became an issue. Decisions thus appeared much less significant at an earlier time. In fact, earlier behavior came to be recognized as decisions made only as time passed and career investments grew to the point where couples faced fairly significant costs if she forsook her career.

Making the Marriage

> It's two separate lives in some ways. It's like a dual carriage way, and we are both going down those carriage ways at more or less the same speed, I would say. While those carriage ways don't cross one another, if

something happens on one of them, something necessarily happens on the other side.

Because both husbands and wives have careers, the marriage can no longer respond entirely to the demands of only one spouse (or spouse's career). Marriage can no longer serve to define a division of labor between breadwinner and homemaker and, with that division of labor, a relative priority or valuation of the different activities. If two careers are to be nourished, they must also be constrained by a set of rules for how competing career demands are to be balanced and how the homemaking or reproductive activities of the marriage are to be organized. Among the couples I interviewed, the predominant mechanism for negotiating individual careers is based upon marriage as a third career. For these couples, marriage represents *both* the social contract entered into by a man and a woman for purposes of gaining intimacy, love, and children, and all the other intangibles of such a union *and* the conjoining of two careers.

This conception of a shared career infuses marriage with a different meaning than the traditional pattern. Couples do not always articulate a clear statement about the equity of careers and the equality of spouses. Yet the practice of balancing the demands of two careers produces an outcome in which, if both careers are to survive, some vision of mutual benefit must be invoked on a daily basis. This criterion serves to distribute or accomplish reproductive/homemaking tasks (broadly and narrowly conceived) and is referred to as a guide when either spouse confronts a situation that challenges or potentially affects the other spouse's career. Marital equity is not taken for granted; it is worked at. As one typical husband put it:

> I certainly don't think this is a gloriously equal marriage marching off into
> the sunset. I think we struggle for equality all the time. And we remind
> each other when we are not getting it.

Put differently, it is not an ideology of marital equality that determines careers; instead, it is because of the two careers that equality becomes an issue. Indeed, couples rarely spoke directly about equality. They spoke instead of trying to strike a balance between careers and family commitments by keeping each other in check so that neither spouse could tip the scale in favor of his or her own career. Although the symmetry may produce feelings of equity, attempts to maintain symmetry provide a constance source of conflict within dual-career marriage. One husband explains how individual career involvement is a catalyst for assessing family involvements.

> There is this constant pressure of trying to balance things, constantly reassessing how much time we spend in family and careers. [Could you give
> me an example?] Sure. Every day. Every week. Trying to figure out how
> much time to spend -- whether you should be with the kids, or with Ann,
> or working... You make definite tradeoffs. You *both* make a tradeoff. It's
> also hard because we both frequently talk about it. How much of a tradeoff
> each one of us should be making -- whether we are both making the same
> amount or whether the other one feels that one of us is spending too much
> time on the job.

Although couples do not keep ledgers, most have instituted rules over job choices and moves. One couple decided to establish a rule a prevent recurrent disagreements surrounding job moves. The wife explained how this is a priori rule reflected their sense of marital equity:

> What we have tried to do is set the ground rules before we are faced with a specific decision. [Why?] To give it some neutrality... Whoever did not have the offer made the basic decision to move. If he had an offer, I had first crack at rejecting the city. It's really a veto power.

Other couples had different mechanisms for achieving parity, including rules about lateral moves as well as promotions.

Although it is difficult to directly assess equality in the household division of labor and in marital roles, these couples exhibit a greater degree of symmetry than has been reported by research on traditional families. Whether these couples are more egalitarian than those studied in previous research -- which suggested that dual career marriages do not always lead to equality -- is difficult to discern (Holmstrom, 1973; Poloma and Garland, 1971; and Pleck, 1977). The findings from prior research and this study are not strictly comparable, and definitions of equality remain to be tightened.

The marriage thus comes to operate as a constraint on the unbridled pursuit of one career to the possible disadvantage of the other. But it also operates as a buffer, cushioning the negative impact of failures or reversal in one or the other career. The unpredictability of careers and responses to them demands such an arrangement, and paradoxically, it forges an emphasis on equity and symmetry for each career. Were it not that marriage is so elevated in importance that it can constrain as well as buffer, then one might refer to the relationship merely as a convenience. But the marital tie operates as a legitimate constraint on careers, and it stimulates a review of the gender roles associated with marriage. Again, as is the case with marital roles, it is the practice of combining two careers, not the articulation of a nonsexist ideology, that shapes decisions and informs change.

A Step Out of Traditional Gender Roles

First-hand knowledge about the organization of family life comes from what we observed our parents doing. Even if couples had friends in dual-career marriages, they were more likely to compare themselves with their parents, not with friends. Like the husband quoted below, the majority of men and women in this study came from families that had clearly defined roles and expectations for husbands and wives.

> I was a product of a family where the mother didn't work ever and whose job, in her mind, and her responsibility, in that marriage, was the maintenance of the household, the parenting function, cooking meals, and keeping things organized. So that when my dad got home he didn't have to put up with anything... Joan [his wife] says, "I'm not going to scurry around here at ten to six and clean up the house so it looks neat and clean when you get home, so you think that's the way it's been all day. You can help clean it up." But that was not the way my mother was. I guess I wouldn't have as honest a view of the world, life, and I wouldn't enjoy it as much if someone with a broom was dusting a path in front of me as I walked.

Gender roles continue to play a part in determining the form of marital relations, and it takes a constant struggle not to fall back on the old ways of marriage -- the old rules and roles -- that these individuals witnessed as children in their parents' homes.

Yet things have changed for these couples. Again, there was no ideological underpinning to their marriages that caused the roles of husband and wife to be dramatically altered. The break with their traditional upbringing is simple to explain: as women's careers became as demanding as their husbands' there was no time for a wife to be a "wife." The initial change, then, was in the wife's role. Thus, as wives and husbands became "duplicates" of one another (at least as workers outside the home), her "new" role altered his. The invisible work of the home is now in plain view, and although couples do hire household labor (and wives were responsible for supervising help) (Hunt and Hunt, 1977; Hertz, 1986), many chores remain to be done around the home. One husband explains how this change came about for him and his wife:

> We don't consciously say that we're going to share, but it just turns out
> with both people working you can't have one do everything. If one of us
> were relying on the other to fix meals, we'd both starve.

Her career alters not only the meaning of "wife" but, in the process, his role as husband. This role expansion is fundamentally different for men and women: she has moved outward, discovering the world of making a living; he has moved inward, discovering the intricacies of running a home. Time, tolerance, and enjoyment determine who performs which tasks. As one husband explained:

> There were no initial arrangements. It was just an agreement that both of
> us would share in the housework. There is nothing like, "You do the laun-
> dry and I'll do the pots and pans." There is just an understanding that we
> were both working and that we both have responsibilities to other things.

Work impacts family life because of time constraints and demands put on each individual. In turn, the couple (both individuals with such constraints) is forced to figure out an organization for running the household that takes into account the work constraints, and that, in the process, accomplishes the equivalent of a frontal assault on the gender-based allocation of duties. This is another way of saying that what is experienced as a breakdown of traditional gender roles in the family need not necessarily be the product of a conscious strategy of confronting gender inequality. Often the role changing is discussed as "new interests" or "hobbies" such as men's interest in cooking when, in fact, the "interest" was generated because those men's wives were not around to cook meals and the men were getting tired of having frozen foods. Similarly, a number of women expressed a real lack of interest in cooking and indicated their relief in not being forced to perform -- precisely because their jobs did not leave them the time or their work provided sufficient income to purchase those services directly.

However, lingering ambivalences are connected with giving up clearly defined husband-wife patterns. These stem from the couple's failure to fulfill what are conceived of as traditional gender roles.

Couples sometimes do fall back on traditional roles. One man uses the derogatory term, "squaw work," to explain his own awareness of the inequality built into a traditional division of labor but nonetheless remains an intermittent feature of their marriage:

You have to realize I was in the 4-H Club with the cows and my wife was in the 4-H Club with home economics. That tells a lot about where we started. But we have migrated away from all that... Even today my wife is not embarrassed by doing the squaw work. She kind of likes to do the housework. It gives us an old-fashioned feeling to our marriage every once in a while and that is a nice touch.

Women in this study also worry about emasculating their husbands by asking them to do more around the house, even when they employ full-time housekeepers. As a result, they retain some aspect of household work as their exclusive turf. One woman reserves one chore for herself, despite her husband's insistence.

I don't like the way he looks doing the laundry. Well, to me it's something that women do. It represents a nurturing activity to me -- something very feminine. Maybe it's my way of showing him I still have that.

This was typical: remnants of a traditional division of labor were defended by the wives as much as, or more than, the husbands.

It is in the emotional arena that men feel most slighted. The attention wives once showered on their husbands is reduced because they no longer have the time or energy, or perhaps even the need to do so. Further, although men are involved in the domestic arena, their feelings are not necessarily aligned with their actions. As one man put it:

You know, I don't consider myself the ultimate liberated man. In terms of the pendulum swing, I'm pretty far in that direction (left). But, you know, when she's had to work on Saturdays or Sundays to finish a big project, I take care of the kids, and I'm not overly thrilled about it. But I do it.

Career Development and Choice

Even if the steps out of traditional gender roles are somewhat tentative and cause some discomfort, the conjoining of two careers does open some real possibilities for change in careers. In most cases, the development of careers is alternating in character. His career comes first and makes possible hers or investments leading to hers. Her career makes possible shifts in his career. Perhaps more important than the alternation of investments is that the large and stable portion of family income coming from the wife's career makes possible career shifts for him. Because the dual-career marriage frees men from sole economic responsibility, the men can be less obsessed by work, less aggressive, and even less motivated because the weight of this responsibility is shared. One man explains how this has made a difference in his life:

I'm not a workaholic. I'm pretty comfortable at what I'm doing. I probably could make more money if I was interested in working a lot harder, but I would have to sacrifice a lot of things for that -- like time with my family, personal time, a lot of things. I'm just not willing to do that, and in part I don't have to do that because my wife works.

A woman describes the freedom she feels her career gives her husband:

The woman who works and makes as much as a man gives the man flexibility and freedom in his job. He doesn't have to worry incessantly: "What if something happens -- what if I die or what if I get fired or what if I hate

259

this career and I'd rather refinish furniture and start my own business?" He has more flexibility because of the economic freedom.

Men did not just fantasize about a career change: several enacted one. For others a career shift was in the talking stages. In all cases the wives encouraged such moves. In this regard, the career marriage paves the way for career choice. One man, after having a disagreement with the president of his company, made good on his intention to "strike out on his own" in the consulting field. He explains how this was possible.

We [he and his partner] went into business with virtually no clients. The fact that Susan was working and making a good income was significant. The decision would have been different if that had not been the case. We couldn't have afforded it. She and I talked about my leaving the company, and she agreed with me.

But the business was not on a solid footing, and this started to affect their marriage.

It's good we started to make money when we did. It took a bit longer than we expected. We'd both reached a point where, if we hadn't started being more successful within a year, I probably would have gone back into the job market. If I hadn't, she would have been pretty unhappy about it. She was feeling the pressure of carrying the financial responsibility and feeling the sacrifice that we were making collectively was beginning to add up.

Shared economic responsibility is these couples' goal, and it is only for brief periods that either spouse is willing to assume full economic responsibility.

In short, the career marriage offers husbands freedom to explore career alternatives and career shifts much like the choice reserved for middle-class women in a more traditional pattern. Women in this study have not yet done the same, but that may be because their careers are newer (in terms of their thinking of their employment as a career and in terms of the number of years they have actually spent in their chosen fields). His career change may eventually make possible alternatives in her career trajectory.

Communication and Support

Despite moments of doubt, ambivalence, and conflict, dual-career couples often develop a communication style that they believe is quite different from that which characterizes traditional marriages. Husbands and wives with careers spend the bulk of their time engaged in similar activities, which, while often drawing on different kinds of expertise, share a rhythm and a structure; this situation is far different from the chasm that separates paid employment and housework. Thus, these spouses understand each other's lives and experience a high degree of empathy: "She has a sense of what I'm doing 'cause she's out there doing the same damn thing every day."

One woman explains how a shared understanding makes her relationship with her husband different from that of traditional husbands and wives:

Another aspect of my traveling and his traveling is that each of us understands what travel is to the other and it's not sitting at home thinking that it's glamorous or exciting and that I'm being left out, as a lot of wives who are very resentful of their husband's traveling. We don't give each other hassles about traveling.

Most couples talk about the day's events over dinner or in bed, whether there is one earner or two. But what is striking in these cases is the similarity of the talk. She talks finance and he talks marketing. It is the content of her end of the conversation that has changed.

Although they can support one another through similar organizational experiences, they are not conduits linking one firm to the next. The majority talk about personal problems, office politics, and unusual events. Unless couples are in the same field, they do not talk about the details of their jobs because of the specialized knowledge needed to understand the finer points. Even when they are in the same field, they do not necessarily talk about the specifics of the work, especially when issues are confidential. The similarity for their employers' organizational structure, however, provides a basis for shared understanding and communication.

> We talk a lot about common problems in respect to interrelating to the other associates. Her study teams are like my study teams. Her problems of having a junior associate who doesn't seem to be able to get his or her game together is the same as my problems, and we are a resource to each other in say, "Have you tried this or that?"

These couples, then, have the quintessential modern marriage -- theirs is truly a companion marriage. Yet there is also the potential for competition for status between spouses. Sometimes spouses pointed out that their talk leads to disagreement about who knows best and who is really the expert. Couples try to resolve this problem by carving out distinct areas of expertise. One man explains how this operates in his marriage:

> Our work coincidentally overlaps an awful lot... But we each have a reasonable working knowledge of where the other person is stronger. There's some recognition that I know more about certain things and she knows more about other things.... Sometimes we interrupt each other when we're talking about things, but if it is my area that I know more about, she backs off, and vice versa.

The carving out of district areas of professional turf allows each partner to avoid getting too close to the world the other occupies outside the home. It is one way in which the marriage buffers the careers and keeps husbands and wives from developing the petty jealousies and conflicts characteristic of co-workers in the same office.

Conclusion

At the outset, I suggested that the dual-career couple represented a situation with two husbands and no wife. However, the epigram ignores synchronous movements in other directions including that of limiting the career aspirations and goals of husbands and wives and opening new avenues of expression for each. This combination of new limits and new openings marks a fundamental departure from traditional marital arrangements for those couples who are willing to undertake the challenge of negotiation. And the negotiation terrain included not just two parties or areas of interest -- his and hers -- but a third: theirs. Their career, the marriage, is a set of shifting boundaries that defines mutual interests in careers *and* a relationship that, more than the traditional marriage, poses a potential counterweight to the influence of employment.

261

The third career forces a clear set of limits on the demands of the other two, offering the possibility that marriage and family could exert some influence on what employers can ask of their employees. But because dual-career marriages are few and far between and careerists tend to be located in organizations that are capable of resisting collective demands from managerial workers, the influence of marriage on work organizations tends to be reduced to selective incidents of individual resistance or, more commonly, individual opportunities forgone in order to sustain the balance between his career and hers. This fact makes even more important the definition of a set of principles that can guide the pursuit of two careers and permit an acceptable union between them and family. In this sense, norms of equity and reciprocity must be much more open to discussion and debate. Since neither husband nor wife can claim sole authority on the basis of bread winning, rules of conduct and a division of labor must be created to service the equally compelling demands of two careers. However, as corporations restructure their employment opportunities to allow some women to become full participants with career mobility, her career emerges alongside his career. This social change in employment opportunities fosters greater symmetry between individual husbands and wives. His and her career are microstructural causes that help create their marriage. But, as I have attempted to show, concerns with equity between husbands and wives rarely precede the construction of dual-career marriages. Rather, those concerns commonly *follow* investments in two careers.

References

Gerson, Kathleen. 1985. *Hard Choices: How Women Decide about Work, Career, and Motherhood.* Berkeley: University of California Press.

Gerstel, Naomi, and Harriet Gross. 1984. *Commuter Marriages: A Study of Work and Family.* New York: Guilford Press.

Hertz, Rosanna. 1986. *More Equal than Others: Women and Men in Dual-Career Marriages.* Berkeley: University of California Press.

Hewlett, Sylvia. 1986. *A Lesser Life: The Myth of Women's Liberation in America.* New York: William Morrow.

Holmstrom, Lynda Lytle. 1973. *The Two-Career Family.* Cambridge, Mass.: Schenkman.

Hunt, Janet G., and Larry L. Hunt. 1977. "Dilemmas and Contradictions of Status: The Case of the Dual-Career Family." *Social Problems 24*: 407-416.

Lorber, Judith. 1981. "On the Reproduction of Mothering: A Methodological Debate." *Signs 6*: 482-486.

Lorber, Judith. 1986. "Dismantling Noah's Ark." *Sex Roles 14*: 567-580.

Papanek, Hanna. 1975. "Men, Women, and Work: Reflections on the Two-Person Career." *American Journal of Sociology 78*: 852-872.

Polma, Margaret M., and T. Neal Garland. 1971. "The Married Professional Woman: A Study in the Tolerance of Domestication." *Journal of Marriage and the Family 33* (August): 531-540.

Pleck, Joseph H. 1977. "The Work-Family Role System." *Social Problems 24*: 417-427.

Risman, Barbara. 1987. "Men Who Mother." *Gender and Society 1*: 6-32.

CREDIT LIST FOR COLLAMER: THE ECOLOGY OF GENDER, 4/e